PRISONERS, SOLITUDE, AND TIME

CLARENDON STUDIES IN CRIMINOLOGY

Published under the auspices of the Institute of Criminology, University of Cambridge; the Mannheim Centre, London School of Economics; and the Centre for Criminology, University of Oxford.

General Editor: Robert Reiner
(London School of Economics)

Editors: Manuel Eisner, Alison Liebling and Per-Olof Wikström
(University of Cambridge)

Jill Peay and Tim Newburn
(London School of Economics)

Ian Loader, Julian Roberts and Lucia Zedner
(University of Oxford)

RECENT TITLES IN THIS SERIES:
Criminal Careers in Transition: The Social Context of Desistance from Crime
Farrall, Hunter, Sharpe, and Calverley

Hate Crime and Restorative Justice: Exploring Causes, Repairing Harms
Walters

Policing the Waterfront: Networks, Partnerships and the Governance of Port Security
Brewer

Traces of Terror: Counter-Terrorism Law, Policing, and Race
Sentas

Reorganizing Crime: Mafia and Anti-Mafia in Post-Soviet Georgia
Slade

Prisoners, Solitude, and Time

IAN O'DONNELL

OXFORD
UNIVERSITY PRESS

3/4/15
WW
$125.00

OXFORD
UNIVERSITY PRESS

Great Clarendon Street, Oxford, OX2 6DP,
United Kingdom

Oxford University Press is a department of the University of Oxford.
It furthers the University's objective of excellence in research, scholarship,
and education by publishing worldwide. Oxford is a registered trade mark of
Oxford University Press in the UK and in certain other countries

© Ian O'Donnell 2014

First Edition published in 2014

Impression: 1

Published in the United States of America by Oxford University Press
198 Madison Avenue, New York, NY 10016, United States of America

British Library Cataloguing in Publication Data
Data available

Library of Congress Control Number: 2014943572

ISBN 978–0–19–968448–9

Printed and bound by
CPI Group (UK) Ltd, Croydon, CR0 4YY

General Editor's Introduction

Clarendon Studies in Criminology aims to provide a forum for outstanding empirical and theoretical work in all aspects of criminology and criminal justice, broadly understood. The Editors welcome submissions from established scholars, as well as excellent PhD work. The series was inaugurated in 1994, with Roger Hood as its first General Editor, following discussions between Oxford University Press and three criminology centres. It is edited under the auspices of these three centres: the Cambridge Institute of Criminology, the Mannheim Centre for Criminology at the London School of Economics, and the Centre for Criminology at the University of Oxford. Each supplies members of the Editorial Board and, in turn, the Series Editor.

Prisoners, Solitude, and Time by Ian O'Donnell is a major addition to the number of outstanding books on imprisonment already published in the *Clarendon Studies in Criminology* series. As the title indicates, its focus is on prisoners' experience of solitary confinement, their handling of time, and the interface between these. Professor O'Donnell brings to bear on these issues a wealth of academic expertise, primarily as a psychologist and historian, as well as experience in penal reform, prison visiting, and as a magistrate. The result is an immaculately written book that is not only scholarly but also thought-provoking, moving, and ultimately inspiring about the potential of human beings to somehow and sometimes transcend even the most cruel and unusual deprivations and pains.

Time is of the essence of prison as punishment, captured in the cliché 'if you can't do the time, don't do the crime'. Yet the vast criminological literature scarcely focuses on the subjective experience of 'doing time'. This was the inspiration for the project reported here, the evolution of which is described in the following way by the author:

My initial ponderings concerned the subjective experience of time passing in prison and how this might relate to rising sentence lengths, growing life expectancy, and an individual's ability to measure time intervals with increasing precision. Did one year in custody feel different to a prisoner in the nineteenth century who was likely to die before he reached the age of 40, compared to his twenty-first century counterpart who could reasonably hope to achieve a lifespan of three score and ten? Are there particular pains associated with indefinite incarceration? And, more generally, what can we learn about the culture of prisons by studying the 'time work' engaged in by their inhabitants? These questions caused me to wonder about solitude and how a strategy for conquering time (or, at least, making it less abrasive) might involve psychological or social withdrawal. Such musings led to a consideration of silence and how it fits into the scheme of things. Solitude is not necessarily silent but, if it is, does it seem less bearable? (p. ix)

O'Donnell begins with an extensive review of the history of solitary confinement in prisons, from its origins with late eighteenth-century reformers (such as John Howard) who encouraged it with benevolent motives, intending to counteract the dangers and harms of the unregulated 'drunken rambunctiousness' (p. 1) of eighteenth- and early nineteenth-century prisons. They were also concerned to foster reform through the severing of prisoners' contact with noxious influences, with exposure only to the supposedly soul-saving ministrations of pastoral workers and the opportunity to commune with one's conscience without external distractions. Whilst the initial intentions of advocates of penal isolation may have been benign, the effects were from the start widely condemned as cruelty amounting to torture. This applies *a fortiori* to the contemporary revival of solitary confinement, justified mainly by a pragmatic security rationale but without any even pretended concern for rehabilitation, with its apogee in the spread of the 'supermax' model. Contemporary solitary confinement raises issues beyond those of earlier centuries, partly because of the greater length of time often spent there (and isolation forces the most direct possible contemplation of the enormity of the problem of time), and partly because of the much more intense sociability and speed of life outside.

After the historical review of the development of solitary confinement, O'Donnell proceeds to analyse in great depth and with acute sensitivity its subjective experience, as recorded over the centuries in a variety of literary forms, including diaries, memoirs, poetry, and fiction. O'Donnell acknowledges this entails some methodological conundrums, although it offers the only windows into souls, especially in the past. In his words:

The first-person accounts which inform the analysis presented in subsequent chapters are by definition the preserve of the more articulate and more highly motivated former prisoners who survived the experience relatively intact and possessed the wherewithal to get their thoughts into print. There are further problems with the fallibility of memory and the range of motivations that lie behind the construction of such narratives. Over-reliance on material of this nature would yield a partial perspective, although it must be acknowledged that these are precisely the kinds of studies in resilience that bring new light to bear on aspects of the captive experience that are central to this book. All prisoners must wrestle with the passage of time and all of those who are placed in solitary confinement must seek out a way to address the lack of human company. Not all are in a position to, or wish to, write about their experiences but study of a wide array of such accounts, written contemporaneously or with the benefit of hindsight, shows clear commonalities despite wide variation in author biographies in terms of age, gender, race, educational attainment, social class, reason for incarceration, duration and location of confinement. These commonalities suggest that what the authors have identified may have a more general relevance. (pp. 56–7)

The dangers of bias are alleviated by recourse to what other sources are available. 'To ensure balance, published prisoner accounts have been tested against newspaper reports, tracts written by prison chaplains and reformers, official publications, academic critiques, field visits, personal communications with prisoners, statistical data, and the documents produced by commissions of inquiry. By weaving together these diverse strands a more complete picture can be painted' (p. 57). O'Donnell also draws on evidence about other experiences of solitary confinement than those imprisoned for crimes: these range from the voluntary isolation of some monks or hermits, to prisoners of war, and explorers.

The book portrays the pains of solitary captivity vividly in disturbing detail. However, its main thrust is to try and identify how some exceptional individuals manage not only to get through the time somehow, but even to draw some positive enrichment. They draw on seven strategies distinguished alliteratively by O'Donnell as: Rescheduling, Removal, Reduction, Reorientation, Resistance, Raptness, and Reinterpretation. The techniques of preserving and perhaps even enhancing personal, ethical, and spiritual integrity are drawn perhaps disproportionality by those who have or find a cause that enables them to transcend the immediate pains they endure. O'Donnell encapsulates the spirit that can do this in a phrase drawn from the psychotherapist and concentration camp inmate, Viktor Frankl, which provides the book with an ultimately inspiring coda. Frankl defined 'tragic optimism' as:

the idea that meaning can be wrought from the direst circumstances and that persons who take responsibility for their decisions can strive to convert suffering into accomplishment. He suggested that the most powerful arguments in favour of this notion are those that can be made from individual cases. To this end, the methodology adopted for this book has been to present a wide range of accounts rather than to concentrate on a few. By a process of aggregation these personal testimonies of unlikely triumph over the least favourable conditions add weight to Frankl's idea. If some can achieve a demeanour of tragic optimism then why not others? Frankl's argument was not that suffering is essential to render life meaningful; far from it. His view was that if suffering could be avoided it should be and that it was only triumph over unavoidable suffering that was meaningful. (p. 278)

None of this of course offers an argument in favour of the acute pains inflicted by involuntary solitary confinement especially over prolonged periods. But it does inspire with the capacity of human spirits sometimes to survive such ordeals, and indeed put the pain to good effect. Perhaps the most celebrated recent example, drawn on several times here, was Nelson Mandela. O'Donnell's book adds much insight and inspiration to criminological studies of penal confinement, and is a most welcome addition to the *Clarendon Studies in Criminology* series.

Robert Reiner
London School of Economics
June 2014

Preface

This book has had a longer gestation period than anything else I have had the pleasure of working on. My first notes were scribbled on a compliments slip in a Barcelona hotel in August 2004. There followed several years of intermittent attention as a potential project began to take shape. During 2010 I drew together the relevant literatures and began to sharpen my focus. A period of research leave in 2011 allowed me to make significant progress with the task of writing and a first draft was completed two years later.

My initial ponderings concerned the subjective experience of time passing in prison and how this might relate to rising sentence lengths, growing life expectancy, and an individual's ability to measure time intervals with increasing precision. Did one year in custody feel different to a prisoner in the nineteenth century who was likely to die before he reached the age of 40 compared to his twenty-first-century counterpart who could reasonably hope to achieve a lifespan of three score and ten? Are there particular pains associated with indefinite incarceration? And, more generally, what can we learn about the culture of prisons by studying the 'time work' engaged in by their inhabitants? These questions caused me to wonder about solitude and how a strategy for conquering time (or, at least, making it less abrasive) might involve psychological or social withdrawal. Such musings led to a consideration of silence and how it fits into the scheme of things. Solitude is not necessarily silent but, if it is, does it seem less bearable?

There are personal reasons for my inquiry also. Having been appointed to the Board of Visitors of HMP Pentonville as it approached its sesquicentenary I have had a long-standing interest in this institution's role in penal history. My experiences as a magistrate in Oxford (which sometimes involved imposing prison sentences), as director of the Irish Penal Reform Trust (where my concern was to challenge the thoughtless expansion of the prison system), and as a professor of criminology (with a particular focus on coercive confinement), have consolidated this interest.

The process of distilling my thoughts into what appears between these covers has itself involved much time, solitude, and silence. It required an unusual degree of intellectual meandering and, occasionally, prolonged absences among academic thickets through which I had not previously hacked. Never before did I have the opportunity to consider what prisoners might have in common with Arctic explorers, what lessons the eremitical life might offer to students of penology, why the temporal dimension of imprisonment has been so neglected despite its critical importance, and the seductive appeal of timetables. If, dear reader, you wonder why anyone would devote so much of the time that is inexorably slipping away from them to a project that would appear to pose unanswerable questions then I will feel vindicated. If your curiosity is piqued and you wish to invest some of your time and intellectual resources in considering what I have to say, I will feel flattered to boot.

Academic life has become progressively more demanding for reasons that are too tedious to review here. The end result is that free thinking can be stifled and an obsession with demonstrating 'impact' can get in the way of chasing ideas wherever they may lead and remaining open to the possibilities offered by serendipity. Bureaucratic demands take on a smothering quality and scholars end up ploughing increasingly narrow furrows of specialization where the yield is poor and excites little interest. To have been able to carve out space in my schedule to write this book has required feats of workload management that would not have been attempted had the subject matter proved less alluring. Whether it has been worthwhile is for the reader to judge.

I have a number of debts to acknowledge. For her assistance in gathering materials that were widely scattered and sometimes deeply buried I am most grateful to Angela Ennis. The staff of the James Joyce Library in University College Dublin, especially the inter-library loans desk, dealt efficiently with my numerous requests. Multiple trips to the Bodleian Library in Oxford and the Cambridge University Library were hugely productive as well as being important reminders of the joys of a well-stocked library, even in a digital age.

I have made many visits over the years to prisons that were built as monuments to silence and separation, especially HMP Pentonville in London (opened in 1842) and Mountjoy in Dublin (opened in 1850). As part of my research for this book I wandered along the tiers of Eastern State Penitentiary in Philadelphia, which received its first prisoners in 1829, was designated a national historic landmark in 1965, and was finally abandoned in 1971. The memories of some who served time there have been recorded and archived and I was fortunate to be allowed access to the transcripts of these reminiscences. The last prisoners at Eastern State were transferred to the State Correctional Institution at Graterford and the Pennsylvanian experiment with extreme segregation was resuscitated in restricted housing units at institutions such as SCI Greene and SCI Rockview. I am much obliged to Bill DiMascio who, during his tenure as executive director of the Pennsylvania Prison Society, enabled me to spend time behind the walls of Graterford, Greene, and Rockview. Auburn Correctional Facility in central New York (opened in 1817 and rebuilt in the 1930s), where prisoners left their cells to work, eat, and worship together but where the rule of silence was vigorously enforced with the whip, famously offered a model to rival the Pennsylvanian one. I am grateful to Harold Graham, superintendent of this institution, for allowing me to visit to see how it has been remodelled over almost 200 years of continuous usage. By walking in the footsteps of those who had served time at Eastern State and Auburn, I felt the ripples of experiments in penal reform that were begun in the early nineteenth century.

A select group of prisoners, including several on death row, who have endured periods of isolation measured in decades rather than years, were gracious enough to share some of their thoughts with me in person and through the exchange of letters. So too were a number of men and women living as hermits or as members of enclosed religious orders in the Christian tradition (such as the Carthusians, Cistercians, and Camaldolese) who have learned to find treasure in stillness. None rebuffed my attempts to communicate and all offered hard-won and valuable insights. I was also fortunate enough to correspond with an experienced Tibetan Buddhist about how joy can be found in isolation. A series of seminars with the Mountjoy Prison Lifers' Group gave me an opportunity to test my ideas against the experiences of those to whom they should relate. I am grateful to the participants for sharing their perspectives and hope that what follows does not lose sight of their concerns. I am also obliged to the Irish Prison Psychology Service for facilitating these meetings.

As part of my effort to understand the rewards that can accompany the rigours of a silent and solitary life—what Patrick Leigh Fermor described as 'the slow and cumulative spell of healing quietness'—I availed of the hospitality offered by the Benedictine monks at Glenstal Abbey and the Cistercians (Trappists) at Mount Melleray Abbey. Indeed, a number of the ideas in this book were refashioned in the guest houses of these austere but edifying establishments which grace the Irish countryside in counties Limerick and Waterford, respectively. These sojourns deepened my appreciation of how life can be affected by a silent rhythm.

For their willingness to respond to my queries, query my responses, challenge my assumptions, strengthen my arguments, and engage with various drafts of my text, I am obliged to Jessica Bird, Mary Bosworth, Ben Crewe, David Doyle, Kimmett Edgar, Rosemary Gido, Barry Godfrey, Deirdre Healy, Tehching Hsieh, Erwin James, Yvonne Jewkes, Helen Johnston, Roy King, the late Norman Johnston, W. Paul Jones, Shane Kilcommins, Sara Maitland, Shadd Maruna, Dan Mears, Eoin O'Sullivan, Keramet Reiter, Lorna Rhodes, Sharon Shalev, Peter Scharff Smith, Hans Toch, and David Ward. Several of the foregoing cautioned against undue length and they will be relieved to find that the final version of the book is half its original size. It remains long but I hope it is less ponderous and meandering than it might otherwise have been. While engaged on this project I was alive to the possibility that a focus on individual resilience and redemptive solitude might be seized upon by proponents of extended solitary confinement to support a practice that should be condemned. I sincerely hope that by teasing out some of the (occasional) benefits I have not downplayed the (almost inevitable) burdens. Whatever else it may do this book does not make the case for penal isolation.

To everyone who helped me to reframe my understanding of time and isolation as they are manifest in prison, I extend my gratitude. To those who have not buckled under the weight of solitariness but have shown, in Brian Keenan's words, 'how in the most inhuman of circumstances men grow and deepen in humanity', I offer my respect.

This book is dedicated to Kirsty Kirkwood with whom I am fortunate to share my time.

Contents

List of Tables

1

Historical Perspectives

Late eighteenth- and early nineteenth-century prisons were crowded, communal, porous places characterized by people milling around the yards shouting, drinking, gambling, carousing, and fighting. Newgate was epitomized by 'noise, contention, licentiousness, and tumult' (Buxton 1818: 76) and Evans (2010: 2) lamented how the same institution was repeatedly used 'to illustrate evil in its natural habitat as a mixture of unbridled crude pleasure, bestiality and filth'. Playfair (1971: 257) observed that, 'Clerkenwell, prior to its being rebuilt in 1834 as a remand prison, was known as a "great brothel" '. Echoing this theme, the renowned prison chaplain, John Clay (1861: 12), painted a picture of drunken rambunctiousness:

Beer clubs and spirit clubs were patronized lovingly; the losels and harlots of the neighbourhood were freely admitted to carouse with their incarcerated pals; all the usual enticements of the pothouse were sedulously offered: cards, dice, skittles, fives, Mississippi, Porto Bello and billiards flourished vigorously. For the due promotion of drunkenness the prisoners were allowed to levy a tax on every new comer.

These were squalid locations where extortion and exploitation flourished. Their occupants were dirty, disorderly, dissolute and, occasionally, dangerous. Nutritious food was in short supply, the ventilation was poor, and the conditions were ideal for disease to fester and spread; the stench threatened to overwhelm. Henriques (1972: 63) listed the defining characteristics of prisons of this era as, 'idleness, corruption, drunkenness and profane jollity'. Debtors and their families were present in large numbers, visitors mingled with prisoners, and there were few staff to enforce discipline. The jailer's major preoccupation was the maximization of profit (from fees charged to prisoners and entrepreneurial activities such as selling food, bedding, alcohol, and tobacco, or charging admission to the public) rather than the humane treatment of those in his charge.

Sex, alcohol, and violence were not unique to the English prisons of the day. Smith (1833: 11) described the Pennsylvanian prison of the late 1700s as a place of 'perfect pandemonium...one revolting mass of festering corruption' and of Walnut Street jail in Philadelphia, Gray (1847: 15–16) observed that:

It is represented as a scene of promiscuous and unrestricted intercourse, and universal riot and debauchery. There was no labor, no separation of those accused, but yet untried, nor even of those confined for debt only, from convicts sentenced for the foulest crimes; not separation of color, age or sex, by day or by night; the prisoners lying promiscuously on the floor, most of them without anything like bed or bedding. As soon as the sexes were placed in different wings, which was the first reform made in the prison, of thirty or forty women then confined there, all but four or five immediately left it; it having been a common practice, it is said, for women to cause themselves to be arrested for fictitious debts, that they might share in the orgies of the place. Intoxicating liquors abounded, and indeed were freely sold at a bar kept by one of the officers of the prison.... Such are the naked facts.

Growing qualms about the propriety of such confinement were reinforced by occasional outbreaks of lethal infection. The crowding and lack of proper hygiene meant that morbidity among prisoners was high and disease spread quickly. John Howard (1777: 16–17), the great calibrator and cataloguer of prisons, remarked in the first edition of *The State of The Prisons in England and Wales* that, based on his observations in 1773 and 1774, he was persuaded that 'the havock [*sic*] made by the gaol-fever' was responsible for more prisoner deaths than 'all the public executions in the kingdom'. Transmissible diseases destroyed the lives not only of prisoners but also of those who came into contact with them; the lice that carried epidemic typhus were indifferent to social status. Evans (2010: 95) gave the example of an incident at London's Old Bailey in 1750 when prisoners brought before the court passed a virulent fever to others in attendance, many of whom perished soon after: 'The death toll included the Lord Mayor of London, two judges, an alderman, a lawyer, an under-sheriff and several of the jury, not to mention 40 others'. Howard (1777: 17–18) wrote of an even more catastrophic 'Black Assize' at Oxford where the presence of infectious prisoners in court led to more than 300 deaths within two days.

The mortality rate on some of the hulks, prison ships which had been introduced as an expedient to accommodate prisoners who could no longer be transported to America, was as high as one in four in the late 1770s, a death toll which their operators described as 'inventory shrinkage' (Ignatieff 1989: 81). Premature death was a persistent problem whether prisoners were held on water or on land. The penitentiary at Millbank in London was temporarily closed in 1823 having been ravaged by typhus, dysentery, and scurvy, with 31 malnourished prisoners dying and another 400 becoming incapacitated (p. 176). In 1842, the satirical magazine, *Punch*, observed that the lethally unhealthy state of Millbank rendered it 'a capital substitute for capital punishments' (cited in Collins 1994: 151).

The need to stop the spread of moral, as well as physical, degeneration added impetus to the reform movement. Prisons were seen as incubators of a kind of disease that, unchecked, might act to deplete the community of God-fearing and law-abiding citizens who came into contact with prisoners, but also of a kind of vice that served to swell the ranks of the criminal classes. The response to this chaotic congregation emerged gradually, and stutteringly, on both sides of the Atlantic. At its heart was the design of a system that, at the same time as preventing contagion, would cultivate introspection. Grass (2003: 22) described how these twin objectives became unified in Howard's scheme of penal reform after his visit to Italy:

Howard argued that moral reclamation should be the principle [*sic*] aim of imprisonment, a sentiment...cultivated during a tour of the prisons, *lazarettos* [places of quarantine], and monasteries of Italy. Howard learned that *lazarettos* employed solitude to arrest the spread of physical disease, and that monasteries used it to inspire introspection, spiritual cleansing and moral awakening. Physical and spiritual cleansing were aims that Howard could advocate in English prison discipline as well, and he argued consequently for a new prison system in which solitary confinement would produce guilty feelings as prisoners were forced to the lonely contemplation of their past wickedness.

Those subjected to solitary confinement would be exposed to the lacerating effects of unavoidable self-examination, into which would be rubbed the salt of remorse. For rough and arbitrary sociality would be substituted clinical aloneness, the latter intended to cause the greater pain. There was no doubting the terror of solitude at the time. In *Solitude in Imprisonment*, published the year before Howard's *State of the Prisons*, Hanway (1776: 42; emphasis in original) wrote of the 'balmy remedy of *solitude*—balmy in the effect; though, for a time, nauseous to the taste or terrible to the imagination'. Ignatieff (1989: 74) cited what he described as a 'chilling phrase' used by John Brewster, who remarked in 1792 that: 'There are cords of love as well as fetters of iron.' Ignatieff elaborated that 'Cords of love bound minds in guilty remorse; fetters of iron bound only the body, leaving the mind free to fester in anger' (p. 74). The prison chaplain played a key role in tying the cords of love by persuading prisoners of their guilt and the righteousness of their punishment.

Those who advocated solitary confinement knew how painful, and occasionally perilous, it would be and the debate was characterized by an emphasis on how much solitude could be borne before the costs would outweigh the benefits. The key questions were when, and how, to dilute it with company, activity, or a combination of both. The individuals who were broken by isolation were seen as the collateral damage of a system that, in overall terms, was considered superior to what it replaced as regards its potential to create a safer society.

Solitary confinement was a form of quarantine that operated on several levels. It kept prisoners apart so they could not communicate diseases or nefarious thoughts; it reduced opportunities for misconduct; and it created a setting where there could be no escape from the pangs of conscience or the ministrations of the chaplaincy. It would prevent criminal contagion as well as curing offenders of their anti-social impulses, effecting a transformation of the prison, which according to the *Journal of Prison Discipline and Philanthropy* in 1856, would cease being 'a pest-house of incurables' and would instead become 'a moral infirmary' (cited in Anonymous 1987: 12). The public would be protected from prisoners, and prisoners would be protected from each other. Segregation by sex, which freed vulnerable women from the risk of exploitation, was a notable step forward and has been described as 'one of the major achievements of nineteenth-century penal reform' (Zedner 1995: 333). The chaplains were the surgeons in these moral hospitals, identifying when prisoners would be most amenable to the curative properties of the gospel message. This was a role they could not have played in the chaos of congregation where, recalling the Sermon on the Mount, the Reverend Clay (1861: 17) described how 'religious teaching in Gaols was mere casting of pearls before swine; the drunkenness and promiscuous intercourse among the prisoners would have thwarted the most zealous chaplain'. In addition, and another welcome development from the perspective of prison administrators, the practice of separation caused the prisoner subculture to fragment and vested much more authority in the staff.

Chatter and its Discontents

Confidence in the rehabilitative potential of silence was rooted in Christian monastic practices. The time of quiet reflection was to be a prelude to prisoners making peace with their God and achieving a state of grace. Once cleansed of their wrongdoing they would emerge from the prison with inner light lit, faith fortified and hope restored, ready at last to engage with the world on mutually beneficial terms. Unlike the anchorite, who sought sanctification in hardship and whose bricked-in existence was indefinite, the prisoner was coercively confined, usually for a determinate period, and while spiritual regeneration was hoped for it could not be guaranteed. There was always a risk that the prisoner would reject the institution's aims or simply mimic the language of penitence while remaining unmoved by it.

The prison philosophy based on segregation, discipline, and solitude as the foundations of moral improvement draws most directly, perhaps, from the *Casa di Correzione* (house of correction) of San Michele, a juvenile prison built in Rome in 1703 by Pope Clement XI. This was not the first cellular prison but it was the most elaborate in scale and design, as well as the most thoroughgoing in its attempt to marry punishment to rehabilitation in its routine operations. Inmates were isolated during the night and worked together in silence during the day, chained to desks in the large rectangular hall that was the building's hub. The young offenders ate, worked, and worshipped at their desks. Their chains were removed if they earned a walk (which took place in the same hall) or if they were to be lashed (the 'place of chastisement' was located at one end of the hall, the altar at the other). The dietary and sanitary conditions were relatively good. The daily routine was organized around prayer, religious instruction, and examination of conscience. Like young monks, the prisoners prayed while dressing, offered the day's work to the Lord, attended Mass each morning (from their desks), sang psalms and recited the rosary together, listened to one of their number reading spiritual literature while they ate their midday meal, and learned their catechism. Also like young monks they experienced mortification of the flesh, but with the significant difference that the flagellation was not self-administered (and as a result was unlikely to be ecstatically received).

According to Cajani (1996: 318) the inspiration for the *Casa di Correzione* was the cloistered abnegation of Catholic monastic life. If men and women of the cloth sought out silent penitence to atone for their sins, why not impose a similar discipline on secular wrongdoers in an attempt to effect a similar transformation? Howard was so favourably impressed by what he observed when he visited Rome in 1775 that he reproduced on the title page of the second volume of his study of European prisons an epigraph that he had seen in the institution's main hall. This read, '*Parum est coercere improbos poena nisi probos efficias disciplina*' ('Repressing villains with punishment is worth little if we do not render them good with discipline'; Cajani 1996: 301).

Evans (2010: 57) suggests that another root of the modern prison is to be found in the writings of Jean Mabillon, a Benedictine monk, 'who announced the principles of redemptive imprisonment' in his *Reflexions sur les Prisons des Ordres Religieux* (published posthumously in 1724; see Sellin 1927). Mabillon's critique of the excessive harshness of ecclesiastical prisons contributed to the emergence of the notion that incarceration, properly tempered with compassion, could provide the basis of a system of rehabilitation for prisoners. Mabillon proposed the construction of monastic prisons modelled on the Carthusian charterhouse where wayward priests or brothers could be brought back within the fold through a combination of isolation, spiritual guidance, and participation in occasional communal rituals. The emphasis was to be on reclamation through reclusion rather than vengeance (see also Wines 1895: 143). In other words, monastic life influenced the architectural forms that prisons would later embrace as well as the underlying penal rationales. Another contributory factor was a cellular prison for minors that opened in Florence in 1677, which was based on perpetual isolation and where, anticipating developments in the nineteenth century, prisoners' heads were covered with tin helmets when they left their cells to attend religious services (Cajani 1996: 320).

The Architecture of Isolation

Much has been written about competing models of prison design and the penal philosophies that underpinned them (e.g. Brodie et al. 2002; Jewkes and Johnston 2007; Spens 1994). No attempt will be made here to review this literature in its entirety, but simply to draw on some of the key elements of the debates about separation and isolation, as they played out in the US and the UK, insofar as they impact on the themes addressed in this book. The aim is not to offer a comprehensive historical account but rather to achieve something akin to what Rhodes (2004: 15), in her ethnography of life in maximum security, described as 'a sense of echo'; showing how the lessons (and mistakes) of the past continue to reverberate in terms of architecture, penological thinking, and human relations.

Walnut Street

The Philadelphia Society for Alleviating the Miseries of Public Prisons was established in 1787 by some of the founders of the Philadelphia Society for Assisting Distressed Prisoners which had been set up in 1776 but dissolved the following year (Smith 1833: 7; it remains in existence as the Pennsylvania Prison Society). Its members were horrified by the sordid, crowded, and corrupting conditions at Walnut Street jail in Philadelphia. The Society's desire was for squalor, filth, and noise to be replaced by the terror of their opposite—a sterile, uncompanionable, and unyielding discipline. This development, which occurred in April 1790 at the instigation of the Pennsylvania legislature, was 'the real foundation of the separate system' (Wines 1895: 146). The county commissioners for Philadelphia were directed to build, in the grounds of the jail, 'a suitable number of cells six feet in width, eight feet in length, and nine feet in height' which would be designed 'to prevent all external communication, for the purpose of confining there the more hardened and atrocious offenders' (p. 146).

   To this end 16 cells for male and 14 for female convicts were constructed in which it was hoped that the legislative intent to reform and to deter (two sides of the same providential coin) would be achieved by joining unmitigated solitude to steady labour. The new regime coincided with a drop in crime in Philadelphia and for a while the experiment was viewed as a success (Smith

1833: 16–17). However, the crime rate soon began to rise again, the prison became overcrowded, and to cope with increasing numbers many of the serving prisoners were pardoned. William Crawford (1834: 8), an English visitor and future prison inspector in his own country, was sceptical about the extent to which Walnut Street ever delivered on its expressed purposes, noting that the new cells were small as well as being 'badly ventilated, and so defectively arranged that the convicts in the adjoining cells could communicate with ease'. He added that there was little in the way of labour carried out in the cells which, in any event, had been appropriated for the punishment of refractory prisoners as evidenced by 'there being in the floor of each cell an iron staple, to which are attached three short chains, for the secure confinement of as many convicts' (p. 8).

But the reformers did not lose confidence in their belief that solitude, and the inward redirection of the person's gaze that it forced, were vital ingredients of the reform process. The challenge lay in discovering the best mode of administration. If the dose could be got right, stimulating enough regretful insight to cause behavioural change post-release, then the hardship would be worth it. Personal transformation would be wrought, not primarily through surveillance, but through enforced aloneness. Quietude would allow the conscience to develop into an effective guide and the fear of it would keep potential malefactors within the law. The prison would act as a 'furnace of affliction' where suffering would allow for the entry of grace and the ensuing characterological reform (see Graber 2011). But when the discipline became too severe the furnace, which was supposed to heat the soul so that it could be remoulded, grew too hot and scorched. If madness and recidivism followed, then a different approach would be required.

Auburn

There followed a more focused experiment when solitude without labour was introduced to a newly built cellblock at Auburn prison in New York in 1821. The chaos of congregation was superseded by cellular control but idle inmates could find little to do in their cramped quarters where the side walls were less than the span of a child's arms apart and some inmates could touch the ceiling with their hands (the cells measured 7½ feet long by 3 feet 8 inches wide and floor to ceiling was 7 feet; Johnston 2000: 75). During the day they were not permitted to sit or lie down (Smith 1833: 36). Even allowing for the fact that people were smaller in the early nine-teenth century, these were still tightly confining spaces or, as Evans (2010: 318) described them, 'claustrophobic cubicles' containing 'closeted convicts'. (It is difficult to imagine that more restrictive conditions might ever have been contemplated, but when Kingston Penitentiary in Canada opened in 1835—the design and construc-tion having been overseen by Auburn's master builder—it con-tained sleeping rooms measuring only 6 feet 6 inches by 2 feet 6 inches (Johnston 2004: 30). The narrowness of the accommoda-tion reflected the narrow view that was taken of the convict's cap-acity to change in a pro-social direction. These were not intended to be places in which the human spirit could flourish and expand. They were places of tight constraint and minimal ambition.)

The initiative at Auburn was a spectacular failure leading within a year to a litany of death, despair, and madness. There were prob-lems with heat (too cold in winter), light (insufficient to read the Bible by), and ventilation (dampness and vermin infestation). Hopelessness soon set in. The consequences, even by the standards of the time, were severe: 'five inmates died, one "became an idiot," and another committed suicide' (Graber 2011: 80). The Governor of the State of New York pardoned 26 prisoners to compensate them for the suffering they had endured. Their subsequent behavi-our showed that as well as being injurious to physical and mental health, the experience of unrelenting solitude had little reformative impact: 14 of the pardoned men reoffended and were reimprisoned within a short period of time. Smith (2009: 82) offers a graphic nine-word summary of this experiment: 'The trial of solitude had become a notorious massacre.' In Franke's (1995: 60) less pungent, but concurring, assessment: 'Completely solitary confinement had brought about death and insanity but not moral improvement.'

The harms of extreme isolation were undisputed. Gustave de Beaumont and Alexis de Tocqueville, who had been commissioned by the French government to visit the United States and to examine its penitentiary system, observed that: 'absolute solitude, if noth-ing interrupt it, is beyond the strength of man; it destroys the crim-inal without intermission and without pity; it does not reform, it kills' (Beaumont and Tocqueville 1833: 5). Adopting a parallel line of argument, Crawford (1834: 15), who had undertaken a similar excursion on behalf of the British Home Secretary, rejected the view that the gravely damaging effects of this experiment could be attributed to solitude, holding that they were due rather to prisoners being confined in tiny cells which they never left even for exercise, with no work and nothing in the way of moral or religious instruction; it was the 'unmixed severity' of the regime which undid the prisoners. This was confinement at its most cramped and least consoling. Solitude leavened by meaningful work, regular exercise, spacious and comfortable accommodation, and directed thought—as recommended by Crawford—was unlikely to be as detrimental.

Crawford recognized that if solitary confinement was to be prolonged 'labour is absolutely indispensable' (p. 38). To be effective its burden needed to be bearable; if the convict was overwhelmed and unhinged by the experience there would be nowhere for the divine light to penetrate. The advocates of solitude and silence were driven by a desire to reclaim souls as well as to deter potential wrongdoers. A regime that drove people mad was inimical to the first of these objectives. The Keeper of Auburn Prison, Gershom Powers, commented on the introduction of absolute isolation—which he had overseen—in the following terms:

There is no doubt that uninterrupted solitude tends to sour the feelings, destroy the affections, harden the heart, and induce men to cultivate a spirit of revenge, or drive them to despair; although such may not always be the effect upon martyrs and patriots, whose devotion to liberty, or religion, may sustain their bodies and minds in health and vigor while suffering in a righteous cause. (Cited in Gray 1847: 41)

This gobbet contains much of what has been found by many others since, namely that solitude makes those subjected to it angry and desperate but if they have a framework in which to make sense of their suffering it can more easily be borne. Given that the men subjected to the regime of unrelieved isolation at Auburn fared so badly at the time and after release, it was decided to abandon it in 1823 and to substitute hard labour in silent association during the day and cellular confinement at night.

Despite the vigilance of the guards, a regime based on silent association was difficult to enforce. Whenever prisoners at Auburn were marching in lockstep, eating together in the mess-room, or at labour in the workshops, there were opportunities to communicate, whether through whispers, notes, hand signals, or other ruses. Each time they succeeded in doing so, or were flogged for attempting to, the system was discredited. The regular use of corporal punishment indicated that this approach could not work and brutalized those subjected to it. The presence of the lash ensured the existence between the prisoners and guards of 'malignant and murderous relations' which changed them into 'fiends and blood hounds' (Prison Association of New York 1845: 48–9). When one man was introducing a whip to the back of another who had been stripped, bent, and tied in place, the finer points of prison discipline soon disappeared in yells, welts, and recrimination. Gruelling labour and cruel treatment, no matter how enthusiastically or half-heartedly they are combined, do not create reformed characters. A beating may result in obedience, but only temporarily; its lasting effects are resentment and anger. The fact that it relied so heavily upon the violence of flogging critically undermined the Auburn system. As Lieber (1838: 88) put it, 'the whip degrades, irritates, exasperates'. By contrast, the submission that follows solitary reflection can endure because it has its roots in a process of individual reorientation that comes from within.

Lane (1835) provided a useful account of life in Auburn. Describing himself on the title page of his pamphlet as 'a discharged and penitent convict', he studied his Bible closely, reading the good book seven times from cover to cover. He wrote of his regrets and the challenges of his spiritual journey. Nevertheless, soon after he was released he reoffended and was reimprisoned; clearly his knowledge of scripture and his desire for salvation failed to keep him sober and law abiding for long. This is an early example of the system succeeding on its own terms (a docile and remorseful prisoner is produced) but failing at the same time (the prisoner returns to serve another sentence). It illustrates many of the complexities associated with creating structures that will lead to change that is enduring and transferable as well as sincere and contrite.

The regime at Auburn was also compromised by overcrowding which frustrated the authorities' desire to eradicate conversation. When occupied by more than one body, as happened when the demand for prison places outstripped the supply of cells, the 'claustrophobic cubicles' became squalid and fetid meeting places. It did not take long for this to occur. Graber (2011: 160) reports that by 1850 New York had more inmates than single cells. The women in Auburn were cramped from the outset, being held in an attic room in very poor conditions. The prison chaplain was sympathetic to their plight, opining in 1833 that while the life for male prisoners at this institution was tolerable, 'to be a *female* convict, for any protracted period, would be worse than death' (cited in Zedner 1995: 338; emphasis in original).

Eastern State Penitentiary

Eastern State Penitentiary in Philadelphia was a hybrid model. It upheld the principles of solitude and labour but the labour was to be carried out alone in cell and not in company with other prisoners as had become the norm at Auburn. The first inmates arrived in 1829 although construction was not completed until 1836. The penitentiary was influential for its design features and for the bold statement it made about human nature. It exemplified the brimming optimism of a generation of penal reformers whose intentions were clear, whose motivations were pure, whose dynamism was undisputed, and whose firmness of purpose was unshakeable. The prisoners whose lives were shaped by this confluence of forces were seen as salvageable and worth salvaging. They were fellow citizens who had strayed but whose life trajectories were amenable to change. The richness and roundness of this vision serve to highlight the pessimism and poverty of imagination that followed in its wake.

Popularly referred to as Cherry Hill after a cherry orchard that was once on the site, Eastern State Penitentiary was a triumph in terms of design, rectifying many of the flaws that had become apparent in the Western State Penitentiary at Pittsburgh where defective construction methods meant that prisoners could easily communicate with their neighbours. The cells were large, measuring 'eleven feet nine inches long, seven feet six inches wide, and sixteen feet high to the top of the arched ceiling' (Crawford 1834: 10). A number were even more generously proportioned, with dimensions of 20 feet in length, 8 in width and 12 in height (Anonymous 1987: 10–11; by volume these large cells could have incorporated ten of Auburn's 'claustrophobic cubicles'). Each was heated, ventilated and equipped with a privy 'constructed in such a manner as to preserve the purity of the atmosphere, and to prevent the possibility of communication from cell to cell' (Crawford 1834: 10). Ground-floor cells had a double door leading to an enclosed yard (8 feet wide by 18 feet long, surrounded by walls that were 12 feet high) where an hour's exercise was allowed each day, except Sunday. The new prisoner was conducted to his cell wearing a hood. When this was removed his eyes rested on the walls that would set the physical boundaries to his world for the years ahead.

Johnston (2004: 25) noted that the prisoners at Eastern State Penitentiary had access to a flushing lavatory before this innovation in plumbing was introduced to the White House. Their quarters were centrally heated and they could avail of showers, again years before such facilities were available to wealthy US citizens. These extras did not come cheap and the enormous construction costs deterred other states from following the Pennsylvania model although, as we will see, these reservations did not carry the same force in Europe and elsewhere, where the achievements of Eastern State Penitentiary in giving physical expression to a clear penal philosophy were acclaimed. Johnston described it as 'the U.S. building most widely imitated in Europe and Asia in the 19th century. No other U.S. building form, until the modern skyscraper, played such a seminal role' (p. 39).

According to Johnston (2000: 74) when the penitentiary opened it was 'an international sensation' attracting scrutiny from delegations sent by the governments of Britain, France, Russia, Belgium, and a variety of other countries. Most reported favourably on the architectural excellence of the buildings and the coherence of the underlying philosophy. They were persuaded by the argument that the rational organization of space could induce rationality in its occupants. The prison also became a major tourist attraction, becoming 'a rival to Niagara Falls and the US Capitol in popularity' with 4,000 visitors in 1839, including school children and groups of Native Americans (p. 74). Admission tickets could be purchased and opening hours were advertised. This popularity did not fade over time, with the prison receiving 114,440 visitors between 1862 and 1872, according to Vaux (1872: 94). The title page of the book about Cherry Hill written by Teeters and Shearer (1957) carries an observation from a Venezuelan lawyer which was recorded in the minutes of the Philadelphia Society for Alleviating the Miseries of Public Prisons on 9 July 1832. It reads: 'The Pennsylvania System is a Divine System.' These seven words capture what inspired the system and how its effects were viewed by those who believed in it.

Crawford (1834) was aware of the view that long periods of solitary confinement were inherently dangerous and this was a matter to which he directed a great deal of attention. His considered opinion was that, properly administered and limited in duration to a maximum of 18 months, solitude had the power to cause a man to change the direction of his life: 'Day after day, with no companions but his thoughts, the convict is compelled to reflect and listen to the reproofs of conscience. He is led to dwell upon past errors, and to cherish whatever better feelings he may at any time have imbibed' (p. 12). Essential to the proper administration of a regime of solitude was the provision of religious instruction. When a convict's mind was clear, and the experience of silence was prolonged, the sound of a human voice was a source of major refreshment. If this voice was imparting a religious message it was to an especially attentive and receptive listener. Crawford felt that Eastern State Penitentiary had not done enough to add this vital ingredient to the mix. Whatever instruction was provided tended to be somewhat patchy and, as illiterate prisoners were not taught to read, there was little they could do to make good the deficit through personal study of the sacred texts.

It is important to note that while the prisoners in Eastern State Penitentiary were to be totally separated from each other they were not entirely deprived of human contact. If they were to recognize their wrongdoing and repent, it was essential that they had available to them role models such as the warden and his staff and appropriate visitors from outside, especially members of the Philadelphia Society for Alleviating the Miseries of Public Prisons. Members of the Society visited regularly. The *Journal of Prison Discipline and Philanthropy* (established in 1845 and continuing to appear as *The Prison Journal*, but no longer a proponent of the virtues of solitary confinement) reported in July 1861 that in a single month the Society's visitors had been in Eastern State Penitentiary on 813 occasions. In 612 of these a prisoner was interviewed in his cell and in the remainder a conversation took place at the door. A later issue of the *Journal* reported that during 1912, the total number of interviews carried out by visitors was 8,400 (cited in Anonymous 1987: 19). Kahan (2008: 37) quoted a report from the September 1854 issue of the *Chambers Journal of Popular Literature, Science and Arts* to the effect that, 'though styled the separate system, the discipline admits of the freest intercourse with respectable visitors. The best people in Philadelphia call upon, and hold converse with the convicts, who doubtless receive no small benefit through such agencies.' These interactions were no doubt brief and somewhat lopsided given the gulf in social status between the two groups but, nevertheless, they broke the monotony and kept open a conduit to the outside world.

In addition, prisoners would have occasional family visits to look forward to, letters to write, and books to read. All had a Bible and a prayer book and some were furnished, in addition, with an atlas and a dictionary. Musical instruments were allowed and, occasionally, pets, and prisoners were permitted to adorn their cells with frescoes, should they have the talent and temperament to do so. Some of the small yards that were available to prisoners were cultivated to grow fruit and flowers. The *Journal* reported in 1848 that one prisoner picked 150 bunches of grapes from the vine in his yard, where he also raised over 100 cucumbers, while others had peach trees, grown from seed, that yielded abundant crops (cited in Anonymous 1987: 10).

Thus, solitary confinement was something of a misnomer; the emphasis was on separation rather than unbroken aloneness and the burden was eased somewhat by the ability to personalise one's living space and to have access to the pleasures that come from reading, playing music, and engaging in a modest level of horticulture. What was at issue in the Pennsylvania system of prison discipline was not idle solitariness (except for the initial phase) but what one of the system's most ardent proponents described as 'uninterrupted confinement at labor', with equal importance attached to the elements of work and solitude (Lieber 1838: 68). As Beaumont and Tocqueville (1833: 23) put it, 'Labour gives to the solitary cell an interest; it fatigues the body and relieves the mind.' Engagement with those who could assist in the moral improvement of prisoners was permitted, and even encouraged. What was prohibited was association with fellow prisoners. Similarly, the silent system practised at Auburn aimed to prevent communication between inmates while keeping open the possibility that they would be receptive to the voices of instructors in trades, education, and religion. Communication between prisoners was seen as mutually contaminating; the possibility of benign exchanges was not contemplated by those pressing for penal reform, whether their preference was for individual separation or congregate silence.

Debate and Dissent

Not every observer was convinced by the merits of the new arrangements. When the great novelist, Charles Dickens, visited Eastern State Penitentiary on 8 March 1842 he was horrified, seeing not an enlightened monument to reform and humanity, but a place of dread. He was unequivocal in his scorn and condemnation: 'The system here, is rigid, strict, and hopeless solitary confinement. I believe it, in its effects, to be cruel and wrong... very few men are capable of estimating the immense amount of torture and agony which this dreadful punishment, prolonged for years, inflicts upon the sufferers' (Dickens 2000: 111). Dickens felt that isolation for any length of time caused unnecessary suffering and was at odds with the aims of the system that embraced it. When he met, during his visit to the prison, a sailor who had been in solitary confinement for upwards of 11 years, he was stunned and dismayed. The man was due for release but appeared not to care. He had lost interest in his life and what his future at liberty might hold and struck Dickens as 'helpless, crushed, and broken' (p. 116). Dickens must also have been staggered by the sheer length of the sailor's sentence, which was a multiple of the longest prison term available in England at the time (see Table 2.1). To Dickens' readers at home, who had been used to seeing transportation as the solution to the convict problem, incarcerating prisoners for terms measuring a decade and more—some even for life—would have seemed like a barbaric curiosity. Interestingly, Dickens felt that the prison's female inhabitants fared better, noting of the three young women whose cells he visited that, 'In the silence and solitude of their lives, they had grown to be quite beautiful' (p. 117).

Dickens' claims were robustly challenged and it was argued that he had exaggerated the psychological effects on the prisoners he encountered. We return in the following chapter to a reconsideration of Dickens' critique but for present purposes it is enough to note that if the solitary system he so deplored had really been in place, he would not have had an opportunity to tour the prison and talk freely with those it held, and that if his lamentation had been taken seriously, the system he so roundly condemned would hardly have been imitated with such enthusiasm in his native country and across Europe.

For all the vigorously expressed views of its advocates the system applied at Eastern State Penitentiary was not adopted by most other states which preferred congregate labour by day in workshops (i.e. the Auburn model). Some, like Maryland, Massachusetts, Maine, and New Jersey, tried separate confinement, but the limited income from prisoners working in their cells set against the high costs meant that they soon switched to the Auburn model and by 1858 the only prison still adhering to the separate system in the US was Eastern State Penitentiary (Johnston et al. 1994: 104). The Auburn system became dominant not least because it cost less (the separate system required cells large enough for the prisoner to work in and individual exercise yards) and was more suited to the kind of factory-like labour demanded by a growing industrial economy (the artisanal work carried out in Cherry Hill, such as shoemaking, was becoming outmoded and inefficient in the age of the machine). Whatever about the underlying penal philosophy the Auburn system won out in terms of the bottom line: it was cheaper to administer and resulted in a more generous profit margin. Johnston (2000: 71) estimated the cost per cell at Cherry Hill at $1,800 compared with $151 for a prison in Connecticut, constructed at around the same time (McElwee 1835: 102 gives different estimates). The strenuous promotional efforts of the Boston Prison Discipline Society also contributed in no small way to the popularity of the Auburn model in the US (Barnes and Teeters 1943: 533–43).

Notwithstanding reservations about its efficacy in the US, 'the Philadelphian system swept through Europe' (Franke 1995: 65). It has been estimated that 'About three hundred prisons worldwide can trace their paternity to Cherry Hill. Its influence was strongly manifest everywhere in the world, except in the United States' (Johnston et al. 1994: 79). At the first International Penitentiary Congress in Frankfurt-am-Main in 1846 it was resolved that separate confinement should be adopted as the norm (Evans 2010: 384). When introduced in the Netherlands in 1851, its proponents repudiated the link between solitary confinement and insanity, with one professor of psychiatry arguing that there would be no threat to mental health even after 20 years in a cell (Franke 1995: 142). By the end of the nineteenth century, there were ten cellular penitentiaries in the Netherlands with prisoners spending the first five years in solitude.

Denmark built prisons according to both the Auburn and Pennsylvania models and continued to operate the distinctive regimes associated with these competing philosophies until the early decades of the twentieth century, long after they had fallen into desuetude in their country of origin (Smith 2008: 1054; for a review of prison historiography outside Europe and the US see Gibson 2011). The Danes clung tenaciously to the principle of isolation and it was not until 1924 that wearing masks was made optional for inmates in Vridsløselille (Smith 2004: 24). The

Belgians were enthusiasts too. When the Royal Commission on Capital Punishment (1953: 485) visited Louvain Prison in October 1950, it found that relics of the system of solitary confinement still survived including the prison's motto, '*accipienti solitudo amica*'. This epigram might be translated as 'solitude is a friend to the one who accepts it' and it captures the optimism that animated penal reformers in the nineteenth century. It must be remembered, of course, that the benevolent intent had a hard edge in the recognition that for those who could not, or would not, befriend solitude, the alternative was bitter enmity.

Crawford (1834: 13) paid particular attention to the 'four insane persons and one idiot' who by his reckoning had been confined in Eastern State Penitentiary in the first four years after it opened. His inquiries left him in no doubt where the blame lay, namely that the prisoners 'had been subjected to mental disorders before they were admitted, and that the disease was in no respect attributable to any peculiarity in the discipline of the penitentiary' (p. 13). Furthermore, he observed that while the prison recorded a small number of deaths each year (one in 1833 and four in 1832, for example) its general effect on prisoners' health was beneficial as they were sheltered from the hazards that characterized their lives outside, such as poverty, bad weather, vagrancy, violence, and excessive alcohol consumption. This was a strong statement to make at the time and one that appears to have been largely forgotten in the intervening period, when the effects of separation have all too often been seen as unequivocally pathological. (Lieber (1838: 72–3) also challenged the assertion that the Pennsylvania system had adverse implications for the health of those subjected to it, noting that 'many who arrive diseased and broken down recover'.) Crawford went on to comment that there was nothing particularly original about the philosophy expressed in Eastern State Penitentiary, the main principles of which were to be found at the Gloucester Penitentiary 40 years earlier and, more recently, in the Glasgow Bridewell. In a sense it was not until the idea of separate confinement had been transplanted to the US (by English architect John Haviland who won the contract to design and build the penitentiary at Cherry Hill) that it was reintroduced to Britain and the rest of Europe for adoption on a much more ambitious scale. As Evans (2010: 318) put it, 'The English rediscovered the reforming power of solitude in America.'

At Eastern State Penitentiary, while the whip was eschewed, devices such as the iron gag—a metal brace that was secured in the prisoner's mouth with a lock and chain—were used instead. Not intended to harm the body, this was seen as a mechanism for bending the inmate's will: 'Like the walls of the cell it restrained the recalcitrant will of the inmate. And, its defenders believed, once in place, the gag, like the cell, eliminated the physical violence and struggle that marked the whipping scene' (Meranze 2000: 318). The subtlety of this distinction was surely lost on the inmate who was forced to yield to its severe discomfort. That a metal clamp like a horse's bit could be resorted to within an institution supposedly guided by benevolence shows how brutality can break through the best of intentions.

Distinctions between the Auburn and Pennsylvania systems are sometimes too sharply drawn. Prisoners at Eastern State Penitentiary from time to time endured the iron gag and the (freezing) shower bath—it was not just at Auburn where the body was distressed. Those at Auburn were sometimes psychologically crippled by the whip—it was not just in Eastern State Penitentiary where the will to live could be broken. In both places opportunities for easy communication and meaningful relationships with other prisoners were non-existent. Both systems sought to subdue through silence, to instruct, to guide, and to reform. They also hoped that inmate labour might defray some or all of the running costs.

Johnston (2004: 27–30) described how the separate system as practised at Eastern State Penitentiary was imperfect from the outset. He gave as examples the deployment of prisoners as assistants to the carpenters and stonemasons who were involved in the institution's construction; the use of prisoners as waiters at staff parties; and the involvement of prisoners in maintenance tasks such as supplying cellblock stoves with fuel (if male) or working in the kitchen or laundry (if female). These violations of the principles underlying the separate system led to a legislative inquiry five years after the prison opened (see McElwee 1835). Prisoners were also adept at communicating with their neighbours by rapping on the walls, shouting into the sewer pipes when they were empty, or throwing notes into adjacent exercise yards. But there was 'a more blatant violation of the system's ideals' (Johnston 2004: 29). This was caused by the presence of prisoners who could not speak English who were sometimes accommodated with a bilingual inmate so that one could act as translator for the other. Similarly, there were reports of the single cell policy being breached if an inmate needed to be observed for medical reasons or if he required instruction in a trade from another prisoner.

But the most serious undermining of the official ethos of silence and separation, what Johnston termed the 'dirty secret' (p. 29) of the Pennsylvania system was that the prison soon became overcrowded, with some cells containing two convicts as early as 1841. According to Teeters (1937: 401): 'By 1860 the system had broken down to the point where a disinterested observer would have admitted that the concept championed by the Society [for Alleviating the Miseries of Public Prisons] was no longer tenable. It broke down first for the very practical reason that it was not only expensive, but difficult of attainment from an administrative point of view.' As Johnston (2004: 29) reported, the heyday of separation did not last long:

Prior to a major building program in 1876, 795 inmates occupied 585 cells. More than half of the prisoners in a penitentiary organized around the principle of separation were sharing cells. Before the turn of the century, the prison's population approached 1,400, with as many as four inmates occupying one cell. The Pennsylvania system, fiercely defended by its local partisans against the rival Auburn system, never maintained strict seclusion for all of its inmates.

Johnston's numbers differ from those reported elsewhere which suggest an even worse situation of 977 inmates in 580 cells in 1876 (Eastern State Penitentiary Task Force 1994: 178, Table 2a). Quibbles about the figures aside, the trend is clear, with more prisoners than cells by the 1860s and an entrenchment of this problem thereafter, despite the provision of additional accommodation. Kahan (2008: 48) cites an attack on the penitentiary's administration made by a local judge in 1881 that was reported by the *Philadelphia Inquirer*. The judge had bemoaned the fact that: 'the prisoners are not in solitary confinement, unless you can call two and three persons in one cell solitary'. However imperfect the Pennsylvania system may have been in terms of enforcing silence and separation, any pretence that the experiment could continue was ended by the doubling up of prisoners. The erosion of the concept of separate discipline to a point beyond which it could not be retained even as a convenient fiction was finally arrived at with its legislative repeal in 1913, bringing law and policy into alignment with what had long been the practice.

Developments on the other side of the Atlantic followed a similar trajectory. The integrity of separation, as exemplified in London by HMP Pentonville, was soon challenged, diluted, and abandoned.

The Model Prison

The Penitentiary Act 1779 formalized the idea that prisoners in England should be lodged in 'separate rooms or cells' at night. Maximum (12 feet long, 8 wide and 11 high) and minimum (10 by 7 by 9) dimensions were specified for these rooms. The Act envisaged the construction of two national penitentiaries—one for 600 men and the other for 300 women—that would involve 'solitary imprisonment, accompanied by well regulated labour, and religious instruction'. The rationale was that this combination of effects would allow the individual to acquire the requisite tools to construct a new life just as solitary confinement worked to obliterate their former self. The impact of this legislative initiative was largely felt at local level in the closing decades of the eighteenth century, where numerous prisons designed with a view to solitary confinement were constructed. The national penitentiaries did not emerge as planned and in the local jails where solitary confinement had been introduced it came under sustained critical attack on the grounds of (high) cost and (dubious) effectiveness and was used less regularly, 'ending up as a special form of discipline for refractory prisoners' (Evans 2010: 192). The enthusiasm for penal solitude waned significantly in the opening decades of the nineteenth century before being revived by Crawford's report of his American visit.

Evans (2010) showed that the reasons for abandoning solitude as a penological principle were practical as much as they were philosophical. As well as exacting a considerable toll on the individual it was difficult to impose successfully. One of the first English prisons to attempt blanket enforcement of silence was Coldbath Fields House of Correction in London. Attempts to communicate were ruthlessly suppressed in the early 1830s. In one year more than 11,600 punishments were awarded for talking or swearing (Playfair 1971: 78). But the governor and staff had to admit partial defeat as, even if they stamped out casual conversation, prisoners managed to convey information through a sign language of winks and hand movements, by tapping on pipes, and other ingenious measures. As expressed by Ignatieff (1989: 178), the prison authorities were limited to 'policing a silence that actually hummed with secret language'. This meant that when architectural solutions emerged to meet the challenges of separation, they found a receptive audience. The experiments in Auburn and Philadelphia gave hope to reformers in England that: 'Silence and separation would yet be the salvation of prisoners' (Evans 2010: 317).

The 1779 legislation allowed imprisonment in a penitentiary for up to seven years as an alternative to transportation, which had been abandoned due to the outbreak of the American War in 1776. But, as the national penitentiaries envisaged by the Act were not built, prison terms remained short. When transportation resumed after 1784, now to Australia, the plans for the penitentiaries were shelved. Work eventually began on a national penitentiary at Millbank in London in 1812. This huge institution, described by Teagarden (1969: 358) as 'a sprawling, shapeless labyrinth of cell blocks and ancillary buildings', was exorbitantly expensive to build and to run, and was plagued by difficulties from the outset. Built on marshy ground and inadequately ventilated, the poorly fed prisoners were vulnerable to disease; disgruntled by the regime, they became rebellious; structural flaws meant that parts of the building were unsafe; public sentiment was ambivalent at best; and the complexity of the layout compromised effective surveillance.

HMP Pentonville, the 'model prison', was intended to overcome these problems and to vindicate penitentiary discipline. It would demonstrate how severity and mercy could be combined in a building that was designed to eradicate communication (of disease as well as of criminal contacts). In this sterile and silent environment those who had done wrong would learn to do right in a way that was cost-effective and served to promote public safety. A flawless institution would eradicate the flaws in its occupants. It would be, in Evans' (2010: 354) words, 'a kind of chrysalis within which the transmutation of the criminal mind was to take place'. When Pentonville opened in 1842 the architectural and philosophical influences of Eastern State Penitentiary were readily apparent in its imposing facade, radial design, individual exercise yards, and relatively large cells. Like its American cousin, Pentonville excited great interest internationally and was used as the blueprint for prisons in many other countries.

Pentonville was the apotheosis of a long process of delibera-
tion, experimentation, failure, and revision. It was the culmination of the desire to connect individual reformation to institutional
design, so that modifications to the latter would impact directly
on the former. According to Evans it was 'more impressive for its
complexity and perfection than for its originality' (p. 363). It was
the epitome of the reformers' credo that a man who has fallen can,
with assistance, learn to stand and to walk straight. It drew on
a long, but inconsistent, commitment to solitary confinement as
a penal objective in Britain and the scrutiny of developments—
especially architectural, but also medical and moral—in the US.
Inmates in the 'model prison' would spend 18 months in separate
confinement, in what was described at the time with alliterative
flourish, as, 'a silent solitary sepulchre of stone' (*The Times*, 29
November 1843, p. 4). They were entitled to a single visit of 15
minutes duration every six months and they could send and receive
two letters each year. At the end of their term they were transported to Australia.

Care is required with the language used to characterize competing penal priorities. As noted already, neither Auburn nor Eastern
State Penitentiary involved absolute solitude as in the former, after
the brief failed experiment with total isolation, there was communal work and dining and in the latter, while denied intercourse with
other prisoners, there were many visitors from outside as well as
regular encounters with the chaplain and other prison staff. Also,
there was a distinction in the British legislation between separate
confinement and solitary confinement. The former was intended
for the prisoner's benefit even if it was felt as punitive, and the latter was intended as punitive, and to be used sparingly, with little
consideration as to its wider impact. Reviewing the situation in
England, Field (1848: 146) drew a sharp distinction between 'solitary confinement' which was purely punitive and unambiguously
harmful, and 'separate confinement' which was intended for 'the
permanent moral benefit of the prisoner'. The former was spent
in cramped conditions, with minimal human interaction and a
reduced diet. It tended to 'harden, provoke, and brutalize' (p. 147).
The latter was spent in a spacious and well-ventilated cell with
decent food and opportunities for work, education, and religious
instruction together with regular visits from those concerned with
the improvement of morals. Its effect was 'to induce reflection,
kindliness, gratitude, and amendment' (p. 147). As Henriques

(1972: 77) put it: 'Separation was from other criminals only, not from the superior moral company of prison governors, chaplains, schoolmasters etc.'

The subtleties of the situation were not always appreciated. A letter to *The Lancet*, penned while Pentonville was under construction, drew attention to some of the adverse consequences of prolonged solitary confinement that had been reported in America and Belgium. The correspondent cautioned that, if true, these reports 'would make the refined cruelty of the silent system appear less humane and merciful than was the Spanish Inquisition' (Simpson 1840). (As will be shown in Chapter 5, technological advances have allowed this 'refined cruelty' to be taken to another level in what have become known as supermax prisons.)

A 'maniac-making system'?

There was adverse commentary in the press in the period after Pentonville opened. A short piece in *The Times* on 27 November 1843—no more than a column inch on page four—was entitled 'Insanity in the Model Prison'. It drew attention to the fact that although the prison had not been open long, and held inmates who were in good health, nevertheless two among their number, John Reeve and John Hill Stone, had become insane during the year and been transferred to hospital. The comment was made that 'It is remarkable that insanity only occurs in the Penitentiary and Model Prison, under Government inspectors, and not in magistrates' prisons.' Madness, it was suggested, seemed to be a problem peculiar to Pentonville. (For a highly partisan, and entertainingly barbed, account of the hostility of *The Times* towards the separate system, see Adshead 1845: 13–93.)

The Illustrated London News described how Pentonville had claimed 'another victim', a convict named Cowle, who was the third within the space of a year to have become insane and been transferred to Bethlehem hospital (13 January 1844, p. 22). Concerns about the model prison incubating madness were made all the more acute by the fact that the rigours of the regime had been anticipated and the prisoners who were sent there were carefully chosen from among those who had been sentenced to transportation. They were young, strong, generally first offenders, and believed to be capable of withstanding the rigours of separation. That a slide into solitary madness was found in an apparently healthy group exacerbated concern in some quarters. As the separate system became more widely established and the ability to preselect prisoners diminished, its adverse implications became more evident. The deleterious psychological consequences of solitude were no surprise. This hazard had always been recognized; indeed the process of reformation, if it was to begin in earnest, required the aversive stimulus of isolation. The question was simply whether the risk was disproportionately large. This was where discussants differed, and prisoners died. (The argument has changed little in the intervening period, namely, how is it possible to establish with any degree of precision the independent effect of isolation, especially among a group where there is known to be a high level of underlying distress and dysfunction?)

Within a year of its opening The Times was describing Pentonville as a 'maniac-making system' where the prisoner became a 'coffined living man' (29 November 1843, p. 4). Indeed, The Times had been pessimistic even before the model prison opened, believing that prolonged separation was 'unnecessarily cruel, impolitic, and injudicious' and that it would cause an unacceptable level of distress: 'Misery will follow the want of excitement, melancholy will give place to despair, and if not relieved by contact with living beings, madness or idiocy must follow' (20 May 1841, p. 8). In the same article, the newspaper warned that, 'if other prisons be built on the same principle, a madhouse will be a necessary adjunct to a county prison' (p. 8).

Table 1.1 summarizes what can be learned about the extent to which this dystopian claim can be empirically validated drawing upon the annual reports to parliament of the prison's commissioners. A complete understanding of medical care in Pentonville would require a detailed archival study but the official figures probably serve as reliable counts of mortality and are suggestive of institutional priorities more generally. The table is limited to the most serious cases—those that led to removal on the grounds of insanity, or where the prisoner took his own life. There were other cases each year—albeit few in number—where prisoners were removed to Millbank or the hulks because they were deemed unsuited to the discipline of the prison. Among this small group were some who showed signs of psychological distress. Other prisoners whose disturbance was insufficient to lead to their removal were treated within the confines of the penitentiary. Table 1.1 shows that, during its first seven years, just two suicides and thirteen cases of insanity

Table 1.1 The 'maniac-making system' at Pentonville

	Admissions	Removed insane	Suicide	Other deaths	Mania/ delusions
1843	525	2	0	2	8
1844	240	1	0	3	0
1845	283	1	0	4	3
1846	243	1	0	2	6
1847	360	0	0	2	2
1848	519	4	1	6	7
1849	599	4	1	1	5
Total	2,769	13	2	20	31

Source: Commissioners for the Government of the Pentonville Prison, second to eighth reports. The figures for 1843 include the final ten days of the previous year; the prison received its first prisoners on 21 December 1842.

were recorded in Pentonville. Ten times as many prisoners died from physical diseases as at their own hands. During the first full year of its operation there were no suicides and two prisoners were removed to Bethlehem hospital on the grounds of insanity. The following year there were no suicides and one insane prisoner was transferred to hospital. If Pentonville was a machine for making maniacs it was not a particularly effective one. Even in the earliest days most prisoners seemed to get by without drawing attention to themselves. Only a tiny minority became floridly unwell and in some of these cases there was a history of mental illness that came to light later. So it is difficult to sustain the argument that the prison *systematically* propelled people towards insanity. Nevertheless, these few cases generated significant interest and the regime was progressively softened, with the period of separate confinement truncated from 18 months to 12 months in 1848 and then to nine months in 1853 (Departmental Committee on Prisons [Gladstone Committee] 1895a: para 78).

The commissioners were at pains to point out in their second report that the first prisoner to be removed to Bethlehem hospital (John Reeve) had not been in custody long and had not been exposed to the rigours of separation. He was admitted on 8 February 1843 and six weeks later (22 March) showed symptoms of melancholy which soon gave way to 'violent religious mania' (Commissioners for the Government of the Pentonville Prison 1844: 9). Discipline was relaxed and he seemed to improve but suffered a relapse and was transferred to hospital on 24 June. According to the commissioners: 'During the short time he was in the prison, and before he became insane, he was almost constantly employed out of his cell and in company' (p. 9). The second prisoner to be removed to Bethlehem that year (John Hill Stone) was reported to have had a history of insanity before his imprisonment and was principally occupied outside his cell (p. 9). There is a defensive tone to these reports; an unwillingness to contemplate that there could be a causal relationship between the regime and the prisoners' mental states. The physician's report to the commissioners for 1844 is emphatic: 'the system of Pentonville presents nothing in itself conducive to the development of insanity' (Commissioners for the Government of the Pentonville Prison 1845: 19). Like the chaplains, prison doctors played an important role in the debate about separation and its effects.

Teagarden (1969: 363–4) was not convinced by the proposition that the regime at Pentonville was 'maniac making', observing that the available records suggest it fared well vis-à-vis comparable institutions in England and the US in terms of rates of insanity and overall mortality. The available data show that the number of prisoners transferred out of Pentonville was very small but that this outward trickle caused a flood of controversy (especially in *The Times*). In addition, there was a less dramatic underlying level of dysfunction that probably resulted in the decision to abbreviate the period of separation. In short, there were few suicidal lunatics but there was much evident distress.

Whatever its effects the infatuation with redemptive separation did not last long. According to Grass (2003: 44), 'Through the rest of the decade [1850s] local officials continued to build separate prisons, and prison chaplains... continued to sing the separate system's praises. At Pentonville, however, the great national experiment in separate discipline was over.' As McConville (1981: 209) put it:

Pentonville sank under the weight of public disapproval, its own unfulfilled promises, and the requirements of the new public works prisons. In 1849 the special selection for Pentonville of the most fit and promising convicts ceased and, with various other changes in the regime, the reformatory experiment was effectively abandoned. Henceforth Pentonville differed little in objectives, methods or population from Millbank convict depot; in both, convicts were disciplined before being sent, as a preliminary to transportation, to labour in association at the new public works prison at Portland, thus irrevocably wrecking the scheme of careful penitential preparation followed by ejection into completely new circumstances.

The abolition of transportation and the loss of faith in the reformative effects of separation meant that the period of isolation that characterized the first phase of the sentence became seen as an entirely aversive experience for a growing number of prisoners. The report of the Select Committee of the House of Lords (1863) chaired by the Earl of Carnarvon, and the Prisons Act that followed two years later, marked the shift towards a uniform system of discipline across local jails and greater emphasis on hard labour, hard fare, and a hard bed. Devices such as the crank and the tread wheel (or 'everlasting staircase' as it was sometimes known), and pointless exertions such as shot drill, became more popular. The food was precisely measured, minimal, and monotonous. The hammock was replaced with a plank of wood. The prevailing wisdom according to Forsythe (2004: 759) was that imprisonment should involve 'rigid, measured severity' and 'carefully graded suffering'. In 1895 the Gladstone Committee ushered in a new era of reform and, once again, the prison system changed tack. The tread wheel and the crank were abolished and the relentless and withering punitiveness of the previous 30 years was jettisoned in favour of more reformative and hopeful measures. What had been accepted was once again discredited (see Harding (1988) for an account of the committee's antecedents and how its work was influenced by differing perceptions of crime and recidivism rates).

In the opening decades of the twentieth century the enforcement of the rule of silence and the rigours of the initial phase of separation were gradually relaxed; the former because it was routinely subverted and the latter because any residual belief in its reformative rationale had evaporated. This is not to say that prisoners were allowed to mingle and communicate freely, but rather that it was generally recognized that the pursuit of absolute silence was futile and had the undesirable side effect of bringing the framework of prison rules more generally into disrepute. Even when silence was a paramount value it was never complete. Prisoners rapped on walls, shouted out windows, banged their doors, or exchanged a few words with a sympathetic guard. When they came together in the chapels of England's separate prisons, they took the opportunity to roar out the responses and to sing the hymns at the tops of their voices (Priestley 1999: 94–5). This served a variety of purposes, none of which was intended. First of all it allowed those who were forced to live by a rule of silence to exercise vocal cords that had been forced to lie idle for too long. Secondly, it provided an opportunity for illicit conversation, camouflaged by loudly insincere singing. Thirdly, it offered opportunities for sacrilegious diversion as ribald lyrics were substituted for Christian verse. Fourthly, the excessive exuberance that characterized the congregation's performance caricatured the chaplains' efforts to bring their flock closer to God; this was divine service as defiance.

The gulf between policy and practice began to widen (see Hobhouse and Brockway 1922: 562–6) and the initial phase of separation was suspended in 1922 as the Home Secretary felt that 'a man brooding alone in his cell became morose and vindictive' (cited in Baxendale 2011: 171). When it was clear that this change did not lead to an increase in indiscipline the suspension was continued until the introduction of new prison rules in 1931 which brought the practice to a formal, and final, conclusion (p. 171). The last vestige of separate confinement had now been stripped out of the system.

When the optimism that surrounded the design and operation of the model prison evaporated, it was replaced by an emphasis on hopeless and pointless discipline. The failure to live up to expectations had profound effects. According to Priestley (1999: 119)

the damage the penitentiary did went deeper than broken promises and hurt minds. The void left by its collapse was progressively filled by a disciplinary timetable from which all humanity and all hope were all but extinguished. The original vision foresaw a dark tunnel of suffering, at the end of which there shone—however distantly—the light of redemption and salvation. When the light went out, the darkness closed in around the Victorian prisoner. It was not to be lifted again for a generation.

The 'darkness closed in' again with the proliferation of supermax prisons in the closing decades of the twentieth century. In another turn of the penal screw, the void created by the disappearance of therapeutic optimism and the pessimism about improving prisoners' behaviour without recourse to the most repressive measures, was filled by harsh hopelessness. As regards prisoner treatment, the view taken was that if nothing worked, then nothing mattered. But, just as the infatuation with hard labour passed, so too the supermax obsession is likely to wane and if the historical precedent is any guide, a more beneficent cycle may lie ahead.

The Hard Cell of Solitude

The separate system was lauded initially and officials at Pentonville and other establishments where it was in place in the UK, such as Reading and Preston, held that prisoners benefited greatly from it. They claimed that former convicts corresponded after release to praise the disciplinary regime to which they had been subjected (Field (1848: 297–8) reproduced some 'specimens'). No doubt this did happen on occasion, but the inmates who had gone mad or returned to crime were unlikely to pen such missives. Also, many reports of the benefits of separation came from chaplains who played an important role in telling prisoners' stories. As Grass (2003: 33–4) argued, taking control of the discourse in this way allowed them to propagate a view of prison discipline in accordance with their own preferences or, at least, to shape the prison narrative so that it became a story of depravity, separation, and religious awakening. Or, as Graber (2011: 187) put it, the writings of reformers and ministers of religion, 'functioned as volleys in a rhetorical war'. This does not negate the value of such publications—the detailed accounts of prison life they yield are important—but their underlying purpose must be kept in sight as an aid to interpretation.

It may be that the more credulous among the chaplains were quicker to go to print with their experiences, so persuaded were they by the success of a system in which they played a central role. By drawing attention to reformed rogues they could bask in reflected glory; not every clergyman could take credit for the spiritual renewal of parishioners who had fallen so far and yet risen so high. Those who laboured among the criminal classes searched hard for virtue among villains and when they found it, it is understandable why some of them were quick to suspend doubt and keen to spread the word. An example of this literary genre is the book of letters and autobiographies compiled by the chaplain of Chester Castle Gaol (Joseph 1853).

Some of the accounts prisoners provided to chaplains of their internal transformations may have been written to curry favour with the authorities but there were others that appeared to be sincere. But why would this be surprising, argued Henriques (1972: 83), given the attention paid to these alienated and barely literate working class men and women who, when they arrived in prison, 'were suddenly overwhelmed by the full impact of self-confident middle class evangelical religious and moral propaganda ... If the pliable merely bent before the wind, some may well have been, at least for the time, subjugated by the solitude and the torrent of exhortation. The techniques described as deterrence and reformation might nowadays be called brain-washing.' In other words, while some did respond to separation as its advocates hoped they would, the range of reactions was wide. In a review of more than two hundred prisoner autobiographies, Priestley (1999: 114) concluded that 'The weight of prisoner opinion is tilted firmly against the chaplains.' Despite the earnestness of their ministrations, and the claims of success made vociferously by a few among them, the chaplains' efforts were, by and large, rebuffed. In a long letter to the editor of the *Daily Chronicle* composed the year after his release from Reading Gaol, Oscar Wilde (1898) described the prison chaplains as, 'entirely useless. They are, as a class, well-meaning, but foolish, indeed silly, men.'

The prison reformers of the nineteenth century believed that enforced silence and solitude would cause prisoners to reflect on the error of their ways and that this reflection would become the springboard for a change of direction in their lives. The first element of this belief was certainly true, but sometimes the regret and remorse that attended hindsight, in conjunction with the limitations of the unbolstered self that solitude laid bare, were too much to bear. Writing of the 15 years penal servitude she served for poisoning her husband, Florence Maybrick (1905: 74–5) offered the following comment about her first nine months, which, in accordance with the practice of the time (Maybrick was convicted in August 1889), she spent alone: 'Solitary confinement is by far the most cruel feature of English penal servitude. It inflicts upon the prisoner at the commencement of her sentence, when most sensitive to the horrors which prison punishment entails, the voiceless solitude, the hopeless monotony, the long vista of to-morrow, to-morrow, to-morrow stretching before her, all filled with desolation and despair.' She saw it as 'inexpressible torture to both mind and body' (p. 81). Maybrick, who was born in Alabama, returned to the US after her release. She was unimpressed by Eastern State

Penitentiary, describing it in 1906 as the worst prison in all of America (Kahan 2008: 71).

Jabez Balfour (1907: 46), a swindler and former Member of Parliament who was sentenced to 14 years penal servitude in November 1895, found the rule of silence to be rigorously enforced: 'The silent system was as strictly maintained as was possible under human organization. I was at Wormwood Scrubbs [sic] for close on seven months, and I hardly exchanged twelve words with a fellow-prisoner during the whole of that time. My conversations were limited entirely to very brief replies to the warder's questions, to an occasional chat with the chaplain, and a passing remark with the then Governor.' One of the problems experienced by the solitary prisoner is retaining a sense of self. This is exacerbated by a lack of company as we tend to make sense of ourselves by comparison with others. When the prisoner is denied access even to his reflection, the grip on identity becomes ever more tenuous. Balfour described how his appearance became foreign to him: 'Curiously enough, I never saw myself in a looking-glass from the moment I left my cell in Holloway, on December 14, 1895, until November 1, 1904—practically nine years. When I did see myself I started back, for I did not know my own face. It was one of the most amazing and terrifying experiences in my life. I had changed past recognition' (p. 37).

Michael Davitt (1882: 10), who began his first period of penal servitude in 1870, with the obligatory nine months of solitary confinement at Millbank, recalled how: 'During the whole of my stay in Millbank my conversation with prisoners—at the risk of being punished, of course—as also with warders and chaplains, would not occupy me twenty minutes to repeat, could I collect all of the scattered words spoken by me...I recollect many weeks going by without my exchanging a word with a single human being.' However, during this period and the years that followed (Davitt was sentenced to 15 years penal servitude in 1870 and released on a ticket-of-leave after seven years and seven months; he was jailed again in 1881 and elected to the House of Commons the following year, while still a prisoner) the Irish patriot was not damaged beyond repair. 'It is his glory' Moody (1941: 525) tells us, 'that, resisting the jail-machine to the end, he was never broken by it— never became insane, or neurotic or embittered or hopeless.'

An account of how the 'jail-machine' is resisted is one of the key aims of this book. It is hoped that a critical examination of the impact of long-term isolation will attest to the durability of the individual under even the most arduous of circumstances. This may act as a prompt to reconsider the rationality of such treatment (to say nothing of its necessity or desirability). Why punish longer and harder if the limits to human endurance are so elastic? Secondly, it is hoped that foregrounding the temporal aspect of imprisonment will stimulate interest in a somewhat neglected aspect of the prisoner's psychological world. Time feels different depending on the individual's age, expectations, and phase of sentence. For solitary prisoners, it has an almost palpable quality, bearing down on them and threatening to crush. For the lonely prisoner the days seem endless and coping with boredom becomes an existential trial. Despite the odds, many discover the wherewithal to cope and their styles of 'time work' deserve closer attention than they have hitherto attracted. Thirdly, by rekindling the debate about silence and separation and returning to the historical precedents, it is hoped that some of the mistakes of the past will not be repeated and once again forgotten. Fourthly, there are lessons for policy and practice. These include the potential for preparing prisoners to mitigate the harshness of solitary confinement and the expanse of time that yawns ahead of them.

The historical message is that unrelieved solitary confinement was a severe burden for prisoners and one that could not be borne for long without running the risk of psychological derailment. When congregate labour was added but the rule of silence remained in place, the enforcement of the rule through corporal punishment created different hardships. Both the Pennsylvania and Auburn systems, but especially the former, came to be seen as embracing approaches to discipline that had few beneficial correlates from the perspectives of those subjected to their demands. But the assumption that the damage caused by isolation was universal and irreversible cannot be supported and there are several aspects of the debate that repay closer scrutiny. These are considered in the following chapter.

2

Reconsidering the Effects of
Silence and Separation

There are five aspects of the historical record that have clouded
scholarly interpretation and that merit re-examination. These are
the greater transparency of madness in the reformed prisons, confusion about causal pathways, prisoner adaptation, subterfuge,
and the provocative insights of a great novelist. Not all of these factors act in the same direction although most lean towards an over-
estimation of adverse psychological effects. They are addressed in
turn next.

Madness becomes Visible

The separate system and associated emphasis on silence meant
that symptoms of madness were likely to be noticed. These would
have been more difficult to detect in the tumult of the prisons
that predated these arrangements; the hallucinating, unhinged
or listless inmate would not have distinguished himself or herself against such a background. In the prisons where madness
became evident, staff were plentiful and better trained, again
making detection more likely even if there were no changes in
behaviour. As well as being present in greater numbers, as sala-
ried employees the staff in modern prisons were not dependent
on the jailer, and in turn on prisoners, for their pay. This allowed
a more detached, objective and professional attitude to emerge,
with staff becoming attentive watchers rather than crowd con-
trollers. Just two turnkeys supervised 114 men and women at
work pounding hemp in Clerkenwell Bridewell in 1779, and in
Newgate in the 1760s there was around one member of staff for
every 100 prisoners. By contrast, for prisons that operated the
Pentonville model, a typical ratio was one custodian for every 10
to 15 prisoners (Ignatieff 1989: 38, 198).

A cellular system with relatively high numbers of staff, no background chaos and confusion, and prisoners who were easy to observe individually, would inevitably lead to an increase in the detection of mental illness, even if there was no change in prevalence. The roaring drunk (or the shuddering delirium tremens of the suddenly abstinent), the obsessive self-mutilator, the taciturn depressive and the syphilitic lunatic will be invisible in the bawdy filth of one and seem strikingly transgressive in the other. Quite simply, the reforms that led to the emergence of penal systems based on silent supervision made the deranged easier to spot. The physician's report for Pentonville relating to 1846 noted that while the 'proportion of mental disease' might appear 'somewhat excessive' it was important to remember 'that most of our cases have been of such a character as would have escaped notice on any system of discipline which did not of necessity enforce so strict a watch upon the mental condition of the prisoners' (Commissioners for the Government of the Pentonville Prison 1847: 53). Furthermore, those with pre-existing difficulties found themselves in conditions (silence) with which they were poorly equipped to deal.

The first cohorts of prisoners committed to Pentonville had been selected on the basis of their robust health, so the more floridly ill would presumably have been screened out at an early stage. Nevertheless, underlying vulnerabilities may have gone undetected in some cases, meaning that ostensibly healthy prisoners would have unravelled in the silence in a way that became readily apparent. Silence allowed the noise of madness to be heard, as well as giving it a distinctive timbre. As the system of separate discipline became more widespread and the prisoner population became more heterogeneous the range and intensity of psychological difficulties can only have been magnified.

In the early years of Eastern State Penitentiary there was a concern that it was a 'dumping ground' for mentally ill offenders for whom there was a dearth of alternative accommodation (Johnston et al. 1994: 60). As public facilities for the criminally insane began to come on stream this pressure eased somewhat, but it did not disappear (for an account of the emergence of institutional care for the mentally ill, see Rothman 1971). The prison's physician stated in 1875 that of 801 convicts received into custody, 59 per cent suffered from impaired physical and mental health or were at risk of becoming unwell due to inherited deficiencies (Johnston et al. 1994: 60–1). This confounding factor is seldom mentioned in the criminological literature although Barnes and Teeters (1959: 343–4) recognized its significance when they cautioned

that in those early days there were mental hospitals only for those who could afford private treatment, that not too much was known regarding mental diseases, and that mental disease and mental defect were confused in diagnoses by some of the best physicians. Due to these factors as well as the extreme partisanship of both groups, this charge [that solitary confinement induces insanity] loses much of its venom as viewed today.

It is also possible that prevailing attitudes when the debate about silence and separation was underway meant there was a rush to see as pathogenic, responses to isolation that elsewhere might be viewed as adaptive. We have learned from work with polar explorers that in a context of extreme under-stimulation a form of psychological 'hibernation' is observed, which is both environmentally appropriate and transient (see Chapter 4). Similarly, the lethargy and withdrawal exhibited by the isolated prisoner can be viewed (positively) as an effective coping strategy as well as (negatively) as an involuntary capitulation to harsh circumstances (see Chapter 3). When circumstances change so, too, do the prospects that 'normal' activities will be resumed. Wherever individuals are found in unavoidable isolation, whether this is sought out or imposed, there are a few who thrive, others who are adversely affected but get by, and some for whom the experience becomes permanently debilitating. It is not possible to estimate with any degree of precision the proportions in each of these three groups but it would seem reasonable based on the extant literature to suggest that the second one is the largest and that while for a minority of prisoners the experience either redounds to their considerable advantage or precipitates a breakdown, most find a way to cope, and wait for the days to merge into weeks, the weeks into months, the months into years and even decades (see Chapters 8 and 10 for an analysis of temporal reorientation and popular survival strategies, respectively).

Madness is Misattributed

One dimension of the relationship between madness and isolation that has received little attention is the perceived role of masturbation in precipitating mental illness and how this may have caused commentators to underestimate the effects of loneliness and hopelessness. Franke (1995: 61) writes that of 18 cases of insanity detected at Eastern State Penitentiary in 1838, 12 were ascribed to excessive masturbation. The following year there were 26 cases of mental illness, 15 of which were believed to have their origin in an unhealthy dedication to the 'secret vice'. The consequences were sometimes believed to be fatal. Examination of the reports of the physician at Eastern State Penitentiary, which refer to prisoners by number rather than name, revealed that for a variety of lethal ailments, there was believed to be a direct causal relationship: '6694...is recorded as having died of *asthma*, produced by masturbation'; '7032...died of *debility*...Persistent masturbation was the sole cause of his death'; even a prisoner who took his own life was considered to have done so on account of 'excessive masturbation' (Johnston et al. 1994: 60; emphasis in original). Kunzel (2008: 22) noted that, 'In accounting for five deaths among the inmate population of a New Jersey penitentiary in 1838, the resident physician reported that "one destroyed himself by Onanism".' When recording deaths in their journals, prison wardens were also acutely aware of the many repercussions of the solitary vice and as late as 1889 Warden Cassidy of Eastern State Penitentiary wrote of a prisoner who had taken his own life: 'primary cause leading to suicide, excessive masturbation' (Teeters and Shearer 1957: 175).

The fearful effects of this practice were widely propagated and officials at Cherry Hill went so far as to hang a printed notice in each cell spelling out its many deleterious consequences, including tumours, digestive complaints, disorders of the heart and lungs, insanity and premature death. The list concluded with a simple exhortation: 'Let all who have been addicted to this loathsome vice thus described, *Stop, at once Stop*' (Franke 1995: 62; emphasis in original). Smith (2006: 458) cites a report to the Boston Prison Discipline Society in 1846 that attributed the incidence of mental illness in Eastern State Penitentiary to the high proportion of 'mulatto' men held there who were 'addicted to those sexual excesses which lead particularly to cerebral derangement'. This echoed a 'finding' made seven years earlier at the same institution that 'the cases of mental disorder occurring in this Penitentiary are, with a few exceptions...caused by masturbation, and are mostly among the colored prisoners' (p. 458). The combination of race, class and what were considered to be deviant sexual practices excited the imaginations of the high minded, comfortably off, white citizens who ministered to the spiritual and medical needs of prisoners. To their genuine concern and disgust must have been added a frisson of anxious curiosity.

Lieber (1838: 82) felt that the 'vice of peculiar vileness... exists likewise in our penitentiaries, both on the Auburn and Pennsylvania plan.' However, he felt that the isolation of prisoners at night that characterized both systems had the distinct advantage of forestalling homosexual relations, which Lieber described as 'more disgusting and unnatural' (p. 82). Given the dire consequences attributed to this practice, the priapic prisoner became a cause of significant interest. Thomas Mott Osborne, Head of the New York Prison Reform Commission, spent a week voluntarily as a prisoner in Auburn in 1913 and came away from the experience convinced that the silent system 'encouraged masturbation and perversion' (Rothman 2002: 120). There was less anxiety about sexual activity among female prisoners, although female staff members were occasionally disciplined for undue intimacy (or 'tampering' as it was coyly described) with the women under their care (Zedner 1995: 345).

Echoes of this concern were to be found in England before Pentonville opened, with one letter writer to *The Lancet* warning that the lesson from America was that prisoners who had experienced prolonged solitary confinement were 'thrown upon the world in a state of complete idiocy, besides having contracted habits contrary to nature and prejudicial to health' (Simpson 1840). In evidence presented to the Gladstone Committee the 'solitary vice' was linked to the 'isolation, monotony, and limited amount of exercise' that characterized the prisoner's life during his time in separation (Departmental Committee on Prisons 1895b: 404). Drastic preventive measures were sometimes taken. According to Forsythe (2004: 764) 'At some prisons, blistering of the penis of young prisoners caught masturbating was practised to stop this.' Prisoners were troubled by their desire because it was widely thought it would lead to insanity and severe debilitation. Smith (2004: 19–21) shows that physicians in Denmark were also preoccupied with the adverse psychological effects of self-abuse and its potential to cause neurological damage. If not already disposed to insanity by reason of heredity prisoners were becoming insane as a result of frequent masturbation. This hazardous habit, not the experience of solitary confinement, was believed to underlie any observed pathology.

Not only was Philadelphia in the vanguard when it came to highlighting the need for penal reform, but by an interesting historical coincidence it was also at the forefront when it came to identifying the supposed harms of masturbation. The first textbook of psychiatry written by an American was Benjamin Rush's *Medical Inquiries and Observations, upon the Diseases of the Mind* published in Philadelphia 1812. Rush, known as 'the father of American psychiatry', was a Philadelphian of Quaker stock and professor of medicine at the University of Pennsylvania. (He was also, of course, a signatory to the Declaration of Independence and one of the Founding Fathers of the United States of America.) His book was to dominate the field for half a century and in it he identifies 'Onanism' as being the cause of a litany of 'physical and moral evils' (p. 33). He noted that it caused madness in young men more frequently 'than is commonly supposed by parents or physicians' (p. 33). The consequences of such behaviour were profound and varied, including 'seminal weakness, impotence, dysury, tabes dorsalis, pulmonary consumption, dyspepsia, dimness of sight, vertigo, epilepsy, hypochrondriasis, loss of memory, manalgia, fatuity and death' (p. 347). There is some overlap here with the behaviours exhibited by prisoners in isolation such as memory loss, digestive problems (dyspepsia) and fatuity (see Chapter 3). This may be why there was sometimes confusion about the most likely causal factors. In addition to his many other achievements, Rush was an influential voice in the debate about penal reform in late eighteenth-century Pennsylvania, speaking out against capital punishment, degrading public labour, and the counterproductive humiliation of the whipping post and the pillory. He was a founder member of the Philadelphia Society for Alleviating the Miseries of Public Prisons (Teeters 1943: 307).

If the mental and physical deterioration of prisoners was regularly attributed to the scourge of Onan, this means that that the harms wrought by silence and separation were to some extent obfuscated. Thus, the horrors attending the system—which were so striking to those whose acquaintance with it was brief—were less apparent to persons who were charged with the daily welfare of prisoners. For the custodians, the enervating effects of cellular confinement were symptoms of unnatural practices; prisoner lassitude resulted not from the lack of intimacy with others but rather from excessive intimacy with oneself. Or as Franke (1995: 160) put it: 'Cellular confinement, instituted in part to prevent immorality in communal prisons, left prisoners with only themselves to fondle.' If matters had not been clouded by what Hunt (1998: 575) describes as 'the great masturbation panic' of the nineteenth and early twentieth centuries, the plight of the solitary prisoner might have been taken more seriously, sooner.

Adaptation and Fearing the Unknown

It is beyond dispute that the early stage of imprisonment is a time when the risk of suicide and self-harm is disproportionately high (e.g. Liebling 1999). In other words, any observed elevation in the incidence of such behaviours may reflect a more generalized process of adaptation to custody rather than a reaction to the pains of isolation. It is important to remember that as well as being characterized by the deliberate imposition of solitude the new prisons were also novel in that they held men and women in custody for periods of time that had hitherto been unimaginable. Previously, corporal or capital punishment (and transportation from the UK) had been the usual sanctions, with prisons used to hold debtors until they made good what they owed, remand prisoners until they could be tried, and minor offenders serving short sentences.

Thus, the high rates of disturbance that became so contentious can be attributed, in some part at least, to a pattern of adaptation to a novel type of incarceration. The difficulties of the early phase were recognized by those who favoured the introduction of the separate system of prison discipline. For example, the Inspectors General of the Prisons of Ireland (1840: 7), who were persuaded of the benefits of separation, commented that, 'it does not increase in gloom as the term of imprisonment is prolonged, but on the contrary, that the Prisoner becomes reconciled to his situation; that his bitterest hours are those in the commencement of his confinement... after a certain lapse of time the severity of separation wears away.'

The challenging nature of this experience was no doubt exacerbated by the fact that no-one had been through it before. There were no cohorts of prisoners who had served their time, tested their resilience to the limit, and emerged to tell the tale. There were no narratives of how the pains of confinement could shape different prisoners differently; until these emerged they would be perceived as terrifyingly procrustean. There was no institutional memory of how best to soften the impact of a regime that was new to both captor and captive. In short, a survival folklore had not yet

emerged. The ideals that drove the new system were freshly triumphant and, as such, dismissive of competing paradigms; it would be
some time before modifications could be viewed as anything other
than admissions of failure and the new dispensation could become
sufficiently flexible (and confident) to yield to demands for change.

The lack of long-term follow-up studies meant that the debate
centred on the most immediate terrors with the inference that if
short bursts of isolation were destructive then longer ones would
invariably be more so. Whether the immediate harms persisted or
prisoners learned to cope with them was not considered. The first
generation to experience the system did not know what to expect
and feared the worst. As other prisoners came to learn that it could
be survived the deterrent effect—general and specific—was weak-
ened. One of the prisoners interviewed by Beaumont and Tocqueville
(1833: 190) described the process of adaptation to the separate system thus: 'at first, solitude was insufferable...but custom overcomes
gradually the horror.' When there was work to be carried out in the
cell, the associated routines further dulled the pains of solitude.

Subterfuge

It was not unknown for prisoners to fake madness by 'putting on
the barmy stick' as Davitt (1885: 142) described it. (Austin Bidwell
(1897: 422) and his brother George (1888: 524), each of whom
was sentenced to penal servitude for life in 1873, referred to this
practice as 'putting on the balmy'.) This was one way to attempt to
avoid the fearful unknown. Davitt wrote witheringly about such
subterfuges believing that they seldom worked and had the unfor-
tunate result that prisoners who really were going mad were overlooked because of the shenanigans of their peers who wished for
the reduced labour and increased diet that accompanied invalidity.
The following is his account of how one prison doctor, who was
known for his ability to identify fraudulent ailments with which
cunning prisoners had successfully duped his medical colleagues,
distinguished the malingerer. In essence what set the latter apart
was a reluctance to engage in coprophagia; sensitivity of palate
was rewarded with a beating:

Upon any convict showing symptoms of insanity, real or imaginary,
he was at once placed under close observation. He would be located in
an empty cell, and the first day's proceedings would commence by the

administration of a powerful aperient disguised in some article of food. The patient would be then hurried into a warm bath, and, during the absence from his cell, an ordinary empty dinner-tin would be slipped inside the door, and the observations of the watching warder continued after the bathing was over. When the medicine began to operate, the patient would utilise the dinner-tin as the only utensil or convenient article to be found in his cell. This would all be noted, of course, through the spy-hole by the warder. Dinner time comes round. The tin is smuggled out of the cell without the act being noticed by the patient, and is, after a while, handed in again as if containing the rations of the prisoner. He is again closely watched. *If he eats of the contents, he is believed to be insane. If he does not, he is reported to the director for a flogging for simulating madness.* (Davitt 1885: 143–4; emphasis in original)

Davitt goes on to report, with a degree of relief, that this practice was confined to a single doctor at one particular institution. But he believed the faking of mental illness to be common and described the lengths that prisoners would go to such as smashing their cells and prison property, attacking other prisoners and staff, wounding themselves, and smearing their bodies with excrement. Others would fake physical ailments by cutting and infecting themselves or even attempting to cause a permanent disability of some kind. Occasionally these self-inflicted injuries led to premature death (pp. 144–6). It has always been the case that prisoners—like rational actors in other environments—will attempt to play the system to their advantage and that those in authority will make this as difficult as possible for them. Priestley (1999: 180) observed that prisoners were quick to exploit the sentiment that separation led to madness:

The temptation to sham insanity was strong in the Victorian prison. Following the events at Pentonville in the 1840s there was a great sensitivity on the part of prison officials to any accusation that their regimes produced mental derangement in those who endured them. Prisoners, alert to the slightest weakness in their masters, soon fastened on insanity as an area that could be exploited to their own advantage.

Why should we be surprised that a population experiencing unwelcome hardship, that contains within its number many who have been incarcerated on account of dishonesty and exploitation, would attempt to take advantage of the situation by mimicking madness if they felt that to do so might be to their advantage? The existence of such gamesmanship, even if no more than a minority pursuit, complicates any attempt to estimate the prevalence and nature of mental illness among prisoners.

The commissioners for Pentonville prison were alive to the possibility that prisoners would feign mental illness in order to escape
the rigours of the regime. For example, in the physician's report
relating to 1845, three cases of attempted suicide were described,
two of which were said to have involved men suspending themselves in their cells when they knew a visit from a warder was
imminent (Commissioners for the Government of the Pentonville
Prison 1846: 36). The third case was portrayed in dismissive and
unsympathetic terms by the prison doctor: 'William J. (Register
No. 606), scraped his throat with his shoemaking knife, which
was very sharp, and would have answered his purpose very well
had he been inclined to commit suicide' (p. 36). Another prisoner,
'Robert B.', was found to have been simulating insanity but when
his bluff was called the physician notes that he, 'at once became
ashamed of the attempt...recovered his good spirits, and is a very
attentive prisoner' (pp. 36–7).

In a review of the mental condition of the prisoners under his
care during the first five years that Pentonville was open, the physician, Dr Owen Rees, opined that:

Our prisoners are occasionally guilty of gross imposition, and, like prisoners in general, can simulate mental as well as physical pain with much
dexterity. Some among them have been well acquainted with the opinion
prevailing out of doors, that the separate system produces insanity, and
they have on more than one occasion told me so. It thus not infrequently
happens, that they will make allusions to the state of their memory, and
to sensations in their heads, talking in a manner which, though it may
prove totally inconsistent with mental disease, yet often succeeds in
impressing careless observers with a fear that they are showing indications of unsoundness of mind. (Commissioners for the Government of
the Pentonville Prison 1848: 52)

There can be little doubt that prisoners suffered then, as they do
now. But they despaired for many reasons unrelated to separation,
such as remorse, harsh treatment, removal from family, and underlying mental illness. Sometimes these pains drove the prisoner to
suicide and again this is an enduring facet of prison life. Priestley
(1999: 180) recounted how, 'The most eye-catching feature of the
later Victorian prison hall was the wire netting suspended between
the galleries that ran round the upper stories of the building.' The
purpose of this netting was to reduce the opportunity for suicide
by jumping from the upper balconies to the hard ground below.

Hobhouse and Brockway (1922: 550) noted that, 'In 1896 strong wire nettings were fastened across the interiors of nine prisons to prevent suicidal prisoners from throwing themselves down from the higher landings to the floor; and since then this device has, we believe, been extended to practically all prisons throughout the country.' No. 7 (1903: 179, with accompanying illustration) described how a prisoner he knew threw himself to his death from an upper landing of A Hall in Parkhurst in the late 1890s. The fact that prison suicide remains a problem indicates that any causal relationship with a particular type of regime is difficult to establish, although it must be noted that it still occurs with disproportionate frequency among prisoners who are being held apart. Sometimes this is because they have been identified as presenting a high risk; sometimes it is because they are in the early stages of their sentence which can be a particularly turbulent time.

Rewriting Dickens

What Dickens wrote about his visit to Eastern State Penitentiary was widely read and hotly contested. *American Notes* sold 3,000 copies in Philadelphia within 30 minutes and another 50,000 in New York in two days, sales figures that the author himself described as 'enormous' (Patten 1978: 131). In contemporary writing it seems to have retained its influence but is no longer challenged with the same vigour. One of the most frequently quoted passages from this book is the author's unequivocal denunciation of solitary confinement:

I hold this slow and daily tampering with the mysteries of the brain, to be immeasurably worse than any torture of the body: and because its ghastly signs and tokens are not so palpable to the eye and sense of touch as scars upon the flesh; because its wounds are not upon the surface, and it extorts few cries that human ears can hear; therefore I the more denounce it, as a secret punishment which slumbering humanity is not roused up to stay. (Dickens 2000: 111–12)

This quotation is often accepted as if it were an unquestionable truth rather than an observation which, despite its rhetorical flourish, is rooted in a series of impressions, fleetingly obtained. Collins (1994: 118) reminds us that Dickens' status as a penal reformer is an ambiguous one and that if some of the penologists who lauded him had studied his body of writing on crime and punishment more generally, 'they would have realised that he was an unreliable ally in the campaign for greater humanity in prison-discipline'. This is because Dickens had little faith in the capacity of individuals to reform themselves and so preferred systems based on deterrence (silent association) over those predicated on internal change (the separate system).

When Dickens visited Eastern State Penitentiary his tour of the institution, according to a newspaper report, lasted for only about two hours (Adshead 1845: 96). The warden, who accompanied Dickens for most of his visit, recalled afterwards that the writer had said much in favour of the institution and 'not one word against the system of Separate Confinement' (Wood 1845: 204). 'Nevertheless', according to Teeters and Shearer (1957: 114) 'what Dickens saw in the prison gave him enough ammunition, aided by his fertile imagination, to indict separate confinement and the Pennsylvania System of prison discipline in such terms of vituperation that the members of the Philadelphia Prison Society were compelled to repair the damage he had wrought throughout the world.' Teeters and Shearer continued:

Dickens was either not astute enough or unwilling to distinguish between the strict solitary confinement that had been advocated by some of the original supporters of the Pennsylvania System and the final system that was adopted, which permitted labor in the cells, books, visitors from the community, and exercise in the adjoining yards. It may have been severe but it was not as bad as the novelist painted it. (p. 114)

Drawing on Dickens' diary entries, Collins (1994: 120) argued in his defence that the novelist spent the full afternoon in the prison and remained there for dinner. Dickens (1850: 100) himself observed that he left his hotel at midday to visit the prison and returned between seven and eight o'clock. While his familiarity with the institution was shallow it was based on more than two hours' exposure. Also, while he was less critical in his initial reaction than he became after a period of reflection, this is hardly a damning criticism. His immediate impressions were no doubt influenced by the generosity of his hosts and the good management of the prison, which impressed him greatly. As Collins (1994: 122) expressed it, 'There was nothing disgraceful in his having, for once, hesitated before arriving at a conclusion, nor in his changing his mind.' Dickens may have been less dismayed by what he saw at Eastern State Penitentiary if he had also visited

Auburn. Had he witnessed the brutal repression that was used to maintain silence when prisoners congregated, his optimism about the silent system may have been dented and his view of the pains of separation may have been revised.

The rejoinders to Dickens' attack sought to address a situation where, as a result of the famous novelist's 'extravagant fancies', there was a concern that the 'benevolent public, at home and abroad, are in danger of being greatly abused and misled' (Tyson 1845: 85). For example, the Prison Association of New York (1845: 48–9; emphasis in original) noted that, 'It is difficult to conceive how any person who has at stake the least *modicum* of reputation for veracity, can invent and set forth, as a matter of fact, a story so utterly void of truth, or even the semblance of it, as the story which *Dickens* gave of his visit to the *Eastern State Penitentiary*. One would think his narrative was too ineffably silly to obtain credit among sober-minded men.' Her Britannic Majesty's Consul General for the State of Pennsylvania observed that what he had seen at Eastern State Penitentiary was 'superior' to anything of the kind he had seen in any other country and that despite numerous visits there, and many conversations with its inmates, he 'cannot recollect having witnessed a single instance of the pains and wretchedness described by Mr. Dickens' (Peter 1845: 86, 88). The Reverend John Field—a prison chaplain described by Collins (1994: 119) as combining 'lavender-water sanctimoniousness towards his flock with a holy combativeness towards his enemies'—poured scorn on Dickens, referring to

the shameful advantage which has been taken of the general want of information on this subject, by a writer whose works have obtained a wider circulation than his veracity deserved. The subject was of by far too serious a nature for discussion in a mere volume of amusement. (Field 1848: 105)

The overall assessment was not that Dickens was trying to mislead his readers, but rather that he was faithfully reporting impressions that had been successfully manipulated by some of the prisoners he met. As Her Britannic Majesty's Consul General concluded:

I have heard Mr. Dickens accused of wilful misrepresentation. Of that I most fully absolve him. I do not think that he would be guilty—knowingly guilty—of a falsehood for any consideration. But all things are not given to all men; and the very faculty which has enabled him so to excel in one species of composition, almost incapacitates him for some others...I believe that he never deceived another without having first deceived himself. (Peter 1845: 88)

The German prisoner referred to at the time as 'Dickens' Dutchman' was a career criminal named Charles Langheimer who, according to Teeters and Shearer (1957: 121), spent 43 years in various US prisons serving a variety of different sentences. He was around 32 when he arrived in America (there is some confusion about his precise date of birth) so may well have had prior prison experience in his homeland. Indeed, Adshead (1845: 102) suggested that he was an experienced prisoner before he emigrated. *American Notes* made him famous and he had a stream of visitors to his cell as a result. Poignantly, he presented himself at the gate of Eastern State Penitentiary on his death bed and asked to be allowed inside to die. He was and he did, drawing his last breaths in the prison that made him a celebrity. Langheimer was older than Dickens when they met and outlived him by 14 years; this despite the many decades he spent exposed to the harsh justice of the US prison system and having been described by Dickens, more than 40 years before he died, as 'a more dejected, heart-broken, wretched creature, it would be difficult to imagine...I never saw or heard of any kind of misery that impressed me more than the wretchedness of this man' (Dickens 2000: 115). Indeed, the year before his death a newspaper article reported that Langheimer was looking 'uncommonly well', being neatly attired and much younger in appearance than his years (Anonymous 1883). Peter (1845: 86) described Langheimer as 'an ingenious and clever fellow, but a great hypocrite' who had duped the celebrated writer with his tale of woe.

It is easy to understand how Dickens' hosts must have felt he acted unreasonably, and discourteously, to the extent that his credulity was taken advantage of by some experienced prisoners. Nor did their memories fade quickly. In 1862, two decades after Dickens' visit to Eastern State Penitentiary, the editors of *The Journal of Prison Discipline and Philanthropy* recalled that what the Englishman had written about the prison was 'so palpably erroneous as to appear to those familiar with that institution and its government to be absolutely absurd' (Bonsall et al. 1862: 34). After yet another decade had passed, the *Journal*, in its response to what it described as the 'remarkable mistakes' in a paper on prisons in Britain and the US by William Tallack, Secretary of the Howard Association in London, reminded readers of the dangers of drawing too much from a superficial acquaintance with a country's penal system (Anonymous 1871: 37). The lack of a properly informed understanding rendered Dickens 'ridiculous to those who know and respect truth ... one whose *fancies* decorated facts with art' (p. 36; emphasis in original; Tallack's paper was reprinted for circulation at the International Prison Congress that took place in London in July 1872).

The Prison Discipline Society of Boston had been arguing against the Pennsylvania System (and in favour of Auburn) for some time and gave a strongly positive reception to Dickens' work, going as far as to reproduce extensive excerpts from his observations on Eastern State Penitentiary in its eighteenth report (Prison Discipline Society, Boston 1843: 97–102). This added weight to a perspective that could have been more easily dismissed if it was simply that of a well-intentioned but naive visitor who had allowed his imagination to run away with him.

American Notes was published two months before Pentonville opened and 'was naturally taken as an attack in advance on the Government's much-publicised experiment with the Separate System there' (Collins 1994: 131). It is difficult to think of any other commentary in the annals of criminology that was as short (a 16-page chapter) and as empirically limited (based on a single prison visit) and yet caused such widespread excitement at the time and continues to reverberate more than a century and a half later.

Extending Temporal Parameters

Two influences coalesced during the latter decades of the nineteenth century to ensure the dominance of the cellular prison, even if belief in its reformative potential had begun to evaporate. These were the evolution of architectural methods to such a point that a truly separate system became a reality, as reviewed in the previous chapter, and the ending of transportation, which is considered next.

The availability of transportation meant that prison sentences in England were relatively brief until the mid-point of the nineteenth century had been passed (see Table 2.1). Then, within a decade, long prison terms were substituted for transportation. Now the temporal dimension of imprisonment became charged

Table 2.1 Time trumps transportation

	1850	1860
Transportation		
Over 10 yrs	404	0
10 yrs and over 7 yrs	805	0
7 yrs	1,369	0
Penal servitude		
Over 10 yrs	0	69
10 yrs and over 3 yrs	0	1,486
3 yrs and under	0	664
Imprisonment		
3 yrs and over 2 yrs	4	7
2 yrs and over 1 yr	551	813
1 yr and over 6 mths	2,770	2,686
6 mths and under	14,277	5,890
Temporal shift		
Custodial terms above 1 yr (%)	3.2	26.2
Custodial terms above 3 yrs (%)	0.0	13.4

Source: Home Department (1851: 53), Home Department (1861: 45). Less serious, and far more numerous, offences such as common assault, drunk and disorderly conduct, and vagrancy (and some minor larcenies after 1855) were dealt with summarily and as a result are not included in this table.

with a novel significance. Not everyone sentenced to transportation had actually been transported: 'Before 1840, convicts sentenced to seven years transportation were seldom sent to penal colonies, but were kept in the hulks at home, and generally discharged after about four years punishment, if they behaved well' (Commission on Transportation and Penal Servitude 1863: para 34). Also, some death sentences were commuted to ten-year prison terms (McConville 1981: 139). But, until 1853, the possibility of sentencing an individual to a prolonged period of incarceration did not exist and so prisoners did not have to think about how they might cope with very lengthy confinement.

The Penal Servitude Act 1853 limited transportation to periods of 14 years and above, including life, but even in such cases the court had discretion to substitute a term of penal servitude, which normally meant hard labour in a convict prison. In 1853, confinement for fixed terms of four to ten years, or for life, became a sentencing option for the first time. The Penal Servitude Act 1857 abolished transportation completely. The small number of individuals who would otherwise have been transported for 14 years or more would henceforth be imprisoned for the same amount of time. This completed a fundamental reorganization of the core spatial and temporal principles underlying punishment in the UK. No longer would serious offenders be sent away from their native shores as punishment and no longer could imprisonment be viewed as a sanction of relatively short duration. The modern prison ceased to be a holding pen for those awaiting transportation and became the site where sentences would be served in their entirety, initially in isolation and then at labour with others. Punishment became less geographically elastic and more temporally elastic.

An appendix to the report of the Commission on Transportation and Penal Servitude (1863: 125) shows that in 1852 there were 2,896 persons sentenced to transportation (down from 4,481 in 1842), of whom 2,541 were actually sent to Australia. In 1853, when the eligibility criteria for transportation were narrowed and penal servitude was introduced, 2,086 sentences of transportation were imposed (of which 600 were carried out) and the first 623 convicts began sentences of penal servitude. The following year the situation was reversed with 360 transported and 2,382 given penal servitude. In 1857, the final year that transportation was available to the courts as a sanction, albeit on a limited basis, it was used on 138 occasions as compared with 2,703 sentences of penal servitude. (This did not bring to a complete halt the export of British criminals to the antipodes as several hundred prisoners each year during the late 1850s and early 1860s were sent to Australia to complete their sentences of penal servitude.)

While brief periods of incarceration continued to dominate, the phasing out of transportation and the emergence of penal servitude meant that sentences of a duration that had not previously been contemplated became commonplace. This disjuncture is shown in Table 2.1 for the years 1850 and 1860, between which transportation ended and penal servitude began. Over this period there was a critical shift in the length of prison sentences imposed on offenders dealt with on indictment. In 1860 more than a quarter of prison terms awarded at the Assizes and Sessions in each county were for over a year and 1 in 8 were for over three years. The respective fractions for 1850 were 1 in 30 and zero. Very quickly, therefore, sentences measured in years rather than months became part of the penal landscape. While people may have been accustomed to hearing of transportation for long tranches of time they now had to become used to the notion that convicted criminals would remain behind bars on home soil for periods that until very recently had not been imagined. This upward shift is to be observed at the other end of the punitive spectrum also with the proportion of persons receiving terms of six months and under shrinking from 81.1 per cent to 50.7 per cent over the same timeframe.

Not only was the US to the fore pioneering large-scale solitary confinement in bespoke institutions, it also set the pace insofar as long prison terms are concerned. While the temporal shift occurred in the UK during the 1850s, US prisoners were by this time already familiar with prison sentences that endured for many years and occasionally for life. The 1829 penal code for Pennsylvania allowed up to 21 years imprisonment for a second offence of kidnapping and up to 15 years for a second offence of arson or burglary; the New York statutory arrangements for 1827 specified not less than ten years for rape, burglary (first degree), robbery (first degree), or forgery (first degree); and according to the Massachusetts penal code of 1830 manslaughter, perjury and assault with intent to rob carried up to 20 years (Kuntz 1988: 24, 42–3, 52–3). The courts were allowed considerable discretion in sentencing and the terms imposed, which were further reduced by good-time laws and gubernatorial pardons, tended to fall some way short of the permitted maxima.

Nevertheless, by the mid-1840s when prisoners in Britain were typically confined for no more than several months, the average prison sentence in the US was just a few days shy of five years— Kuntz (1988: 184) gives it as 4 years, 11 months, and 26 days—and some prisoners were serving much longer than this. In New York's Sing Sing penitentiary in 1849, for example, 14 (2 per cent) of the 655 men in custody were serving life and 145 (22 per cent) were serving ten years or more (Kuntz 1988: 180; New York courts also imposed brief periods of incarceration that were served at local jails rather than penitentiaries). There was considerable variation across the states with prisoners in Pennsylvania's Eastern State Penitentiary

Table 2.2 Long time, no see: US prison terms in the 1840s

State	Year	Average term	Life sentences
Pennsylvania (Eastern State Penitentiary)	1845	2 yrs, 9 mths, 11 days	0
District of Columbia	1846	3 yrs, 5 mths, 1 day	0
Pennsylvania (Western Penitentiary)	1845	3 yrs, 6 mths, 0 days	0
Maryland	1845	4 yrs, 0 mths, 3 days	0
Vermont	1845	4 yrs, 0 mths, 21 days	2
Maine	1845	4 yrs, 4 mths, 14 days	7
Michigan	1845	4 yrs, 6 mths, 11 days	1
New York (Auburn)	1846	4 yrs, 11 mths, 5 days	9
Massachusetts	1845	4 yrs, 11 mths, 9 days	14
Kentucky	1846	5 yrs, 0 mths, 0 days	0
Ohio	1846	5 yrs, 0 mths, 22 days	6
New York (Sing Sing)	1845	5 yrs, 3 mths, 21 days	9
Mississippi	1845	5 yrs, 4 mths 0 days	1
Tennessee	1845	5 yrs, 7 mths,. 9 days	9
Rhode Island	1844	5 yrs, 11 mths, 10 days	3
New Hampshire	1845	6 yrs, 4 mths, 20 days	11
Connecticut	1846	6 yrs, 10 mths, 8 days	19
Virginia	1845	7 yrs, 3 mths, 2 days	12

Source: Kuntz (1988: 183–4).

serving less than half the time of their peers in Connecticut, New Hampshire and Virginia (see Table 2.2). But the general pattern is clear: prisoners in the US were sentenced to longer terms, earlier. England exported the idea of separation and then re-imported it. It did not import the idea of long prison sentences but found the need for such foisted upon it when transportation was abandoned.

By the 1850s the penitentiary was so well-established that it was beyond challenge. It seemed to strike a balance between the need to treat prisoners humanely and with a view to their reformation but in a context where this transformation was forged in silence and solitude, each of which were characterized by their own particular terrors. The goal of the prison was simultaneously to deter and to reform. Ignatieff (1989: 213) felt that these arrangements became ascendant because the ideal of reform was appealing to the middle class as 'it implied that the punisher and the punished could be brought back together in a shared moral universe'. Nobody was too villainous to re-enter the fold and those who were unlikely ever to darken the door of a prison could comfort themselves with the idea that what was being inflicted in their name was for the good of individual prisoners, even if the latter were yet to see their pain as disguised benevolence. Although enthusiastic advocacy of cellular confinement was waning by the end of the nineteenth century, the system still received occasional plaudits. Smith (2009: 7) cites the Belgian insistence at an International Prison Commission conference in Brussels in 1900 that solitary confinement, 'even prolonged ten years or beyond... has no more unfavourable effect upon the physical or mental health of prisoners than any other mode of imprisonment'.

Given the role of the monastery in shaping spatial (cells and the centrality of the chapel) and temporal (the primacy of the clock and the unchanging rhythm of the daily timetable) aspects of imprisonment it is surprising that the reformers felt there could ever be a place for undiluted solitary confinement. Monastic life, of whatever variety, strikes a balance between prayer, work (often manual), and reading (usually of theological texts). This dual emphasis on 'ora et labora' (prayer and work) allows for the regularity that is essential for shared living and the variety that acknowledges an individual's corporeal, intellectual, and spiritual needs. While the number and timing of the religious offices each day has changed over the years and differs across congregations and orders, and the kind of work and reading that is permitted has evolved (the scriptorium was supplanted by the printing press and later by the personal computer), the three ingredients of worship, reading, and work have remained in place since laid out by St Benedict in his sixth-century Rule (in chapters 8–19, 42 and 48, respectively). The wisdom of the Rule is shown by the fact that it is still being followed 1,500 years later and that, when deviated from—as in the experiments with unmediated solitude—institutional life quickly becomes unbearable. Even the Carthusians, the most austere and unflinching of Christian religious orders, knew that communal activities were important, hence the singing together in church, the weekly group walk where monks could converse, the occasional community meeting (for example, to discuss whether a novice should be permitted to take his first vows), an annual opportunity for close family members to visit, and the coming together to eat (in silence, but listening to a scripture reading) on Sundays and feast days. Maguire (2006: 80) stated that, 'When St Bruno built the first Charterhouse in the French Alps [in 1084] he invented a hermit life with some communal activities—to keep the hermits from going crazy.'

In summary, the enthusiasm for silence as a policy imperative waxed and waned and a combination of pragmatism and pessimism eventually overcame any principled adherence to the disciplinary demands of a silent system, whether separate or congregate in nature. The variety of penitential life chosen for the penitentiary had not secured the goals of its originators. When it was found wanting it was allowed to slide into desuetude, its lessons grudgingly acknowledged at the time but, as we shall see in subsequent chapters, not remembered.

Then and Now

The foregoing should not be taken to imply that solitude does not cause harms independently. As Chapter 4 will show, it carries risks, even if welcomed. The purpose here is simply to highlight that there are other factors at play that are seldom accorded the weight they deserve. It is also to introduce an important theme of this book, namely that isolation may feel more painful now than it did in the past. Solitude is more difficult to bear today because the world outside is more connected and moves faster, thereby accentuating the penal contrast. For this reason, and because it is so deliberately devoid of hope (or, more precisely, what is hoped for is stripped of any redemptive quality, it is no more than the shaping of a different stimulus–response relationship), solitary confinement in the twenty-first century—as exemplified by the supermax prison—is qualitatively different from what preceded it. But people are more resilient than we might allow; the range of human reaction is wide. For all its horrors, many prisoners adapt to solitary confinement without suffering irreparable damage, and some—a fortunate few, admittedly—are fortified by it. The key to understanding what silence and separation mean is found by placing them in the wider network of expectations of those who endure, and those who enforce, these penal rationales.

Accounts from the nineteenth century show that prisons were quite impermeable places, especially when one considers the limited access to visits, letters, and news from outside. Today we know what maximum security prisons are like because television cameras regularly go inside. What is different about today is that the new technologies of surveillance and control allow staff to withdraw even further to the margins (a process that continues, even in prison systems where there has traditionally been an emphasis on the dynamic security that emerges from close relationships between the keepers and the kept). This means that the eye at the door is replaced by the camera; and the occasional word of comfort or disparagement is replaced by a blanket of silence. The distancing is dehumanizing for all concerned. While not suggesting a return to corporal punishment, this brutal practice at least had the virtue of reminding staff and prisoners that together they occupied a flesh and blood world and allowed them to react to each other in a way where otherwise concealed strengths and weaknesses came to the fore (e.g. the prisoner who showed fortitude or humour in adversity; the prison officer whose enthusiasm for the lash was subdued or extravagant). Of such things are characters formed. When a man is being carried away after a flaying it is difficult for those involved not to see him as a fellow human in distress; caricatures soon fade in the presence of real emotional engagement. When men (and more recently women) enforced discipline it had to be personal; cameras, sensors and other technological gadgetry serve to remove the person from the disciplinary equation. The prisoner who is immobilized by the sting of a taser or fastened to the concrete plinth of his bed in four-point restraints by a team of officers clad in body armour excites less sympathy than his bruised and bloody forebear.

It could be argued that prisoners are less isolated today but feel the sting of separation more sharply. They are allowed frequent visits, but these may take place behind a screen or over a video link; they are allowed letters, but these may be censored; they can petition the warden but why bother when the best that can be offered is a barely adequate minimum; they can litigate but this takes time and courts are reluctant to interfere in what are seen to be matters of internal prison administration. Suggesting that the deprivations of today are somehow a radical break with the past is misleading. The prison rules regarding communication in the nineteenth century were highly restrictive and they were enforced with the whip and a variety of dietary and other penalties. What has changed is the sheer number of prisoners in solitary, the timing and logic of the silent period in the context of the overall sentence, and the length of time spent alone.

In general, prisons have become increasingly porous places, with home leave, telephone calls (sometimes made using devices that have been smuggled into the prison), often unlimited (incoming) correspondence, financial support for visitors, in-cell television and so on. This relieves much of the monotonous misery that characterized earlier times. Just as some of the prisons which were supposed to keep their occupants apart and in silence, allowed easy communication because they were poorly built, so too today do most prisons allow, even encourage, regular interaction with the world outside. But prisoners may *feel* more marooned from loved ones today given the plethora of ways of keeping in touch, virtually instantaneously and regardless of the degree of geographical separation, many of which require only rudimentary literacy skills (e.g. text messaging, emailing, tweeting, updating social networking sites). Compared to the pen and paper that were the only options until the end of the twentieth century this is a far greater degree of relative deprivation. In an age where communication is defined by simultaneity, prisoners may feel more cut off than ever (see Johnson 2005). In addition, many of them, especially in the US, are serving sentences so long that a return to the outside world is highly improbable.

The debate about the relative advantages and disadvantages of the Auburn and Pennsylvania systems and the rise and fall of the associated prison regimes transformed prison architecture, administration, and discipline. Despite their manifest limitations they heralded the professionalization of punishment and brought an end to chaos, arbitrariness, and neglect. They introduced a seriousness to the field that had not previously existed and their legacy, while greatly diminished, remains evident.

The first-person accounts which inform the analysis presented in subsequent chapters are by definition the preserve of the more

articulate and more highly motivated former prisoners who survived the experience relatively intact and possessed the wherewithal to get their thoughts into print. There are further problems
with the fallibility of memory and the range of motivations that
lie behind the construction of such narratives. Over-reliance on
material of this nature would yield a partial perspective, although
it must be acknowledged that these are precisely the kinds of studies in resilience that bring new light to bear on aspects of the captive experience that are central to this book. All prisoners must
wrestle with the passage of time and all of those who are placed
in solitary confinement must seek out a way to address the lack
of human company. Not all are in a position to, or wish to, write
about their experiences but study of a wide array of such accounts,
written contemporaneously or with the benefit of hindsight, shows
clear commonalities despite wide variation in author biographies
in terms of age, gender, race, educational attainment, social class,
reason for incarceration, duration and location of confinement.
These commonalities suggest that what the authors have identified
may have a more general relevance.

To ensure balance, published prisoner accounts have been
tested against newspaper reports, tracts written by prison chaplains and reformers, official publications, academic critiques,
field visits, personal communications with prisoners, statistical
data, and the documents produced by commissions of inquiry.
By weaving together these diverse strands a more complete picture can be painted. Not every literary genre is represented in
the analysis. The keeping of a diary, even if permitted by the
prison authorities and not considered by the prisoner as render-
ing him or her vulnerable to threats, reprisals, ridicule or exploitation should it fall into the wrong hands, is largely antithetical
to the prison experience. A contemporaneous record serves as a
constant and painful reminder of one's predicament. According
to Symes (1999: 360, 376), a diary can be seen as 'a reminder
machine' and 'an anti-amnesic device' and imprisonment is a
time when reminders are either redundant (one's schedule is
fixed and externally imposed) or unwelcome (the past and future
are displaced by the imperatives of the present) and amnesia is
not necessarily problematic. Also, the kind of confessional writing for which diaries are suitable requires a degree of emotional
lability which prisoners tend to avoid in the interest of maintaining an equable course through their sentences. At a more

practical level, in an environment where little changes, finding something worth saying each day, and then saying it with brio, requires a rare combination of keen observation, insight, and literary prowess. Prisoner accounts, almost always of necessity written retrospectively, require a level of post-release stability, commitment, patience, and support for their successful execution. One would predict therefore that certain kinds of prison writing, such as fiction, poetry and narrative accounts of pre-prison life would be more popular among prisoners with literary predilections than diaries.

The pains and pleasures of solitude, as experienced in a variety of extreme environments are the focus of the next two chapters and a number of the themes raised are revisited later in the book. There has been much concern about the proliferation of supermax custody in the US, its open-ended nature, and the manifold harms it inflicts on individual prisoners. These developments are addressed in Chapters 5 and 6. The origins of supermax are reviewed in Chapter 7 with a particular focus on two prisoners whose actions catalysed the lurch to lockdown. The temporal dimension of imprisonment is the topic of Chapters 8 and 9 and this is followed in Chapter 10 by an examination of what we can learn from prisoner accounts about the most successful approaches to countering the potential harms of solitude and a temporal terrain that is distinguished largely by its sameness. It is hoped that exploring how this environment is negotiated will generate insights into the structure and organization of the prisoner society. The final chapter explores the role of hope in prisoner narratives and considers the possibility that adverse circumstances create an opportunity for individual accomplishment in what Frankl (2004: 55) characterized as 'the art of living'.

3

The (Certain) Pains and (Uncertain) Pleasures of Solitude

Terry Waite experienced profound and prolonged isolation. During almost four years in solitary confinement as a hostage in the Lebanon he received a single communication from the outside world. This was a postcard—from a stranger—that comprised 24 words in total including salutation and signature. Having spent little time alone prior to his captivity this was a degree of social disconnection for which he was totally unprepared. One would imagine that after such an experience, the solitary life would have held only aversive connotations but this was not the case. Waite (1994: 251) described solitude as a 'gift' and despite uncertainty about when his incarceration would end and fears of interrogation, torture and execution, he concluded that there were positive aspects to being alone that it was incumbent upon him to discover. After his release Waite described how, 'One part of me longs for the solitary life, longs to go to the desert with my books and papers and devote myself entirely to the interior journey. Another part recognises that I must find a balance. A balance between family, solitude and community' (p. 460). Having unlocked the creative potential of solitary life, the challenge was to find an appropriate place for it in a world that demanded a level of sociability. From this account it seems that, once mastered, solitude exercises a continuing allure. The fact that it remained seductive when it was no longer enforced attests to the existence of benefits that alleviate the burdens.

For those with the right temperament solitude can become 'the luminous silent space of freedom, of self and nature, of reflection and creative power' (Koch 1994: 299). Not all of those who choose solitude are rewarded with this luminosity and many of those upon whom it is foisted find that it takes time to identify where the treasures may be hidden. For prisoners who are young, impulsive

or mentally ill, time spent alone may be nothing other than corrosive to the self. But, while many are adversely affected, not all are;
and even for those who experience the pains there are occasional
glimpses of the potential pleasures. The real problem for prisoners is that they cannot juxtapose solitude with encounter in order
to make the most of each; they are prevented from establishing
an equilibrium between these two states and then attempting to
maintain it. The challenge is much greater for them than for the
solitary in the community because the dilution of their solitude
lies beyond their immediate control. Life entails a combination of
solitude and encounter; neither makes sense without the other and
each has positive and negative aspects. But too much of either is
wearing for all but the hardiest few.

Studies of the Solitary Prisoner

The opening words of a paper by Lucas (1976: 153) in the
Australian and New Zealand Journal of Criminology were
unequivocal: 'Solitary confinement is a form of torture.' This
theme was recapitulated 33 years later by Gawande (2009) in an
essay for *The New Yorker*, where he stated that, irrespective of
the location, 'all human beings experience isolation as torture'.
But matters are somewhat more ambiguous than such statements
allow. While under certain circumstances isolation can be torturous (or intended as such but resisted), under others it is experienced
as offering a partial route to self-actualization. Its effects are not
exclusively malign. The coercive use of silence and separation, as
reviewed in the previous chapters, offers many causes for concern
but closer scrutiny of the historical record in juxtaposition with
contemporary accounts, suggest that its effects were uneven and
that many individuals emerged surprisingly intact, even from periods of solitary incarceration that were mind-bogglingly long.

Suedfeld (1978) provided a brief, but useful, riposte to the attacks
made by critics of solitary confinement on those, like himself, who
were open to the therapeutic possibilities of solitude, but were
sometimes mistaken, or misrepresented, as apologists for punitive
segregation. (By writing this book I risk being bracketed in a similarly artless fashion.) Suedfeld was impatient with the claims made
by Lucas which he saw as based on a selective reading of the literature and an unscientific approach to the evidence. He strongly
rejected the view that solitary confinement was invariably 'a form

of torture', offering instead the opinion that: 'It is, on the contrary, a promising and humane tool to help disturbed individuals with various kinds of problems, including the criminally insane, to regain control over their behaviour and thus of their own lives' (p. 111).

Suedfeld was not advocating the use of solitary confinement as a punitive measure. Indeed, he opposed its use in this way on the basis that it was ineffective and ethically dubious and that this 'detracts from its potential utility in therapy' (Suedfeld 1974: 14). What he had in mind was the therapeutic use of isolation as an adjunct to other measures such as relaxation training and psychotherapy, and in combination with appropriate safeguards, for prisoners who wished to volunteer for such treatment. He submitted that, 'The potential benefits of isolation, properly used, should not be permitted to camouflage the horrors of its misuse; nor, as is more common, *vice versa*' (p. 18). It would be quite a stretch to find support in Suedfeld's work for the extremely harsh and isolating prison environments that emerged in the years after its publication. The supermax prison, which has taken penal separation to a new level, is the subject of subsequent chapters.

Suedfeld was guilty of undue optimism just as Lucas was of undue pessimism. Whatever promise solitude might offer in a prison setting has not been tapped and it has seldom been used as a 'humane tool' that can be deployed in the prisoner's interest. It is probably fair to say that in correctional contexts the relationship between solitary confinement and prison indiscipline has not been severed, and the potential of carefully calibrated periods of isolation to benefit suitable and willing prisoners as part of a broader rehabilitative programme, has not been systematically tested. With the advantage of another several decades of research it seems reasonable to suggest that critics of solitary confinement still tend to overstate the universality and depth of its harms, that the evidence base remains limited, and that accounts of its positive aspects are glossed over.

In a review of the effects of solitary confinement on prison inmates, Smith (2006: 488–93) suggested a fivefold categorization of the 'symptoms' they exhibited. This is a useful way of thinking about the range of impacts concerned, namely:

1. Physiological: headaches, heart palpitations, muscle pains, digestive problems, diarrhoea.
2. Cognitive: impaired concentration, confusion, memory loss.

3. Perceptual: hallucinations, illusions, paranoia, fantasies.
4. Emotional: depression, anxiety, panic, despair.
5. Motor: lethargy, chronic tiredness, apathy.

To Smith's five categories I would add a sixth, being a miscellany of positive effects. These include clarity of thought, heightened feelings of personal accomplishment, enhanced status among other prisoners, and an improved internal life. I would also add the caveat that there is more than one interpretation of some of these patterns of symptoms. (Indeed, describing them as symptoms suggests that there is an underlying illness and predisposes the reader to view them as adverse effects.) For example, withdrawal and poverty of speech can be seen as pathological or as forms of psychological hibernation that are rational and adaptive given the prevailing conditions. As a prisoner commented shortly after leaving solitary confinement in Maine State Prison, 'In such an environment, it is normal to act abnormal' (cited in Benjamin and Lux 1975: 30). Memory loss can be seen as cognitive failure or a strategy, common among prisoners, of restricting their temporal focus to the present (see Chapter 8). Hallucinations can be seen as facets of emotional breakdown or mystical, transcendental experiences. The possible disintegration of one's identity can be seen as thrilling or terrifying. Rumination can be a constructive process of reflection, searching for meaning and re-authoring one's life, or a destructive process of disconsolate brooding.

This is not intended to downplay the harms of penal isolation but rather to extend the debate by drawing attention to the capacity that some solitaries possess to grow in maturity and wisdom at the same time as they recoil from repeated assaults on their identities. Solitary confinement, even when prolonged, is not always intolerable. Viktor Frankl (2004: 55) showed how, 'it is possible to practice the art of living even in a concentration camp, although suffering is omnipresent'. Prisoners who come to realize that the 'art of living' can be practised anywhere, however unpropitious the circumstances, fare better during their confinement.

As for how many prisoners are affected, Smith (2006: 493) opined that: 'Some suffer from all or most of the symptoms described, some suffer from one or two, and others exhibit no visible ill effects.' He added the qualification that: 'It has to be remembered, of course, that many ... [segregated] prisoners may be mentally ill on arrival' (p. 493). In the absence of before and after measures it is difficult to be conclusive about the effect of isolation per se on prisoner mental health, and researchers run the risk of committing the *post hoc ergo propter hoc* fallacy. Nonetheless it has become almost an article of faith that the consequences of solitary confinement are solely negative and that the longer the exposure the greater the harm. Kupers (2008: 1005–6) observed that 'for just about all prisoners, being held in isolated confinement for longer than 3 months causes lasting emotional damage if not full-blown psychosis and functional disability'. In a lengthy review of the evidence Haney and Lynch (1997: 500) arrived at the unequivocal assessment that, despite the methodological shortcomings of much of the research, 'The empirical record compels an unmistakable conclusion: this experience is psychologically painful, can be traumatic and harmful, and puts many of those who have been subjected to it at risk of long-term emotional and even physical damage.' They continued, 'There is not a single study of solitary confinement wherein non-voluntary confinement that lasted for longer than 10 days failed to result in negative psychological effects' (p. 531).

This contrasts with the conclusion reached by Hinkle and Wolff (1956) in a review of Communist interrogation techniques which was funded by the Central Intelligence Agency (CIA). These authors noted that despite the rigours of isolation and the attendant uncertainty about what lay ahead, 'there are wide differences in the capacity to tolerate the isolation regimen. Some become demoralized within a few days, while others are able to retain a high degree of self-control for months. In addition to this, most men possess the capacity to adapt to isolation, and those who experience the isolation regimen a second time almost always tolerate it better, and longer' (p. 127). Individual differences, in other words, were strikingly apparent as was the diminishing impact of repeated exposure; as a nineteenth-century prisoner quoted in Chapter 2 expressed it, 'custom overcomes gradually the horror'. In an early letter to his parents from Tegel prison in Berlin, where he was held for 18 months before being transferred to the Gestapo prison in Prinz Albrecht Strasse and onward to Flossenburg prison camp where he was executed, Dietrich Bonhoeffer (2001: 1), a theologian and pastor, described solitary confinement as an enriching experience, 'a good spiritual Turkish bath'. But what cleanses one man can degrade and destroy another.

Smith's (2006: 502) considered judgement based on a careful sifting of the research evidence was that: 'between one-third and more than 90 per cent experience adverse symptoms in solitary confinement.' The corollary, of course, is that between 10 per cent and two-thirds do not. The extent of this variation, while often acknowledged, is seldom probed. When we add to this the over-representation of the mentally ill among isolated prisoners, the fact that even if multiple symptoms are present, they are not necessarily of clinical significance and seldom endure for long when the prisoner is restored to company, the role of staff in adding to the pressures by creating a context in which the bad behaviour that is expected is regularly manifest, and the other brickbats and caveats highlighted throughout this chapter and elsewhere in the book, a somewhat less dystopian view emerges.

The closer we look and the more seriously we take the limitations of existing research, the less certain we become about the inevitability of solitary confinement causing irreversible and unmitigated harm, however strenuously it may be objected to as a practice. Or more precisely, the closer we look the more cautious we must be about inferring that it is isolation that causes mental deterioration, rather than the selection of prisoners with underlying vulnerabilities, their treatment by staff, the pathological interpretation of observed behaviour patterns, and so forth. The harms of isolation are exacerbated by so many other factors that their relative significance is difficult to establish. These issues are returned to in Chapters 5 and 6 when the effects of supermax incarceration are examined.

The Social Imperative

Solitary confinement strips away the possibility of meaningful social interaction. While prisoners are not completely alone in that they have contact with staff and may be able to hear a neighbour's muffled shouts, such exchanges do not come close to meaningful engagement. A person's sense of self is forged in a social context and is maintained through interaction with others. Even the most solidly constructed identity needs occasional reinforcement or else it will be undermined, the extent of the damage depending on the quality of the original structure. In solitude, without the mirroring effect of others, the personality—what Cooley (1902: 184) memorably termed the 'looking-glass self'—can threaten to fracture; a terrifying prospect when not anticipated. When this process is understood it can be resisted or accepted (allowing the individual ego to be subsumed by something greater). According to Robert Kull (2008: 170), himself an experienced solitary, 'Solitude is liberating because the only limiting factor is your own capacity, but difficult because there are no other people to help catalyze growth.'

A very good account of the looking-glass self is to be found in the following prisoner account: 'The first three years of my sentence I spent in solitary confinement on death row. It's like what I perceive blindness to be: you kind of lose your balance; there's nothing that steadies you. When you lose contact with other people, it leaves you in a kind of darkness, a limbo' (Sharon Wiggins, cited in Zehr 1996: 112). We need the steadying effects of others to be fully human. From time to time we need confirmation that we exist, and to be reassured that our existence has meaning and, possibly, value. Solitary confinement is fundamentally inhumane because it distorts and impoverishes human relations. Without intimate attachments the individual cannot flourish. It is not just the presence of others that is necessary—all prisoners have their jailers—but the availability of companions and confidants.

As a species, human beings are 'obligatorily gregarious' (Cacioppo and Patrick 2008: 63) and to deny them opportunities to be sociable is to strike at the very heart of personhood. Does this imply that to conquer loneliness is to triumph over a fundamental aspect of what it means to be human? If we achieve this are we diminished as social beings however much we might exult as individuals? The answers to these questions are Yes and Yes. Humans evolved to be sociable (loners were more vulnerable to predators) and learn about themselves through their social interactions. This is why denying connection with others causes a very particular pain. It is how we see ourselves reflected in our relationships that helps us to fashion an understanding of who we are and what sets us apart. When we are set apart, literally, the structures that sustain our view of ourselves begin to crumble, and it is the ensuing disintegration of identity that prisoners fear. When the range of social contacts is reduced, and interactions become tense and combative, the prisoner is left with a limited range of possibilities, prominent among which are truculence and withdrawal. But because belligerence requires energy and because isolation begets listlessness, a state of passivity often results.

To survive over time in the absence of direct and meaningful engagement with others requires a well-developed personal sense of self and, ideally, identification with a group (e.g. the experienced prisoner who shares a political agenda with others). For the prisoner who has no connection with a wider collective and whose sense of self is fragile at the outset, the removal of tangible social relationships is hugely destabilizing; there is nothing to fall back upon or to reach out to. Deprived of interpersonal support and devoid of a sense of purpose they cannot recover their balance. Instability of this kind can have pathological consequences. In testimony to the US Senate Judiciary Subcommittee on the Constitution, Civil Rights, and Human Rights Hearing on Solitary Confinement, Haney (2012: 9–10) gave examples of the extreme behaviours that are sometimes exhibited by those who are thrown back on their own resources but found wanting:

I recall a prisoner...who was floridly psychotic and used a makeshift needle and thread from his pillowcase to sew his mouth completely shut. Prison authorities dutifully unstitched him, treated the wounds to his mouth, and then not only immediately returned him to the same isolation unit that had caused him such anguish but gave him a disciplinary infraction for destroying state property (i.e., the pillowcase), thus ensuring that his stay in the unit would be prolonged. A prisoner...who had no pre-existing mental disorder before being placed in isolation, has suffered from severe mental illness for years now. While in solitary confinement he has amputated one of his pinkie fingers and chewed off the other, removed one of his testicles and scrotum, sliced off his ear lobes, and severed his Achilles tendon with a sharp piece of metal...Another prisoner...has several times disassembled the television set in his cell and eaten the contents.

Haney observed that, 'the extreme deprivation, the isolating architecture, the technology of control, and the rituals of degradation and subjugation that exist in solitary confinement units are inimical to the mental health of prisoners' (p. 13). This makes the fact that some prisoners can overcome them all the more noteworthy. My intention is not to justify the continuation or, worse, exacerbation of a set of arrangements that can inflict such a mighty quantum of pain, but to explore what can be learned about the outer bounds of resistance from the experiences of those who have been held apart for prolonged periods. To state that solitary confinement does not invariably have the psyche-shattering consequences that are attributed to it is not to offer an apologia for penal extremism.

    There are numerous accounts throughout this book, a selection of which is listed in the Appendix, of individuals who overcame the most appalling circumstances, where they were denied company, adequate food, clothing or medical care, experienced torture and routinely degrading treatment, did not know when, if ever, they were to be freed, and sometimes believed that they faced execution. This strong statement of the human capacity to overcome adversity is too seldom made with sufficient vigour in writing about solitary confinement. It is hoped that by identifying points of convergence and divergence in accounts written by men and women who had little in common other than experiencing extended coercive isolation, the key elements of a robust analytical framework have been deduced. This approach was preferred to a close examination of a limited number of narratives because the fragmentary nature of the evidence—when the passage of time, alone, is addressed it is often obliquely or sparingly—meant that an argument had to be built, piecemeal, from numerous disparate materials. While two prisoner stories are revealed in some detail in Chapter 7, the emphasis throughout the remainder of the book is to layer excerpt upon excerpt, drawing upon accounts written far apart in time and space, so that by a process of accretion, an apparatus for understanding is constructed and general conclusions are reached.

The Trials, Tribulations, and Triumphs of Being Alone

Solitary confinement forces existential self-examination in a way that the buzz of activity among the general population precludes. Denied diversion and distraction, even the most reluctant and unreflective prisoner will be drawn to scrutinise the hinterlands of the self. The Trappist monk, Thomas Merton, wrote of deep silence bringing the individual to a place where 'he sits on the door-step of his own being' (cited in Kenny 2011: 224). What lies over the threshold is tantalising for the willing contemplative who has been readied (and steadied) for it but terrifying for the prisoner who must cross it unaided and unprepared. Silence can be viewed as 'a fertile pause' (Prochnik 2010: 13). But when uninterrupted for too long, its fecundity threatens to overwhelm. Some find unbearable the internal life that is revealed to them and respond through withdrawal, fantasy, drug use, or violence; avoidance is not an option in the isolation cell. Others learn to look

at their lives dispassionately and emerge triumphant and philo-
sophically enriched. Toch (1992: 8) put it well when he observed of
the variegated impact of imprisonment that: 'Paradoxically, some
offenders flourish in this context. Weaklings become substantial
and influential; shiftless men strive and produce; pathetic souls
sprout unsuspected resources.'

Even the most determined, astute and politically driven prisoners find the deep thinking that accompanies solitude to be testing.
Nelson Mandela (1994: 494) recounted in his autobiography how,
'I found solitary confinement the most forbidding aspect of prison
life. There was no end and no beginning; there is only one's own
mind, which can begin to play tricks. Was that a dream or did
it really happen? One begins to question everything. Did I make
the right decision, was my sacrifice worth it? In solitary, there is
no distraction from these haunting questions.' Despite the hardship, he found that he could prevail, continuing, 'But the human
body has an enormous capacity for adjusting to trying circumstances. I have found that one can bear the unbearable if one can
keep one's spirits strong even when one's body is being tested.
Strong convictions are the secret of surviving deprivation; your
spirit can be full even when your stomach is empty' (p. 494). Toch
(1992: 330) wrote about the 'cold, suffocating vacuum' that is the
isolation cell and how 'it remains a tragic fact that our ultimate
tool for dealing with fear-obsessed persons defies and defeats their
regeneration: We isolate such persons, make them feel trapped,
and seal their fate. We place those who are their own worst
enemies face to face with themselves, alone, in a void.' For those
who find the burden of self-examination unbearable the consequences can be catastrophic.

But the cell can also be seen as a sanctuary and sometimes
isolation is sought out by prisoners who feel that they need an
opportunity to consolidate a self that is in danger of unspool-
ing. In this way segregation can be identified as a survival strategy of sorts. In her study of women in Canadian prisons, Martel
(2006: 608) observed that the segregation unit was seen by some
as 'a dual space—a space that punishes and a space that saves'.
Solitude, then, can nourish as well as poison and this is recognized
by those who seek exposure to it when the stresses of congregation
become too onerous.

One of the political prisoners surveyed by Hobhouse and
Brockway (1922: 492) recalled a variety of benefits and burdens: 'A

certain amount of solitary confinement I found pleasant and rest-ful. It gave one a chance of dreaming a little. As time goes on, however, one becomes faced with two alternatives: either one can go on dreaming, in which case one's mind stagnates, or one can attempt to force oneself to think. In the latter case one is very soon at the end of one's stock of ideas.' When the 'stock of ideas' has been exhausted there can be a tendency to brood over perceived grievances which become magnified to such an extent that they eclipse positive thinking. This is when despondency becomes suffused with anger, either directed inward through gestures of self-harm, or outward by way of aggressive behaviour displayed towards staff.

A prisoner in Maine State Prison who had spent eight months in solitary confinement and did not know for how much longer he would be isolated, wrote with psychiatric precision that, 'I am aware that I have reached the stage of depressive lassitude and seemingly cannot shake it' (cited in Benjamin and Lux 1975: 29). Another prisoner on the same unit for the same period of time and facing the same uncertain future described how he was giving serious consideration to cutting off his left hand in order to bring attention to his predicament. He acknowledged that this would be a 'barbaric' act but felt that it would be worthwhile if it led to his release from isolation as, in his view, 'The segregation environment seems designed to break the human spirit, to destroy dignity, and to drive men into psychosis' (cited in Benjamin and Lux 1975: 30). A premeditated act of madness, therefore, would prevent a gradual slide into derangement.

Ignatieff (1989: 9) noted in his study of Pentonville that 'men came apart in the loneliness and the silence'. This cannot be gain-said. One of the key issues addressed in this book is how some manage to remain intact, how they demonstrate what Goodman (1970: 370) characterised as a 'bouncy resiliency'. Describing the Jewish Anarchist Alexander Berkman's long and painful incar-ceration, Goodman identified the most impressive lesson to be learned from the experience of his subject and other prisoners as that: 'Given any resources of physical health, moral conviction, or intellectual alertness, they make do in a shaking bad environ-ment without being personally destroyed' (p. 370). Brian Keenan was held hostage in Beirut for four and a half years, the first three months of which were spent in solitary confinement. He described how, alone in a tiny cell, his imagination ran riot, presenting him with a diverse array of images, 'some beautiful, some disturbing and unendurably ever-present' (Keenan 1992: 32). This was a kaleidoscope that was being twisted by forces outside his control and he oscillated between feeling grateful for the 'compensations of this gift' (p. 32) and bewailing the strangeness and incoherence of the visions and sensations with which he was being assailed.

The harmful effects of penal isolation have been described in similar terms for almost 200 years. So too can be found occasional references to prisoners' capacity to adapt successfully to its rigours such as the observation made by the Secretary-General of the Belgian Ministry of Justice about the strict solitary confinement at Louvain that

> most of the men subjected for years to that regime of isolation passed through a period of depression or of excitement, according to their individual disposition. But after that period they generally adapted themselves to their new life. I have known several cases of criminals who, after many years of that existence, readjusted themselves to normal life. (Royal Commission on Capital Punishment 1953: 484)

The prisoners seemed to adapt to their isolation, but whether this was an endorsement or an excoriation of the system, which was enforced with rigour between 1831 and 1920 and less rigidly thereafter, was not clear. Prisoners sentenced to life imprisonment in Belgium spent the first decade working alone in their cells, and wore a hood when allowed out for exercise or to attend chapel or class. Thereafter, they had a decision to make regarding the future administration of their sentence:

> But, after a period of 10 years, they had a right to choose between the continuation of their cell regime, or to be transferred to the old prison of Ghent with isolation only by night and work in association by day. In fact, very few elected to be transferred. This may be explained by the fact that they were satisfied with their isolated life in a cell, or it may also be that after 10 years of such an abnormal existence, most of the prisoners were too deeply adapted to that abnormal life and preferred to continue rather than to make the effort to mix with other human beings again. In the latter case, it would be a clear condemnation of this solitary method. (p. 484)

In a review of the German literature on prison psychoses from the first mention of this phenomenon in 1853 (by Delbruck, the physician of Halle prison) to the end of the first decade of the twentieth century, Nitsche and Wilmanns (1912) anticipated many of the issues that continued to cause concern a century and more later. They saw solitary confinement as a powerful agent for change (of a positive nature), but one that was fraught with danger. They debated whether the risk of mental disorder increased along with the duration of solitary confinement, or whether it was more acute in the early stages and then dissipated as the prisoner became accustomed to an abnormal environment. They found that recovery was generally complete. They questioned whether the constellation of observed symptoms should be seen as a new form of insanity or whether it could be accommodated within the existing nosology. They highlighted the difficulty, when measuring the impact of isolation, associated with separating out pre-existing problems from those induced by the prison setting, in other words how to deal with persons who were insane before being imprisoned.

With a nuance that was sometimes lost in later discussions, Nitsche and Wilmanns (1912: 8) declared:

Here one has to deal with an emotional effect evoked by the self-contemplation due to being alone—the deepest expression of an intense tumult in the emotions of the isolated prisoner. The emotional shock must often be hailed as the turning point towards reform in the life of the prisoner, but at the same time it furnishes the transition between mental health and disease, and emphasizes the dangerous side of solitary confinement.

When things went wrong the prisoner found it difficult to concentrate, became hypersensitive to noise and was observed to be 'uncertain, depressed, irritable, suspicious...he sinks into an apathetic brooding, is painfully affected by unpleasant bodily sensations, and perplexedly faces the indefinite illusions and hallucinations' (p. 15; drawing on the first stage of prison paranoia as defined in 1884). When prisoners deteriorated in isolation the symptoms they exhibited included disturbed sleep, poor appetite, headaches, irritability, moroseness, anxiety, and hallucinations.

These patterns of symptoms observed in German prisoners in the late nineteenth century are virtually identical to those exhibited by prisoners in solitary confinement in the US in the late twentieth century and beyond. In a review of the psychopathological effects of solitary confinement, based on his clinical assessment of 14 maximum security prisoners involved in litigation against the Massachusetts Department of Corrections, Grassian (1983: 1452) highlighted a number of themes that he found to be 'strikingly consistent' and wholly negative. They included generalized hyper-responsivity to external stimuli; everyday sounds and smells became amplified and unbearable. Prisoners reported perceptual distortions and hallucinations, hearing voices and seeing impossible things happening. They experienced massive free-floating anxiety, sometimes leading to panic attacks, as well as problems with thinking, concentration, and memory. They were troubled by paranoia and aggressive fantasies involving torture and mutilation of prison guards. They exhibited a lack of impulse control, leading to self-harm or damage to their cells.

There was one other consistent finding. This was the rapid diminution of difficulties, usually within a matter of hours, when the period of isolation was terminated. Even the most severe symptoms were found to dissipate quickly, thus emphasizing their reactive nature. Grassian believed that these symptoms formed a 'major, clinically distinguishable psychiatric syndrome' (p. 1450). While he did not give the syndrome a name, in a later paper with Nancy Friedman, he described this constellation of symptoms as constituting 'solitary confinement psychosis' (Grassian and Friedman 1986: 55). As Smith (2006: 481) noted, Grassian's study, 'is methodologically problematic because of the small sample size, the lack of a control group, and the obvious selection bias.' Nevertheless, because he painted a picture that showed a degree of consistency with what had been portrayed in some of the nineteenth century literature, Grassian's work became influential despite its shortcomings.

More recently, Grassian (2006: 337) suggested that these symptoms were so seldom found in other psychiatric samples, but clustered together so often among prisoners in isolation that they could be considered to constitute a distinct syndrome, one that was 'strikingly unique'. He argued that this syndrome shared many of the characteristics of delirium, an acute, organic brain syndrome. Grassian wrote of solitary confinement having 'profound psychiatric effects' (p. 330), a 'devastating psychological impact' (p. 343), and being 'almost uniformly terrifying' (p. 347). Even the most robust individuals experienced 'a degree of stupor, difficulties with thinking and concentration, obsessional thinking, agitation, irritability and difficultly tolerating external stimuli (especially noxious stimuli)' (p. 332). Many, including some who do not become overtly ill during their period of isolation, 'will likely suffer permanent harm as a result of such confinement' (p. 332). Furthermore, he argued, 'Even those inmate [sic] who are more psychologically resilient inevitably suffer severe psychological pain as a result of such confinement' and these harms 'may result in prolonged or permanent psychiatric disability' (p. 354). While Grassian acknowledged that there were significant individual differences in how individuals responded to solitary confinement, the way his argument is structured leaves little room for countenancing the possibility that some of those who experience penal isolation might be unaffected at the time or afterwards and that others might even benefit.

The onset of these symptoms was rapid, with some prisoners becoming 'grossly symptomatic in only a few hours' (Grassian and Friedman 1986: 55). An onset this speedy would suggest that the individual's expectations were at least as significant as the change in environmental conditions. Otherwise the swings in mood and behaviour of prisoners and staff as they moved between different locations within a prison would make the institution unmanageable. It also suggests a degree of environmental determinism somewhat at odds with the same authors' statement that the 'individual response to sensory deprivation is remarkably variable' (p. 63).

Available studies of women, while few in number and small in scale, report similar patterns. Korn (1988a: 14) described the women in the Lexington High Security Unit as experiencing 'psychotic flight reactions and feelings of unreality', chronic rage, depression, hallucinations, withdrawal, apathy, and blunting of affect. This is the classic symptom checklist of the solitary and is accompanied by a range of physical reactions including weight loss, dizziness, heart palpitations, and visual disturbances (see also Zwerman 1988; Shaylor (1998: 386) offers 'a challenge to the masculinist manner in which control units are generally discussed'). There is another issue to consider here, namely that what disturbs prisoners when they are placed in isolation is that it is more difficult for them not to confront the temporal dimension of their confinement. As there are so few distractions they must face up to the expanse of time yawning ahead, and the hurdle of each empty day, with a directness that can be avoided by their peers among the general prison population; it is not only the pain of isolation that must be tempered but also the pain of facing time. These factors can operate independently but the solitary experience foregrounds the former.

When Isolation is Invited

The symptoms listed by Grassian (1983) have been found in many types of isolation over many years. It would appear that whenever men or women are denied human company for long, they become irritable and aggressive fantasists. In the silence they brood and turn malevolent. In Fyodor Dostoyevsky's (2004: 208) words, prisoners become 'taciturn and morose to the point of vindictiveness'. In her account of a 40-day silent and solitary retreat on the Isle of Skye, Sara Maitland (2008) noted a range of experiences that paralleled those reported by prisoners in isolation. These included 'an extraordinary intensification of physical sensation' (p. 48) whereby smells, sounds, and tastes became much more vivid. She experienced a kind of disinhibition where, 'I found myself, for example, overwhelmed by seriously bizarre sexual fantasies and vengeful rages of kinds that I had never "dared" admit' (p. 55). There were auditory hallucinations of singing; sometimes a young woman, sometimes a male voice choir. There were some peak experiences, occasions of great connectedness. There was a sense of boundary confusion. It became difficult to distinguish internal from external events and clock time became unimportant. She had the 'thrilling' fear that her identity might be overwhelmed by the experience (p. 73). There was a sense of profound joy and blissfulness.

The silence to which Maitland exposed herself was an absence of human interlocutors rather than noiselessness. As John Cage demonstrated so effectively in his provocative composition *4'33"*, when expected sources of sound do not materialize they are invariably replaced by an alternative auditory soundscape (see Gann 2010). Even in conditions of sensory deprivation where external auditory stimuli are scientifically removed, the beating heart and the swelling lungs and the sucking and blowing mouth and nose all provide an existential backing track. Maitland's experiences can be viewed as concomitants of solitude which emerge even when a lack of company is sought out rather than externally imposed. What is qualitatively different for the prisoner is that these experiences are unlikely to be anticipated and often cause an already fragile psyche to disintegrate further. It could be argued that hypersensitivity, hallucinations, aggressive fantasies, and fear of identity breakdown, are 'symptoms' of solitariness more generally which feel particularly painful in the unnatural, unwelcome, inescapable surrounds of the prison. Again, it is worth making the point that some of these reactions are normal adaptations, akin to the tendency to withdraw and conserve psychological resources.

There were empty, bleak times also during Maitland's self-imposed six weeks of reclusion. It was not all serenity and ecstatic highs. On occasions she felt that the silence threatened to overwhelm her: 'I felt that the silence was stripping me down, desiccating, denuding me. I could hear the silence itself screaming' (Maitland 2008: 81). There were moments of intense anxiety and panic. While disturbing, these were relatively infrequent: 'I can only recall with great effort the extraordinarily powerful feelings of abandonment, desolation, fury and madness that swept over me at times. It did not last very long. My negative experiences have been little ones, but they have been enough to give me some small understanding of how overwhelming and destructive silence can be, and how closely the terrors seem to follow the same paths and patterns as the joys' (p. 86).

Kull (2008) spent a year in extreme isolation on a small, remote island on the Pacific coast of southern Chile. He had previous experience of lengthy retreats but this was far and away the most demanding. He reported how being alone was sometimes a frightening experience: 'in the afternoon I felt a dark ominous *presence*, and tingled with fear as it approached. The fear was not my usual anxiety, but deeper and not associated with anything physical... Will this darkness come for me? Is it madness?' (p. 110; emphasis in original). Kull described how before his first long retreat into wilderness solitude he had not been prepared for the inner turmoil he would face, and 'nearly went insane as a consequence' (p. 130).

Maitland (2008: 90) was familiar with Grassian's work and, reflecting on her own experiences, noted that 'his [Grassian's] whole list of symptoms is extraordinarily close to the list of positive effects of silence that I drew up in Skye, with the not altogether surprising absence of bliss. Even though we each give them different names and they clearly have different emotional meanings, as experiences they are more or less identical'. Maitland showed how the same patterns of thinking, feeling and behaving can be seen as debilitating or potentially liberating. For example: 'What I experience as a thrilling sense of risk or peril he [Grassian] diagnoses as "overt paranoia". An experience of "disinhibition" can be a profound freedom or a "problem with impulse control".

"Auditory hallucinations" can just be there in an interesting and thought-provoking way, or they can be experienced as "perceptual distortions" suggesting an unusual psychotic state' (p. 91). Social withdrawal and lassitude can be seen as an adaptive strategy of hibernation or psychomotor retardation. Which interpretation is taken depends on, and in turn influences, one's perspective. The same epiphenomena—by-products of silence—can be pathologized or valorized.

Maitland was at pains not to trivialize what Grassian had described but wished to raise the possibility that the same experiences can be viewed in non-pathological ways. She concluded that: 'it would make as much or more sense to say that these were not symptoms of madness or any other illness, but the effects of silence itself, occurring within a dangerous context' (p. 91). When Maitland experienced what the solitary prisoner experiences she interpreted it differently. This demonstrates that being isolated is not necessarily a psychologically destructive experience; to be understood it must be contextualized and interpreted. Solitude can be positive, or negative, or a mix. Long et al. (2003) identified nine types of solitude of which seven were experienced as positive, namely: anonymity, creativity, inner peace, intimacy, problem-solving, self-discovery, and spirituality. One was negative (loneliness) and one was neutral (diversion). Positive experiences were more frequent, giving rise to the remark that: 'Psychology's almost exclusive emphasis on loneliness, while understandable, seems disproportionate' (p. 580). The tendency to focus on the aberrant and the pathological, which is ingrained in psychology (and which defines psychiatry) impacts adversely on a fuller understanding of the phenomenon in question.

If prolonged, solitariness always elicits a strong reaction, but how this is perceived and handled depends on subjective interpretations and the context within which it emerges. The consequences of being alone will be felt differently in the monastic cell and in the prison cell. Why the denial of company occurs, and the degree to which it is welcomed by the individual, are important determinants of how it is felt. Religious conviction makes solitude safer because it offers a sense-making framework for the experience. Similarly, those who have a context in which to place their captivity tend to cope better with it. Maitland's (2008: 187) argument is that silence is not just an absence, which by implication is often seen as something negative, but that it has qualities of its own: 'Silence can be calm or frightening; lonely or joyful; deep or thin'. How it is felt depends on a combination of the context and the individual's expectations, powers of discernment, and adaptive skills. Some prisoners can reconfigure their internal environment in a way that redefines external realities. This can help transform a frightening void into a space for self-actualization. (As Beckett (2006: 302–3) put it in his novel *The Unnameable*: 'For it is all very fine to keep silence, but one has also to consider the kind of silence one keeps.')

Haney (2009: 15) was critical of those who attempted to downplay the adverse effects of prolonged solitary confinement. By his reckoning the anguish of isolation is evident to anyone who cares to look, even if it does not always reach clinical intensity and if prisoners' fears of psychological deterioration are exaggerated. At the same time he acknowledges the degree to which there is individual variation in reaction: 'But whether and how often long-term solitary confinement makes healthy people "crazy" or drives those predisposed to mental illness across some diagnostic line, it certainly appears to cause significant distress and even anguish in many people, and puts them at risk of serious psychological harm.' It is a risk factor, in other words, rather than a causal agent. (On the challenges of identifying, classifying and responding to mental illness in a maximum security environment, see Rhodes (2004: 131–59).)

But these experiences are by no means unique to criminal populations, being found among prisoners of war, hostages, reluctant monks, and inhabitants of extreme environments such as the Antarctic (see Chapter 4). There is a historical constancy to them and also a repetitive, if underplayed, acknowledgment that harsh experiences, coupled with profound aloneness, are not inevitably or solely destructive. The purpose here is to examine the range of responses with a particular emphasis not so much on the accompanying disintegration and degradation—which is usually the focus of such inquiries—but on the factors that promote resilience.

This book is a celebration of the human capacity to overcome even the most unprepossessing circumstances rather than an attempt to diminish the potential harms of social isolation. As Waite (1994: 225) said of himself during the years he spent alone in chains in makeshift cells: 'I have no deep thoughts, no great insights, no outstanding qualities. I am a very ordinary man chained to a wall and attempting to struggle through another day of boredom and uncertainty.' The extraordinary fortitude that ordinary men (and women) can display is a central focus of this book. Towards the end of his memoir, Waite again remarked on his ordinariness: 'I look back over the years of my captivity. I have had no great thoughts, no illuminating inspirations. Better men than myself would have been able to dig deeper into their inner experience. All I seem to have done is keep afloat and withstand the storms' (p. 398). But keeping afloat is all that anyone can do and who is to say that 'better men' would not have drowned? By bobbing along on a sea of adversity and remaining weatherproof Waite achieved as much as anyone could hope for under the circumstances. That he considered his achievement so underwhelming serves to underline its significance.

It is possible that solitary confinement is psychologically harmful for most of those who are forced to endure it, but that it becomes disabling only for a few. It is also important to remember that it may be simultaneously harmful (in terms of lethargy, depression, hallucinations, difficulties concentrating) and beneficial (in terms of insight, reflexivity, awakening of intellectual, artistic, and spiritual sensibilities). One set of outcomes does not rule out the other. By accentuating the positive the harms of what is being endured are not negated. Even those rare individuals who triumph spectacularly over the most adverse conditions are not completely unimpaired in the process. It seems reasonable to argue that there are (certain) pains and (uncertain) rewards in every case and that much of the criminological literature has tended to downplay the latter. My intention is not to disregard the significance of the harms that solitary confinement causes but to frame them differently by juxtaposing the benefits that can accrue simultaneously and, also, by arguing that while the negative side effects tend to disappear with a change of environment the positive ones can be long lasting (see discussion of post-traumatic growth in Chapter 11).

Crippling Lethargy

Even the most highly motivated prisoners, who exult in solitariness and have a context in which to locate their suffering, must combat the exhausting ennui that accompanies undistracted isolation. The prisoner and the cell become locked in a melancholic embrace, with the restrictions of the physical environment finding behavioural expression in a severely limited repertoire of movement, emotional constriction, and poverty of speech. The solitary cell becomes part of the fabric of the prisoner's personality. It confines the body and trammels the mind, smothering individuality and making it difficult for the person subjected to it to retain the sense of uniqueness that is central to being human. It shrinks the core of personhood to an unadorned minimum and whether the prisoner looks inward or outward they are confronted by a vista that is uniformly bleak. As Jack Henry Abbott (1981: 45), a man who was well acquainted with the violence of incarceration, put it: 'Solitary confinement in prison can alter the ontological makeup of a stone.'

Drawing on his personal experiences of imprisonment, Nelson (1933a: 342) described 'prison stupor' as 'a species of bodily and spiritual anemia. It is largely self-induced, a kind of unconscious habit of self-dramatization or auto-hypnosis.' Nelson was not the originator of this term, which he also described as 'prison paralysis'. It is to be found in prisoner writings at least as early as 1923 (see Nelson 1933b: 236), and has a more recent analogue in what one maximum security prisoner described as 'autistic thinking, or total absorption in fantasy for an extended period of time' (cited in Baxter et al. 2005: 214). The prisoner withdraws into a world of their own creation, over which they have some control, and in which they play more active, self-expressive, roles than their conditions of captivity allow. These flights of fancy offer a mixture of stimulation and consolation and few prisoners are immune to their attractions. As Nelson (1933a: 342) expressed it, 'No matter what form his dreams may assume, he is always trying to compensate himself for the hurts and shocks and hungers of the present unbearable life. He seeks happiness in the spurious world of his imaginings, and sometimes this gives him a certain mild and temporary relief.'

The listlessness and absent-mindedness that accompany such activity occasionally become entrenched and are viewed as symptoms of mental illness; for some prisoners the border between fantasy and reality dissolves. This is the 'reverie-plus' described by Clemmer (1940: 244) which can veer from harmless daydreaming into pathological fantasizing accompanied by profound lethargy and social disengagement. For Nelson (1933b: 241) the cure for prison stupor was an injection of 'meaning' into prison life. If a prisoner's life was not somehow rendered meaningful the threat of stupor could never be eliminated.

Of course, absolute solitude for the prisoner does not exist. Cells are visited by guards delivering meals (however uncommunicative they may be); there are opportunities (however infrequent) to engage with the warden, chaplain, or health care professionals; there are phone calls to, and visits from, families and lawyers (however irregularly they may occur). Solitary confinement is accompanied by surveillance and the organization of the latter can have a deleterious psychological impact. Adjusting to the level of scrutiny that characterizes imprisonment can be difficult, sometimes terminally so, and what seems like an intrusive but irritating facet of life for some can become a destructive obsession for others. Writing about the peep-hole that punctures every solid prison door, Zeno (1968: 13) made the acute observation that its existence 'denies a man the privacy of his solitude'. To the pain of solitariness is added the intrusive burden of an unwelcome gaze. The prisoner in solitary confinement loses out in two ways. By being denied the opportunity for meaningful contact with others, and by being denied the opportunity for real privacy, he or she is prevented from being fully human. This is where voluntary isolates have a distinct advantage; their every move is not potentially observed by an unsympathetic eye.

The body is subdued but the mind seeks revenge

One of the side effects of solitude, especially if it is imposed and the imposition is seen as illegitimate as well as unwelcome, is simmering resentment. Korn (1988a: 14) described the 'barely suppressed rage' that was visible in the body language of the women held at the Lexington HSU. This had the unintended but predictable result that those subjected to it—often because they were seen to pose a threat to institutional order—came to exhibit a plethora of 'risk factors' that were taken as proof that the decision to segregate them was well founded and should be upheld. Whether or not they were dangerous before, there is little doubt that many prisoners spend their time in 'the hole' consumed by violent fantasies, the targets of which are the staff in charge. These revenge fantasies can be accompanied by auditory and visual hallucinations. To prevent this deadly rumination finding an outlet requires a dehumanizing degree of barrier handling.

During his long and lonely captivity in Peking, Anthony Grey (1988: 228) described 'the gathering sense of fright felt after seven months absolutely alone in confinement'. This feeling of dread sometimes results in lashing out in an effort to find relief. Gawande

(2009) instanced the case of Bobby Dellelo, who served 40 years of a life sentence, including a continuous period of five years in isolation which was imposed for escaping. He became obsessed with one particular correctional officer and 'spent hours imagining cutting his head off and rolling it down the tier'. Rhodes (2005: 393) quoted a supermax prisoner in Washington State: 'All day long I was thinking about chopping people up, chopping their families up and stuff like that...If I keep going that way, I'm going to get out and be a serial killer.' Dostoyevsky (2004: 209) described this kind of brooding malevolence thus: 'When he has lost all hope, all object in life, man often becomes a monster in his misery.'

Abbott (1981: 50; emphasis in original) reported that his verbal dexterity disappeared while he was in solitary: '*I do not want to talk any more.*' This was because his entire being had been crushed by the experience; the words had been squeezed out of him. But while language might have been extinguished, anger flourished: 'I was slow and slack-jawed and confused—but beneath the surface I raged' (p. 51). The desire to communicate remained but it would find expression in a grammar of violence, punctuated by hard fists and cold steel. This is taciturnity, corrupted.

Learned helplessness and the depression that accompanies it are found in circumstances where aversive outcomes are perceived to be uncontrollable; no matter what the individual prisoner or any similarly situated individual does, they cannot influence what will happen to them. Furthermore, even when a measure of control over their environment is returned to them, they do not avail of it, having become resigned to adversity. Those who have written about concentration camps describe a cohort of prisoners who appear to lose the will to live and display abject passivity. They were known as Muselmänner (muslims) 'because of what was erroneously viewed as a fatalistic surrender to the environment, as Mohammedans are supposed to blandly accept their fate' (Bettelheim 1960: 151). By ceasing to respond they denied the environment the power to influence them but by so doing they denied their own capacity to impinge on their surroundings in any meaningful way. This rejection of life hastened their demise.

Prisoners held in solitary confinement cannot exercise the avoidance option so, strictly speaking, it is difficult to determine to what extent the situation that is foisted upon them results in learned helplessness until the burden of isolation is removed. But it would seem that they are acutely aware of the ontological threat associated with becoming habituated to a painful situation that causes an ebbing away of their capacity to resist. This is why prisoners sometimes go to extreme lengths including self-harm or goading guards into pre-emptive strikes to prove to themselves that they retain some power, however residual, to influence their environment. Such actions can be interpreted as attempts to prevent helplessness being transmuted into hopelessness.

Silent and Solitary Virtues

Those who persevere can find riches in silence. Writing of time spent with the Benedictine monks of the Abbey of St Wandrille de Fontanelle and the Cistercians of La Grande Trappe, Leigh Fermor (2004) described 'the clarity of spirit' that defined the silent monastic life (p. 7) and the 'slow and cumulative spell of healing quietness' (p. 89) that even a visitor to a monastery could discern. By his reckoning these treasures were there to be found by anyone who went in search of them regardless of their propensity for religious belief. But it must not be thought that such rewards come immediately or easily. The silent life is not for the faint-hearted and Leigh Fermor spoke of 'a mood of depression and of unspeakable loneliness' that overcame him and 'suddenly felled me like a hammer-stroke' (p. 19). He sat at his desk in the monastery 'in a condition of overwhelming gloom' (p. 22). He complained of restlessness, depression, broken sleep and nightmares, followed by extreme lassitude and hypersomnia. When this phase passed he found himself possessed with uncommon vitality and returned to his work with new vigour.

It is hardly surprising that prisoners find the early stages of isolation difficult if a well-educated, fit, and capable person like Patrick Leigh Fermor, who has opted for a period of monastic solitude to work on a book, exhibits many of the self-same symptoms. In other words, the pain is greatest, earliest, for everyone, but can be overcome. To fully understand the impact of solitary confinement on the prisoner requires paying close attention to the longitudinal dimension of his or her experience. If first impressions are assumed to have an enduring quality the impact will be overestimated. It is not surprising that the initial phase in a radically new environment, such as a solitary confinement cell, is temporarily unsettling. Just as it would make little sense to assume that the traumatic early days define an entire prison sentence, so too must the early days in solitary be seen as unusually turbulent.

It is not only those in certain varieties of religious life who can turn being alone to their advantage. In an evocative celebration of solitude, Koch (1994) argued that it does more than simply provide an opportunity for restoration, respite from the hurly burly, and a chance to refresh the self between social encounters. In addition to allowing 'restful retreat' (p. 6) solitude can be liberating in that it unhooks one from the demands of others and opens new directions for the unhindered self to travel.

For Koch solitude is characterized by physical isolation, social disengagement and reflectiveness. But each of these can be qualified: solitude is possible in a crowd; an isolated person can have imaginary companions and form relationships with non-human animals; unthinking aloneness is possible. The most important feature, according to Koch, is social disengagement: 'Solitude is, most ultimately, simply an experiential world in which other people are absent... Other people may be physically present, provided that our minds are disengaged from them' (p. 15). This is why solitude can be part of life in a crowded prison. One can be troublingly (even terrifyingly) lonely in the midst of other people. Although surrounded by prisoners Dostoyevsky (2004: 234) felt his isolation keenly, but came to see its beneficial aspects: 'I was fearfully lonely, and at last I grew fond of that loneliness. In my spiritual solitude I reviewed all my past life, went over it all to the smallest detail, brooded over my past, judged myself sternly and relentlessly, and even sometimes blessed fate for sending me this solitude, without which I could not have judged myself like this.'

Solitude is neither positive nor negative. It is not an emotional state like loneliness, which is intrinsically painful (and which according to Cacioppo and Patrick (2008) has profoundly adverse health consequences). Rather, it is open to a variety of competing interpretations and accompanying moods: 'solitude is not, in its essence, either serene or not serene: it may be especially propitious for attaining serenity, but is not itself a kind of serenity. Sometimes it is turbulent, sometimes threatening, sometimes exhilarating' (Koch 1994: 33). At the root of solitude is a state of disengagement (intellectual and experiential, if not always social) from other people that persists over time. The prisons literature has tended to focus on the harms of solitude, on sensory deprivation and unwelcome isolation. This does not do justice to the richness of the human imagination or the variety of possible responses to similar situations. To reiterate, it is not my purpose to deny the pains of solitude but simply to assert the value of a concept of solitude that is neutral as regards accompanying emotional states. Bodily isolation is not accompanied by exclusively negative psychological sequelae.

Koch (1994: 99–135) identified five virtues of solitude. These are the characteristics that make it restorative and allow it to act as a balm. The first is *freedom* from the demands of others and the constraints and expectations of society. This is the freedom to be oneself; to do as one pleases, when one pleases. The second virtue is *attunement to self*. This does not equate to self-understanding but is more the openness to one's inner processes that becomes possible in the absence of the distraction of others. It is about being open to the self, even if this is sometimes accompanied by discomfiture rather than peace and harmony. The third virtue is *attunement to nature*. Solitude allows powerful connections to the natural world. There is an otherwise difficult to attain clarity of perception, and a dissolution of the barriers between oneself and nature. The fourth virtue that solitude brings is *reflective perspective*. This involves recollection, musing, sense-making of the past and present, contemplation without borders and without restriction of time, and, for the lucky few, enlightenment. The fifth and final virtue is *creativity*. The solitary life acting as a spur to creativity is found in the biographies of many artists and geniuses (for a series of case studies see Cobb 1977; Storr 1988). But creativity in solitude is not limited to a few extraordinary individuals. All who experience solitude and find resources they did not know they possessed make the most of them. Sometimes this results in writing, drawing or other artistic endeavours that reveal to the prisoner a potential they had not previously recognized in themselves and that might otherwise have continued to go unnoticed.

Living according to Koch's virtues is difficult in prison, but it is not impossible. Prisoners can use their imaginations to escape, in their own time, from surroundings which severely limit their room for manoeuvre. They can become attuned to their own internal processes and the associated pains and pleasures, and many former captives have written of the fortifying nature of their isolation. Although they live within tiny worlds of concrete and steel, prisoners in solitary confinement show a heightened sensitivity to the natural world on the occasions when they are reminded of its splendour. Breyten Breytenbach (1984: 130) spent the first two of his seven years in prison in South Africa in solitary confinement. He remembered how for the solitary prisoner, 'the smallest sign of life from outside becomes a gift from heaven, to be cherished'. So too are isolated prisoners prone to the kind of deep reflection that brings clarity to their past lives and can imbue their presents with a sense of meaningfulness and serenity. Arthur Koestler (1942: 203; emphasis in original), thinking back upon his time spent incommunicado, awaiting execution, in a Spanish prison cell, remembered occasions when he overcame his fears and managed to slough off the routine tribulations of life, to achieve a unique sense of lightness and freedom: 'Often when I wake at night I am homesick for my cell in the death-house in Seville and, strangely enough, I feel that I have never been so *free* as I was then.' Finally, they also show the kinds of creativity that are one of the beneficial correlates of a solitary life.

For all of the valid concerns about the pernicious consequences of penal isolation, there are potentially positive aspects to solitude in whatever context it is experienced. Koch (1994: 134) described these as 'the perennial gifts of solitude, rich treasures whose powerful intrinsic value cannot possibly be denied'. Prisoners who discover these treasures find that they can temper the effects of an experience that might otherwise threaten to be overwhelmingly aversive. But we must not lose sight of the fact that prisoners' solitude is different because it is externally imposed and cannot be relieved by encounter at times of their choosing. Sometimes they exist in a sphere where there are no meaningful relationships to kindle, even at a distance. They cannot create the necessary balance between the presence and absence of company that is desired and meaningful.

4

Pathological Loneliness

The cluster of behavioural, emotional, and cognitive changes that accompanies enforced isolation is so well recognized that it has attracted a variety of labels according to the environment where it is exhibited. These include the close confines of the cloister, the prisoner of war camp, the shelter of a polar research station, the furthest reaches of the wilderness, and the locks, bolts, and bars that define the modern solitary confinement cell. When stepping outside is impermissible or impossibly dangerous, the intensity of self-examination can become difficult to withstand.

Accidie

In her monograph on medieval English nunneries, Power (1964) described how what might be called the 'reluctant religious', those who had no particular vocation but entered the monastery while still children or found themselves taking the cowl or the veil because they were not preferred for inheritance or marriage, bucked against the routine. They failed to attend services, turned up late and dozed, or rushed through their prayers and hymns in an irreverent fashion. As well as carelessness in their devotions, they sought out worldly amusements to enliven their days. This rebellious deviation was known (in Latin) as *accidia or acedia* (accidie in English), 'that dread disease, half ennui and half melancholia, which, though common to all men, was recognised as the peculiar menace of the cloister' (pp. 293–4). This was a cause of significant concern: 'Against this sin of intellectual and spiritual sloth all the great churchmen of the middle ages inveigh, recognising in it the greatest menace of religious life, from which all other sins may follow' (p. 294).

The consequences of this 'moral disease', induced by the strictures of institutional life and not limited to those who were unsure about their vocation, were boredom, irritation, and depression; a kind of corrupting lethargy that reduced the sufferer to a debilitating state of despondency. Sometimes this led to suicide. There are clear parallels with the kind of mental and emotional shutdown and associated withdrawal that are found among prisoners who have for too long existed under a set of precepts and rules for daily living which are imposed upon them, the repetition of which can become tedious, and against which resistance is futile. To keep accidie at bay required discipline, routine, and activity, the study, work, and prayer recommended by St Benedict to his monks and followed by their successors since the sixth century.

For Paget (1896), accidie was characterized by despondency. This was accompanied by 'resentment, fretfulness, irritation, anger' (p. 41) or as itemized in his sermon, 'The Sorrow of the World', the three main elements of the sin are '*gloom* and *sloth* and *irritation*' (p. 54; emphasis in original). These elements combined to cause individuals to lower their sights so that there was a lazy acceptance of what could easily be attained rather than a determined striving for what was noble or worthwhile. The sufferer was robbed of strength and became listless and uninterested. Its common characteristics were irritability, weariness, sluggishness, and an inability to concentrate. It was a kind of bitter gloominess, a resentful withdrawal from the world and an evaporation of interest in the higher things in life as well as a lack of motivation to strive for improvement (generally in a spiritual sense).

The mind becomes crowded with negative thoughts about those with whom the sufferer is brought into contact; a cynical, ungrateful and mirthless disposition emerges. When it strikes the religious they become careless, even contemptuous, of holy exercise; they yawn when singing the psalms; perceive the worldly life as better than their own and come to regret and even hate their profession. The mind is weighed down, the body is sluggish and the individual is plunged into a bitter torpor. In Paget's words, 'a sullen, heavy, dreary mist about the heart, chilling and darkening it, till the least thing may make it fretful and angry—such was the misery of the "accidiosus" ' (p. 55). This kind of exhausting despondency accompanied by irritability, joylessness, anger towards others, and a marked lack of drive or ambition, which Paget identified as appearing with greatest force among those who dwell in solitude, has clear parallels among prisoners in solitary confinement. The novice monk or nun experiences similar emotional challenges to the incarcerated felon.

The notion of accidie may have fallen out of favour because, according to Huxley (1923: 22), it morphed from being a 'deadly sin' to a 'disease' and then a 'lyrical emotion' that inspired much modern literature: 'Accidie in its most complicated and most deadly form, a mixture of boredom, sorrow and despair, was now an inspiration to the greatest poets and novelists'. Huxley felt that the tragedy of the First World War had created such a profound sense of dislocation, despair, and hopelessness that accidie became 'a state of mind which fate has forced upon us' (p. 25). It was no longer a vice or a disease or a literary expression of ennui but rather an understandable outcome of communal disillusionment and pessimism. While the debate about accidie might be viewed as a historical curiosity, a recent book by Norris (2008) shows that the concept continues to offer something of explanatory value.

Barbed Wire Disease

In his account of the psychological impact of confinement in a prisoner of war (POW) camp, the Swiss surgeon A.L. Vischer (1919) found that living cheek by jowl with other men for a prolonged period of time had a range of adverse consequences. What he was concerned with differed from the usual prison experience in several pertinent ways. First of all, it was mass confinement where solitude was impossible and the craving for privacy could never be satisfied. As Sartre (1947: 92) would write in his play *Huis Clos* (No Exit), perhaps influenced by his own experience as a prisoner of war between 1940 and 1941, '*l'enfer, c'est les Autres*'. Similarly, and drawing on his four years in a Siberian prison camp, Dostoyevsky (2004: 7) observed: 'I could never have imagined... how terrible and agonising it would be never once for a single minute to be alone.' Autonomy is crippled by interaction over which one has no control just as it is by forced isolation. Secondly, it involved healthy and obedient young men from a variety of backgrounds (rather than the sickly and defiant urban dwellers who tend to make up prison populations). Finally, it was indeterminate (no-one knew when the war would end so the time until release could not be calculated). There were similarities also, including the deprivation of heterosexual relationships, the poor diet, the loss of liberty and personal autonomy, the fracturing of relationships with family and friends, and the imposition of an institutional regime.

Vischer observed a pattern of behaviour in the confined men which was sufficiently constant to suggest the existence of a specific disorder, which became known as 'barbed wire disease'. Its symptoms included irritability: 'the patients cannot stand the slightest opposition and readily fly into a passion' (p. 50), difficulties with concentration, exhaustion, memory failure, poverty of speech, brooding, paranoia, insomnia, disturbing dreams, and loss of libido. In combination these led to a state of 'utter weariness' (p. 49). It seemed that few were immune to the effects of barbed wire disease, with Vischer suggesting that it was present, to a greater or lesser degree, in most who had been in the camp for over six months. Nor was the prognosis good. Once established, the sheer fact of release was not enough to allow a return to normal functioning. Recovery took time and was not always complete; some would bear 'traces of the disease to the end of their days' (p. 60).

While there are elements of Vischer's scheme that are clearly unsatisfactory, such as issuing such a negative outlook without the benefit of any follow-up (his paper appeared the year after the First World War ended), the listlessness, apathy, irascibility, and dependence that he describes are also to be found in other captive populations. Drawing on his experience as a POW in Germany from 1940 to 1945, Gibbens (1961: 47) endorsed the view that barbed wire disease was a 'normal reaction'.

Deaton et al. (1977) surveyed 137 US airmen who had been POWs in Vietnam. All but one spent time in solitary confinement and the average duration was 39 weeks (max: 286 weeks). Deaton et al. argued that while prolonged isolation had consequences such as hallucinations or obsessive rituals that would normally be considered pathological, coping strategies were also present. POW studies allow us to answer questions that no (ethical) experimental study could ever dare to ask. They illustrate facets of human resilience under the most appalling conditions of disease, torture, malnutrition, and uncertainty.

The aviators studied by Deaton et al. differed in important ways from prisoners. They were well educated (most were college graduates), mature (average age at capture was 31), socially stable (three quarters were married), and in high status occupations (all were naval officers). This distinguished them from the socially isolated and low achieving young men so often found in prisons, many of whom have their first experience of detention during childhood. Also they were assertive, energetic men, who were more likely to try to achieve mastery over their environment than to yield passively to its demands. The threat to survival faced by POWs was great and this, together with their view that they were still 'at war' while imprisoned and remained in a chain of command, meant that there was a degree of cohesion across the prisoner of war society that is seldom found among civilian prisoners.

Despite the stresses associated with their captivity (both physical and mental) and its indefinite nature, the POWs adapted successfully. Deaton et al. felt that the experience of solitary confinement and the opportunity it presented for reordering personal priorities and reconsidering value systems was beneficial and 'may have set the stage for significant positive personality and behavioral changes' for the men involved (p. 255). If in these most unpropitious of circumstances solitary confinement can have downstream benefits, there is no reason to believe that it might not have a similar effect for other types of prisoner.

A less upbeat assessment than that offered by Deaton et al. comes from Ursano et al. (1981: 310) whose study of US Air Force POWs uncovered 'a significant degree of psychiatric readjustment problems.' At repatriation, and at a five year follow-up, almost a quarter of the group were given a psychiatric diagnosis. Most of the clinical problems were in the areas of interpersonal, marital, and occupational adjustment. This was a group of men that had been carefully screened for flying; they were free of psychiatric difficulties before they were captured. They were intelligent, highly motivated, successful, well trained, and patriotic. If, despite all of these protective factors, they showed long-term adjustment difficulties due to the extreme conditions to which they had been exposed, what hope is there for the prisoner who lacks many of their strengths and is often accompanied into custody by a history of mental ill-health? Ursano et al. concluded that 'under maximum stress few if any sociodemographic factors are protective' (p. 313).

A study by Sledge et al. (1980: 430–1) of US Air Force personnel still on active duty who had been prisoners in the Vietnam war found that while research about former POWs tended to focus on the pathological consequences of captivity, most of the men in their sample reported that in a number of important ways their experience had been beneficial:

They responded to the challenge of captivity as an opportunity to experience their human limits, and they defined their abilities and limitations more sharply than most people ever will. They often report feeling more self-confident and stronger than before their captivity. For some, the experience has been a dividing line between an old and a new life, sometimes dramatically different—with a new family, job and orientation to the future.

There was a positive correlation between the degree of suffering and the perceived benefits with even the most appalling treatment being seen by many as a stimulus for growth. Some of these men, especially those captured in the early years of the war suffered greatly, experiencing torture, disease, routine abuse, and malnutrition as well as solitary confinement, but emerged fortified. The men involved, of whom there were over 200, recounted how they had become more inwardly directed. Through introspection they gained substantially in terms of self-awareness and self-understanding. Sledge et al. concluded that, 'This report is further evidence that some individuals who experience extremes, or the unusual, or who must make a great sacrifice, may believe they grow from or are advantaged by the experience' (p. 443).

Winter-over Syndrome

The polar literature is littered with accounts of the deleterious effects of spending winters on ice. As Strange and Klein (1973: 410–11) summarized matters in their analysis of interviews conducted over several years with personnel who had spent prolonged periods cut off at research stations in the South Pole, 'a basic and axiomatic observation remains true: The physical deprivations and dangers of Antarctic life are remarkably well tolerated. It is the isolation, with its related social and psychological stresses which requires the most adaptive effort and causes human adjustment problems.' They introduced the term 'winter-over syndrome' to describe a typical adjustment pattern which comprised the four elements of depression, hostility, sleep disturbance, and impaired cognition. These problems were widespread, with 72 per cent reporting depression; 65 per cent reporting problems with hostility and anger; 60 per cent complaining of sleep disturbance ('big eye' is the term used to refer to the chronic insomnia experienced by those living in an environment which is devoid of sunlight); and 41 per cent suffering from diminished concentration and memory, absentmindedness and a more general intellectual torpor. An unfocused gaze into the middle distance accompanied by a wandering mind is known as 'long eye' (Suedfeld and Steel 2000: 231).

This cluster of difficulties was not usually disabling and, while causing discomfort, it did not prevent station members carrying out their duties. It was rare for severe psychiatric problems to emerge and, when they did, they reflected an underlying pathology rather than being environmentally determined: 'The stress of isolated Antarctic duty does not make psychiatrically healthy people psychiatrically ill. It may, however, exacerbate or make apparent emotional problems which already exist' (Strange and Klein 1973: 411). Underlying difficulties, in combination with heavy alcohol consumption, created a toxic mix. Taylor (1989: 239) described how spending the winter in the Antarctic 'has long been known to have at best a lethargic effect and at worst an occasional psychopathological effect'. Reviewing the results of observational, clinical, and experimental studies as well as journal entries, Taylor concluded that wintering produced a 'hibernating' effect that had two important characteristics. First of all, it was an adaptive response to the environment rather than a symptom of some underlying disorder; it was an effective way of getting through a period where sensory inputs were greatly reduced, and it was not necessarily harmful. Secondly, it was transient; while the poverty of behaviour associated with this state might cause observers to become concerned, when circumstances changed so too did the individual's behaviour.

While most seemed to suffer from winter-over syndrome, becoming listless, apathetic and hostile, some thrived in these conditions, a group that might be called 'professional isolates' (p. 243). There are parallels here with the prisoner in solitary confinement, namely an unchanging external environment and reduced sensory input. Indeed, some of those writing about their polar experiences describe it as 'imprisonment'. Taylor provided a range of extracts from the diaries of polar explorers, going back almost two centuries, that show what one diarist described as the 'brain cracking' impact of social isolation and unrelieved boredom (pp. 240–2). The consequences of such conditions are consistently the same: lethargy, difficulties concentrating, and despondency. Suedfeld and Steel (2000) cautioned against exaggerating the significance of winter-over syndrome. Acknowledging the existence of depression, irritability, disturbed sleep, withdrawal, personal neglect, and cognitive impairment, they argued that any such changes 'are temporary and seldom interfere seriously with work and other activities' (p. 231). As Strange and Klein (1973) noted, for persons without a pre-existing psychopathology, these ranked as occupational hazards that were unpleasant, but not clinically significant.

The Antarctic winter-over experience results in emotional flatness, impaired concentration and memory, weariness, sleep disturbance, and hostility. There is little *joie de vivre* and instead a kind of angry apathy. As for prisoners the process of adaptation is patterned, with initial anxiety followed by withdrawal, irritability and disrupted sleep, and finally agitation as the departure date draws near. This is a useful way of viewing behaviours that are sometimes seen as pathological, or at the very least as maladaptive or symptoms of mental deterioration. On the contrary such processes of shutdown (or, perhaps more accurately, standby) could equally be seen as adaptive responses to a monotonous environment. These are transient states and the tempo can be raised when the environment changes.

The same surely applies to prisoners in isolation whose lassitude makes sense given the poverty of their external environment. These behaviours may be situational rather than reflecting permanent psychological shifts; it makes sense to power down when environmental demands are low. To the untutored observer, what appears to be a profound adjustment difficulty or a pathological symptom, may be a way of conserving resources in a hostile environment. Newspaper editor and publisher Jacobo Timerman (1988: 34) who was imprisoned for 30 months during Argentina's 'dirty war', described how, to cope with the impact of solitary confinement and regular torture sessions involving electric shocks, he learned to adopt 'an attitude of absolute passivity'. He believed that by not venting any emotions he was conserving the energy required for survival. By not fighting back he found the strength to survive. In his words, 'The vegetable attitude can save a life' (p. 35). While his passivity might have suggested despair and capitulation, in reality it meant the opposite. 'I kept going', he wrote, 'and here I am' (p. 92).

In a similar vein, Meisenhelder (1985: 52; emphasis in original) suggested that prison reverie was adaptive and that if used wisely, daydreaming and fantasy helped prisoners to cope: 'what is often described as a prisoner's deplorable habit of withdrawing regressively into a private fantasy world is more accurately seen as a way of *actively resisting* the impositions of the institution of prison'. This is purposive adaptation rather than pathetic withdrawal. It is a question of degree, of course, and there is a world of difference between the inane mumblings of a prisoner for whom a fantasy life trumps interpersonal relations, and the prisoner who chooses to while away an afternoon, allowing dreamy wish-fulfilment to effect a temporary detachment from a grim reality. By keeping the dream alive the dehumanizing effects of imprisonment are combated.

Grey (1988: 287) remarked that 'total isolation dulls and blunts the edges of the emotions somewhat while the isolation lasts, puts them on ice to a degree, and this is perhaps a saving factor'. The dulling of affect has adaptive significance. The danger is that it goes too far and the individual cannot return from passivity. Waite (1994: 134) found the value in quietude but was aware of the potential harms: 'I am learning to be quiet and still within, perhaps calm is a better word. I don't want too much stillness as I need a certain inner tension to keep my mind alive.' As long as an apparently inert exterior conceals an episodically active interior, all is not lost.

A conscientious objector who gave evidence to the Prison System Enquiry Committee, established in January 1919 by the Executive of the Labour Research Department in the UK, described how he found a partial shutting down of his mental faculties to be adaptive: 'I gradually discovered that, half consciously and half sub-consciously, I was drifting (and perhaps partly forcing myself) into a condition of mental and nervous "hibernation," which proved the best possible protection against the mental and nervous strain of prison conditions' (Hobhouse and Brockway 1922: 646). Writing of his experience as a political prisoner in a Soviet labour camp, which included periods on hunger strike and in solitary confinement, Gluzman (1982: 60; emphasis in original) observed that:

Although situationally induced changes of mood—feelings of loneliness and distress—are not rare here, they are not manifestations of a psychic disorder. They are a natural, healthy reaction to gloating brutality and trampled justice, to abuses of power, to the insensitivity of God and the world. Psychological inadequacy or deficiency under such conditions would manifest itself by the *absence* of such negative emotions.

Once again, what appears to be pathological can be an appropriate, and proportionate, response to trying circumstances.

Capsules and Frontiers

In their account of the negative impact of long-duration space missions Kanas et al. (2009: 665), were quick to acknowledge that 'isolated and confined environments can also be growth enhancing', and listed among the positive effects 'increased fortitude, perseverance, independence, self-reliance, ingenuity, comradeship, and even decreased tension and depression'. Sometimes, transcendental experiences or religious insights are reported by space travellers, whose view of the world changes (literally). One Russian cosmonaut, after a 438-day stay on the space station Mir, showed that during a brief period of adjustment (lasting around two weeks) there was evidence of impaired performance and subjective well-being, but thereafter mood and performance returned to pre-launch levels and remained stable. The initial decline in functioning was attributed to increased workload and the unfamiliarity of living in microgravity. It is not surprising that prisoners can go through similar kinds of personal transformation given that they, also, are faced with an out-of-the ordinary experience of isolation. One major difference is that many prisoners are mentally ill at the outset thus limiting their options for self-actualisation, while potential space travellers are screened for pre-existing psychiatric conditions.

Despite all of the preparatory work, and the finding that space travellers can return to earth with heightened sensibilities, on occasion the experience affects them in a negative sense to the extent that medical and psychotherapeutic remedies are required to effect a return to normal functioning. If this is the case for even the most well-adjusted and carefully chosen space travellers, how much truer must it be for prisoners in isolation who are often unstable beforehand and many of whom share the kinds of characteristics (aggression, insubordination, mental ill health, alcohol and drug dependency, weak family and social ties) which are used to screen out individuals who opt for isolation in other settings?

Capsule inhabitants find 'empty' time difficult to manage as there is no distraction from the unpleasantness and monotony of their cramped surroundings. In these circumstances there can be a tendency to slow down the tempo of cognitive and motor activities and altered states of consciousness are sometimes observed. In the Russian space programme most long-duration cosmonauts are believed to suffer from asthenia, a disorder that is not fully recognized by US psychiatrists, but which entails many of the symptoms that are found in others who experience extreme isolation. These include 'fatigue, irritability and emotional lability, attention and concentration difficulties, restlessness, heightened perceptual sensitivities, palpitations and blood pressure instability, physical weakness, and sleep and appetite problems' (p. 665). Again, if the brightest and most carefully preselected space travellers experience such a constellation of problems it is reasonable to expect that the prisoner in his enforced reclusion will feel at least as bad. If the occupant of a prison isolation cell is thought of as orbiting normal life, it is not surprising that he shares some experiences with the astronaut, who is also orbiting the real world, far removed from those he loves, and anxious about re-entry and the attendant perils.

In their exploration of the psychology of being alone, Long and Averill (2003) highlighted four benefits, which closely resemble the virtues described by Koch (1994), as outlined in the previous chapter. These are freedom (to make choices, unhindered); creativity (uncluttered thinking, dreaming, imagining a new self); intimacy (feelings of connection with others); and spirituality (meditation, an unimpeded search for one's God). One factor that is important in determining whether solitude is viewed as positive or negative is the degree of control an individual has over their separation from others. The beauty of the external environment is another relevant consideration, with the awesomeness of nature enhancing the perception of solitude. Prisoners are singularly bereft of either of these consolations. Generally speaking, they are involuntarily confined in ugly surroundings, unaffected by the passage of the seasons or the wonder of the natural world. While some prison buildings evince a certain architectural sophistication when viewed from above or outside, the corridors and cells upon which the prisoner's gaze rests seldom inspire; drabness is integral to the design.

The voluntary isolate has the added advantage of being able to choose a space which allows reflection to be combined with vigorous and varied physical activity, following the Benedictine injunction to combine 'ora' with 'labora', something that the prisoner's cramped quarters rarely permits. Voluntarism is important but its role should not be exaggerated. As we have seen, those who opt to be alone have many of the same experiences but interpret them differently, with the result that they are less malign in their effects. In other words, it is not the fact that prisoners experience solitude against their will that causes the damage but how they view this.

According to Long and Averill those who cope best with solitude have successfully negotiated attachment issues during early childhood and possess a capacity for both advanced reasoning and reflexive thought. These are triumphs that many prisoners are unlikely to have experienced given their typical backgrounds of family and educational disadvantage. As a result they are perhaps more likely to find solitude painful. Nevertheless, the human variation in responding to solitude led Long and Averill to conclude that: 'Whatever one's opinion of solitary confinement and its potential misuse (e.g., as an adjunct to brainwashing), from a prisoner's perspective it may not always be the "cruel and unusual punishment" often depicted' (p. 36).

Even those who cope recognize the dangers. Mason (1918: 134) put it well when he observed that: 'Prison either makes or blasts a man. It either makes him self-reliant or else it stuns him into a coma, a mental vacuity which time and habit turn into an inability to do anything except under obedience. Unless one has something self-assertive within one that thwarts the ravages of silence and isolation one will be surely damned.' Austin Bidwell (1897: 393) remarked of his separate confinement that: 'Of my experience in Pentonville during my year of solitude it suffices to say that, passing through a great deal of mental conflict, I found I had grown stronger.' Keenan described being a hostage as a time of 'crucifying aloneness' (cited in Anderson 1994: 347). This language is symbolically loaded, but nuanced, implying as it does the possibility of resurrection, of bleakness and abandonment followed by joy and reunion.

Jenny Schreiner, an activist with the African National Congress, spent six months in solitary confinement in South Africa beginning in September 1987. She was isolated so that she could be interrogated before being brought to trial. During this period she became so dejected that she attempted suicide. Even so she did not view the experience as unequivocally bleak, writing from her prison cell that: 'I found one can adjust even to what the psychologists call sensory deprivation...It's true that through facing ordeals and adversity one develops one's personality and strength. I have matured, I think. I appreciate life, people in their strengths and weaknesses, with a new depth' (cited in Schreiner 2000: 62).

Wilderness Narratives

Those who search for enrichment in isolation do not necessarily find it. In his controversial book on the peripatetic Chris McCandless who sought deeper self-understanding in the remoteness of Alaska but perished in the process, Krakauer (2007: 156) quoted historian Roderick Nash: 'The solitude and total freedom of the wilderness created a perfect setting for either melancholy or exultation.' The journal entries penned by McCandless certainly show evidence of the latter, as he put himself to the test in an unforgiving environment. But ultimately it would appear that as he faced death, utterly alone and not contactable, he came to the profound realization that humans are inherently social; by fleeing the world he discovered his inextricable connection to it. In one of his final comments, an annotation to the text of *Doctor Zhivago* which he had just finished reading, McCandless wrote 'Happiness only real when shared' (Krakauer 2007: 188). These words were jotted down beside Boris Pasternak's (1991: 161) observation that 'an unshared happiness is not happiness'. Tragically, McCandless never had an opportunity to seek happiness in company, dying within weeks of making this note.

Similarly Zeno (1968: 66) realized, after long reflection in his prison cell, that 'Content and peace of mind may be found on a desert island, but happiness, true happiness, can only be reached through human relationships.' And Brian Keenan (1992: 277), whose relationship with fellow hostage John McCarthy was characterized by deep reciprocity and an unshakeable rapport observed that: 'We are all made of many parts; no man is singular in the way he lives his life. He only lives it fully in relation to others.' Tom Leppard, a former British soldier who had his entire body tattooed with the markings of a leopard (and changed his name to reflect his new, feline, identity) lived alone for more than two decades in a tiny hut on a remote Scottish island. Leppard reported that he never felt lonely and was always more than satisfied with his situation but that the emotional highs and lows that accompany life with other people were denied him. There was a flattening out of affect, but the overall feeling was one of peace and contentment. In his own words: 'For me, to be extremely happy or extremely sad I need to be around people. If you're alone I think you can only be content. You don't get real highs and lows. But being alone gives you much greater inner joy' (cited in Hemming 2008: 49). Solitude might lead to internal calm and a pacific mind but it does so at the price of being fully human.

Laing and Crouch (2009) argued that frontier travellers are attracted by solitude; this is part of their reward for journeying so far. The social isolation that they strive hard to find facilitates reflection, resulting in feelings of freedom, authenticity, self-actualization, and spiritual growth. They learn what remains of themselves when society's support structures are stripped away and when external stimuli are reduced to a minimum. They gain insights into what life means to them and where they fit in the greater scheme. But solitude, and the silence that accompanies it in truly remote locations, can be a source of anxiety also. Acquiring the independence required to withstand the most unforgiving environments occasionally causes the individual to fear that they might become so self-referential that interactions with others will have an indelible blandness about them. As Arctic explorer Jonathan Waterman expressed it, 'I am concerned about sacrificing some vital part of myself to solitude...I have to hold myself together, tightly, so I don't disappear into a world inhabited only by me' (cited in Laing and Crouch 2009: 335).

The ultimate achievement for frontier travellers is to remould themselves in the crucible of isolation; by shaking off the shackles of society they are free to examine what emerges without the need for conformity or impression management. This allows a degree of uninterrupted self-absorption which is absent (or easy to avoid) in normal life. Similarly, prisoners can wring meaning and a new perspective from a long prison sentence through a combination of the maturity that comes with advancing years, self-examination, and a sense of personal efficacy that accompanies survival in a harsh clime. For those without the inner resources that allow self-transformation, anger, struggle, and madness are the alternatives.

One of the themes in Anthony Storr's book, *Solitude*, is that the enormity of being alone can allow an individual to forge a deeper understanding of their place in the world. The more complete the isolation, the more potentially profound the accompanying revelation. Storr gives the example of Admiral Richard Byrd who insisted on manning an Antarctic weather station, alone, for five months in 1934. (As Koch (1994: 2) put it, 'he charted the weather and measured the sort of man he was.') Quoting from Byrd's account of his experience, which he explained as a desire to 'taste peace and quiet and solitude long enough to find out how good they really are', Storr (1988: 35–6) relayed a mystical experience which the polar explorer felt gave him insight into his being part of something greater, something universal:

Harmony, that was it! That was what came out of the silence—a gentle rhythm, the strain of a perfect chord, the music of the spheres, perhaps...In that instant I could feel no doubt of man's oneness with the universe...It was a feeling that transcended reason; that went to the heart of man's despair and found it groundless. The universe was a cosmos, not a chaos; man was as rightfully a part of that cosmos as were the day and night.

(It is possible, of course, that solitude 'tastes' different if it is forced upon one.)

Cohen and Taylor (1972) quoted Byrd also, in particular his observation that to survive he focused all of his attention on the present moment and his immediate surroundings and avoided thinking of the future or the past. His goal was 'Full mastery of the impinging moment' and this was accomplished through routines that were designed to 'increase the content of the hours' (p. 92). The polar explorer realized the importance of immersion in the 'now', a realization shared by the wise prisoner (see Chapter 8). The individual who masters time takes an important step towards achieving mastery over his or her life.

Self-examination, described by Halpern (1993: 202) as 'solitude's true vocation', is akin to a confrontation as the psychological carapace that has accumulated over the years splinters under scrutiny. This is a confrontation which it can take even the most pious monks years to win (or more accurately, perhaps, to fight to a standstill). What unremitting self-reflection reveals is an image that is often unflattering and discomfiting to contemplate. This is why solitude can feel threatening whether entered into willingly or under duress. Even John Howard, the impressively ascetic and unswervingly focused penal reformer, wilted occasionally when he applied the rule to his own life. His cold self-examination, after his cold early-morning bath, and on a perennially grumbling stomach, sometimes resulted in 'flashes of self-laceration' where he saw himself as a 'vile worm' or a 'fruitless, barren, cold, dead, vile creature' (Ignatieff 1989: 51). Howard felt a sense of kinship with the confined. They were all sinners and the penitentiary offered a 'technology of salvation' (p. 57).

Breytenbach (1984: 309) wrote about how one effect of prolonged solitary confinement was that beauty is found in the banal: 'once you have been totally isolated and undone—then you will find the most permanent comfort in humble things... that fluff of wool in the corner, a cloud, a tin, the hoarse cry of panic slicing through the night... these things have a terrible one-by-one beauty.' Mason (1918: 174; emphasis in original) noted that prison provides an opportunity for thoroughgoing reflection that is seldom found, and never for long, in everyday life: 'In prison one is forced to think and deal in essentials, whereas in civil life one is in a whirlwind of disconcerting *ephemera*'. He argued that this view was shared by other prisoners: 'all, I think, were exhilarated and invigorated by their prison experiences, and being forced to concentrate upon life's essentials, gained a greater insight into its problems. I think, I *know*, that I did' (p. 175; emphasis in original). Mason was also alert to the fact that beyond a certain point, such concentration would become counterproductive and the insights less plentiful. By his estimation three months was time aplenty for what he termed a 'rest-cure' (p. 175). It is notable that even those who sing the praises of isolation are aware that, if prolonged, its curative properties are extinguished.

Good food, welcome company, purposeful activity, natural beauty, wise rules, and careful mentoring; these are vital elements of the penitential life that are absent from the penitentiary. The companionable and communicative silence enjoyed by the monk in his cell is a burden more easily borne than the suffocating aloneness of the isolated and ignored prisoner. The fact that some prisoners can survive prolonged separation in the absence of these protective factors makes their achievement more remarkable still.

Interim Conclusion

It is probably fair to say that solitude is *often* damaging if it is involuntary, *sometimes* damaging if it is an unavoidable corollary of a chosen course of action, but *seldom* so if it is sought out. What is less clear is whether the mark it leaves is indelible, or deleted when normal living circumstances are restored. This depends on the duration of confinement, the reasons for it, the individual's prior mental health status, how well it is administered, and how transitional arrangements (before and after) are managed. At a fundamental level the isolated prisoner fears that he will lose the authorship of his life (something that the entrant to religious life might seek); that he will become little more than a vessel upon which a penal policy is inscribed, and overwritten—the prisoner as palimpsest—that he will become a minor character in another's story.

Isolation could be considered along with sleep deprivation, extreme noise, silence, and temperature alteration as a form of what McCoy (2006: 7) described in his account of CIA interrogation techniques as 'no-touch torture'. This echoes Dickens' condemnation of the separate system of prison discipline as a 'secret punishment' to be all the more denounced because 'it extorts few cries that human ears can hear' (see Chapter 2). Physical pain has clear parameters. Its marks are visible. Cuts can be stitched and injuries dressed. Scars are sometimes worn as badges of honour. By contrast the intangible, internal wounds of anguish are discernible to none but the bearer and, if revealed, may signal weakness or madness, either of which increase vulnerability in a social world where toughness is king. Reyes (2007: 607) described how:

> In Uruguay, in the 1970s and 1980s, leaders of the MLN-Tupamaro movement were imprisoned in harsh conditions of solitary confinement for several years without being allowed to communicate with anyone. Meals were delivered through a hatch by guards who were strictly forbidden to say even a word to them. Several of these prisoners confided that for them solitary confinement had been the worst form of torture. 'Electricity [torture]', said one, 'is mere child's play in comparison to prolonged solitude.'

As Reyes put it 'the worst scars are in the mind' (p. 591).

McCoy (2006: 8) observed that the impetus for the CIA to develop new ways of extracting information was interrogators' consistent experience over many hundreds of years that 'mere physical pain, no matter how extreme, often produced heightened resistance'. Sensory deprivation (or disorientation) and 'self-inflicted pain', such as standing for a prolonged period with arms extended, were found, in combination, to create a form of trauma that acted as 'a hammer-blow to the fundamentals of personal identity' (p. 8). Because victims feel partially responsible for their pain they capitulate more readily. In addition to being efficacious this approach does not require the interrogator to strike, cut, throttle, electrocute, or drug the subject of their attention. As there are no obvious marks, allegations of torture are easy to refute and, indeed, whether such practices constitute torture can become a matter of debate and interpretation. There are fewer grey areas as far as bruises, burns, and broken bones are concerned. If a succession of such 'hammer-blows' could shatter the resistance of an enemy agent, trained in counter-interrogation and determined to resist, how much easier will it be to splinter the defences of a disorganized individual, possibly suffering from poor mental health?

It is probably not a coincidence that the country whose Central Intelligence Agency has pioneered 'no-touch' approaches to torture, and resisted their labelling as torturous, has developed a capacity to inflict similar treatment on its prisoners. If isolation, reduced sensory input, and unpleasant ambient heat and light are used to elicit information from those whose lives (and possibly their nation's security) depend on not imparting it, it is absurd to think that analogous processes—whatever their ostensible objectives, and however clearly they fall within legally permissible limits—will have a null effect on prisoners.

There are factors that help to neutralize the impact of prison isolation. For example, the realization dawns on some prisoners that while being in prison is unpleasant and fraught, they faced, and posed, greater threats on the street. Although suicide rates are elevated, prisoners are less likely to die at the hands of others when they are inside (see Table 6.1). Similarly they are protected from the ravages of alcohol, drugs, homelessness, and poor diet. While prison food is unattractively presented and lacks variety, it generally meets minimum nutritional standards. They are insulated from community disdain and the disappointment of those close to them. They are removed from a context where they see themselves as adversely impacting the life chances of family members. They sometimes achieve a status among their peers that had been absent outside. They discover talents that were smothered by the imperatives of the present that define life on the street. These can be artistic, or legal, or political, or scholarly, or physical—the mind can be built as well as the body. For some offenders prison is a place of respite and safety, an oasis of predictability in a world that is loosely structured and open-ended. Cells are seen as secure enclosures. As one prisoner expressed this sentiment, 'It gives me a sense of comfort to be here. I like it . . . the way it . . . well it wraps me up and makes me feel safe' (Medlicott 2004: 111).

In his account of writing *The Magic Mountain*, which started off as an idea for a short story and became a two-volume novel,

Thomas Mann (1996: 725) described how the book's protago-
nist, Hans Castorp, went through a process of 'heightening' or
Steigerung. An ordinary young man, indeed 'a simple-minded
hero' (p. 725), he became capable of sensual, moral, and intellectual adventures that would otherwise have remained beyond
his ken. This resulted from his experience of a 'charmed circle
of isolation and invalidism' (p. 721) in the comfortable confines
of a Swiss sanatorium, where time was stretched to such a point
that the individual became disconnected from external realities,
allowing a transformation of character to occur. Castorp visited
the sanatorium in Davos to spend three weeks with a tubercular
cousin, but ended up remaining there for seven years. Some of the
prison writers whose work informs this book seem to have gone
through the process of *Steigerung* also, arriving in what for them
might be better described as charmless isolation but discovering
within themselves a hitherto unknown capacity to produce works
of beauty and subtlety (see Appendix for a selection of the texts in
question).

When reaching a balanced assessment of the consequences of
solitary confinement it is important not to lose sight of the fact
that some of those subjected to it see it as offering life-enhancing
opportunities which they are keen to accept. The longer the term
and the greater the self-examination the more likely it is that a
nuanced appraisal of this kind will emerge. This is not to deny
the manifold harms associated with the deprivation of liberty, and
their intensification in solitary confinement, but simply to state
that in some cases, when prisoners look at the trajectory of their
lives they conclude that had imprisonment not intervened they
may have gone on to cause the kind of devastation to themselves
and others that, if they survived, would have been a cause of perennial regret. Prison, even in its harshest and most corrupting manifestations, does not ruin all of the people all of the time. For some
it replaces the kamikaze course that their life was following with
a better guarantee of arriving at middle age with bodily integrity
intact and future prospects, however limited, in place. Which state
of affairs is preferable is to some extent in the eye of the beholder
but the point is that perspectives differ.

Central to this book is a concern with penal isolation when it
is enforced and when it endures. It is also about making explicit
how the temporal dimension of incarceration is managed in terms
of how the passage of time is felt and fought. These two aspects

of prison life necessarily overlap and intermesh and it is the individual in long-term solitary confinement whose identity is most severely tested by the challenges of space and time. Before considering in more detail how solitary prisoners grapple with time (Chapters 8 and 9) and the approaches they devise to lightening its burden (Chapter 10), it is necessary to complete the chronological analysis begun in Chapter 1 by addressing how enforced isolation is manifest in the modern prison, especially in the species of institution known in the US as the 'supermax'. This is addressed in the following two chapters.

5

The Apotheosis of Solitary Confinement

As outlined in Chapter 1, solitary confinement has long been part of the practice of imprisonment. What has changed over time is the rationale behind it, the enthusiasm with which it is embraced, and the identity of its champions. Shalev (2009a: 22–5) described three waves of solitary confinement. The first was led by religiously motivated prison reformers, the second by psychologists who had become intoxicated by the promise of behaviour modification, and the third by prison administrators. The shift in the breadth and locus of debate is noteworthy. A discourse that took place outside the prison gates and featured many voices has been replaced by one which is almost entirely intramural and one-sided. Prisoners contribute to the debate intermittently through coordinated actions such as law suits and protests which, if seized upon by pressure groups and the media, can prise the matter open for wider consideration.

Generally speaking, there are three kinds of circumstance when prisoners are isolated. *First*, there is protective custody, often at the prisoner's request. A return to the general population can be difficult if a prisoner has been segregated because of vulnerability due to the nature of his or her offence, the accumulation of debts that cannot be discharged, or a perception that he or she has communicated information to staff. *Secondly*, there is disciplinary detention for breaking prison rules; generally the duration is relatively short. *Thirdly,* there is administrative segregation. This can be short term (e.g. for medical or psychological observation, while an investigation is being carried out or pending transfer to another institution) or long term (if a prisoner is deemed to present a risk to self or others or to the smooth running of the facility). These prisoners are deemed to be the 'worst of the worst', a group described by Collins (2004: xi), in a report for the US Department of Justice, as 'the most dangerous, recalcitrant, aggressive, and antagonistic inmates in a prison system'. For such men (and, very occasionally, women) there is little sympathy among prison administrators, politicians or the public. As a result, what passes for an acceptable level of treatment falls short of any humane minimum standard, with predictably awful consequences for those who are already vulnerable and whose internal resources, and external supports, are scant. Prisoners with 'validated' gang associations can spend an indeterminate term in administrative segregation. The route back to the general population is not always clear (Metcalf et al. 2013) and sometimes it is predicated upon satisfactory 'debriefing' with staff which may jeopardise the individual's safety and lead to the substitution of protective custody for administrative segregation; a dubious result at best from the perspective of the prisoner. The debriefing process can be lengthy, sometimes taking up to three years to complete (King et al. 2008: 150).

There are other routes into solitary confinement which are minor in the overall scheme but mentioned for the sake of completeness. Prisoners occasionally seek the respite of the solitary cell as a way of easing psychological pressures. In such cases the stay is generally brief and prisoners return to their usual place afterwards. There may be stigma associated with behaviour of this kind, in the sense that it betrays an inability to cope, but not such that it will invite the opprobrium of one's peers in the same way as a spell in protective custody. In some jurisdictions, prisoners are held in solitary confinement during the pre-trial period. This practice, which has been roundly condemned, is associated with Scandinavian countries otherwise applauded for the temperate nature of their penal climates. Indeed, Evans and Morgan (1998: 247) described pre-trial solitary confinement as a 'peculiarly Scandinavian phenomenon'. Very occasionally a court imposes solitary confinement as part of a sentence and the time period here can be lengthy. In some central European states, and in Mongolia, prisoners sentenced to life imprisonment are kept in solitary confinement (United Nations 2011: para 41) and in the US prisoners on death row can be segregated for decades as the legal process runs its course. There is perhaps nothing to match the experience of Iwao Hakamada who spent 45 years in solitary confinement on death row in Japan before doubts about the safety of his conviction led to his release (McNeill 2014).

It is long-term administrative segregation where the challenges of isolation are greatest. It is likely that punitive or protective segregation is less psychologically threatening even if the physical conditions are not dissimilar, because the reason for its imposition is clear, and there are usually boundaries around duration together with due process safeguards. Also, those isolated for offences against prison discipline or for their own safety, while perhaps denigrated on account of their offending history or their misbehaviour are spared the burden of expectation that comes with the 'worst of the worst' label, a misleading shorthand term that facilitates harsh treatment by stripping away shared human characteristics.

Being selected for administrative segregation is different. The criteria for admission and discharge are loose and unspecific, prisoners can feel unfairly targeted, and there is a greater air of illegitimacy around its use. Ronald Del Raine (1993: 1), who spent more than two years on the control unit at Marion in the early 1970s, described how prisoners were assigned there for 'reasons so nebulous and evanescent as to defy articulation'. Korn (1988a: 13) described the lack of clarity around what is required of prisoners to transfer out of administrative segregation as 'the condition beside which all other pathogenic factors fade in comparison'. In another paper the same author described this as the 'condition of interminability: it was the lock without a key' (Korn 1988b: 21; see also United States Government Accountability Office 2013). Further exacerbating matters, the environment in which it is administered can become toxic because of the depth of animosity that exists between prisoners and guards. The apotheosis of this kind of incarceration is found in the supermax prison, where the solitary period can be extensive. Figures from the California Department of Corrections and Rehabilitation showed an average population of 1,106 in the Pelican Bay Security Housing Unit during 2011 of whom 513 had been there for at least ten years. Among this group were 222 who had been there more than 15 years, and 78 who had lived for more than 20 years in these conditions of extreme isolation, their misery unrelieved as the years slid by (*Ruiz v. Brown* 2012: para 33).

Separation Redux (and Redoubled)

Wacquant (2013: xiii; emphasis in original) described supermax as 'a species of *meta-prison*, a prison for the prison'. This is a

good way of thinking about the intensification of penal austerity that supermax involves. It is a deeper, heavier, tighter, experience, in less forgiving surroundings, which is reserved for those
who are perceived as too menacing to be handled in any other
way. Synonyms and euphemisms abound. They include 'administrative maximum penitentiary or ad-max or ADX', 'maxi-maxi',
'security housing unit or SHU', 'administrative close supervision',
'restricted housing unit', 'special control unit', 'extended control
unit', 'intensive management unit', and 'correctional adjustment
center' (Metcalf et al. 2013: 3; Riveland 1999: 5; Shalev 2009a: 9).
While there may be local variations in terminology, all of these
facilities share a regime based on extreme, and largely unrelieved,
isolation where the human contact that does exist is fraught and
distant. This is boredom, screwed down tight.

The lack of a standard nomenclature means that it is difficult
to be absolutely sure how widely the supermax phenomenon has
spread. In particular, some states define as 'maximum security' the
kind of confinement that is elsewhere called 'supermax'. By one
calculation, 44 states had supermax prisons or their equivalents
by 2004, up from 34 in 1996 (Mears 2006: 4). While estimates of
the number of prisoners subjected to this extreme form of penal
discipline may vary (Naday et al. 2008), there is no disputing that
a lurch to lockdown occurred in the US. Correctional authorities
are in lockstep with a practice that has marched them to a model
of confinement that attracted well-intentioned (but misguided)
reformers two centuries earlier but was then de-emphasized for
generations.

In a study of how corrections commodities are marketed in
trade journals, Lynch (2002: 310) found that the phrase 'maximum security' first entered the criminal justice lexicon in 1960
in an advertisement for a key control system. In 1984 the word
'supermax' made its debut in conjunction with an advertising campaign for a lighting system that was touted as more
tamper-resistant than any competitor: 'Tougher than any hardened criminal, Supermax was built for abuse. The guards like
Supermax. The cons leave it alone' (cited in Lynch 2002: 313;
according to the Oxford English Dictionary online, the term
can be dated to a 1975 newspaper report). The marketing of
actual supermax units and the associated paraphernalia, such
as perforated metal walls and doors with feeding slots ('cuff
ports'), began in 1988 and has been unrelenting since. This was

the year after the Special Management Unit (SMU) opened in Florence, Arizona. According to Lynch (2010: 5) this was 'the first state-level newly constructed (as opposed to retrofitted) supermax facility in the country.' Its architects took advantage of cutting-edge technologies to design spaces for indefinite solitary confinement.

However, the language of super-maximum-security custody echoed faintly across the penal landscape even when the ethos was avowedly rehabilitative and security concerns jostled for ascendancy with treatment, training, and the maintenance of inmate morale. The control unit at Marion was described as 'super-maximum-security' in the 1970s (Bronstein 1981: 73) and decades earlier Alcatraz had been known as 'the super-maximum-security prison in San Francisco Bay' (Barnes and Teeters 1959: 461). It seems reasonable to suggest that prior to the 1980s such facilities were reluctantly accepted as a necessary response to a few exceptional prisoners; they were islands, sometimes literally, of austerity in a system with an overall focus that was more optimistic. Also, they were not designed to enforce the degree of separation between inmates and others that characterizes the modern supermax.

When 'H' unit at Marion was designated a control unit in June 1972 (King 1999: 167), this marked a return to the practice of holding prisoners in long-term solitary confinement which had been abandoned after the failure of the previous century's experiment with isolation. While isolation was used to enforce discipline at Alcatraz, and the conditions of confinement were indisputably severe, life on the Rock was more communal than in the supermaxes that succeeded it, with prisoners dining, working, and spending recreation time together. They had daily contact with other prisoners and guards as well as regular exposure to the elements, whether walking to work or associating in the yard. When Alcatraz opened it was intended to operate a silent system with conversation prohibited at work, during meals and in the cell block. Talking was permitted during yard time at the weekends and during the eight minute rest breaks allotted to workers twice a day. But this system was discontinued within a year or so as it proved to be unenforceable (Ward and Kassebaum 2009: 107–8). All of these small mercies made life there feel less cruel. Also, Alcatraz was seen as a regrettable anomaly in a federal prison system that was otherwise guided by a rehabilitative ethic while Marion became a model that was widely admired and emulated. Alcatraz was an admission of failure. Marion was a statement of intent.

Supermax facilities are restrictive places but the isolation is not total. Despite the best efforts of prison architects and corrections staff, prisoners who are supposed to be in solitary confinement still find ways to communicate and their lives are characterized by much clanging, banging, and haranguing, despite the superficial impression of sterile quietude and complete enclosure. Occasionally, due to pressure of numbers, prisoners in restricted housing share a cell and solitary confinement is replaced with enforced—and highly cramped—company. Reiter (2012: 544) noted that at least one-third of the prisoners in the SHUs at Corcoran and Pelican Bay prisons in California had been 'double-bunked' since the institutions opened in 1989. In recent years the problem has been more acute in Corcoran where, in 2010, 58 per cent of the SHU population was double-bunked compared with 11 per cent in Pelican Bay (p. 546).

Supermax is defined by the almost total removal of contact that is meaningful in a social sense. When added to severe restrictions on movement and highly limited sensory input this creates a substantial cumulative psychological burden. There is a world of difference between a family visit that takes place across a table and one that occurs over a video link or where the parties gather together in the same space but behind a shatterproof screen. Similarly, an occasional brief exchange—whether gruff words or banal pleasantries—during the delivery of food to a cell or on an escort to an exercise cage is not the kind of conversation that nourishes an individual. When the only physical contact with another human being comes during a forcible cell extraction—and even this involves collisions with dehumanized 'extractors' carrying shields and clad in gloves and body armour—this is a far remove from the melees of the past, where fisticuffs at least meant the possibility of meaningful, even if potentially harmful, touch.

Shalev (2009a: 163) described how prisoners in the SHU at Pelican Bay engaged in an occasional 'finger shake' with their friends. This involved a prisoner who was on his way to a solitary shower or exercise period pressing his finger against one of the holes in a perforated steel cell door while the prisoner on the other side did likewise. This allowed a momentary touching of skin on skin. It was observed of one of the litigants in a 2012 case involving the Pelican Bay SHU that he had 'not shaken another person's hand in

13 years and fears that he has forgotten the feel of human contact. He spends a lot of time wondering what it would feel like to shake the hand of another person' (*Ruiz v. Brown* 2012: para 54). This contrasts unfavourably with the past and is another indication that supermax is more encompassing than what went before. Prisoners at Eastern State Penitentiary had many visits from citizens concerned for their welfare. Prisoners at Auburn were beaten severely for any attempt to communicate, but as they marched around the prison in lockstep, holding the man in front and being held by the man behind, they were reminded that they were members of a flesh and blood world, however unnatural and coercive.

As typically defined, supermax involves administrative rather than punitive or protective segregation. The use of long-term segregation for administrative purposes has created, for a small minority of US prisoners, a hugely restricted life-world within an environment where the parameters were already tightly drawn. The gulf between themselves and their peers living in the hurly burly of congregate prison life has widened. What is under consideration in this book is both more and less than supermax: less in that those doubled up in restricted housing are excluded, and more in that those in prolonged solitary confinement for non-administrative reasons are included. The isolated prisoner who must find ways to deal with the passage of time is the key concern, whatever the reason for his or her isolation. But the re-emergence of penal separation in the guise of supermax, even if the solitude is sometimes imperfect, has been so emphatic that it demands attention.

What sets supermax apart from the nineteenth-century experiment with enforced separation is that it is targeted at particular prisoners or types of prisoner, rather than being seen as appropriate for the generality; it involves separation from the (potentially benign) influence of staff as well as the (potentially malign) influence of peers; it is held out as a regrettable necessity rather than heralded as a new approach to prisoner reform; it is careless as to the consequences for those subjected to its rigours; and it has not been as widely imitated abroad. There has been a shift in the rationale ascribed to such treatment (optimism in the capacity of the individual to reform has been supplanted by a corrosive pessimism) and a reversal of the trend towards enforced isolation as solely a disciplinary, or protective, strategy.

Doing time is also doing space. Both of these dimensions are brought into sharp relief in supermax. Confined in a small box made of concrete and steel, the enormity of the time yawning ahead is amplified. What might be bearable (just) in company or in comfort becomes an agonizing trial. Beauty is beneficent and we should not be surprised to find brutal behaviour being exhibited in brutalist buildings. In subtle but significant ways, the ordering of space influences the geometry of relations between people. Ugly, bleak, uninspiring buildings give expression to a penal policy that is denuded of hope and sets expectations at a low level. The segregation unit is created as a deliberately disenchanting space where the potential for architecture to soften, civilize, and nurture interpersonal relationships is eschewed (on penal aesthetics see Fiddler 2010; Jewkes 2012).

The grim, repressive nature of supermax calls to mind two comments made a century apart. The first is Jeremy Bentham's description, in a letter written in 1791, of the Panoptican prison as 'a mill for grinding rogues honest and idle men industrious' (Bentham 1843: 226; Burns 1966: 107). The second is Oscar Wilde's (1891: 301; emphasis in original) lament in his essay, 'The Soul of Man under Socialism', published several years before his imprisonment, that the sickening lesson of history is not 'the crimes that the wicked have committed, but...the punishments that the good have inflicted; *and a community is infinitely more brutalised by the habitual employment of punishment, than it is by the occasional occurrence of crime'*. The bottomless ingenuity for coming up with new ways of inflicting pain, in whatever guise it is presented, shows this lesson has not been learned. What has been forgotten is the pretence that punishment may be used to leverage industriousness. Like so many tread wheels and cranks, the supermax is designed to grind to no useful end, leaving bitterness and broken bodies in its wake.

Deeper, heavier, tighter

Crewe (2011: 522) suggests that the metaphor of 'tightness' captures some aspects of the contemporary experience of imprisonment better than the ideas of 'depth' and 'weight' as conceptualized by King and McDermott (1995), who adapted the idea of depth from Downes' (1988) comparative study of Dutch and English penal policy. King and McDermott (1995: 90) reserved the concept of depth for 'the extent to which a prisoner is embedded into the security and control systems of imprisonment,' while weight

connoted, 'the degree to which relationships, rights and privileges, standards and conditions serve to bear down on them'.
These variables can be negatively correlated in that life in a
high-security prison can be tolerably light.

As Crewe acknowledges, it could be argued that tightness is
a product of the interaction of the other two variables, being
the personal experience of depth and weight. However, he suggests that tightness differs in the sense that it better describes
a carceral experience where power is exercised more softly, but
grips the prisoner in manifold ways such that wriggling free of
it becomes impossible. In other words, it is feasible for the depth
(i.e. security level) to be moderate, and the weight to be bearable
(i.e. good relationships and conditions exist), but for the prisoner to feel tightly enmeshed. By this account a reduced dependence on direct oppression in prisons is accompanied by a more
concerted attempt to connect prisoners in myriad ways to the
administration of their own sentences. They become necessarily entangled in the interventions, programmes, and procedures
that dictate how they will progress. While their lives may have
improved in many material respects, when they are recruited as
agents in their own transformation they become vulnerable to a
new range of pressures; they are encouraged to believe that they
can play a role in directing their own futures and become responsible, in part, for decisions about the timing of their release. This
can have a stifling effect.

Prisoners in supermax have few opportunities to become
involved in shaping the nature of their own prison experience
and it is probably fair to say that, for them, custody is defined by
extremes of depth (i.e. security and control) and weight (i.e. feeling the sentence as a burden that cannot be lightened or displaced
through the amelioration of conditions or relationships with
correctional staff). But it is also tight in the sense that progression out of administrative segregation and back to the general
population is predicated on satisfactory debriefing; in this way
they are invited to play an unwelcome part in their own prison
careers. This combination of conditions feels hugely oppressive
and it is not surprising that some prisoners in solitary confinement describe it as akin to being buried alive. Supermax is heavy,
deep, and suffocatingly tight. It creates a sense of powerlessness
among prisoners, a feeling that they are impotent in the face of
a penal apparatus that has demonstrated its unwillingness to

turn and where there is a readiness to tighten the screw beyond a point that would previously have been considered unnecessarily inhumane.

For long-term prisoners, the pain of incarceration is not dulled until the temporal angle has been dealt with. Only then is the tightness bearable and can they breathe freely. For short-sentence prisoners, there can be weight and depth, and even a measure of tightness, but because the temporal dimension does not come to exercise an oppressive independent presence, this can be handled once the initial turbulent phase is past. Time is the missing ingredient in this analysis. It is like a leavening agent—once added to the mix as it is in Chapter 8—understanding expands.

Measuring Madness

In Chapter 3 the (certain) pains and (uncertain) pleasures of isolation were considered. Much of the extant literature predates the advent of supermax and the huge elongation of periods of penal isolation that accompanied it, and many of the early studies were carried out in Canada, a country characterized by a relatively parsimonious approach to harsh treatment. The critique that follows relates specifically to what we know about the situation in the US, where penal extremes are more marked than elsewhere.

In his work at the Pelican Bay SHU, which involved interviews with 100 randomly selected prisoners, Haney (2003) found levels of psychological trauma that were significantly out of line with those present among the non-incarcerated population and in other prisoner samples. There were two interesting conclusions to be drawn from his findings. The first was how much higher the prevalence rates were among the incarcerated samples than the general population. To some extent, of course, this reflected the particular characteristics of prison populations with their disproportionate representation of violent and distressed citizens. But there was more to it than this. High levels of psychological disturbance have also been found among other isolated groups in extreme environments. As reported in the previous chapter, Strange and Klein (1973: 411–12) found insomnia, depression, chronic irritability, hostility and anger in the majority of personnel who spent the winters in Antarctica, and a more general diminution in intellectual activity in almost half. While these problems were widespread they led to severe psychopathology only in those rare cases where there was a pre-existing vulnerability. Also they tended to be transient, subsiding when circumstances changed.

The second conclusion was that the prisoners in supermax fared worse than prisoners in protective housing, although the physical conditions endured by the two groups were broadly similar, involving segregation and severely limited regimes. Haney (2003: 135) posited that the reason for this difference was that the prisoners in protective custody, while isolated and stigmatized, had opted for protection and as such had some control over their status. (In Chapter 11 we return to the importance of prisoner values and perceptions in mediating environmental impacts.) Even so they were an unhappy, angry, and anxious group. When the isolation was coerced, rather than chosen (however reluctantly) and when the reason for it was administrative rather than protective, the levels of trauma increased further. It is also noteworthy that symptoms such as hallucinations, delusions and talking to oneself reported by prisoners in protective custody were only counted if they happened frequently and were a cause of concern; in other words these are minimum estimates (Brodsky and Scogin 1988: 273–4).

In addition to clinically significant changes, Haney (2003: 138–40) reported a number of other, more subtle, transformations that emerged in supermax prisoners. He described these as 'social pathologies'. They included an exaggerated form of the dependency that long-term prisoners tend to exhibit. When prisoner autonomy is reduced to a minimum, future freedom is particularly difficult to negotiate. The lack of initiative is exacerbated by the lethargy and emotional exhaustion that accompany the supermax experience. The depth of isolation also makes normal relationships difficult to re-establish and there is an air of unreality around social interaction as the inmate goes through the difficult process of reinventing himself or herself in the eyes of others. The stripping away of the kind of social contact that is vital to forming and sustaining a coherent identity and self-image, activity that most humans engage in continuously and often unthinkingly, takes time to repair. There are negative consequences for others too as sometimes the anger and frustration that have built up over a period of solitary confinement find expression in explosive acts of violence. It takes time for prisoners who have spent many empty days preoccupied with fantasies of revenge to realign their internal life with the demands of a new environment.

Metzner and Fellner (2010: 104) reported that solitary confinement can be 'as clinically distressing as physical torture'. This has been a constant refrain of penal reformers, going back to the observation in *American Notes* that the psychological impact of the regime in Eastern State Penitentiary was 'immeasurably worse than any torture of the body' (Dickens 2000: 111). In a court declaration in 1993 Terry Kupers stated with regard to supermax that: 'Every prisoner... eventually begins to lose touch with reality and exhibit some signs and symptoms of psychiatric decomposition' (cited in Shalev 2009a: 189). We are not told how significant or enduring this decomposition is or, importantly, how it compares to the experience of being held in the general population of a maximum security prison, with all of its stresses, threats, and potentially mind-altering pressures. To evaluate the harms of supermax requires comparing them against the harms of alternative environments. In supermax facilities prisoners are less likely to be attacked by other prisoners but may suffer more psychological damage. How are these effects to be weighed, one against the other? Kurki and Morris (2001: 393) opined that, 'While there is no proof of positive effects of the supermax on prisoners or on prison systems, evidence of its negative effects is also scant.' This is because the accumulated body of knowledge is insufficient to tease out the relative importance of individual characteristics and environmental factors and to examine their interplay, longitudinally.

Meta-analyses show significantly elevated rates of medical and psychiatric morbidity among prisoners across countries and over time (Fazel and Baillargeon 2011). In other words, the problems that become apparent in supermax reflect, to some extent at least, the prevalence of mental illness in the prison population. Also, given the focus on the psychologically disturbing potential of supermax, symptoms that go unnoticed in company may appear vivid when an individual is isolated. It is also possible that the 'disturbed disruptive inmate' (Toch 1982) is more likely to elicit a response when among the general population than the mentally ill prisoner who is symptomatic but well behaved. Consequently, it may be that particular types of serious mental illness are more likely than others to result in a transfer to segregation.

Abnormal environments evoke abnormal responses in normal people so it is not surprising that supermax confinement leads to behavioural extremes. While virtually everyone suffers, the intensity of the pain is greater for those with a pre-existing mental illness for whom the experience can be more immediately incapacitating and more permanently disabling. But the emphasis on damage and the suggestion of its universality has drawn attention away from studying the characteristics of those who can survive, and perhaps even thrive, in isolation. The withdrawal, apathy, and emotional numbing that characterize life in supermax could be seen as adaptive, akin to the psychological hibernation of polar explorers, which by definition is time-limited. Also, the fact that the harms are environmentally determined means that when circumstances change more appropriate behaviours will follow. The risk is that the damage proceeds beyond a point where it is reversible or the prisoner takes actions during this period of adaptation that reduce his or her life chances afterwards (e.g. deliberate self-harm, injuries sustained during altercations with staff or inflicted on other prisoners). Finally, the focus is often on the early phase of confinement, which we know to be destabilizing whatever form it takes.

Many prisoners adapt, are restored to previous levels of psychological functioning when their solitary confinement ends, and sometimes report being strengthened by the experience. This is what would be expected according to the body of work emerging in the field of post-traumatic growth (see Chapter 11). There are three additional considerations. First, as shown in Chapter 4, there is evidence of harm even when isolation is voluntary. Secondly, some involuntary isolates (e.g. hostages and political prisoners) have not experienced lasting damage; group membership and what this signifies provides a shield. Thirdly, there are extraordinary individuals for whom long periods of penal isolation act a stimulus to creative endeavour. While not numerous we can learn much by examining their survival stories; they are akin to the 'tragic optimists' about whom Frankl (2004: 139) wrote. By turning the spotlight onto survival factors, new interpretations become possible. That people can endure appalling treatment, or that they can be trained to withstand some of its rigour, is testimony to the capacity of humans to adapt to changing circumstances. It is not a justification for even deeper deprivation. The reality of post-traumatic growth is not an argument in favour of trauma. It is simply a reminder that some of the changes flowing from adversity are viewed as positive by those in whom they are wrought.

Positive aspects of the solitary experience tend to be downplayed by critics who may fear that acknowledging them will reinforce a practice that should be condemned without equivocation. But it is important to locate harms precisely if they are to be challenged effectively. The argument advanced in this book is that the sheer fact of survival and the indomitability of the human spirit that it indicates show that isolation does not work, especially if it is intended to extinguish the flame of individuality and resistance (but also if it is designed to ignite an inner light). The denial of meaningful human relations is inherently destructive of individuals' identities and is an affront to the dignity of the person. For these reasons, extended solitary confinement, whether in supermax or elsewhere, should be opposed. Whether men and women display mastery over their environment, or crumble, or simply cope, they should not be treated in this fashion. Even if prolonged isolation could have a demonstrably positive effect on prison order, it should be resisted. Jeffreys (2013: 106) is one of the few scholars in the field to have recognized the limitations of a critique based solely on consequentialist considerations.

Methodological problems with studies of supermax confinement generally include small sample sizes, lack of control groups, no before–after measures, no standardized instruments, variations in conditions, duration, and reasons for isolation. A key question is how additionally stressful is supermax compared to routine life in a maximum security prison? What is the extra margin of discomfort? It is possible that supermax units where there is a high level of reported distress are located in prisons where the maintenance of physical and psychological integrity is generally more difficult on account of fraught relationships with staff and entrenched interpersonal violence between prisoner groups. Also, while some signs of disturbance may be regularly observed, they are not necessarily at a level that would make them clinically significant. When we add to this the fact that many of those in solitary confinement have pre-existing mental conditions, that the solitary environment provides a backdrop against which deviant behaviours are strikingly evident, and that much of the available academic research derives from litigation challenging the constitutionality of the arrangements, it becomes clear that despite the virtual consensus about its harmful nature, the situation is more nuanced than we might care to believe. (Perhaps matters are expressed more starkly in legal argument than the conventions of academic writing would permit. In a telling phrase Grassian and Friedman (1986: 50) described the world of the courtroom as 'polemical'.)

Claim and Counterclaim

Some of the shortcomings of previous work were addressed by O'Keefe et al. (2010) who sought to establish whether the high level of mental illness observed among prisoners who were administratively segregated in Colorado State Penitentiary (CSP) was caused by the environment in which they were held or resulted from selection bias such that mentally ill prisoners were more likely to be placed in administrative segregation (AS) on account of their inability to adapt successfully to life among the general population. The sample size was larger than in earlier studies, the refusal and attrition rates were lower, the time period was longer, there were more testing intervals and a greater range of tests was used. As a result the findings, however unpalatable they might appear to some parties, must be taken seriously. O'Keefe and her colleagues hypothesized that offenders in segregation would develop a range of symptoms consistent with 'SHU syndrome' as elaborated in the academic literature and articulated in prisoner accounts. The primary concerns were anxiety, cognitive impairment, depression/hopelessness, hostility/anger control, hypersensitivity, psychosis, somatization, and withdrawal/alienation. The existence of malingering, self-harm, trauma, and personality disorders was also explored. Self-report measures were supplemented by ratings from clinical and correctional staff and data from official records. The researchers further hypothesized that prisoners would deteriorate over time, the mentally ill among them declining further and faster; and that the rate of deterioration would be greater than for matched groups in other prison environments. Contrary to expectations they found little evidence to support these hypotheses.

O'Keefe et al. concluded, echoing Zinger et al. (2001) and Suedfeld et al. (1982), that segregation was not highly detrimental to those forced to endure it. The inmates housed in AS at CSP exhibited high levels of psychological impairment but so too did members of the comparison groups who remained among the general population in other prisons, suggesting that the AS environment was not uniquely problematic in this regard. Over time there was an initial improvement in all groups, followed by stability. The only measure where deterioration was observed was withdrawal, but this was found for non-mentally ill offenders whether or not they were in AS. Mentally ill offenders fared worse on virtually every measure but the pattern was not of rapid decline. Indeed,

while the non-mentally ill offenders in AS did not change significantly, the mentally ill prisoners actually improved. Symptoms
of SHU syndrome were found in all of the study groups with
the exception of non-mentally ill offenders who remained in the
general population. In the great majority of cases the symptoms
remained the same. In a few cases (7 per cent) they worsened and
in others there was an improvement (20 per cent). The authors
concluded that: 'this study cannot attribute the presence of SHU
symptoms to confinement in AS. The features of the SHU syndrome appear to describe the most disturbed offenders in prison,
regardless of where they are housed' (O'Keefe et al. 2010: ix). The
authors were careful to note that their findings did not legitimate
the use of segregation for offenders, including those suffering from
mental illness. They cautioned that a different pattern of results
might be found if the study were to be replicated in a prison that
was more restrictive and offered fewer programming resources
than CSP. They also observed that an absence of harm might be
an inadequate measure and that prison systems should be trying
to improve the behaviour and psychological functioning of segregated inmates; to aim for a null effect was aiming too low.

    While the Colorado study avoided a number of the limitations of
other work in this area in that it was longitudinal, there were comparison groups, and a variety of measures was taken and repeated,
it also suffered from obvious weaknesses, and its publication was
greeted with 'angry concern' by several commentators (Fellner
2011: 5). The problems related to the lack of generalizability (which
the authors readily acknowledged) and a fear that it would give
succour to supporters of supermax who were unlikely to become
embroiled in controversies around measurement and interpretation and would conclude, simply, that AS did less harm than might
have been expected. As Shalev and Lloyd (2011: 5) expressed it,
there is 'a real risk that the Colorado study will be used to justify
the warehousing of large numbers of mentally ill prisoners in solitary confinement.'

    More specific concerns relating to the research were that prison-
ers with low levels of literacy or learning difficulties were excluded
and this group may find solitary confinement particularly vexing;
that the improvement observed in some cases may have reflected
the amelioration of conditions and accrual of privileges that accompanied progress through the three different levels of regime that
are available in CSP; that many of the general population inmates

also had experience of solitary confinement; that the true harms of supermax will only be revealed when the prisoner is attempting to reintegrate into society post-release; that the vast array of test results presented in the report made it difficult to discern important trends; that the involvement of the Department of Corrections in the research may have influenced respondents; that the literature review was incomplete; that the fieldworker was inexperienced; and that self-report measures and scores on standardized inventories which are not rooted in data gathered through clinical or qualitative interviews give an inadequate sense of what it feels like to spend time in supermax conditions (see Lovell and Toch 2011; Shalev and Lloyd 2011; Smith 2011). Grassian and Kupers (2011: 10) went further claiming that the report's authors 'chose to ignore critical sources of data' and that they failed to perform statistical analyses that would have caused them to reinterpret their findings.

Despite these criticisms the study is valuable because it prompts reconsideration of the consequences of supermax, how best they might be grasped, the importance of between-group differences, and the significance of context. Some people are more resilient than others, even in conditions that appear crushingly harsh. But, also, what might appear to be small gradations of misery can make a huge difference from a quality of life perspective. For example, AS in CSP, after an initial week or so at the lowest privilege level, was an improvement on the punitive segregation that prisoners had to endure, usually for several months, prior to transfer there. Also, while harsh in the extreme to one unused to such practices (e.g. there is no open air recreation) CSP has more to offer than equivalent facilities in other states. All of these variations are critical to any overall assessment. It is possible that the kind of supermax custody provided at CSP is less damaging than that available elsewhere.

The Colorado study, whatever its failings, highlights the individual's capacity to adapt and the need to take account of shades of difference. Given that there is no (ethical) way to demonstrate the effects of supermax with sufficient scientific rigour to satisfy everyone, research findings will always be contestable. As Fellner (2011: 5) correctly observed, 'If the Colorado study had found serious psychological deterioration...it would no doubt have been met with criticism, but presumably from different quarters.' Circumspection regarding the interpretation of scholarly findings is especially important when it comes to issues that excite strong, and sincerely held, standpoints. It is unfair to lambast researchers because their findings might be expected to elicit a particular kind of response, especially when they are aware of this possibility and caution against drawing broad policy conclusions from a narrowly focused piece of work. As the lead author reflected in an article written with a professor of psychiatry: 'it would be an improper use of this study to state that it either advocates for the use of long term segregation or indicated that there is no harm in the use of such confinement' (Metzner and O'Keefe 2011: 14).

Research that has been less pessimistic about the harms of solitary confinement may have been unduly neglected in a field where there is passionate objection to the subject of study. It is understandable why the null effects (or even positive possibilities) of solitary confinement might be ignored given the widespread revulsion that such practices have been allowed to continue—even become consolidated—as a corollary of the US incarceration binge. Supermax is seen as epitomizing a prison system gorging itself on pointless pain; in such circumstances it appears obscene (or, at best, wilfully contrarian) to consider that it might be anything other than invariably, and hugely, damaging. The fight against supermax is a fight for improved conditions more generally and as such there may be a feeling that to highlight any associated beneficial effects, however rare, would be politically naive and counterproductive.

But it seems reasonable to argue that the extent to which solitary confinement is uniformly harmful may have been over-emphasized. Indeed the competence and articulacy shown by some of those who have been isolated for many years, gives the lie to the inevitability of mental deterioration. Anyone who reads the memoirs listed in the Appendix will be struck by the soundness of mind required for such activity and by the swiftness with which critical faculties are restored after release. This is not to minimize the major readjustment required to get used to human company and to reassume responsibility for the structure of one's day, but simply to make the point that where intellectual functioning is concerned, it can sometimes peak during a lengthy period of isolation, and if dampened down it seems to bounce back quickly when the conditions are changed. Smith (2006: 497) summarized the evidence on post-isolation effects as follows: 'The overall conclusion must therefore be that symptoms generally recede and people generally get better when they get out of solitary confinement.' If the exhibited behaviour is seen as adaptive hibernation rather than pathological withdrawal the lack of enduring negative effects is less surprising.

There are two reasons why some people might benefit from administrative segregation. First, the clarity of thought that solitude forces upon one and the feeling of self-confidence that accompanies coping with adversity are referred to in many prisoner accounts. Ward and Kassebaum (2009: 119) commented on the change process as follows: 'the absence of visual and auditory stimuli on Alcatraz and the many hours spent in quiet contemplation were cited by many convict interviewees as important factors in their decisions to end their criminal and prison careers'. Uninterrupted reflection accompanied by maturation led to cessation. Secondly, there is the finding in psychological research that a variety of severe forms of trauma are sometimes accompanied by an improvement in functioning (see further Chapter 11). We must take care not to underestimate human resilience and the strength that comes from being recognized as a survivor. King (2005: 129–30) was surprised to find that over half of the prisoners he interviewed averred that their experience in supermax had some beneficial effects: 'it had given them time to think and reflect, and in so doing they had learned patience and control, or had been given an opportunity to turn themselves around away from the influence of their peers. In some sense, at least, some of them could conceive that they might come out of the experience the better for it.' The great majority of interviewees reported multiple effects and the potential benefits must be seen against a background of negative ramifications, particularly of the psychological variety. Furthermore, they remained in supermax long after any benefits had been reaped.

In the words of a prisoner who, at the time he was writing had spent 27 years continuously in maximum-security confinement in California: 'The supermax is the ultimate whetstone of human behavior, sharpening those who survive its rigors and deprivations to a keen edge' (Hartman 2008: 172). Those who survived acquired a new status among the general prison population; they had been tested and not found wanting. Hartman again: 'Prison is a great compressor of experience, and intensifier of the human condition for good or ill: mostly ill. The supermax is, likewise, an intensifier, but by another order of magnitude. The hard prisoner who enters emerges harder still. The mentally unbalanced, after a stint, leave all the more unbalanced' (p. 173). This analogy captures much of what we know about supermax: it is isolation as intensification, as amplification. Benjamin La Guer (2000: 165), another veteran of the isolation unit, concurred with this view, noting that:

> No matter how much I have, in the past, spoken of my belief that twelve years in solitude has left me unaffected, truth now told, I am a creature inextricably tied, in both failures and accomplishments, to what has happened to me in prison. It is here, in solitude, that a man attains what is nearest to his nature, where he battles to deliver himself either to his God or his devil. In whatever mold, a man emerges from his battles with scars of honor or wounds of disgrace.

Carceral Creep?

There was cautious optimism in the early 1970s that a legal prohibition on solitary confinement might be forthcoming. Although the courts had been reluctant to take such a step, some scholars felt that there were strong grounds for moving in this direction based on the typically poor physical conditions associated with prison segregation, the degree of associated mental anguish, the disproportionate nature of the measure, the possibility that the same penal objectives could be more parsimoniously achieved, the length of time prisoners could spend so confined, and the lack of due process safeguards associated with the procedures by which a period of solitary confinement could be imposed. A review of legal developments by Singer (1971: 1251) opened with the following statement:

> It seems remarkable that, in this the last third of the twentieth century, we still send men to small dank closets, deprive them of human companionship, sanitary needs, and clothing, feed them on a starvation diet, force them to sleep on thin mattresses, and then, after an unspecified period, remove them from this environment and proceed in the hope that they have been 'rehabilitated'. Yet in virtually every prison in the country this is what we do in that hell-hole called solitary confinement.

What seemed 'remarkable' in 1971 became so well established thereafter that despite some improvement in the physical conditions, men are still being sent to small 'closets' where they are stripped of much of what it means to be human, and expected to emerge the better for it. Singer closed his article with a clarion call for reform:

It would seem, therefore, that the present system of prison discipline, particularly as embodied in solitary confinement, is an eighteenth century concept draped in nineteenth century clothes, yet alive and well as we approach the twenty-first century. Solitary is inhuman, degrading, and pervasive in the prison system. It affords a too-ready and easy answer to difficult issues which prison personnel would rather not face. Its use has been marked by gross excessiveness and widespread abuse. It is time it is outlawed. (pp. 1295–6)

Singer would no doubt be alarmed that more than 40 years after his paper was published, the 'eighteenth century concept' that he described as 'draped in nineteenth century clothes' has been given a makeover and now, often disguised as administrative segregation, continues to exist as a blot on the penal landscape. What Singer could imagine as an aspect of imprisonment ready to be robustly challenged and perhaps even removed is now even more firmly fixed in the penal firmament.

The spread of supermax has led to the normalization of approaches to security and control that would have shocked (or only been dreamed about by) the previous generation of correctional administrators (but not by their more distant forebears for whom the screw was kept tight). Most prisoners are spared the solitary experience most of the time and, on average, 95 per cent of US prisoners are not held in restricted population units, whether for protective, disciplinary or administrative reasons (Bureau of Justice Statistics 2008). Nonetheless the idea of supermax has become deeply ingrained and there are more prisoners in the 'separate system' today than ever there were when the ideology of separation was bidding for penal supremacy. Despite being excessively harsh and poorly targeted, the idea of administrative segregation has taken hold, and may be responsible for a clamping down across the board. Mushlin (2012: 269) described the increased use of solitary confinement as 'one of the most pressing issues in American corrections'.

According to King (1999: 164), by the late 1990s supermax facilities in the US held around 20,000 prisoners. This compared with fewer than 50 prisoners held at the highest security level in England and Wales, usually in close supervision centres (for a critique of the origins and operation of these centres see Clare and Bottomley 2001). There was wide interstate variation, with around one in 3,500 (0.03 per cent) prisoners in Georgia being held in supermax confinement compared with one in eight (12 per cent) in Mississippi (King 1999: 175, Table 1; the rate for Georgia in King's table is mistakenly given as 0.3). The wide variation in the usage of supermax likely reflects decisions about definition and allocation as well as the margin of tolerance for disruptive behaviour, rather than the proportion of dangerous and unmanageable inmates in a state. It is hardly credible that there are 400 times as many (12 per cent vs. 0.03 per cent) of the 'worst of the worst' in Mississippi than Georgia. The figures used by King (1999: 164), which build on a survey carried out on behalf of the US National Institute of Corrections in 1996 (LIS 1997), were conservative. Even limiting consideration to those administratively segregated, the census of state and federal correctional facilities carried out in 1995 showed that there were almost 28,000 prisoners so confined, with another 10,000 in protective custody and 20,000 held apart for disciplinary reasons. This implies an even greater disproportion between the US and England and Wales than described by King. The two jurisdictions differ in more ways than scale. What constitutes 'extreme custody' in England and Wales is more reluctantly accepted, more independently monitored, and more therapeutically orientated (e.g. HM Inspectorate of Prisons 2006; for an account of life in a high-security prison in England, and how it has changed, see Liebling et al. 2011).

Supermax facilities are not places to which carefully selected individuals are removed for the benefit of others, but omnium gatherums of troubled and troublesome prisoners. They have been described by Cohen (2008: 1031) as 'sterile, human wastebins mixing the "worst of the worst" with political prisoners, suspected gang members, high-profile prisoners, and the inept or incautious.' LIS (1997) found a diversity of views around what supermax custody entailed, for which classes of prisoner it was best utilized, what kind of programming should be made available, if any, and how long prisoners should spend in segregation. Reflecting this dissensus there was wide variation in the extent to which states reported needing supermax accommodation with estimates ranging from 0 per cent (e.g. Kansas, Kentucky) to 20 per cent (Mississippi) of overall bed capacity (pp. 4–6). Mississippi, in other words, was already resorting to supermax custody more regularly than other states and anticipated a significant increase in demand. This makes the sudden and substantial reduction in its supermax population after 2007 all the more extraordinary (Epps 2012; Goode 2012; Kupers et al. 2009).

Censuses carried out by the Bureau of Justice Statistics at the US Department of Justice show that between 1995 and 2000 the proportionate increase in the number of prisoners in restricted population units (40 per cent) outstripped the rise in the overall prison population (28 per cent). The Commission on Safety and Abuse in America's Prisons (2006: 53) described this as suggestive of 'a troubling shift in practice'. But this upward movement was largely accounted for by a rise in the use of disciplinary action. The level of administrative segregation grew only marginally (from 2.7 per cent of all prisoners to 2.8 per cent) and protective custody fell (from 1.0 per cent to 0.8 per cent). Furthermore, this shift did not endure and the trend went into reverse during the following quinquennium when the number of prisoners in restricted housing fell by 17 per cent and the overall prison population increased by 10 per cent. The fall in the numbers held apart was most marked in the levels of protective custody and disciplinary segregation; the numbers administratively segregated declined modestly. The population in solitary confinement in the US in 2012 was estimated as being in excess of 80,000 (http://solitarywatch.com/2012/02/01/how-many-prisoners-are-in-solitary-confinement-in-the-united-states/; site accessed 26 February 2014).

So what might we conclude from this brief statistical survey? First, that the use of administrative segregation has become an established part of the repertoire of prison administrators in the US, and accounts for how around 1 in 40 prisoners is held on a given day. Secondly, that protective custody was used half as frequently in 2005 as in 1995, but the slack was not taken up by administrative segregation as the numbers in both categories fell after 2000. Thirdly, that neither was the fall in disciplinary detention due to a displacement effect, as administrative segregation fell in tandem.

When the boom in supermax construction ends the numbers held in administrative segregation will be slow to fall even if the demand tapers off because these blocks within prisons, or entire prisons, will be expensive to modify for alternative uses. Perhaps they will be called into service for other categories of prisoner, as in California's grossly overcrowded prison system where administrative segregation has been used for periods of six months and more to locate mentally ill prisoners awaiting a scarce treatment bed (*Brown v. Plata* 2011: 21). There is an awful irony in that the very class of prisoner for whom such confinement is deemed to be constitutionally unacceptable (e.g. *Madrid v. Gomez* 1995; *Ruiz v. Johnson* 1999; *Jones 'El v. Berge* 2001) ends up there under a different guise, with predictably deleterious consequences. There is a lesson here for prison architects and administrators about designing institutions that are so inflexible in layout, and inspired by such darkly pessimistic views of human nature, that they remain as monuments to misery long after their original rationale has become redundant. This recalls the 'jaded disillusion' that Evans (2010: 402) ascribed to another era. Even when the reformatory impulse had ceased to beat strongly by the late nineteenth century the buildings that were its legacy remained in operation, busy but untethered from their original sense of purpose. Some of the prisons that were inspired by a philosophy of silent separation were still in use 150 years later, often characterized by a reversion to the noisy, crowded, and chaotic intermingling they were designed to efface.

6

Making the SHU Fit (for Purpose)

Shalev (2009a: 47–50) suggested that supermax prisons have five official goals which can be summarized as follows. First, they control risk by incapacitating the most dangerous. This protects staff and other prisoners. Secondly, by filtering out the 'worst of the worst', conditions for those who remain in the general prison population can be relaxed. Thirdly, when disruptive prisoners are not in a position to exercise their malign influence, their peers are free to take advantage of rehabilitative programmes that they might otherwise forswear. Fourthly, they exercise a deterrent effect, both specific (those who have been subjected to supermax do not wish to repeat the experience) and general (other prisoners are so frightened by what supermax offers that they toe the line). Finally, they disrupt gang communication channels with the result that organized criminality behind bars is frustrated.

To these might be added a sixth, namely that the advent of supermax returned to prison administrators a degree of control over prisoners' lives which they felt had ebbed away from them during the period of rehabilitative optimism that characterized the 1960s and 1970s. During these decades prisoners' feelings, attitudes, and beliefs were accorded a significance that they had previously been denied. They became politicized and began to organize and agitate for their rights, sometimes with riotous results (Useem and Kimball 1989). This created conditions where staff felt that the balance had tilted too far in favour of the prisoner.

Even the most enthusiastic advocate of supermax confinement would probably concede that these goals are achieved, at best, imperfectly. Shalev (2009a: 220) goes further, concluding that: 'Supermax prisons fail to meet most of their declared goals. They impose a heavy human, financial and societal cost, and by operating on what even a non-interventionist judicial system considers to be the verge of psychological torture, raise profound moral questions about whether they befit a civilised society.' Rhodes

(2004: xiii–xiv) offers a similarly bleak assessment, namely that 'these expensive prisons are profound in their effects on inmates and workers and useless for other purposes'.

Adopting a policy evaluation framework, Mears (2008) addressed five central questions: Are supermaxes necessary? Are they implemented as intended? Do they have the desired effect? Do they have a sound theoretical basis? Are they cost-efficient? His assessment of the evidence is that there is minimal support for the first three questions and none for the final two. The Commission on Safety and Abuse in America's Prisons (2006: 59) saw supermax facilities as 'expensive and soul destroying'. Of course, proponents of supermax could eschew effects-based reasoning and offer a purely retributive argument along the lines that problematic inmates deserve to have the screw twisted tight. That such a position is seldom articulated suggests that the desire for supermax is rooted in a sincere belief that it delivers important correctional goals and that this belief does not depend upon unequivocal empirical support for its sustenance.

In its recommendation on the management of life sentence and other long-term prisoners the Council of Europe (2003) set out half a dozen fundamental principles which are worth considering in light of supermax. These are:

1. *Individualization.* Consideration should be given to the diversity of personal characteristics to be found among life-sentence and long-term prisoners and account taken of them to make individual plans for the implementation of the sentence.
2. *Normalization.* Prison life should be arranged so as to approximate as closely as possible the realities of life in the community.
3. *Responsibility.* Prisoners should be given opportunities to exercise personal responsibility in daily prison life.
4. *Security and safety.* A clear distinction should be made between any risks posed by life-sentence and other long-term prisoners to the external community, to themselves, to other prisoners and to those working in or visiting the prison.
5. *Non-segregation.* Consideration should be given to not segregating life-sentence and other long-term prisoners on the sole ground of their sentence.
6. *Progression.* Individual planning for the management of the prisoner's life or long-term sentence should aim at securing progressive movement through the prison system.

With the exception of the fourth, all of these principles are violated by supermax confinement, which is procrustean, abnormal, infantilizing, segregationist, and regressive. Even the emphasis on security and safety tends to eschew the risk to the prisoner's mental or physical health. By any reasonable yardstick supermax falls short of an acceptable standard. In a report on the US, the United Nations Committee against Torture (2006: para 36) recorded its concern regarding, 'the extremely harsh regime imposed on detainees in "supermaximum prisons". The Committee is concerned about the prolonged isolation periods detainees are subjected to, [and] the effect such treatment has on their mental health.'

The Committee urged the US to review the regimes in force in supermax prisons, especially the practice of prolonged isolation. In 2011, the UN Special Rapporteur on Torture, Juan Méndez (who had himself been a victim of torture and administrative detention in Argentina in the 1970s), called for an absolute prohibition on prolonged solitary confinement, which he defined as any period in excess of 15 days when an inmate was isolated for at least twenty-two hours each day. The Special Rapporteur chose 15 days as the cut-off, 'because at that point, according to the literature surveyed, some of the harmful psychological effects of isolation can become irreversible' (United Nations General Assembly 2011: para 26). This seems to be overstating the case given what we know about how people return to normal when restored to company.

For juveniles and prisoners suffering from mental disabilities Méndez went further, stating that the imposition of any period of solitary confinement whatsoever amounted to torture or cruel, inhuman or degrading treatment or punishment (paras 77 and 78). This is an emphatic declaration of what constitutes unacceptable treatment and it applies to a large number of prisoners, especially in the US, but also in a variety of other jurisdictions (the Special Rapporteur identified the use of pre-trial detention in Denmark in this regard and listed other countries where there was excessive recourse to this mode of penal treatment). If 15 days is torturous what term captures the collective experience of more than 200 men who have spent over 15 years in the Pelican Bay SHU in California? As the litigants in *Ruiz v. Brown* (2012: 150) put it: 'Plaintiffs and class members have been held in solitary confinement for at least 250 times this duration.'

When attempting to assess whether the experiment with extreme segregation, described by Tapley (2010: 35) as the creation of an 'archipelago of agony', has been a 'success', one important consideration is the weight attached to post-release behaviour. Proponents of supermax might argue that its existence allows other prisoners to be managed effectively and that recidivism rates are, at best, a marginal consideration. The problem with much of the research in this area is that counterfactual logic is absent: we do not know what would have happened in the absence of supermax prisons or in the presence of an alternative intervention. Nevertheless, the small number of studies that have examined reoffending suggest a null effect when the analysis controls for pertinent prisoner characteristics.

Recidivism

Toch (2001: 381) warned that the 'Perception of capricious deprivation and custodial overkill predictably engenders bitterness and alienation. For this reason, supermax prisons may turn out to be crucibles and breeding grounds of violent recidivism. The graduates of such settings (often released directly into the community) may be time bombs waiting to explode. They may become "the worst of the worst" because they have been dealt with as such.' The limited available data indicate that—mercifully—this dystopian forecast has not come to pass.

In their follow-up study of men held at Alcatraz, the grandfather of the modern supermax (with Marion as its only son, the latter institution being much more promiscuous when it comes to offspring), Ward and Kassebaum (2009: 390) found that despite the complete absence of rehabilitative programming, and the fact that prisoners were sent there because of their perceived dangerousness and incorrigibility, most fared well post-release, with half of those held at Alcatraz between 1934 and 1963 never returning to prison. The outcomes were best for the men who had served time there during the first decade when conditions were the most punitive, who 'did what no one expected them to do: they succeeded in building productive lives in the free world after years of imprisonment under the harshest conditions that the federal government could devise' (p. 455).

As the authors acknowledged, these were not typical prisoners, even for the time. They exhibited unusual qualities of determination, self-confidence, leadership ability, and group solidarity. They had been convicted of a narrow range of offences that required skill, risk-taking, and ingenuity. They were imprisoned during an era where hard drugs had yet to make their mark. They retained networks of friends and associates throughout their sentences. They were unwavering in their opposition to staff. Their experiences in Alcatraz were a source of pride to many, who drew strength from surviving the most severe environment that the federal prison system could devise. Some made careers of their fortitude. The prisoner society they constituted offered protection to its members and valorized psychological strength. Withdrawal and 'going crazy' were looked down upon; the inmate code added to the pressure to retain psychological integrity, however difficult the circumstances. 'Real men' wanted to prevail and the tougher the conditions the greater the desire to overcome them. In combination, these factors offered a protective buffer.

But, as supermax proliferated it began to embroil prisoners who were less robust, less well able to withstand its rigours, and less likely to have reputations to protect. It is also possible that singling out prisoners for especially harsh treatment may have had the paradoxical effect of helping them to survive by emphasizing their individuality. Bruno Bettelheim (1960) noticed a similar phenomenon at work around him in the concentration camp where aristocrats targeted for particular contempt and humiliation by the SS did not appear to suffer the same degree of damage to their self-esteem as other prisoners. An unintended consequence of SS brutality was the creation of an opportunity for transcendence on the part of their victims: 'By remaining special, even if only in the way they were abused, they remained individuals' (p. 188).

The Ward and Kassebaum study was marred by the absence of a control group; it is not known how similar inmates held elsewhere fared after release. In an attempt to remedy this deficiency and identify the specific contribution of supermax confinement to recidivism, Lovell et al. (2007) compared inmates released from supermax housing in Washington State with a matched comparison group. Prisoners who were directly released from supermax, without an opportunity to readjust to life in the general prison population, were more likely to reoffend than their peers who were not directly released. For the latter group the recidivism rate, defined as the acquisition of a new felony conviction within three years, did not differ from the rate for the matched sample of non-supermax prisoners. In addition, the direct-release group reoffended sooner than other prisoners. To the authors' surprise the amount of time spent in supermax did not affect the likelihood of recidivism. This reinforces the idea that prisoners can readjust quickly to a change of environment. Public safety is enhanced if this turbulent period is spent in a custodial setting prior to release.

There are two possible interpretations of Lovell et al.'s findings. The first is that the prisoners who were directly released were more combative, impulsive and antisocial and this is why they were so confined until their departure date. This offers, at best, a partial explanation as the supermax prisoners had been carefully matched with a sample of other prisoners to control for this kind of variation. The second, more plausible, explanation is that, as Lovell et al. concluded: 'Evidently, many inmates can recover their equilibrium if they spend time in social prison settings before release' (p. 650). Given that there is little evidence to show that supermax prisons achieve many beneficial results, the argument in favour of ameliorating their demonstrable harms is difficult to resist. One practical implication is that prisoners such as gang members who, under present arrangements, are required to 'parole, snitch or die' (Reiter 2012) in order to vacate their supermax cells, pose an elevated threat to the public under the first of these three conditions, and an alternative mechanism should be found for their phased reintegration into the wider prison community before they are returned to the streets.

Insofar as supermax custody per se inflated reoffending, Lovell et al. (2007: 652) observed as follows: 'this study provides little support for the hypothesis that the likelihood of recidivism is exacerbated by supermax assignment by itself. Opponents of the supermax institution, therefore, may prefer to use arguments other than recidivism in support of their position.' The fact that experiencing supermax may have a null effect on offending behaviour post-release as long as there is a transitional period spent back among the general prison population says a great deal about the individual's capacity to adapt and the critical importance of the early phase of adjustment, whether it is upon arrival in prison, assignment to supermax, or release to the community.

Mears and Bales (2009) compared recidivism rates among Florida prisoners who had spent more than 90 days in supermax with prisoners who had not. They found higher levels of recidivism in the supermax group over a three-year follow-up period.

However, when prisoners were matched according to a variety of characteristics known to influence the likelihood of recidivism, these differences largely evaporated, leading the authors to conclude that: 'It thus seems that any observed differences in the recidivism of supermax inmates derives [sic] largely from selection effects, which, once taken into account, either eliminate the differences, or, in the case of violent recidivism, substantially reduce the difference' (p. 1151). Furthermore, the authors cautioned that the modest observed difference for violent recidivism may have been a statistical artefact.

Like Lovell et al., Mears and Bales found no evidence that the length of time spent in supermax influenced the likelihood of recidivism. 'In short,' they concluded, 'the total amount of exposure to supermax incarceration does not seem to influence recidivism of any kind, violent or otherwise' (p. 1152). Unlike Lovell et al., Mears and Bales found no relationship between recency of supermax incarceration and reoffending. Prisoners who had experienced supermax shortly before release were no more likely to reoffend than those for whom the experience was remote. This study is important because it is an empirical demonstration, albeit in one state (Florida), but adding weight to another single state study (Lovell et al. in Washington), that apparent differences in recidivism rates between supermax prisoners and non-supermax prisoners disappear when selection effects are taken into account. The two studies are also united in finding that the amount of time spent in supermax is not related to recidivism post-release. These findings call into question the notion that supermax custody has a brutalizing effect that endures, enraging inmates, who emerge vengeful, angry, and primed to reoffend. Where they differ is on the relevance of the timing of release. Lovell et al. found an elevated rate of recidivism for prisoners released directly from supermax while Mears and Bales found no such relationship.

More important than recidivism reduction, at least from the perspective of prison administrators, who know that many of the prisoners held in supermax may never be released, is the impact on institutional safety. This is a very pragmatic concern.

Staying Alive

Shalev (2009a: 91) stated that if supermax was supposed to be making prisons safer, it had been a failure, at least in California, which in terms of absolute numbers has the second largest prison population in the US after Texas (West et al. 2010: 16). This was because 'prison violence there is constantly increasing' or 'steadily increasing' (Shalev 2009a: 91, 209). But the evidence is not so clear cut. Shalev's conclusion is based upon a review of trends in assaults by prisoners on staff and other prisoners in prisons and jails. The latter institutions have been explicitly omitted from consideration in the rest of her book and their inclusion in this analysis makes interpretation difficult—why would supermax be expected to reduce violence among the short-term and often volatile jail populations from which it does not draw prisoners? To answer this question adequately would require a focus on prisons, and in particular the maximum security estate.

Furthermore, the data presented by Shalev for the period 1980 to 2006 do not suggest an unequivocal upward trend in violence. Inmate-on-inmate assaults recorded by the California Department of Corrections and Rehabilitation, which are clearly an underestimate of the total number given the reluctance on the part of prisoners to report their victimization, increased in frequency, but they would appear to have decreased in seriousness. Between 1980 and 1988 most of these assaults involved a weapon. In 1989, the year when the SHU at Pelican Bay was opened, this ratio was reversed and thereafter assaults without weapons dominated. Examination of the data presented by Shalev shows that the number of prisoners fatally injured each year averaged 14.3 during the 1980s. During the 1990s, despite substantial growth in the prison population, the annual average number of such fatalities fell by one quarter to 10.7. When prisoners who were shot are excluded, as would seem appropriate in a test of whether prisoner-initiated violence was increasing, the change is even more pronounced: the average number of prisoners stabbed, beaten or strangled to death each year fell from 12.5 (between 1980 and 1989) to 7.6 (between 1990 and 1999). Again, if the increase in prisoner numbers was taken into account the gradient of the decline would be even steeper.

Turning to violence against staff, killings by inmates are rare events—an officer in California died after being stabbed in 1985 and two decades elapsed until the next killing in the state, again by stabbing, in 2005. As for non-lethal violence, where the magnitude of under-recording will be less pronounced than for incidents between prisoners, the annual average rate of assaults on staff fell from 1.43 (per 100 prison population) during the 1980s to 1.28

during the 1990s. It rose to 1.99 between 2000 and 2006, but it would not be sensible to attribute such a lagged effect to the introduction of supermax confinement more than a decade previously. In other words, the very least that can be said is that the data lend themselves to competing interpretations but an obvious upward spiral in violence is not discernible in Californian prisons in the years after the introduction of supermax. Figures are not available for the rate of assaults on inmates by staff, a category of prison violence that segregation may make more likely. Given the role played by correctional officers as perpetrators of crimes as serious as sexual abuse (Kaiser and Stannow 2013) there is little room for complacency in this regard.

Briggs et al. (2003) offer partial support for Shalev's view, finding no relationship between the availability of supermax and a reduction in aggregate levels of violence across three state prison systems. According to these authors, the primary rationale for supermax is its reductive effect on prison violence, namely that tight controls 'will effectively incapacitate the most incorrigible offenders, thereby reducing institutional violence by dramatically limiting opportunity' (p. 1345). In addition, it is believed that the threat of supermax confinement will deter those in the general prison population from misbehaving, and that anyone who has already experienced it will comply with the rules for fear of being sent back. But they found that, 'the results uniformly indicate that the supermaximum security facilities included in this study failed to reduce levels of inmate-on-inmate violence within the three prison systems studied' (p. 1365). There were inconsistent results insofar as inmate violence against staff was concerned with a decrease in one state, no difference in a second, and a mixed pattern in the third. The overall conclusion was qualified, but clear:

Although the findings obtained here must be buttressed with analyses from other states—and more contextually informed analyses of trend data from the three states studied herein—this study presents strong preliminary evidence that supermaximum prisons cannot be justified as a means of increasing inmate safety. Our findings with regard to officer safety are more equivocal, but the necessary onus of evidence in support of the use of supermax certainly has not been met here. (p. 1370)

In other words those in favour of supermax will need to come up with another justification as it does not deliver the desired effect in terms of prison safety; it is still a 'solution in search of a problem'

(King 1999: 163). In a follow-up study, this time focusing on a single state—Illinois—Sundt et al. (2008: 94) found that the opening of a supermax at Tamms did not affect levels of inmate-on-inmate violence but, 'resulted in an abrupt, permanent reduction in assaults against staff'. There was also a reduction in the use of lockdown across the prison system which meant an improvement in living conditions for those held in the general population.

Analysis of national-level data suggests a more positive trend in levels of prison violence. Based on prisoner mortality in 2002, Mumola (2005: 11) found that prisoners were safer than a matched demographic group outside prison. In particular they were ten times less likely to die as a result of homicide. (Standardized suicide mortality rates were found to be lower for state prisoners but this situation was reversed for prisoners in local jails, for whom there was an elevated rate.) Safety had improved over time with homicide and suicide rates in state prisons and local jails falling steeply. The homicide rate in state prisons declined by a remarkable 93 per cent between 1980 and 2002 (Mumola 2005: 1) and changed little between 2002 and 2010 (Noonan 2012: 14). The rate of suicide in jails continued to fall until 2007, with a slight upturn in 2010, while the homicide rate remained low and relatively stable (Noonan 2012: 6). These trends are summarized in Table 6.1. The precipitous drop in prison homicide means that there is no longer a dramatic divergence between the rate for prisons and the rate for jails. The substantial decline in jail suicide means that, while the rate is still higher in jails than in prisons, the gap has narrowed.

Mumola's analysis is important because it shows that prisoners are less likely to be victims of homicide when in prison than when outside. It is perilous reading too much into the analysis of a single variable but it certainly could not be said that prisons in the US have become more violent as the number of prisoners has grown and security has tightened. On the contrary they have become safer, certainly insofar as homicide and suicide are concerned. It would seem therefore that when it comes to lethal violence, prisoners in the US are safer than a comparable group at liberty and have become increasingly so.

While it is not possible to construct a full time series it is clear from the available data that the decline in inmate suicide and homicide occurred during the 1980s, after which time the downward trajectory was less marked. This was the decade when the idea of supermax took hold and when the first tranche of prisons built on

Table 6.1 Prisoner mortality in the US (selected causes). Rates per 100,000, average population

	Suicide		Homicide	
	Jails	Prisons	Jails	Prisons
1980	—	34	—	54
1983	129	—	5	—
1990	—	16	—	8
1993	54	—	4	—
2000	48	16	3	5
2003	43	16	2	4
2010	42	16	3	5

Source: Mumola (2005: 2), Noonan (2012: 6, 14).

the principle of long-term separation came into existence. But it was also a decade which saw a striking decline in the community homicide rate across the US (e.g. Rosenfeld 2000). The relative importance of these factors (and intra-prison variables such as changing patterns of drug use and gang affiliation, fewer weapons in circulation, curtailment of prisoner movements, enhanced staff training, quicker response times, better screening of vulnerable individuals, the application of crime prevention principles to design out opportunities for violent behaviour, and improvements in prison emergency medicine) remains to be disentangled, so it would be premature to assign a determining role in increased prisoner safety to tighter prison security. Putting matters of interpretation aside, and accepting that a more fine-grained analysis might reveal that identifiable prisoner subgroups have benefited disproportionately from the safety dividend, there is no doubting the direction and the magnitude of the trend. The Commission on Safety and Abuse in America's Prisons (2006: 6) accepted that, 'America's correctional facilities are less turbulent and deadly violent than they were decades ago.'

McCleery (1961: 287) opined that isolation and withdrawal were 'likely to mature into either homicidal or suicidal behaviour'. If such predictions were valid, the spread of supermax would have led to human carnage. But given the large number of isolated prisoners and the small—and declining—number of homicides and suicides, some of which are committed by non-isolated prisoners, such a claim has proven to be without foundation. The proliferation of supermax has not been associated with a relentlessly rising prisoner death toll. One thing appears clear therefore: for whatever combination of reasons—and the causal relationships are complex—prisoners in the US are not increasingly at risk of meeting a violent death while in custody. Of the many harms associated with the arrival of supermax, an exacerbation of lethal violence is not one.

Degrees of Isolation

The variables set out in Table 6.2 capture some of the principal dimensions of isolation as practised in the twenty-first-century prison. They characterize the solitary cell in a supermax environment as well as places where prisoners are held apart for reasons of indiscipline or vulnerability rather than due to administrative necessity. They are amenable to observation (and modification) and interact with the personal attributes of the prisoner, in particular their expectations and any pre-existing mental health problems, to shape the response to solitary confinement.

However similar environments may appear on the surface there exist significant sources of variation in how life is interpreted, lived, and felt. A visit with family members feels different wearing shackles. A polite correctional officer who uses a shared passion for sport as a way of building rapport may defuse a situation which would be ignited by curt indifference. A corridor where the occupants of cells on either side can communicate without roaring at each other seems less chaotic. The noisy ranting of a mentally ill neighbour— and the hostile responses it may elicit—jars against long intervals of hushed inactivity. Tasty food and occasional access to fresh air revive jaded senses. Managers who treat requests promptly and fairly and are prepared to explain their decisions ease the irritation that accompanies a perception of arbitrariness or bias.

The room for manoeuvre may be limited, but how it plays out has major implications for the occupant of the isolation cell. Even small differences in the way outdoor exercise cages are arranged can have a significant effect; a higher ceiling and an unimpeded view of the sky create a feeling of space even if the floor area remains the same (see photographs in United States Government Accountability Office 2013: 21, 24).

Table 6.2 Shades of difference

Rationale	Route into solitary confinement. Does prisoner subscribe to a belief system that makes isolation more likely but at the same time renders it more bearable? Includes degree to which isolation is desired or sought out.
Legitimacy	Fairness and transparency of rules governing entry to and exit from segregation. Compatibility with prevailing legal standards. Does process feel arbitrary to prisoner?
Duration, termination, repetition	Is the stay fixed (how long?) or open-ended? Can the individual's behaviour extend or truncate the experience? Has he or she been assigned to such conditions on more than one occasion?
Communication with peers	This ranges from face-to-face exchanges, to muffled shouts through pipes, tapping on walls, sign language, and written messages surreptitiously delivered.
Communication with outside world	How many weekly telephone calls are permitted? Is the prison so far from inmates' homes that visits are unlikely? Is the prisoner required to conduct his visit via video link while chained to the floor, or unshackled, but behind a screen, in a booth? How easy is it to add new visitors to one's list?
Relationships with staff	Those working on the unit cannot be ignored given their role in supplying prisoners with life's necessities. Are they viewed with indifference, disdain, antagonism, hatred, grudging respect, or warmth? Are certain members of staff singled out for particular vilification or gratitude?
Room to roam	How emphatic are the spatial restrictions on movement? What are the dimensions of the individual's living quarters? If there is a separate area for outdoor exercise, how is it configured (yard vs. cage), and does it facilitate interaction with others?
Sensory inputs	Range and variety of sensory stimuli, including access to fresh air, tasty food, and views of the external world. Degree to which these are amenable to individual control (e.g. being able to open and close one's own window, extinguish one's own light, supplement the official dietary with purchases from the prison shop).

Ambient noise	How regularly is the silence disturbed by clanging gates and doors, blaring radios and televisions, roaring mentally ill neighbours, raucous staff, crashing cell extraction teams?
Safety	Secure environments can be places where prisoners feel fearful, sometimes with good reason. How concerned are isolated prisoners regarding the maintenance of their bodily integrity against the threat posed by their peers and staff?
Agency	Scope for self-expression and self-efficacy including creativity (e.g. drawing, writing, litigating).
Personal effects	To what extent are prisoners allowed to possess and display mementos such as photographs and letters from loved ones? How easily and regularly can they refresh this stock of reminders of another life?
Support	Availability of social, psychological, medical, and educational resources. Is there any human touch (literally) from the caring professions?

Korn (1988a: 9) described how at the High Security Unit for women in the federal penitentiary in Lexington, Kentucky there were 16 rooms, eight of which had a southerly aspect, and a view of green lawn and distant trees. The other eight faced north, had smaller windows and no view. All five of the women in the facility, when it became the subject of a formal assessment by the National Prison Project at the American Civil Liberties Union Foundation, were housed in the north-facing rooms. The better accommodation was left vacant. Understandably this added to the inmates' collective sense of grievance. The ACLU found that there existed on the Unit 'a level of administrative cruelty and callousness that is gratuitous, unnecessary, and extreme' (cited in Freeman and Aiyetoro 1988: 2). For a detailed account of the effects of this small group isolation, by one of the women who was confined there, see Rosenberg (2011: 73–102).

What is at issue here are shades of difference rather than major divergences, but in an environment which is impoverished in so many ways, small variations can have large effects. Echoing Tolstoy's famous observation about happy families with which he opened his novel *Anna Karenina*, Fellner (2011: 6) noted that, 'While all supermax prisons impose misery, each imposes its own version.' As Table 6.2 shows, there is more to supermax than oppressive architecture. Two prisoners on the same unit can have quite different experiences based on an accumulation of marginal effects any one of which, considered independently, might have a negligible influence. The consequences differ too: one might unravel and confirm their vulnerability to their peers while the other finds that their view of the world and their place in it is clarified and they return to the general population with reputation enhanced.

'Fetters of iron' Without 'cords of love'

The perceived intent behind solitary confinement is important and the risk of psychopathological consequences is elevated when isolation is seen as part of a strategy of disinterested segregation rather than an attempt to ameliorate an individual's circumstances. The most appalling physical conditions are easier to endure if the rationale behind their imposition is widely understood, even if not accepted by those on the receiving end. A long stretch in solitary is likely to be more bearable if prisoners and staff know that this is underpinned by a belief—however wrong-headed or disagreeable—that it is intended to be for the prisoners' benefit; that the authorities have designed this painful system because they think that it will bring those subjected to it closer to God and equip them with the capacity to see the error of their ways and choose a different path in the future. Eighteenth- and nineteenth-century notions of solitude were that it was intended to reform but also had a deterrent value. Today these have been reversed—it is intended to deter and whether or not it reforms is a barely relevant consideration.

Following this logic it is reasonable to posit that nineteenth-century penal isolation was less painful than its twenty-first century analogue because prisoners were guinea pigs in a trial of benevolent intent. They can have held few illusions about what their treatment was intended to achieve, namely, redemption and a return to law-abiding community life. The best that many of their counterparts today can look forward to is an unsupported return to the general population of a maximum security prison where they will spend the rest of their natural lives, always at risk of revisiting supermax should the authorities determine that such a transfer is an administrative necessity.

Returning to the distinction made by Brewster in 1792 (see Chapter 1), they are held in 'fetters of iron' without the potential amelioration of the 'cords of love' which constituted the other essential feature of the prisoner's bondage. They are contained in buildings that have been designed to crush the spirit (or at best that are indifferent as to their human effects) rather than to encourage it to take flight. There are two parts to this argument. First, that the harms of the nineteenth-century experiment with isolation may have been exaggerated (not least due to Dickens's intervention and the heated nature of the debate at the time). Secondly, that the late-twentieth-century manifestation of solitary confinement, notwithstanding that some people show remarkable resilience and that the effects are often time-limited and occasionally transformative, is more determinedly pernicious.

When the introduction of the separate system of prison discipline was under consideration, there was an explicit recognition that separation required vital safeguards such as work, education, instruction in trades, spiritual guidance, and interaction with prison staff who were 'humane and intelligent' and who brought a 'consolatory and beneficial influence' to bear (Inspectors General of the Prisons of Ireland 1840: 6). Otherwise it would be unremittingly gloomy and destructive to the individual. As one correspondent noted, 'there can be no doubt but that [solitary confinement] may be an excellent mode of punishment, when carried to a certain extent, but beyond that it is highly injurious' (Simpson 1840). This had been recognized as early as the Penitentiary Act 1779 where the imposition of solitary confinement was to be accompanied by 'well-regulated labour, and religious instruction' so that it would accustom prisoners to 'habits of industry' as well as acting as a deterrent. The twin emphases on benevolence and hard work have evaporated. Supermax prisoners have few, if any, opportunities to engage in labour, whether for the purposes of training, industry, or diversion. Bentham's mill for grinding rogues honest, at a profit, has been replaced by an inherently loss-making facility for grinding down the 'worst of the worst'.

John Howard was impressed by what he saw during his visits to prisons in Holland during the latter part of the eighteenth century. Ignatieff (1989: 53) remarked that the Englishman's evolving philosophy was captured in an inscription carved above a prison doorway that he would have walked through in Amsterdam. This read (in translation): *My Hand is Severe but my Intention Benevolent.*

This motto captures the sentiments that motivated the penal reformers of the era. Today the first four words apply to supermax but the qualification has disappeared: it is a severe but indifferent hand that guides and disciplines. Stripped of a reformative rationale, the solitary prisoner today is abandoned, not to his conscience and his God, but to the peculiarities of a legislative framework that has been designed to crush rather than to empower. He is cast aside and thrown back on his own, often meagre, resources. Some of those who experienced enforced solitude in its various guises in nineteenth-century prisons were broken by it, despite its lofty intentions, the debates that had preceded its introduction and the disease and disorder it replaced. It is not surprising then that their counterparts a century and more later, who lack even the cold comfort of a chaplain's concern, so often feel overwhelmed by a regime that seems based on the preconception that they are beyond hope, rather than being fallible mortals for whom the possibility of redemption is never exhausted.

Just as Eastern State Penitentiary and Pentonville were the architectural expression of optimism about the individual's capacity to change, so too were the US Penitentiary Administrative Maximum Facility (ADX) in Florence, Colorado (the 'Alcatraz of the Rockies') and Marion (during the lockdown phase; see Chapter 7) manifestations of defeat and despair. They communicated a view of human nature guaranteed to shrink the hearts of those close to it, whether captors or captives. The idea that those bound by 'cords of love' would find the chords to sing hymns of praise would be ridiculed by many penal reformers if expressed today. But even an analogous philosophy is absent. Florence ADX has been described as 'a chamber of sensory deprivation, designed to press inmates to the brink of insanity by its very architecture' (Perkinson 1994: 125) and more memorably by Ray Levasseur, a veteran of 13 years solitary confinement, as a 'proto-techno-fascist's architectural wetdream' (cited in Franzen 2004: 236). The fetters of iron are still in place (literally) but supplemented by twenty-first-century technologies. The cramped, artificially lit, stimulus-poor, cage-like environment of the supermax may create the very behaviours that perpetuate its existence. Despair about the capacity of individuals to change—or disregard as to their efforts to make good—has resulted in the emergence of places of confinement where optimism is anaesthetized.

This tendency is defined by a deeper attachment to technological solutions than to the human problems they are designed to counter; it is the expression of supreme indifference in steel and concrete. Hope was designed into the early penitentiaries. These were intended to be places of instruction and transformation where separation was a prelude to reconnection with (spiritual and temporal) society. Any such hope has been obliterated from the architecture of supermax, but it bubbles up with reassuring regularity in the lives of the prisoners from whom it has supposedly been eradicated. Just as the early penitentiary did not grind all rogues honest, neither has the supermax extinguished every trace of humanity in its occupants. As later chapters will demonstrate, there are some remarkable individuals who can overcome the most hostile environments.

While the prisoners held in silence and separation in the past were being prepared to re-enter society, the best that most supermax prisoners can hope for, if they are not released directly to the streets, is a return to the general prison population. Pentonville was seen by its creators as 'the portal to the penal colony' where a productive new life could be created (Departmental Committee on Prisons 1895a: para 77). By contrast, today's supermax offers a portal to nowhere for those who will never be released and a portal to an unwelcoming and potentially un-navigable world for the others. For anyone who decides to take the opportunity to 'debrief' as a route out of supermax (i.e. to inform on other prisoners, especially gang members; also described as performing a renunciation (Kurki and Morris 2001: 402), the perceived sincerity of which is positively correlated with the quantum of useful intelligence provided), the place where they can most likely be relocated safely is in protective custody, another form of solitary confinement. This is a fundamental distinction between the nineteenth century and the twenty-first; the imperative to protect society from released prisoners is diluted in a system where sentences have become elongated to the extent that many solitary prisoners have no realistic prospect of release.

The number of US prisoners serving life without parole (LWOP) more than trebled between 1992 and 2008 (from 12,453 to 41,095; Nellis and King 2009: 10). This is another remarkable shift in US penality. Never before were there so many people for whom incarceration marked not a stage in their lives or a temporary interruption, but a permanent rupturing, an irreversible exclusion from society. Consider that the number of life sentence prisoners in the US in 1992 (69,845 according to Nellis and King 2009: 7) exceeded the total population of state prisons and penitentiaries a century earlier, which stood at 45,233. (If prisoners held in county jails, city prisons, workhouses, houses of correction, asylums, and military and naval prisons are included, as well as prisoners leased out, the total prisoner population for 1890 comes to 82,329; Department of the Interior, Census Office 1896: 130.)

Looking at LWOP prisoners specifically, there were more of them in Angola prison in Louisiana in the early twenty-first century—3,660 according to Ridgeway (2011: 48)—than there were prisoners serving terms of life imprisonment across the entirety of the US at the end of the nineteenth century (2,766 in 1890 out of 70,295 prisoners who had been sentenced and for whom further particulars were available; Department of the Interior, Census Office 1896: 199). This prison now has a hospice as well as a more traditional death-row. In the former, death is certain and comes soon after arrival there. In the latter, execution is far from inevitable and the wait for it, in maximum-security conditions, is long and fraught.

Just as nineteenth-century reformers saw prison buildings as instrumental in the reform process insofar as they could give physical effect to notions of silence and separation, so too does the supermax incorporate the latest technology to shape the conduct of its inhabitants. The difference is that the supermax can avail of technology which allows separation to be even more complete, and its buildings generate a massive, suffocating inertia. In Auburn, prisoners worked and ate together. In Eastern State Penitentiary they were separated from their criminal peers but received regular visits from persons concerned with their moral reclamation. These institutions were not solitary places in the same way as today's supermax. There is an important qualitative difference also. In the past isolation was a means to an end. Today it has become an end in itself. As Evans (2010: 327) put it in his study of English prison architecture between 1750 and 1840, 'Solitude was a force unleashed, separation was the same force in check.' It is striking how this lesson has been unlearned and how supermax has unleashed this force, heedless of the all too predictable consequences.

What sets solitary confinement in supermax apart from the experiments with penal isolation that preceded it is that there is no attempt to mitigate the harms that are known to ensue and there is no concern for replacing what isolation strips away with anything better. To use an analogy that would have made sense to the early religiously motivated reformers, this is crucifixion without the prospect of resurrection; it is faith, flawed. This is what makes the modern experience different: it is harm unmitigated by benevolence. It is what remains when optimism has evaporated and in its place resides a blend of pessimism and unconcern. A narrative of change may be implicit in how supermax operates, but supermax is about modifying behaviour regardless of any underlying motivational transformation. It is about enforced compliance rather than willing obedience. This is a significant distinction. Much of the debate about supermax revolves around the conditions, which are rightly condemned as deplorable, and the psychological consequences, which can be significant, but the adverse impact of a lack of purpose is seldom addressed. To hold someone in awful conditions because it is believed to be beneficial, even if it turns out not to be, is a world away from the disregard that characterizes supermax.

7

Lockdown, Infamy, and Inhuman Relations

It is probably fair to say that the impetus towards supermax was driven by the actions of two prisoners, Thomas Silverstein and Clayton Fountain, each of whom killed a correctional officer in the same prison (USP Marion, Illinois) on the same day (22 October 1983). Fountain died in July 2004 but a decade later Silverstein remained alive and litigating. As the individual to whom an epidemic of excessive penal austerity can be traced, he can be thought of as Prisoner Zero, drawing an analogy with the medical term for the originator of a disease. Silverstein deserves this mantle because he struck first on the fateful day.

Marion was held out as the citadel of secure confinement in the US, replacing Alcatraz as the place where difficult prisoners could be concentrated in an escape-proof and tightly controlled environment (for an account of its controversial early years see Gomez 2006). In 1979 Marion was designated the only 'level 6' penitentiary in the US and its control unit became the destination for the most problematic prisoners from across the Federal system (see Bronstein 1981: 73–5 for an account of life on this unit, which Haney and Lynch (1997: 489) described as 'perhaps the most secure and oppressive correctional facility in the world'). Marion was intended to neutralize the threat these men posed to staff and other prisoners. The killings in October 1983, and the background against which they occurred, vitiated this claim to safe custody. Within days the prison went into lockdown and, as time passed, the use of indeterminate solitary confinement to deal with problem prisoners was normalized.

Murder and Mayhem

In their report for the Committee on the Judiciary of the US House of Representatives, Ward and Breed (1985) provided a detailed analysis of the events that preceded the Marion lockdown. What is striking about their account is the volatility of the prison in the time that led up to the killings and the somewhat equivocal nature of the administration's initial response. The latter would seem to indicate a tolerance for disorderly conduct that would not be found today. However, it is understandable when viewed against the violent traditions of Marion.

Table 7.1 shows the level of violence in Marion during two 18-month periods in the mid to late 1970s leading up to its designation as a 'level 6' penitentiary, for a nine-month period on either side of the lockdown, and for the six subsequent years. The figures in the table relate to the most serious assaults only, those that involved lethal force or the use of a weapon. Many violent incidents occurred that are not shown in the table. Between January 1978 and June 1979, for example, unarmed attacks by prisoners occurred almost on a daily basis with 445 in total recorded (181 on other prisoners and 264 on staff). These are minimum estimates given that prisoner fights unobserved by staff and not resulting in obvious injuries no doubt went unrecorded. The figures should be viewed in light of the relatively small number of prisoners held at Marion, which was designed with a capacity of 435 (Human Rights Watch 1991: 75) but usually held fewer, with 373 in custody in 1983 (Ward and Breed 1985: 11). This was a lot of aggravation for such a small population.

It is interesting to note that when prisoners assaulted other prisoners they usually had a weapon, whereas when they assaulted staff they usually did not, perhaps believing that a hard blow against one would elicit a response from all. This suggests a high degree of fear and violent intent; it was risky to leave one's victim in a position to strike back if he was a fellow prisoner. It may also indicate a degree of forethought or simply reflect the fact that prisoners were routinely armed. (Between January 1976 and June 1979 there were 692 assaults by prisoners on other prisoners that involved a weapon and 338 that did not—a ratio of 2:1. For assaults on staff the respective figures were 135 and 412—a ratio of 1:3). It is clear from Table 7.1 that, during the late 1970s, when Marion was a level 5 maximum-security prison where inmates were generally free to congregate unless they were held in the control unit or the disciplinary segregation unit, it was a dangerous place with at least one homicide, on average, each month. Its transformation into an institution where supervision of inmate activities was intensified

Table 7.1 Levels of violence in USP Marion. Number (annual average)

	Assaults with weapons		Homicides
	Inmate on inmate	Inmate on staff	
January 1976 – June 1977	337 (224.6)	55 (36.7)	23 (15.3)
January 1978 – June 1979	355 (236.7)	80 (53.3)	25 (16.7)
*** Marion becomes 'level 6' penitentiary			
February 1983 – October 1983	11 (14.7)	8 (10.7)	—
*** Lockdown initiated			
November 1983 – July 1984	4 (5.3)	4 (5.3)	—
November 1983 – December 1989	—	—	6 (1.0)

Source: Ward and Breed (1985: 3, 12), Coid (2001: 288). Missing homicide data requested from Federal Bureau of Prisons in October 2012 under Freedom of Information Act, but deemed to be unavailable.

and movement anywhere in the penitentiary was much more restrictive reduced the overall level of violence substantially but did not eliminate it. According to Ward and Breed (1985: 5): 'Staff reports indicate that from the end of February, 1980 to the middle of June, 1983, along with 14 attempted escapes and 10 group disturbances, there were 54 serious inmate on inmate assaults, that 8 inmates were killed by other prisoners and that there were 28 serious assaults on staff.'

The situation at Marion began to deteriorate during the summer of 1983. Ward and Breed (1985: 5–7) described the sequence of events beginning in July when two officers were taken hostage, one of whom was stabbed as he attempted to free himself. The following week a prisoner suffered multiple stab wounds and several days later two officers escorting a group back to their unit from the main dining hall were attacked, one of them being stabbed a dozen times. The prison was placed on lockdown status after this incident. On 21 July visits, recreational activities, and a full meal service were reinstated for most prisoners. But a fight in the dining hall on the same day led to the suspension of normal activities once again. On 1 August there was a relaxation with inmates being permitted to take some of their meals in the dining hall and to avail of a limited amount of outdoor recreation. Two days later an inmate en route from the dining hall was stabbed but communal dining and recreation were allowed to continue. On 8 August recreation time was increased and prisoners were allowed to have all of their meals in the dining hall. In September an officer was assaulted and a prisoner was found murdered in his bed. In early October there were a number of fights causing injuries to prisoners and staff.

But on 22 October, on the control unit, matters took a catastrophic turn for the worse. Thomas Silverstein, who was being escorted by three officers from the shower back to his cell, stopped momentarily to talk with another inmate. The latter provided him with a key to unlock his handcuffs, and a knife. Silverstein ran to officer Merle Clutts and stabbed him repeatedly. Clutts died an hour later. Silverstein, reputed to be a leader of the Aryan Brotherhood prison gang, had a violent past, having been transferred to the control unit in Marion Penitentiary in 1980 following his conviction for the murder of another prisoner in Leavenworth, a decision later overturned on appeal (see Grann 2004). In 1981, and again in 1982, he killed on the control unit; on each occasion the victim was African-American. This was followed by the attack on Merle Clutts who, like Silverstein, was white. According to Radic (2011: 32) the killing of Clutts was motivated by his strict enforcement of the rules which included the confiscation of Silverstein's art supplies as a punishment for having contraband in his cell. Earley (1992: 232) described how Silverstein and Clutts 'locked horns almost from the moment they met'. By Silverstein's own account this killing was personal.

After the murder of officer Clutts all activities were temporarily halted in the control unit and other parts of the prison but later in the day they were reinstated in most places. That evening Clayton Fountain, a friend of Silverstein's and another multiple murderer who was believed to be associated with the Aryan Brotherhood, was being escorted to the C Range recreation cage by three officers. He paused in front of a cell and when he turned around his handcuffs had been removed and he was armed with a knife. He attacked all three officers, one of whom, Robert Hoffman Sr, was fatally injured, dying just before the arrival of his son, who served alongside him. When asked why he did it, Fountain, who took pride in his accomplishment as a killer, is said to have declared, 'I didn't want Tommy [Silverstein] to have a higher body count than me' (Radic 2011: 33; see also Earley 1992: 239). On 23 October virtually all inmate activities were cancelled but the following day they were restored. On 27 October a knife fight on D Unit resulted in the death of inmate Jack Callison. An hour later as a group of prisoners from another unit was being released to go to the dining room four of them rushed down the corridor and attacked several staff members.

Lockdown

A state of emergency was declared by the warden the following day (28 October), with all activities cancelled apart from visits. The administration's patience had been stretched beyond breaking point and Marion was now on full lockdown status. Prisoners were strip searched whenever they left or returned to their units and were escorted in handcuffs and leg irons by a party of three officers. Prisoners who were suspected of concealing contraband, or who had to leave Marion for a court appearance, were forced to submit to digital rectal examinations, known colloquially as 'finger waves'. These searches were a source of huge anger and resentment, being viewed by prisoners as a form of 'anal rape'. (In the months after the lockdown 67 digital examinations were ordered and in 13 of these items of 'hard contraband' such as hacksaw blades, handcuff keys and small knives were found—Ward and Breed 1985: 23; see also Olivero and Roberts 1990: 36–7.) Silverstein's lethal strike against Clutts and Fountain's copycat killing of Hoffman were the catalyst for the move to indefinite lockdown. Their actions were of pivotal importance but they were not the final acts of lethal violence preceding the lockdown. It seems to have taken the murder of Jack Callison to stiffen the authorities' resolve and to convert anger into intransigence.

In his foreword to the report on Marion prepared for the Committee of the Judiciary of the US House of Representatives the chairman of the committee, Congressman Peter Rodino, noted that Marion had implemented 'the longest lockdown in the history of the Bureau of Prisons' (Ward and Breed 1985: iii). These words were written in December 1984, 14 months after it had been initiated. It was to remain in place until 2007 when the 'mean little house' was re-designated as a medium security institution (Richards 2008: 6).

The longer prisoner movement was curtailed the more difficult it was to reinstate it. There were several reasons for this. Correctional officers recruited in Marion after October 1983 had never faced an inmate who was not behind bars or in chains. For them, freedom of movement would constitute a frightening departure from normal practice. Their more experienced colleagues remembered the mayhem that had preceded the tightening of control in 1979 and again, with greater determination, in 1983. As Table 7.1 shows, in the 1980s the level of lethal violence in the prison was a fraction of what it had been in the 1970s, with one homicide per year as opposed to at least one each month. Non-lethal assaults with weapons declined dramatically also, from several hundred each year to a small handful. Staff also knew how vulnerable they would be to prisoners who had experienced harsh treatment and were biding their time to retaliate. These anxieties, coupled with the predictability that accompanied working in an environment where the ascendancy of staff was indubitable—this was a prison that could be run without the consent of prisoners—meant that any relaxation of the rules would meet with employee resistance.

Silverstein had shown that even the control unit at Marion provided ample opportunity for murder and mayhem. If prisoners in the most secure part of the most secure prison in the US could kill guards this sounded an alarm bell that could not be ignored and allowed a dramatic intensification of control. (For a prisoner's account of life in Marion during the lockdown see Griffin (1993: 1) who defined the penitentiary as 'a penal cesspool where other institutions discarded their waste'. Del Raine (1993) describes life there before and after the terrible events of October 1983 and Gomez (2006) provides an overview of the origins of the prison's control unit, its role in dealing with rebellious and politicized prisoner activists, and the resulting tumult.)

The lockdown regime was challenged in the courts (*Bruscino v. Carlson* 1987) but found not to violate the constitutional prohibition on cruel and unusual punishment. The finding was upheld on appeal. Olivero and Roberts (1990) provided a detailed account of the circumstances that gave rise to this class action and the impoverished and brutal nature of the Marion lockdown. These authors were critical of the court's decision, questioning its impartiality and describing it as 'shortsighted' and creating 'a troublesome precedent' (pp. 4, 23). Olivero and Roberts feared that, in light of the decision in *Bruscino*, 'it may be no large leap in logic to assume that other state and federal prisons in this country may adopt this organizational procedure' (p. 50). And indeed they did. As a result of this legal validation the lockdown regime was mimicked by prison authorities across the US, whose representatives flocked to Marion to see what a prison looked like when prisoners remained behind their doors. They returned home impressed, several commenting that they had 'died and gone to heaven' (Ward and Werlich 2003: 59). For corrections officials, whose sincere, but often thwarted, desire was to devise predictably safe custodial environments this was an opportunity not to be missed.

Shalev (2009a: 21) attributed to the events of 22 October 1983 'the birth of the supermax doctrine', a view that is widely shared. The American Bar Association (2011: 100) commented that it was, 'The 1983 lockdown at the federal penitentiary at Marion that inaugurated the current wave of supermax confinement.' The lethal conduct of Silverstein and Fountain led to what has been described as the 'Marionization' of the US penal system (Human Rights Watch 1991: 3; see also Immarigeon 1992). In 1986 the Federal Bureau of Prisons opened a 16-bed high-security unit for the administrative segregation of women at the penitentiary in Lexington, Kentucky. Zwerman (1988: 32) described this facility as 'akin to the "maxi-maxi" secure prison for men at Marion, Illinois'.

The proliferation of supermax occurred quickly, with momentum added by new concepts of prison design and the emergence of technologies that made possible surveillance at arm's length. Cameras, computers, motion detectors, electronic doors, and a range of non-lethal weaponry all meant that the security which had hitherto been delivered through human contact was now administered remotely. The fist and boot, as well as the banter and occasional act of kindness that punctuated daily exchanges between prisoners and staff, were replaced by a disembodied voice over an intercom and the automatic opening and closing of exits and entrances. Modern technology allows a studied indifference to be paid to prisoners; they command less personal attention than did their nineteenth-century predecessors and this reinforces their status as socially redundant. This extra distance was appreciated by correctional officers. Coid (2001: 294) found that staff working at Florence ADX felt in control and safe; their working lives were 'relatively stress-free'.

According to Kurki and Morris (2001: 385), 'In 1984 there was only one prison in the United States that would now be called a "supermax"—the federal penitentiary at Marion, Illinois, after the October 1983 lockdown. In 1999, by various counts and various definitions, between thirty and thirty-four states had supermax prisons or units, with more building apace.' There may be a little more shade here than Kurki and Morris acknowledged. A survey carried out in 1996 listed several institutions that would have satisfied the definition of supermax confinement, even if they were not described in such terms at the time. The most long-standing of these was Unit 17 at Mississippi State Prison, Parchman which opened in 1954 (LIS 1997: Table 1, pp. 4–6).

If it had not been Silverstein and Fountain it might well have been some other prisoners in some other prison on some other day. After all, these were violent times in the US penal system and states such as Arizona were already experimenting with units that isolated prisoners for long periods and minimized their contact with correctional staff (Lynch 2010: 135–8). But as things happened it was them and this is why their subsequent prison careers are of interest. The long-term ramifications for these individuals encapsulate many of this book's key themes about the burdens and benefits of solitary confinement.

Dramatis Personae

Thomas Silverstein holds the record for long-term isolation in the US federal prison system. Albert Woodfox, the sole member of the Angola Three remaining in custody at the beginning of 2014, holds this grim record for the state system. In March 2008, after 35 years and 11 months alone in a 6 x 9 foot cell, Woodfox was transferred to a maximum security dormitory. After eight months he was returned to solitary. A judge in 2007 observed that she could not find 'anything even remotely comparable in the annals of American jurisprudence' to match this treatment (Amnesty International 2011: 10. Robert King was freed in 2001 after 29 years in solitary. Herman Wallace spent 41 years in solitary and died at liberty in October 2013, days after his court-ordered release.) Like Silverstein, Woodfox had been convicted of killing a correctional officer.

The opening paragraph of a court declaration made by Silverstein stated: 'I have been held in solitary confinement for the past 10,220 days, which is 336 months, or 28 years. I am 59 years old and have spent almost half my life in solitary confinement' (Silverstein 2011: 1). Silverstein maintained that the dehumanizing conditions he experienced inside the prison system were responsible for the murders he committed as he had not killed anyone before he was sentenced to 15 years for armed robbery in 1977. There was a clear escalation in Silverstein's violence the deeper he went into the prison system. Fountain, by contrast, had been incarcerated for killing his staff sergeant while serving with the US Marines.

In November 1983 Silverstein was moved to USP Atlanta where he was placed in a 'no human contact' cell, sealed off from the other prisoners. The cell was small, 'almost exactly the size of a standard king mattress' (Silverstein 2011: para 66). Earley (1992: 121–2) described it thus:

> The lights in his cell were kept on twenty-four hours a day, and during the first nine months he was in Atlanta, Silverstein was not permitted a television, radio, newspaper, magazine, book, or writing material. Provided only with meals and a single set of clothing, which he wore, Silverstein was given nothing else to help pass the time. He sat alone in an empty cell with two guards watching his every move. Out of respect to Officer Clutts, the guards refused to speak to him.

During his time in Atlanta, Silverstein began to study the Bible and Buddhist philosophy as well as continuing his artistic endeavours. He became dedicated to yoga and believes that this was critical to his psychological survival: 'Yoga allowed me to exercise both my body and my mind in spite of being confined in such a tiny cage. It brought me a feeling of peace, at least occasionally' (Silverstein 2011: para 95).

In December 1987 Prisoner Zero was transferred to Leavenworth, where his accommodation for the first 18 months or so was a desolate, and continually lit, basement cell. In July 1989 he was moved to a specially constructed cage in the same building as the Leavenworth SHU, but with its own entrance and no opportunity to communicate with other prisoners. This was known as the 'Silverstein Suite'. The lights were never switched off, the surveillance was constant and the 'no human contact' rule continued to apply. Silverstein spent 15 years in the 'suite' during which time he was allowed out only on rare occasions, such as for a dental examination. On such days he was heavily chained and escorted by a large party of correctional officers.

Silverstein was moved to Florence ADX in July 2005, where he was placed on Range 13. He was still denied human contact and, by his own account, the conditions were even worse than in Leavenworth (Silverstein 2011: para 173). There was one other prisoner on Range 13 and after 22 years of not communicating Silverstein was relieved to be able to shout occasional comments to this person, but staff insisted on quietude and to enforce it a solid steel door was constructed in the hallway (Silverstein 2011: paras 175–7). Given his advancing years, it was hardly credible that Silverstein posed the same physical threat in 2011 as he had 30 years earlier, but the authorities were unyielding in their response to his pleas for an amelioration of conditions.

Craig Haney interviewed Silverstein and acted as an expert witness in his case, which he described as 'the most isolated form of long-term confinement I have ever encountered' (Haney 2011: Attachment 2, p. 4). For over a quarter of a century Silverstein had not eaten a meal in company, touched another human being with affection, or had a meaningful social interaction. Nor did he ever know when his isolation would end or what he could do to expedite matters. After more than two decades without a single disciplinary infraction he was still being held in conditions of almost complete solitude. Silverstein described solitary confinement as 'a slow constant peeling of the skin, stripping of the flesh, the nerve-wracking sound of water dripping from a leaky faucet in the still of the night while you're trying to sleep. Drip, drip, drip, the minutes, hours, days, weeks, months, years, constantly drip away with no end or relief in sight' (cited in Prendergast 2007).

Haney (2011: Attachment 2, p. 5) applauded Silverstein's 'psychological resiliency and his remarkable ability to survive these harrowing experiences, apparently without becoming profoundly debilitated or developing a serious mental illness'. The lengthy statement that Silverstein (2011) submitted to the United States District Court for Colorado, and the drawings that accompanied it, suggest an organized mind. That such an articulate account has been written by a man who has been held in extreme isolation for so long is a striking instance of the human capacity to overcome adverse circumstances. Notwithstanding this apparent robustness, Haney argued that the full range of effects may not yet have been witnessed.

After the killings in Marion on 22 October 1983, Clayton Fountain was moved to a specially constructed isolation chamber in the SHU of the federal medical facility in Springfield, Missouri. He remained in solitary confinement there until his death in July 2004, aged 49. Robert Stroud, the so-called 'Birdman of Alcatraz', another long-term isolate and killer of a prison guard, passed away in the same institution in 1963, the year Marion opened. Stroud had been in prison for 54 years, including more than four decades in solitary. He thrived intellectually in prison. Having completed only three years of schooling as a child he became a self-taught expert in avian diseases, developing international renown for his work with canaries, and publishing two books, the better known of which was his *Digest on the Diseases of Birds*. In the latter part of his life he produced a substantial manuscript about prison life, having turned his attention to men in cages. This was passed on to his lawyer with the rest of his possessions but efforts to find a publisher proved unsuccessful. Stroud was sustained by anti-authoritarianism, the confidence of the autodidact, the meticulousness of the laboratory scientist, the determination of the writer with an unfinished project and the wherewithal to see it through, deep emotional reserve, a hard-won status among other maximum-security prisoners, and unfamiliarity with any other kind of existence. By keeping busy and maintaining a tension with those who held him captive (through his public profile as an expert on avian pathology and his activities as a litigant) he kept psychological disintegration at bay (see Gaddis 1962).

Like Silverstein, Fountain's actions earned him the disdain of prison staff, who out of loyalty to their murdered colleague, ensured that the solitariness of his confinement was as near total as they could make it. Rarely during his 21 years in the facility was he allowed out of his cell and when he was, no chances were taken. Reflecting his status as the 'most dangerous' prisoner in the federal system he 'was restrained with two pairs of handcuffs securing his hands behind him, an electric belly belt (constructed so that any abrupt movement would render him temporarily senseless), and two pairs of leg shackles' (Jones 2011: 25). Just in case these precautions were insufficient he was escorted by up to half a dozen guards.

Fountain described what he experienced during the first phase of this unmitigated solitude as a 'five-year trial by fire' during which he came to the realization that to survive he would have to change (p. 27). The change involved a process of religious conversion that began in December 1989 and the incorporation of a radically new perspective on his predicament. Fountain recast his forced solitary confinement into a form of spiritual reclusion. He followed a daily regime of prayer and study. On Easter Sunday 1992 he was baptized and confirmed into the Roman Catholic Church. Later he pursued advanced studies in theology and at the time of his death was enrolled on a master's degree programme with the Catholic Distance University and hoped to gain admission to the doctoral programme.

Fountain became determined to pursue a monastic lifestyle and as a result he withdrew his petition to be released into the prison's general population, asking rhetorically, 'What more could I want, than my own quiet study cubicle, with no cell mates to distract me with television and chatter, able to pray and work as the Spirit moves me? I am a blessed man' (p. 77). This decision was also perhaps influenced by an appreciation of the dynamics of prison violence. Fountain must have known that were he to be allowed to re-enter the general prison population he would be vulnerable to attack from men wishing to avenge his victims. In such circumstances he could have become embroiled in conflict once again, an eventuality he wished to avoid.

It is not altogether surprising that the variety of religious life that appealed to Fountain was that offered by the Order of Cistercians of the Strict Observance (generally known as Trappists). Many prisoners who have been isolated for prolonged periods lose the desire to talk, and consider frivolous what would have been the stuff of their conversation in the past. The parsimonious approach to conversation that typifies the life of a Trappist monk must have exercised a strong attraction. By seeking to become a monk Fountain was redefining in a fundamental way his relationship with his environment. His cell became his hermitage, his life became a pilgrimage, and the solitude that was imposed on him came to direct his progress. In a letter to his spiritual adviser he disclosed that, 'I've certainly learned to convert punitive isolation into constructive solitude' (p. 62). He chose the Apostle Paul as his saint because, 'He felt an affinity with someone who had been instrumental in killing Christians and then experienced a shattering conversion' (p. 46).

In February 2004, the Abbot of Assumption Abbey suggested that Fountain might be interested in pursuing the possibility of becoming a Family Brother. Assumption Abbey is 75 miles east of Springfield, Missouri where Fountain was incarcerated. Fountain was as isolated in his cell in the middle of town (on Sunshine Street!) as the monks whose lifestyle he aspired to emulate were in their abbey among the trees in the rugged landscape of the Ozarks. Fountain was keen to establish a formal relationship with the monastic community as he believed that for the previous five years he had been living as a 'functional monk' and he wished to 'complete the transition from a situation of ultimate punitive isolation meant for his destruction to a situation of constructive and contemplative solitude' (p. 96). In June of the same year he was accepted by the monastic council of the abbey and his candidature was voted upon by the monks the following month. The vote was unanimously in favour and Br Clayton was received into the monastic community on the basis that he would live in his prison cell under the Rule of St Benedict, wear the short habit and hood provided by the abbey, be kept informed of important developments in the community, and be buried in the abbey cemetery.

As matters transpired the vote was taken posthumously; Fountain had died of a heart attack the previous week. The habit that he looked forward to wearing had been sent to the prison while the deliberative process was underway given that the indications he would be accepted were strongly positive. However, due to a 'mix-up in the postal room' this was returned to the abbey along with a breviary that the monks had wished him to have so that he could synchronize his worship with theirs (pp. 109–10). His early death meant that he never had the opportunity to wear his religious garb, or coordinate his prayers with those of his new brothers. Nor did he live long enough to have his cell blessed by a priest as a hermitage, a ritual which the prison authorities had agreed to permit. He suffered a final misfortune. The suddenness of his death deprived him of the opportunity to inform the prison and his family of his desire to be buried at the abbey with the other monks and he was interred instead near his father. However, a white cross bearing his name was placed in the abbey cemetery in memoriam.

Fr Paul Jones, Fountain's spiritual adviser for six years, accompanied him on his journey from reviled multiple killer to monk, describing him as 'one of God's masterpieces of redemption' (p. 110). Jones' account of Fountain's life after Marion is the redemption narrative writ large. It shows how a prison cell can become a crucible for spiritual transformation and how a prisoner can become a 'functional monk'. This is the kind of story that John Howard would have drawn much comfort from, should his commitment ever have wavered. A letter such as the one Fountain wrote to Assumption Abbey requesting acceptance as a Family Brother would have caused many nineteenth-century reformers to feel that their religiously inspired efforts had been vindicated (however lukewarm their feelings might have been about his denomination of choice). The letter read: 'All I have to offer is to be a witness: that if you will have me, by far the least worthy of any who ever dared to ask, may my grave be a living declaration that no person is beyond the forgiving and reconciling mercy of God in Jesus Christ' (Jones 2011: 119).

Thomas Silverstein and Clayton Fountain, the two men singled out as responsible for the intensification of control that led to supermax, made a lasting contribution to our understanding of how men cope with, perhaps even triumph over, protracted solitude. Knowing they would never be released, and denied meaningful human interaction for decades, they were thrown back on their own internal resources. As relatively young men when they brought their murderous careers to a dreadful culmination (Fountain was 28 and Silverstein was 31), they forfeited human contact as well as any wafer-thin prospect of liberty. (The Federal Bureau of Prisons online 'Inmate Locator' reports Silverstein's release date as 2 November 2095, a few months ahead of his 144th birthday; http://www.bop.gov/iloc2/LocateInmate.jsp, site accessed 26 February 2014.)

To carry on, day after unchanging lonely day, required steely determination and a radical reappraisal of the situation. Silverstein chose yoga, art and litigation as his props for life. Fountain opted for Christian monasticism. Unsurprisingly, given the strictures under which they lived, neither of them killed again. Each reshaped his individual character, despite the apparently totalizing effects of the environment. These were men who, however warped by external circumstances, however barbarous their prior conduct, and however compromised psychologically, managed to retain a vestige of humanity. This demonstrates that people can survive enforced isolation, often damaged, bitter and terrifyingly angry (as Silverstein and Fountain were during their time in segregation on Marion's control unit) and sometimes damaged but anxiously reconciled to their lot (as Silverstein and Fountain became).

The protagonists of the fateful day in Marion in October 1983 have been unduly neglected. This matters because if we take a longitudinal perspective it becomes clear that the prison careers of the 'worst of the worst', the two men who were the tipping point for supermax, did not continue along paths of destruction and mayhem. One found Art and the other found God. Both produced something of value. Silverstein's ink drawings are well-executed, characterized by what Haney (2011: para 48) described as 'emotional maturity'. A monstrance purchased with the money left in Fountain's education account after his death will display the consecrated host in the monastery to which he had committed himself. Neither is mentioned by name in the criminological literature and their victims have been likewise effaced from the record, although not from the collective memory of correctional staff. Merle Clutts and Robert Hoffman are memorialized by the Federal Bureau of Prisons in its roll of honour of 'fallen heroes' (http://www.bop.gov/about/history/fallen_heroes.jsp; site accessed 26 February 2014.) The list of staff who fell in the line of duty in Federal prisons shows four names in the 1970s and six in the 1980s, but only two in the 1990s and one in the first decade of the twenty-first century—a sign of a prison system that is becoming safer for those who spend time within it.

An Ecology of Cruelty

Penal philosophies are articulated partly through architecture and partly through the actions of correctional staff and the responses that they elicit. When it comes to the latter, Haney (2008: 958) has described how staff in supermax prisons contribute to what he terms an 'ecology of cruelty' and how their expectations and actions influence the experience of those in their 'care'. Kurki and Morris (2001: 420) observed how, 'In a democracy, few powers of one human being over another come closer to absoluteness than the powers of supermax staff over supermax prisoners.' This is a recipe for the corruption of human relations that is not always addressed directly, especially in studies where the emphasis is on prisoner psychopathology and the role of the built environment rather than on prisoners' relationships with the men and women who control gates, watch monitors, patrol corridors.

Given that prisoners in supermax have so little contact with other human beings, their encounters with staff are invested with huge significance. As a species that is 'obligatorily gregarious' (Cacioppo and Patrick 2008: 63) the denial of engagement with others leads to human relations that are hostile in affect and effect.

When staff and prisoners interact as a matter of course they come to see each other as rounded individuals with unique combinations of positive and negative attributes. When viewed occasionally and through a steel mesh or a perspex sheet, their mutual humanity is never given an opportunity to grow. In places that are far removed from scrutiny and where staff put an exaggerated value on mutual protection and *esprit de corps* the conditions are in place for a slide towards lower standards that is accompanied by a growth of impunity. This potentiates abuse no matter how benign, or noble, are the sentiments of those who spend their days in charge of 'the worst of the worst' and whose daily routine involves subjugation, degradation, and humiliation.

When the staff is required to treat any interaction with prisoners as potentially hazardous, and when prisoners are often preoccupied with violent fantasies regarding staff, encounters become charged and anxiety-provoking for both sides. Toch (2001: 382) described the resulting atmosphere as 'a climate of trench warfare' where staff 'view their charges with trepidation or contempt'. In the words of a prisoner who had spent time in a special management unit at the Arizona State Prison Complex in Florence: 'If they only touch you when you're at the end of a chain, then they can't see you as anything but a dog' (cited in Dayan 2011). It is no coincidence that in this institution the tiny exercise yard to which prisoners were allowed regular, if brief, access was referred to as the 'dog pen'. It requires extraordinary resourcefulness for a prisoner to behave with dignity in such an environment; the same is true, to a lesser extent, for staff. Cohen (2012) described how Jose Martin Vega remained shackled at the wrists and ankles while staff attempted—unsuccessfully—to resuscitate him after a suicide attempt in the control unit at Florence ADX in May 2010. Vega's chains remained in place while his body lay on a slab in the mortuary awaiting an autopsy. Even in death his humanity was not acknowledged.

There are few aspects of the inmate's existence that the rule book does not touch. This means that the nature of the prisoner–guard relationship assumes added importance, not so much in terms of the scope for discretionary treatment, which is severely limited, but in terms of the tone and conduct of prescribed interactions. Is food served on time and with civility? Are mocking remarks made within earshot of those to whom they refer? Are the formalities of the day dealt with courteously and efficiently? Are searches carried out with the minimum degree of intrusion? Are inmate requests taken seriously and handled efficaciously?

When the staff group will brook no dissent and their charges are despised en masse, the scene is set for abuse, denial, and cover up. The filter through which prisoners at such institutions are viewed is one that stresses infamy and dangerousness; alternative perspectives are seldom found and this creates a gulf between a security-preoccupied staff and a collective of prisoners that must be treated with extreme caution. A publication of the American Correctional Association stresses that care must be taken when selecting staff to work on supermax units to avoid those who might be considered 'door warriors' (Greco 2003: 38). These are correctional officers who take advantage of their position to taunt, or otherwise interact unprofessionally with, prisoners. Such brazen reminders of the marked asymmetry that exists between the two groups create resentment and provide the pretext for an aggressive response should the opportunity arise. King et al. (2008: 156) contended that 'an officer subculture supporting objectification of inmates, excessive use of force against inmates, and loyalty to the code of silence exists in the SHU in Pelican Bay and is supported by the administration'. The toxic relationships that fester in supermax are aggravated by a built environment which is designed to disenchant, to disempower, and to disrespect. These are places where people are caged, cramped, and coerced with little regard for the consequences.

The micro-regulation of everyday life—what Foucault (1991: 198) described as 'the capillary functioning of power'—may have been the aspiration in the early days of Eastern State Penitentiary and Pentonville where the hope was that repeated intrusions into the subject's mind would induce compliance: the model prison would mould the model prisoner. But, as shown in Chapter 1, these aspirations were never more than partially realized. This project has been abandoned in supermax where the threat of brute force carries the day. Far from attempting to engage with prisoners as other sinners seeking salvation, correctional officers pull on surgical gloves whenever there is a possibility they will come into bodily contact with them. When skin touches skin our common humanity is asserted; circumventing this possibility makes the empathy gap potentially unbridgeable. (In an ironic twist, the original staff in Eastern State Penitentiary, who aimed to correct, were called keepers while their equivalents today are called correctional officers, although their primary aim is simply to keep.) Every prisoner movement is recorded but the purpose of the recording is to protect staff against false or malicious allegations of misconduct rather than to induce compliance in inmates (Riveland 1999: 15).

In the Panoptican, prisoners could never be sure if they were being observed by an interested member of staff. The 'unverifiable' nature of the surveillance was its strength and if this arrangement was perfected the actual exercise of power would be unnecessary (Foucault 1991: 201). In the supermax, prisoners can be confident that their movements, even cell extractions, are disinterestedly captured on camera, but there is no pretence that this is for their benefit and no guarantee that what is recorded is ever viewed.

Prisoners' days are timetabled in the sense that meals are served according to a rigid schedule but this is often arranged to suit the staff roster and for the most part prisoners exist in a state of bored inactivity. There is a curious coming together of huge time surpluses and enforced punctuality. Whether captive bodies evince 'docility' is largely irrelevant given the massive coercive power, and array of non-lethal and lethal weaponry, available to staff. They may learn to be helpless and acquiescent but if they do not, resistance against such overwhelming odds is futile and both sides know this. Whatever chances a pugilistic prisoner in times past may have had against a few baton-wielding officers in his separate cell have disappeared. Even the fittest and most courageous of prisoners cannot withstand the sting of a taser, the eye-wateringly incapacitating effects of pepper spray, or the latest techniques of control and restraint. Given the power imbalance that exists between them, and the relative availability of equipment and reinforcements, the almost certain victor in any such encounter is the member of staff. There is nothing subtle about this. Returning to Foucault's cardiovascular analogy, this could be described as arterial rather than capillary power; it is surging, pumping, pulsating rather than creeping or leaching.

Good staff can ameliorate poor conditions. As Grassian and Friedman (1986: 62) put it, 'the effects of treatments prescribed hinge as much on the perceived humanity of the caregiver as on any other variable'. Conversely, poor staff can negate the possible advantages of good conditions. When Gendreau and Bonta (1984: 474) argued that brief periods of solitary confinement

were not necessarily destructive they were alive to this important
dimension of prison life, noting that: 'Where people are consider-
ate and courtesies are the rule, then the dullest of environments are
perceived differently. The reverse is also true.'

To transform an ecology of cruelty into an ecology of courtesy
requires an attitudinal shift as much as a modified built environment. Supermax is pernicious not only because prisoners are
cocooned in concrete coffins but also, and at least as importantly,
because they are seen as unworthy of better. This is not to deny the
possibility of humane treatment and decent relationships, or the
occasional blossoming of friendships across the divide, but simply
to acknowledge the existence of deep fault lines in situations of
coercive confinement. Both captive and captor become indifferent to the other's humanity with the result that their interactions
are characterized by callousness, hostility, and, occasionally, violence. Supermax involves almost entirely situational rather than
relational control. Perhaps the best that can be hoped for is an
uneasy, and imperfect, peace.

In an account of women held in the SHU at Valley State Prison
for Women in California, one of the largest prisons for women
in the world, Shaylor (1998) showed how routine sexual harass-
ment added to prisoners' feelings of violation. This was particularly acute during cell extractions, usually carried out by teams
of male correctional officers, which Shaylor described as 'highly
sexualized: women are rendered immobile, placed in a position of
extreme vulnerability, stripped of all of their clothing, and then
subjected to a full body search' (p. 392). This had the effect of
recalling past experiences of trauma and abuse. There was a casual
violence to the language also: 'Guards constantly use racial epi-
thets, many of which are gendered, to refer to the women. They
call the prisoners "dogs," "niggers," "bitches," "whores" and
"black bitches" ' (p. 396). These humiliations exist on top of all of
the quotidian distresses that are part of life on an SHU.

Mutual hostility and incomprehension create a context for robust
verbal exchanges, violent cell extractions, fights, meticulous rule
enforcement, and recrimination. The staff is permanently on alert
and the quality of the relationship with prisoners, already starved
of social contact, does nothing to relieve the tension. A parlous
situation is exacerbated by florid mental illness (on the part of some
prisoners) and a conviction that 'wicked' people deserve what they
get (on the part of some staff). Prisoners are seen as responsible

for their own predicament. There is an element of self-selection in that the correctional officers who opt to work with 'the worst of the worst' may be predisposed to view them negatively. Haney (2008: 975) argued that

the dysfunctional adaptations of supermax prisoners are often attributed to their dispositions—antisocial traits, character flaws, or predatory natures—rather than the characteristics of the setting in which they are forced to live. Those kinds of attributions tend to harden over time. Supermax prisoners are often judged and demonized so effectively that some of them grow into their reputations, and those who acted in ways that warranted those reputations initially find they cannot grow out of them.

There is little room for personal development; dysfunction is set in aspic. Similarly, prisoners are likely to infer that the behaviour exhibited by staff reflects innate predispositions rather than being a product of their work environment, and this further increases the level of fear and antagonism.

Prisoners and guards are dragged down by the same dynamic into what Keve (1983: 47) depicted as the 'quicksand prison' where they remain, struggling but stuck. They are participants in a toxic routine where each party is locked into a way of thinking that pits them against the other. The gulf between the two groups becomes so wide that it cannot be straddled. There are no shades of grey, there is no room for nuance; it is 'us' against 'them'. Any perceived slippage will be exploited, with potentially disastrous consequences, so vigilance becomes the watchword. As Haney (2008: 979) summarized the situation, 'All too often, supermax brings together a perfect storm of social psychological pressures and influences, and a set of counterproductive interpersonal dynamics that cannot be transcended by either the prisoners or the guards.' In combination these factors create a milieu where cruel treatment is expected by prisoners and meted out by staff. Respect is extended in neither direction. There is a degree of callousness about everyday encounters that brutalizes all concerned.

When prison staff rely heavily on handcuffs, leg irons, belly chains, restraint techniques, taser guns, batons, pepper canisters, and firearms, it is understandable that they view those whose lives they oversee as being less than human. Otherwise why would such weaponry be required? In recent years technology has displaced the kind of 'dynamic security' which saw safety in the cultivation of strong relationships and easy rapport. Why bother trying to listen and persuade, let alone to understand, when there is so little common ground to be found, and when order can be restored with the flick of a baton or the release of a spray? When poor treatment becomes the norm, what was previously unconscionable becomes all too easy to defend and new levels of depravity cease to shock; the slide is difficult to arrest. This situation is sustained by a code of silence among staff which mirrors the code against 'snitching' to which prisoners subscribe. In closed environments where outside scrutiny is rare, and where employees depend upon the support and loyalty of their colleagues, blowing the whistle on rule breaking is seen as betrayal. Where ranks (and lips) close tightly under pressure, a culture of impunity can emerge. When cruelty has no foreseeable consequences, it becomes ingrained.

Corrupting human relations

Loathsome as it might be to contemplate, some prison guards will derive satisfaction from the power they wield over those in their custody especially perhaps if in other contexts, such as on the street, their dominant position would be far from guaranteed. This is not a phenomenon that has emerged with the advent of the supermax; it was ever thus. But in the tightly locked-down world of supermax, the opportunities for causing humiliation are significant and in the absence of robust oversight an exploitative environment can evolve.

In some prisons health care professionals have begun to mimic the obsession with security that dominates prisoners' lives. This has led to grotesque situations such as the construction of cages into which prisoners are locked being arranged in a semicircle for a 'group therapy' session, or clinicians having cages installed in their offices so that they can work their curative magic from the comfort of their desks, but safely out of harm's way at the same time (Haney 2008: 973). In California, the preferred term for these cages is 'therapeutic modules', which must count as one of the most ludicrous criminal justice euphemisms (for a photograph see Amnesty 2012: 36). Once installed in their individual modules, 'Steel mesh and a plastic spit shield separate the patients from the therapist, who sits in front of the enclosures wearing a shank-proof vest' (Dolan 2010; see also King et al. 2008: 151). Sometimes space constraints mean that the therapy modules are arranged in the

middle of cell blocks where their occupants are taunted and vili-
fied by the bored prisoners who look down upon them (literally
and figuratively).

An account of a session with a psychologist at Vacaville prison
would be hilarious were it not so disturbing. The *Los Angeles
Times* described how the therapist, 'wearing a herringbone
sports coat over his body armor, sat just out of urination range
of the cages with an acoustic guitar, trying to engage the inmates
with a sing-along of "Sitting on the Dock of the Bay"' (Dolan
2010). Such developments violate in the most uncompromising
fashion the principles of voluntarism, empathy, congruence,
confidentiality, and unconditional positive regard that are vital
to any authentic therapeutic relationship. They are a further
example of the distance that the supermax regime has moved
from being 'client-centred'.

Shalev (2009a: 125) reports that 'telemedicine' equipment exists
in all of California's prisons and allows psychiatric, and other,
examinations to be conducted via video conferencing. This further
reduces the possibility of human contact and removes the reassur-
ance that a skilled doctor can provide with a kindly word accompanied by a firm handshake. (A class action taken by severely
mentally ill prisoners in Florence ADX described how their needs
were addressed by the distribution of 'books with such titles as
Anger Management for Dummies, Choose Forgiveness—Your
Journey to Freedom, and Why Zebras Don't Get Ulcers' (*Bacote
v. Federal Bureau of Prisons* 2012: para 66.) In the same institution
a psychologist, clad in full riot gear, participated in the cell extraction of a prisoner who had attempted suicide by hanging (para
69).) In an environment where mental illness is prevalent it is counterproductive to prevent the development of meaningful therapeutic relationships. This demonstrates how far non-custodial
staff have allowed themselves to be captured by the 'ecology of
cruelty' within which they work.

In her ethnographic work in supermax Lorna Rhodes
(2002: 452, 451) noted how some mental health workers viewed
prisoners as 'evil in the biblical sense of good and evil', that it
was as if 'ice water is running through their veins'. The language
of psychopathy was used to label certain prisoners as inherently
dangerous and deserving of the harsh treatment that was meted
out to them. In a melding of moral and clinical discourses, individual prisoners were reduced to diagnostic categories, their

behaviours were reinterpreted in light of this labelling, and the resulting gulf between captor and captive became too great to bridge.

This distancing, as well as being dehumanizing, created a context where staff treated all interactions with suspicion, fear, and sometimes hostility. They did not want to allow a situation to develop where they might be manipulated by the cunning predators in their charge. The tragic irony was that by treating prisoners without empathy or kindness or discretion they were acquiring the very traits which they saw as so characteristic of the psychopath. By hardening their attitudes in this way they contributed to the development of an environment where relationships based on anything other than security and control became difficult to foster and where mutual antagonism was often the order of the day. For staff this confirmed the wisdom of their preconceptions and reinforced the culture of 'us' against 'them'. The staff became hostages of their own fears.

The view of supermax prisoners as a breed apart, ready to spring into violent action if given the slightest opportunity, impacts on every aspect of their lives, from the design of their cells to the food on their plates. To provide such fiendishly clever and dangerous people with something as apparently innocuous as a balanced diet is to offer them a potential armoury. Even the humble apple contains within its flesh the seeds of destruction. According to Shalev (2009b: 23) supermax prisoners 'will not be served ... fruit with pips because of a concern that these may be fashioned into weapons'. Damien Echols (2013: 343), who spent time on death row in the Varner Unit supermax in Arkansas recalled how, 'The prison used to give everyone two apples and two oranges on Christmas, but then they stopped, said it was a "threat to security".'

Victim Precipitation

Sometimes prisoners who have been held apart for a prolonged period will go to what might appear to be perverse lengths to elicit a predictably negative response. This is because a reaction of any kind demonstrates that they still count, that their actions have human consequences, that they remain part of a social world, however attenuated the ties that bind. To be attacked their existence must first be acknowledged. This is one way of maintaining identity, and a feeling of self-efficacy, in the face of concerted attempts to strip it away through seclusion.

Nien Cheng, who spent six and a half years in solitary confinement in a Chinese prison, recounted how when she became depressed in her solitary cell in Shanghai she would deliberately provoke the prison guards into using violence to silence her. This was a most unequal contest between a defenceless and malnourished woman of mature years and a party of fit, angry, and strong guards. Why did she invite such brutality? As Cheng explained (1995: 188): 'Though my arms became bruised and my legs bear to this day scars inflicted by their heavy leather boots, I always enjoyed a period of good humour and calm spirits after fighting with the guards. Then tension would gradually build up in me again. I believed that what I needed was human contact; even encounters with the guards was [sic] better than complete isolation. Besides, fighting was a positive action much more encouraging to the human spirit than merely enduring hardship with patience.' When Cheng felt her fighting spirit was beginning to wane she would engineer conflict with the guards in order once again to screw her courage to the sticking-place. Bettelheim (1960: 150) remembered how he provoked an SS concentration camp guard because: 'I believe that in order not to collapse, I had to prove to myself that I had some power to influence my environment. I knew I could not do it positively, so I did it negatively.' The risk that the response to such provocation would be fierce was worth taking because it confirmed to Bettelheim that he retained some capacity for initiative. Eisenman (2009: 38) described how a young male prisoner in Tamms supermax in Illinois, 'became so desperate for physical contact that he often refused to return his food tray through the slot in his door so that the "tag team"—a squad of masked and helmeted officers—would come to his cell to tackle and extract him.'

While the elderly Chinese woman, Austrian survivor of Nazi persecution, and young American may have little else in common they shared a need for contact and were prepared to risk harm to themselves to achieve some, however brutal, cruel, and perfunctory it might prove to be. By inviting attack they showed a desire to remain fully human. Even when resistance is futile and appears contrary to the prisoner's best interests it is not pointless. Sometimes self-harming behaviour has its origins in the same need to be reminded that one is a human being with a capacity to feel, even if what is felt is pain, tinged with a mixture of relief and regret.

In a world where toughness is prized, the use of sprays, electricity, batons, shields, and body armour to quell prisoner resistance is another way of diminishing the human capital of the prisoner. It also contributes to the staff attitude that they are dealing with a subhuman form of animal that needs to be held at arm's length and crushed with tools rather than engaged with interpersonally. The physicality of fighting acted as another reminder that prisoners and staff had something in common. There is a capacity for empathy during an exchange of blows that does not exist when weapons and overwhelming force enter the equation.

Where to From Here?

Riveland (1999: 1) opened his review of supermax prisons by wondering whether they were 'fad, trend, or wise investment?' At this stage the question might be answered by suggesting they are too well established to be a 'fad', too costly to be a 'wise investment', and if they are a 'trend' it is one that does not have an obvious destination. It could be argued that they are a small but intensely problematic element of the US penal landscape that, if anything, may have reached a plateau in terms of popularity and perceived utility. Whatever the future may hold for the supermax prison, this form of containment merits close scrutiny because it shows how a form of extreme custody can become an integral element of the repertoire of prison administrators despite deep concerns about its likely effects. Supermax custody is based on a bleak vision of human nature and while it does not invariably involve solitary confinement, when it does it poses a major challenge for those subjected to it in terms of conquering profound boredom and maintaining a sense of self in the absence of meaningful social reinforcement.

It was argued in Chapter 2 that the effects of separation and isolation in Eastern State Penitentiary were perhaps overestimated at the time and that greater distance from the debates has allowed their parameters to be drawn in starker and more caricatured terms. In particular, the softening effects of a benevolent ethos tend to be overlooked. In the past the separation was from other prisoners and the visitation of concerned citizens ensured a degree of human contact, however superficial.

Supermax isolation feels different. It is intended to be absolute and technological advances allow a kind of existence from which meaningful human interaction can be eradicated. While Dickens' (2000: 123) account of Eastern State Penitentiary may have been, in some key respects, a distortion, his conclusion that 'there is surely more than sufficient reason for abandoning a mode of punishment attended by so little hope or promise, and fraught, beyond dispute, with such a host of evils' would seem to apply without modification to supermax.

The next chapter deals with one of the most pressing challenges of isolation, whether in supermax or elsewhere, namely, the passage of time and how to ease it.

8

Time Passes, Inescapably

The passage of time can feel painful when we lose the wherewithal to impose our own stamp on it. Prisoners feel this pain sharply because they, more than most, have lost sovereignty over time. A prisoner's relationship to time is sundered by his or her imprisonment. Time has been taken from them along with their freedom, but unlike liberty it can never be won back. It is no longer a resource that they decide how to deploy but a burden that they must learn how to discharge. Time is over-abundant. It must be frittered away in large quantities so that it does not become excessively onerous. Despite its centrality to their lived experience, little is known about how prisoners negotiate time. When this critical aspect of the captive life is addressed it is often either implicitly or superficially. It is surprising how many scholars appear to have been deaf—or indifferent—to the heroic efforts made by prisoners to effect mastery over an aspect of their lives that cannot be seen, tasted, touched, smelled or heard but that nevertheless bombards, and threatens to overwhelm, the senses. Prisoner narratives evince a more wholehearted engagement with the profound challenge of calling time to account and that is why autobiographical voices are louder than those of academic commentators in many places throughout this book.

Solitary prisoners, with little to distract them, feel time's passage all the more acutely. The experienced among them, who know what lies ahead in all of its suffocating bleakness, feel that they are being buried alive. This is hibernation, but without the accompanying revivification. It is a deep sleep, without the repair that usually follows. As Abbott (1981: 4–45) put it, 'Time descends in your cell like the lid of a coffin in which you lie and watch it as it slowly closes over you.' For Gomez (2006: 61), writing of life on the Marion control unit, this was akin to existing in 'a breathing coffin...a space of permanent living death'. Koestler (1942: 107) also drew on the image of the grave to describe his ime in solitary confinement: 'The cell was like a vault enclosed

nge. The sense of being entombed dates back to the origins of

risoner in Eastern State Penitentiary: 'He is a man buried alive; to

e dug out in the slow round of years; and in the mean time dead to

everything but torturing anxieties and horrible despair.'

The pain of isolation is exacerbated by the burden of time and
vice versa. The latter presses down more heavily on an individual who is otherwise unoccupied and temporal pressures build,
unabated by many of the usual sources of distraction. Jackson
(1983: 75) cited Richard Korn's expert evidence in litigation taken
by Canadian prisoners about their experiences of solitary confinement: 'Prison time is almost palpable. It...has mass and weight.
Too heavy a sentence can suffocate...[In solitary confinement]
time stops and begins to crush and you have that suffocation, you
have the tiny space, the relative inaction, and that crushing experience and then the mind begins to play its tricks to save itself.' One
of these 'tricks' is to drag one's temporal focus to the present and
to avoid the backward or forward glance.

Calling Time to Account

It is discombobulating for prisoners to view time in linear terms,
relentlessly advancing, as this only serves as a reminder that their
own development has been frozen. Their lives have been put on
hold; they cannot share in the futures of those they care about as
they unfold, so forward thinking is best avoided. Meisenhelder
(1985: 53) captured it well when he noted that, 'the most significant aspect of the lived temporality of prison is its lack of a future'.

Grey (1988: 136) described how he smoothed out the major
fluctuations in mood that characterized the early months of his
captivity, 'I gradually learned to throw my hopes and expectations further forward so as to avoid the bitter disappointment of
nothing happening over and over again.' Reflecting this temporal
reorientation he lost interest in the past even to the extent of ceasing to read back through entries made in the diary he concealed
from his guards. This disregard for past and future is typical.
'The future is blank, there is no present, and the past is dead' was
Wilfred Macartney's (1936: 37) lament after his appeal failed and

he waited in London's Wandsworth prison to be sent to Parkhurst on the Isle of Wight to begin his sentence. This indicates massive temporal dislocation which if not addressed will compromise successful adjustment and threaten psychological survival.

Serving a 58-year sentence for possession of guns and explosives, Susan Rosenberg (2011: 200) was well aware of the dangers of retrospection: 'I knew that unless I was actively engaged in the business of living, my past would become all-consuming.' But she also knew that adopting a forward perspective was likely to be counterproductive: 'To live for the future made no sense to me, but to live in the present with ongoing meaning demanded that I effect change in myself' (p. 202). Temporal reorientation is not easy, but it is essential. As Rosenberg elaborated: 'These lines of demarcation [i.e. knifing-off the past and future] functioned to limit my emotions of joy and agony, happiness and sadness' (p. 287). The highs and lows of euphoria and despair are sacrificed to the safety of monotony. Emotions are flattened when the amount of time spent alone is prolonged; this is life lived parenthetically.

Based on an analysis of prisoner writings from the late nineteenth and early twentieth centuries Brown (2003: 31) argued that the relatively static nature of prison life, where each day unfolded like its predecessor, 'resulted in a perception of the present which was considerably extended and which increased the burden of imprisonment.' She went on to observe that, 'One repercussion of this was to increase the strain and frustration inherent in a long sentence and to increase the likelihood of prison disorder' (p. 31). This analysis is moot. There is no disputing that prisoners live in an extended present but it could be argued that this *reduces* the burden of imprisonment. Looking backwards to a non-prison past becomes increasingly difficult, even if it is still desired, as time spent in custody increases, and a forward orientation is fraught with anxiety as too many of the variables required for effective planning lie outside the prisoner's direct control. For this reason the past becomes an undifferentiated prison past as time progresses, and the future is eschewed.

Stretching the present and remaining within it is an important form of adaptation. Such a temporal orientation does not appear to increase the inherent stresses of a long sentence or to make disorder more likely. Indeed the opposite seems to be the case, with prison life being most comfortable for the person who has managed to refocus his or her attention on the present and has found a way to allow the days slip by, almost unnoticed. It is prisoners serving short sentences for whom temporal reorientation is not a priority, or those in the early or final stages of a long sentence where a focus on the past or future is unavoidable, whose equilibrium is most affected and for whom 'strain and frustration' are increased.

The desire to avoid contemplating an uncertain future or drawing attention to the contrast between the bleakness of what is and the richness of what might have been means that the options for reflection are limited to the present or the past. If a prisoner is serving a long sentence the currency of the past is soon spent and this means either submitting to the despondency of retrospection or, the route more often taken, becoming immersed in the present. Even prisoners who are equipped with prodigiously well-stocked minds find that, with time, the furrows of their previous lives can no longer be ploughed with profit. The past cannot be relived, and the official version of it that has set the prisoner's course is difficult to challenge. Neither can the future be contemplated without anxiety. As a result, much of the richness of human life, which involves re-narrating one's past and re-imagining one's future, is negated by imprisonment.

At a fundamental level therefore prisons will always be dehumanizing, no matter how good the physical conditions or the relationships between prisoners and staff, because they curtail the individual's capacity to look ahead, to plan, to efface the marks of the past, to wonder, to project themselves into new futures. They become tied to an interpretation of their life based on their criminal character and rooted to an unpromising present.

Molineux (1903: 24) captured this shift in temporal perspective when he wrote of his time in the hushed solitude of death row in Sing Sing, where guards and prisoners alike wore felt-soled shoes to muffle the sound of their movement, as a 'sort of noiseless purgatory in which, as the months go by, past experiences, the hopes and fears and happinesses which were, grow fainter and fainter, till, like the future, they inspire us with nothing but indifference, leaving only the present to be endured.' Waite (1994: 297) came to realize the necessity of seeking refuge in the present during his time as a hostage in the Lebanon: 'It's probably better not to worry too much about release. What I need to do is accept the moment for what it is.' Similarly, Ward and Kassebaum (2009: 296) described how in Alcatraz, 'many prisoners developed a coping strategy that involved focusing on the here and now'. This involved cauterizing contacts with the outside world and redirecting their focus to the minutiae of prison life, where daily activities were imbued with new intensity.

This attempt to live within a prison-present is a strategy that has long been favoured by canny prisoners. It becomes a more pressing consideration when the denial of human company is protracted. Schroeder (1976) describes the importance of shutting down the remnants of life outside in the interests of avoiding the distress associated with trying to live (emotionally) in two places at once. The sooner this is done, he argues, 'the sooner your time eases into that long, mindless lope which makes a year only marginally longer than six months' (p. 136). This 'long, mindless lope' is the preferred stride pattern of the prisoner serving a lengthy or indeterminate sentence who needs to be parsimonious about the expenditure of energy because there is a long road ahead.

Timerman (1988) coped with confinement by deliberately avoiding any speculation about his fate, the safety of his family, or the wider political context, and refusing to contemplate anything that might bring his real life to mind. He kept his gaze on the immediate context, recalling in his memoir that, 'Memory is the chief enemy of the solitary tortured man' (p. 36). By disconnecting himself from any consideration of the past or the likely turn of events in the future his task was reduced to manageable proportions. If he could direct all of his energy to the current moment he would be carried forward to the next one and so on and so forth. But a relentless focus on the present can be accompanied by a sense of time dragging. Time repays close attention by slowing down and speeds up if it is ignored. Thus, another 'trick' the solitary prisoner must master is that of speeding time's passage.

In his essay on the perception of time, William James (1890: 624; emphasis in original) observed with his usual limpidity of expression:

In general, a time filled with varied and interesting experiences seems short in passing, but long as we look back. On the other hand, a tract of time empty of experiences seems long in passing, but in retrospect short. A week of travel and sight-seeing may subtend an angle more like three weeks in the memory; and a month of sickness hardly yields more memories than a day. The length in retrospect depends obviously on the multitudinousness of the memories which the time affords. Many objects, events, changes, many subdivisions, immediately widen the view as we look back. Emptiness, monotony, familiarity, make it shrivel up.

This captures the prison experience superbly: it is arid ground upon which to expect to cultivate a fertile supply of memories from which to chronicle a life. It is the shrivelling up of time that the prisoner seeks. This becomes easier with advancing years because, as James explained, '*The same space of time seems shorter as we grow older*—that is, the days, the months, and the years do so; whether the hours do so is doubtful, and the minutes and seconds to all appearances remain the same' (p. 625; emphasis in original). The reason for this is that for a ten year old, one year is one-tenth of his or her life, whereas for a fifty year old the same interval is only one-fiftieth of life. Also, an individual has most new experiences early in life and over time many of these become routinized and are no longer worthy of notice; the days meld, the weeks merge and, as James expressed it, the lack of variety and content cause the years to 'grow hollow and collapse' (p. 625). As we get older and there is less variety in our environments, time seems to speed up (see also Draaisma 2004). This process is accentuated in prison where a backward glance reveals that time has flown and there is little to show for it.

Flaherty (1999: 13) is critical of James, noting that his model omits the important fact that, under certain conditions, a busy interval of time can seem to pass slowly giving a sense of 'protracted duration'. There is an exception to the rule that when we are absorbed in what we are doing time passes quickly. When attention is focused to a very intense degree on an activity the opposite happens and time slows down. During highly stressful or highly eventful situations the seconds expand and the lived experience of time slackens. The individual becomes preoccupied with time which, as a result of the close attention it is given, is experienced in slow motion. Examples include witnesses to serious crimes who tend to overestimate how long the incident lasted, and top sportspeople such as racing drivers for whom time is elongated (Taylor 2007: 88–91). When we attend more than we ordinarily would to what is (or is not) going on around us the experience of duration is protracted. This applies as much to a stimulus-rich situation where a dramatic sequence of events is unfolding as it does to the excruciating bleakness and boredom of a solitary cell.

To make sense of how time is lived and felt requires the incorporation of a subjective dimension. This allows for the possibility that time is perceived to pass slowly when the level of overt activity is abnormally high *or* when it is abnormally low. The causes of protracted duration are: (i) suffering and intense emotions; (ii) violence and danger; (iii) waiting and boredom; (iv) altered states of consciousness; (v) concentration and meditation; and (vi) shock and novelty (Flaherty 1999: 43). What unites the various elements of the foregoing list is that they are all departures from ordinary circumstances, characterized by individuals becoming engrossed in what they are doing. When these conditions are in place, time is magnified and people report that what they knew to be brief episodes felt like they had a greatly extended duration. These elements are present for the first-time prisoner and it is only when they have waned, and the individual is back in synchrony with objective time, that it is possible to devise methods for dealing with the temporal challenge of continuing imprisonment.

The key to understanding why some busy intervals are experienced as passing quickly and others as passing slowly is to grasp that there are two qualitatively different kinds of busy time. The first is what Flaherty characterizes as 'routine complexity' (p. 106). This is the kind of activity that, even if it requires a high level of skill, has become habitual for the individual and can be executed without much emotional or cognitive involvement. Time passes quickly under such circumstances. The second is 'problematic complexity' (p. 109) which requires that more than normal attentional resources are brought to bear. Under such conditions, the experience is one of protracted duration.

For the isolated prisoner who can introduce a level of routine complexity into his or her day, time will pass more easily. Prisoners who survive, or even thrive, in solitary confinement manage to do this. The prisoners who fare worst are those who keep on attending to time, who mark the days on the wall, who watch the minutes crawl past. They are saturated by an awareness of time and feel powerless to do anything to accelerate its passage. Winston Churchill recalled of his brief stay in a Boer prison how: 'The minutes crawl by like constipated centipedes' (cited in Kurki and Morris, 2001: 401). George Foote (1886: 116), imprisoned for 12 months for blasphemy, described how when he began his sentence, the absence of external stimulation bore down on him and the passage of time had a viscous quality: 'How the time crawled, weary hour on hour, like a slow serpent over desert sands.' A prisoner who spoke to Medlicott (1999: 220) put it as follows: 'Literally, the seconds ticking away, that's the Chinese water torture of what it's like.'

By paying such close attention to time these inexperienced prisoners extended its duration. Koestler (1942) was vividly aware of this phenomenon, describing how during a period of illness he was unable to read, write or otherwise distract himself. This meant that he could not ignore time but rather became painfully aware of its dreadfully slow progress, concluding that 'an inexorable law prevails: increasing awareness of time slows down its pace' (p. 155). If prisoners succeed in ignoring time they can create a context where they are so busy that they might need a watch to keep track of the routine complexity that they have laid on top of an environment free of social distractions. Under these circumstances the timepiece loses much of its power to tyrannise.

Time Flies, in Retrospect

One of the key paradoxes of time is that intervals that seem to drag as they pass appear to have flown in retrospect. According to Flaherty (1999: 104–12) temporal compression is greatest when activities are habitual, the process being further intensified by the erosion of episodic memory. For the long-term solitary prisoner whose days are defined by unchallenging and unremarkable repetition, and where there are few external activities to recollect, the past contracts rapidly. An unchanging routine leaves but a faint trace in memory or, as Victor Serge (1970: 101) expressed it, 'The bitter minute drags on eternally; the empty months fly, leaving no more than a bit of dust in the soul.'

Tenzin Palmo, a Buddhist nun, spent 12 years meditating in a tiny cave (6 feet wide and 6 feet deep) in the Himalayas. She had no bed, spending most of her time in a meditation box measuring 2 feet 6 inches square. Every day she ate the same meal of rice, lentils, and vegetables supplemented by bread and the occasional piece of fruit. The last three years were spent in complete reclusion without any human contact. Tenzin Palmo spoke afterwards of how, looking back, time seemed to have flown: 'The thing that struck me most was where had all the time gone? Time just condensed. The last three years in particular just flew past. It seemed like four months at most' (cited in Mackenzie 1998: 146).

Periods of profound boredom generate few memories, so when looked back upon there is little to distinguish them from the similarly empty periods on either side. In Klein's words (2006: 124), 'Time changes as we look back on it. Expanses of time that once seemed endless get so compressed as to be nearly unrecognizable. An experience that went by like nothing balloons in our memory.' Each solitary prison day feels excruciatingly long in the absence of a 'programme of distraction' (Macartney 1936: 194). But in retrospect even the years seem to have flown past. Because of the unchanging external environment long periods appear to merge. This pattern is commonly found in the autobiographical writings of prisoners. It is also to be discovered in other literary forms, with a particularly apposite example being the exploration of time, and its elastic nature, in *The Magic Mountain*, from which the following passage, redolent with psychological insight, is taken:

In general it is thought that the interestingness and novelty of the time-content are what 'make the time pass'; that is to say, shorten it; whereas monotony and emptiness check and restrain its flow. This is only true with reservations. Vacuity, monotony, have, indeed, the property of lingering out the moment and the hour and of making them tiresome. But they are capable of contracting and dissipating the larger, the very large time-units, to the point of reducing them to nothing at all. And conversely, a full and interesting content can put wings to the hour and the day; yet it will lend to the general passage of time a weightiness, a breadth and solidity which cause the eventful years to flow far more slowly than those poor, bare, empty ones over which the wind passes and they are gone. (Mann 1996: 104)

The author continued: 'Great spaces of time passed in unbroken uniformity tend to shrink together in a way to make the heart stop beating for fear; when one day is like all the others, then they are all like one; complete uniformity would make the longest life seem short, and as though it had stolen away from us unawares' (p. 104). These excerpts capture the twin terrors of solitary confinement as it is lived (painfully slow—when will the day end?) and as it is remembered (agonisingly quick—where did the months go?). Koestler (1942: 120; emphasis in original) was impressed by *The Magic Mountain* and described the paradoxical nature of his time in solitary confinement during the Spanish Civil War in words similar to Mann's:

Time crawled through this desert of uneventfulness as though lame in both feet. I have said that the astonishing and consoling thing was that in this pitiable state it should pass at all. But there was something that was more astonishing, that positively bordered on the miraculous, and that was that this time, these interminable hours, days and weeks, passed *more swiftly* than a period of times has ever passed for me before.

The time that was felt to drag on account of its dreary uneventfulness was remembered as having rushed past. When Koestler arrived at this insight, he drew solace from it: 'There was a bizarre consolation in the knowledge that these interminable, torturing hours, as soon as they had ceased to be the present, would shrink to nothing, like an india-rubber pig when the air escapes from it with a squeak' (p. 121). Echols (2013) spent 18 years in prison awaiting execution for crimes he did not commit. Much of this time was spent in solitary confinement and he recalled how:

Time has changed for me. I don't recall exactly when it happened, and I don't even remember if it was sudden or gradual. Somehow the change just crept up on me like a wolf on tiptoe. Hell, I don't even remember when I first started to *notice* it. What I *do* remember is how when I was a kid every single day seemed to last for an eternity…I swear to God that I can remember a single summer day that lasted for several months…Now I watch while years flip by like an exhalation, and sometimes I feel panic trying to claw its way up into my throat…I truly don't understand how it happened. How it *continues* to happen. (pp. 206–7; emphasis in original)

The 'wolf on tiptoe' analogy is apt. By the time one becomes aware of the danger it may be too late to take evasive action. So too is the image of years flipping by 'like an exhalation', the solitary prisoner gasping in the realisation that so much life has slipped by beneath awareness and that it cannot be recovered.

Ingrid Betancourt (2010), another innocent person who was coercively confined, gives an excellent sense of how time is distorted in captivity. The transition in her case was particularly traumatic. As a presidential candidate in Colombia she was captured by the FARC and held in the jungle for six years in conditions of dreadful, and unrelenting, hardship. She spent long periods chained by the neck to a tree and forbidden to speak to any of the other hostages. A life that had been defined by public service, politics, family commitments, and a whirlwind of activity became stagnant overnight:

I was aware of how distorted my sense of time had become. In 'civilian life'…the days had gone by with staggering speed and the years had passed slowly, giving me a sense of accomplishment, of leading a full life. In captivity my perception of time was the exact opposite. The days seemed endless, stretching cruelly and slowly between anguish and boredom. In contrast, the weeks, months, and, later on, years seemed to accumulate at breakneck speed. (p. 120)

The finding that monotony stretches time as it passes and squeezes it on reflection is robust. In his study of philosophical approaches to boredom, Svendsen (2005: 55) captures the same idea thus: 'Because time is not filled out in boredom, the boring span of time appears afterwards to be short, while it is experienced as unbearably long during the actual span of time. Life becomes short when time becomes long.' When a monochrome existence is interrupted by a burst of colour, the vivid details are remembered long after; novelty dilates time.

There is a soporific quality to sameness which adds to the inertia that characterizes many isolated prisoners. 'The flatness of life, the boredom, time that was forever starting over again just the same—it all acted like a sedative' (Betancourt 2010: 494). After three and a half years as a hostage of the Islamic Jihad, Anderson (1994: 292) mused: 'The days go so slowly, yet pile up so quickly. It's hard to conceive of forty-two months just gone, evaporated.' Time seems to accelerate in a monastery just as it does in a prison where the unchanging routine lends an impression of speed. As Leigh Fermor (2004: 38) put it, based on his experience as a lay person who regularly availed of the hospitality of monks:

Time passes in a monastery with disconcerting speed. Except for the great feasts of the church, there are no landmarks to divide it up except the cycle of the seasons; and I found that days, and soon weeks, were passing almost unperceived. The speed of this temporal lapse is a phenomenon that every monk notices: six months, a year, fifteen years, a lifetime, are soon over.

In an exploration of the relationship between mood states and perceptions of duration Wittmann (2009) noted that individuals with depression reported a slowing down of the pace of time. The argument is that their psychological distress makes it difficult to focus on meaningful thoughts and actions; all that is left to attend to is time creeping slowly past. The relationship between time perspective and different forms of psychiatric disorder is discussed by Melges (1982: 135–6) who argues that 'it is possible to look at temporal disintegration as either a manifestation or mechanism of psychotic illness' and that 'once a time distortion takes place, whatever its underlying cause, it alters the organization of consciousness at the psychological level'.

These findings are of relevance to the prisoner. Those held in solitary confinement routinely exhibit symptoms of depression such as withdrawal, poor sleeping, and fatigue and this can be expected to impact on their time perception by stretching the empty moment. Similarly, boredom-prone individuals are more likely to over-estimate the duration of time intervals. The young men who end up in prison are often distractible, become bored easily and need diversion. Again this can be expected to elongate their perception of time's passing. As Andrew and Bentley (1976: 179) put it in their survey of young offenders, 'For delinquents, time seems to pass slowly.' Finally, following Melges, by adjusting their temporal horizons unwary prisoners may be inviting adverse mental health effects.

One of the prisoners Dickens (2000: 117) met in Eastern State Penitentiary, whose release after two years of separation beckoned the following day, pronounced that the time had passed 'pretty quick—considering'. Dickens seemed sceptical of this account, judging that the man found it easy to speak uncritically of the system that he was about to leave and that his excitement at the prospect of putting it behind him was causing him to be unduly positive about his prison experience. However, it is perfectly plausible, as made apparent by so many other prisoner accounts, that a backward glance over a period of time undifferentiated by novelty gave the impression that it had raced past. Although Dickens would likely have found it difficult to accept, given his abhorrence of the Pennsylvania system, hours that seem to unfold in interminable, excruciating succession are looked back upon as having tumbled swiftly along, giving way to a rapid passage of days, weeks and months.

Another of the prisoners Dickens met had built himself a clock out of odds and ends with a vinegar bottle as its pendulum. He cut a pathetic figure, with trembling lip and quiet, deliberate speech. When asked if time passed quickly, he replied to his visitors, 'Time is very long, gentlemen, within these four walls!' (p. 114). But these are not irreconcilable perspectives. For the second prisoner, who had served six years and had a further three ahead of him, and whose attention was focused on his homemade clock, each tedious solitary day was a test of endurance. For the first man, on the cusp of release and looking back on his sentence, time seemed to have collapsed.

This perceptual distortion has implications for understanding deterrence. It is only when an individual actually returns to prison that the unbearable weight of the empty moment is once again fully felt. This helps to explain why long prison sentences do not necessarily deter. The corollary is that a sentence packed with varied and interesting activities would seem longer upon reflection and might thereby exercise greater influence on ex-prisoner decision making. There is a delicious irony here about how lengthy, austere, and monotonous prison terms, beloved of law and order politicians, collapse when reviewed by those subjected to them and so seem to have flown, thereby diminishing their potential deterrent value.

Exceptions to the rule

Writing about his experience of Auschwitz, Frankl (2004: 79) described a 'deformed' sense of time: 'In camp, a small time unit, a day, for example, filled with hourly tortures and fatigue, appeared endless. A larger time unit, perhaps a week, seemed to pass very quickly. My comrades agreed when I said that in camp a day lasted longer than a week. How paradoxical was our time experience!' At first glance this perspective may seem to conflict with the finding that days filled with activity are felt to pass more quickly. But this apparent contradiction is resolved when we recall Flaherty's (1999: 106–10) distinction between routine and problematic complexity. The uncertainty and horror that characterized life in a concentration camp meant that engrossment with the moment was essential for survival. The coexistence of intense suffering, violence, danger, waiting, concentration, shock, and novelty—all causes of protracted duration—ensured that every hour seemed to be cruelly stretched.

As another camp survivor put it, 'A day begins like every day, so long as not to allow us reasonably to conceive its end, so much cold, so much hunger, so much exhaustion separate us from it' (Levi 1987: 69). When every day might be one's last, the immensity of the struggle to survive is such that routine complexity never becomes remotely feasible. Nor is the paradox revealed by the backward glance surprising: when viewed retrospectively, even by those suffering the most appalling persecution and degradation, monotony leads to temporal compression. Primo Levi (1987: 109) recalled 'those usual immemorable days, so long while they are passing, and so short afterwards'. Days that seemed inexorably long when they began left hardly a trace in the memory once they had been endured.

J. E. Nardini served as a medical officer in prison camps in the Philippines and Japan along with 30,000 American prisoners captured by the Imperial Japanese Army with the fall of Bataan and Corregidor. His imprisonment lasted for three and a half years, by which time only around 12,000 of the prisoners were still alive. Nardini (1952: 244) suggested that the most adaptive time perspective was one which minimized the significance of the present: 'It was important to look forward and backward and retain an active identification with one's home countrymen instead of with the miserable prisoner group...These men had to overlook, repress, or ignore the present, and place undue emphasis on past and future.'

This is an exception to the general prisoner strategy which is to stretch the present and become immersed in it to survive. It is no doubt explained by the particular horrors that accompanied life in these camps where the conditions of confinement were awful, mortality was high, disease was rampant, beatings and abuse were regular, there was no indication when the war might come to an end or who would emerge victorious, and food was in short supply. In such a context the relative psychological disadvantages of a future or past time orientation (which can be crippling to regular prisoners) are less emphatic; any distraction from the horrors of the present—however insubstantial or troubling—is to be welcomed.

Chronophobia

The temporal aspect of imprisonment has attracted less attention than the morbid effects of isolation but there has been at least one attempt to describe it as a species of prison neurosis— 'chronophobia' (fear of time)—and to find a place for it in the taxonomy of psychiatric disorders. Russo (1943: 581) was unambivalent about the detrimental impact and universal significance of chronophobia, which he described as a condition peculiar to the prison setting, 'from which almost all inmates suffer sooner or later, although it is more pronounced in individuals with long sentences'. He claimed that this was 'the most common problem' confronted by mental health professionals in prison (p. 581). The prisoner panics because of the immensity of time ahead. He knows that his debt to society must be paid in units of time, and that these are non-negotiable; time 'cannot be hurried or telescoped; it cannot be bartered or sold; it has no substitute' (p. 581). The panic does not set in at once. During the early phase of a sentence there are plenty of distractions for the prisoner as he settles in and learns the routine. A month or a year may pass or even several years but then, inevitably, there is an attack of fear about the time left:

He is now in a panic and suffers from chronophobia. It usually attacks him while in his cell, but it may come in the mess hall, the showers, anywhere. He fears his enclosure, his incarceration, the confining walls, the restraining bars. But this apparent claustrophobia is only an expression of his panic; it arises from his fear of time, which is represented by the prison. (p. 583)

The first attack is followed by anxiety, restlessness, insomnia, digestive problems, chest pain and a host of other symptoms, including belligerency and withdrawal. This pattern of responses is very similar to that found in prisoners who have been subjected to solitary confinement, suggesting that some of the adverse effects attributed to isolation may have their roots in anxiety about time rather than the absence of social intercourse. Prisoners in solitary confinement find it more difficult to avoid thinking about time; the issue cannot be dodged, they must confront it. Again, an underlying process, common to all prisoners, however accommodated and wherever located, may become more visible among those held apart. So it is not the pain of isolation that is at issue as much as the pain of facing time. Russo quoted from a story written by an inmate who had identified the source of his disquiet:

Have you ever felt the weight of time? Thicker than the darkness of night, heavier than the walls of stone. So thick that it could not be cut by light or penetrated by rays of thought. I awoke and found that my cell was filled with time. It seemed to have body and weight, it permeated the whole room and oppressed me on all sides. It was like a monster clutching at my throat. My heart beat wildly and I gasped for breath. I was overcome by a nameless fear of something I could not understand. It threw me into a panic. (p. 584)

Russo commented that the author of this story, a recidivist offender, 'can face anything but the contemplation of the time he must put in' (p. 586).

When it came to the treatment of chronophobia, Russo acknowledged that the cause of the disturbance cannot be removed as there is no alternative to the prisoner serving his sentence, but the situation can be ameliorated with a change of location, occupation, exercise or diet and the addition of some clinical attention and sympathy. All of these go some way towards helping inmates 'who suffer from the tension of time' (p. 590). The prisoner can also be helped to gain insight into the root of his problem by thinking of his sentence in manageable chunks, rather than as a yawning expanse of time that threatens to engulf him. 'Contemplating a long stretch of time is an evil. The inmate is not asked to serve a ten-year sentence all at once, but merely to put in one day at a time; he has to live only one day in twenty-four hours. Thinking of ten years of durance as a single block of time is a form of self-pity not to be indulged in; it brings on a neurosis' (p. 590).

Some chronophobic prisoners became belligerent and others withdrew. While the crisis remained intense for a relatively brief period (several months at most) mild relapses were common. Once the initial panic had subsided the prisoner simply went through the motions for the remainder of his sentence:

The men are phlegmatic, indifferent; they have only shallow interests, and a deadened sense of taste, smell, and visual perception. To all outward appearance, they are automatons. This is as it should be; it permits time to pass more smoothly. It distresses them to look before and after; they must live discreetly in the present, only one day at a time. (p. 584)

The pattern that Russo described is at variance with the usual trajectory of prisoner adaptation which shows the highest levels of disturbance around the entry and exit points. Russo's model suggests a peak in anxiety some way into the sentence after the prisoner has adapted to prison life, with ripples of panic thereafter including a mild attack just before release. Russo's argument about the need to take chronophobia seriously did not generate much debate in the literature and the existence of this neurosis in prisoners is now referred to about as often as its alphabetical cousins chiroptophobia and coulrophobia. That is, hardly at all.

Styles of Time Usage

Brian Keenan (1992: 69) wrote that during the three months of isolation that marked the beginning of more than four years spent cheek-by-jowl with fellow hostage John McCarthy he began to think about time in a new way: 'The idea, the concept of time enthrals me...Time is different now. Its flux and pattern is new, seeming so clear, so precise, so deeply understood yet inexplicable.' This is a good example of how when people begin to think hard about something that they have long taken for granted it remains understood at one level but becomes impossibly complex at another. This is St Augustine's dilemma—'What, then, is time? If no one ask of me I know; if I wish to explain to him who asks, I know not'—expressed by a hostage in Beirut 1,600 years later. While the nature of time remains elusive, we can learn something about how it is deployed from work carried out in non-penal settings.

In a study of patients in a rehabilitation institution in San Francisco, Calkins (1970: 494–500) identified six distinct styles of time usage. The variety of styles reflected the mixed nature of the population which included the physically handicapped, alcoholics, old and senile patients, and a number of volatile young adults with learning difficulties. The average age was 59 years. The prison social context is quite different in that the population tends to be younger and less infirm, the degree of coercion is greater, and there is little that most prisoners can do to influence the timing of their release through participation in rehabilitation programmes. Nonetheless, Calkins' scheme is a useful way of thinking about the range of opportunities that people have to interact with time when it is abundant and they are sequestered from normal life. Her styles can be summarized as follows:

1. *Passing time.* The individual accepts the imperatives of the institution's schedule and finds activities within it to fill the day, without reference to the achievement of future goals.
2. *Waiting.* The institution and its staff are held in disdain, activity is avoided and the day is spent observing (self and others) and daydreaming.
3. *Doing time.* Little is done beyond that which the institution demands. The individual sits and waits, often solitary and sullen.
4. *Making time.* This is the option chosen by the institutional entrepreneur, the opportunist for whom time is a resource. Tasks are completed at speed so that new ones can be taken on. An effort is made to exert control over one's own outcomes and to be recognized as so doing.
5. *Filling time.* This is a hybrid style. The priorities of the institution and its programmes are accepted half-heartedly, empty time is not considered aversive, little effort is directed towards rehabilitation.

6. *Killing time.* Disruption and subversion are of central importance. The values of the institution are rejected and the approval
of staff is not sought. Crises are generated, rules are broken and
attempts are made to buck the system.

Prisoners also pass, do, make, fill, and kill time as well as waiting. Like the patients studied by Calkins they evince a variety of
styles, but the more repressive nature of their confinement gener-
ates responses to time management that are more extreme in range
(from catatonic withdrawal to violent rebellion), more variegated
in expression (the entrepreneurial prisoner can make time through
devotion to intellectual pursuits in ways that were not open to
Calkins' sample), more uniform in motivation (the overwhelming
need is to drag one's temporal orientation to the present), and more
potentially life-enhancing in outcome (the rewards that accompany self-examination can be substantial).

Lauer (1981) set out an approach to the study of social time that
viewed it as having three aspects that required analysis, namely,
pattern, orientation, and perspective. Temporal pattern comprised
the five basic elements of duration, tempo, sequence, timing, and
periodicity. The value of such an approach is that it moves attention
away from a preoccupation with time as a unit of measurement.
It also highlights how different prison time is to time in the free
world. To a great extent *duration*, or the length of time devoted to
an activity, is determined by others for prisoners. Where they have
room to manoeuvre is in terms of how duration is perceived and
it is the manipulation of perceived duration that is central to the
solitary prisoner's existence.

Prisoners remain largely oblivious to changes in *tempo*, or the
speed at which activities take place. The acceleration of time which
technological innovation has allowed—and the accompanying
intensification of experiences—has barely penetrated the penal
realm, where prisoners are 'cavemen in an era of speed-of-light technology' (Johnson 2005: 263). The idea of prisoners remaining in a
time warp is captured by a poignant photograph in *Still Life: Killing
Time*, a photographic essay on a wing for elderly prisoners in an
English prison, which depicts an illustration that has been cut from a
newspaper showing how to make sense of the new price system that
accompanied the introduction of decimalization (Clark 2007: 60).
The clipping carries the legend, 'cut out and keep for handy reference', advice which the prisoner to whose cupboard it was neatly

affixed has clearly taken to heart. The photograph was taken more than 30 years after the currency changeover, suggesting that the clipping had been kept carefully by an individual for whom coinage that had long disappeared from circulation continued to be significant. This did not appear to be an exercise in nostalgia but rather, a desire to keep in touch, however tenuously, with a world that had, in many important ways, changed beyond recognition. Goffman (1961: 63) described how, for the duration of their sentences, inmates felt 'exiled from living'; this elderly prisoner is just such an exile.

When it comes to the *sequencing* of activities, again prisoners fare poorly compared with their peers outside. They cannot reorder what they do to take account of shifting priorities. For example, a prisoner could not decide to go to the yard earlier one day so as to have more time for leisure in the evening or to 'multi-task' during the day so as to make simultaneous progress on several fronts. Nor is the prisoner free to determine the *timing* of his or her activities so that they are in synchrony with others. They are locked into a timetable that has changed little in its essentials over almost two centuries. Finally, when consideration turns to *periodicity*, or the rhythm of an activity, prisoners are once again at a relative disadvantage, having little scope to deviate from patterns that are prescribed for them.

For all of these reasons there are few opportunities for prisoners to engage in the types of 'time work' that people are so adept at when it comes to sloughing off external constraints and customizing their temporal experiences. The prospects are more severely reduced again for the individual in solitary confinement who must confront a penal juggernaut that flattens the scope for individual decision making. As Austin Bidwell (1897: 459–60) expressed this relationship in the closing years of the nineteenth century, the prison can be viewed as: 'a vast machine in which a man counts for just nothing at all . . . Move with it, and all is well. Resist, and you will be crushed as inevitably as the man who plants himself on the railroad track when the express is coming. Without passion, without prejudice, but also without pity and without remorse, the machine crushes and passes on.' But as Frankl (2004) has shown, no matter how steeply the odds are stacked against them, prisoners retain the capacity to make decisions, even if these are simply choices between equally unattractive options; their agency is crushed but not completely obliterated; their repertoire of responses is limited but not non-existent.

Prisoners in solitary confinement come up with a variety of ways to put their own stamp on their temporal lives, particularly how they experience duration. They do this because the stakes are so high; to relinquish the belief that one can continue to engage with time is to give up hope and to be diminished as a human being. Solitary prisoners strive to be survivors, not victims, of circumstance. Given the vast scale of the institution's power over the individual there are many aspects of temporality where any attempt to wrest back control is predictably futile. But this is not always the case. Prisoners work hard to make intervals feel shorter than the clock or calendar would suggest and in this respect they meet with a measure of success as Chapter 10 will show. In the words of Flaherty (2011: 23): 'In manifold circumstances, human beings wield the weapons of creativity against the forces of time.' In the stimulus-poor environment of the solitary cell these weapons are used first to focus the temporal gaze firmly on the present and secondly to truncate perceived duration.

Other dimensions of temporality are usually predicated on interaction, on the coordination of activities with others, so they are of limited relevance to the isolate. So, too, they involve the introduction of temporal variety, not something that necessarily appeals to the solitary prisoner for whom one eventual payoff of relentless sameness is a feeling that time has rushed past. Finally, people try to tweak time in an effort to make the most of a scarce resource, often to find a temporal niche for themselves among many competing obligations. Again this is not a major consideration for the prisoner who exists in an abundance of time.

In other words, of the various dimensions of time that are open to manipulation such as sequence, timing, tempo, and duration, it is how duration is perceived that is of greatest moment for the prisoner in solitary confinement. The individual may not be in a position to determine how long he or she spends in isolation but there is scope to influence how this feels. Cohen and Taylor (1972: 51) noted that: 'Prison involves an involuntary migration to a region in which the dislocations of life are not necessary costs of the move, but are rather deliberately engineered insults to the self.' One of the most significant of these insults is the removal of control over how to spend one's time and the negation of any value associated with time. For the prisoner in solitary confinement the lack of meaningful engagement with others may add injury to insult.

Clock Time and Prison Time

In a classic paper, Sorokin and Merton (1937) offered a conception of time that stressed the importance of social phenomena, and the relationships between them, as temporal measures that could take precedence over days, weeks, months, and years. 'Social time', they argued, 'expresses the change or movement of social phenomena in terms of other social phenomena taken as points of reference' (p. 618). Social time can be contrasted with astronomical time in that it has a strong qualitative dimension: 'these qualities derive from the beliefs and customs common to the group and...serve further to reveal the rhythms, pulsations, and beats of the societies in which they are found' (p. 623). As the field of interaction of the group expands, the need to coordinate activity between the different elements of a wider society becomes more pressing, and this leads to the adoption of a common and mutually understood means of designating time intervals, based on the certainty provided by the calendar and the clock. Local time systems, with their idiosyncratic emphases on events of local significance, conflict with the kind of synchronization and predictability required by differentiated industrial societies and so, over time, they are effaced.

It might be hypothesized that social time would remain relevant in prisoner societies given their smallness of scale, lack of geographical mobility, homogeneity in terms of class background, relative lack of internal differentiation, and paucity of opportunities to interact with other groups. And indeed prisoners do mark time by reference to events, rather than simply by the accumulation of days, weeks, months, and years. The arrival of a new warden, an outbreak of violence, a period of lockdown, a concert; these are all important markers of time for the community that experiences them. They might be thought of as 'time anchors' that act as points around which to gather recollections. Their precise location on the calendar, or the actual duration of the intervening intervals, is of no great significance.

Because prisoners are constrained in the extent to which they can determine the occurrence of the kinds of social activities they deem to be important, it is challenging for them to impose their own social time on top of the clock time that sets the rhythm of their days and the calendar against which their sentences are plotted. There are practical problems too. Social time depends on a degree of population stability and reciprocal trust that is not always found in prisons. Where there is a high turnover of inmates the opportunity to share significant experiences and commit an agreed version to institutional memory is severely limited. Nonetheless, the qualitative attractions of social time remain relevant—especially when a release date is some way distant and purely quantitative measures are overwhelming—but the fact that prisoners are forced to march to the institution's disciplinary cadence means that the challenges associated with maintaining parallel time-reckoning systems are not inconsequential. Where prisoners live together for prolonged periods, shared conceptions, and a sense of social time, are more likely to be found.

Hans Castorp, the hero of *The Magic Mountain*, learns from the older sanatorium inhabitants the importance of marking time by events rather than by days and weeks: 'Christmas, like other holidays in the course of the year, served them for a fulcrum, or a vaulting-pole, with which to leap over empty intervening spaces' (Mann 1996: 270). This image of a vaulting-pole is a useful one. Many prisoners learn to measure their sentences by the occurrence of regular events from each of which they leap forward to the next, soaring over—and indifferent to—the expanse of time beneath. This allows a sense of easy velocity, a feeling of covering ground without being unduly distracted by the terrain. Reflecting on many years in isolation on death row, Echols (2013: 276), observed how 'each moment is meaningless because it has no context'. As the quantity of unremarkable days piles up prisoners become oblivious to each new increment. It is events that pattern time and synchronize memories; these are the time anchors that become part of the prisoner's subjective calendar.

For men and women in isolation time has a treacle-like quality that makes its presence felt by preventing an easy passage through the day. A determined effort is required to trudge through the morass and to add meanings and milestones to a journey that would otherwise become arduous in the extreme. Describing a period of solitary confinement as a political prisoner in Argentina in 1977, Timerman (1988: 5) recalled that time became 'that dangerous enemy of man, when its existence, duration, and eternity are virtually palpable'. The same author described life in his isolation cell thus: 'only time remained, all of time, time on all sides and in every cranny of the cell, time suspended on the walls, on the ground, in my hands, only time'

(p. 37). Grey (1988: 225) recounted how after six months he began 'to find the weight of isolation pressing on me increasingly'. Waite (1994: 204) described the boredom of his daily life as a hostage held in extreme isolation for years as 'crushing'. As well as compressing the mind the lack of stimulation is felt as a physical burden; more and more effort is required to stand up and face the day. Simple tasks take longer to execute and are disproportionately wearying. Unless the prisoner takes decisive action the weight of inertia will grow as the isolation is prolonged; body and mind will lose vim and vigour together.

While difficult, the prisoner's plight is not hopeless. Those who have the resources to create complex but unproblematic routines for themselves, whether rooted in their exterior or intrapsychic worlds, find it possible to speed time's passage. For those who do not develop this talent, or whose routines remain problematic, time crawls and madness beckons.

There is also what might be described as 'spiritual time', a concept that has been defined by someone with many years experience of living in isolation in a cell in the following terms:

'I am so many years of age.' What does such a statement mean? It means only this: that the earth has gone round the sun so many times since I came into the world. That is the normal measure of what the world calls time. But there is another 'age' which consists in interior movement and progress proper to each individual, as opposed to periodic movements which are from without, and are the same for all. Our real age depends on the interior events which have taken place within the soul, upon their rhythm, and upon the greatly varying reactions, entirely personal and unique resulting from them. That is our true age, and it is an age which varies with each individual. (A Carthusian 1975: 38–9)

This is time marked by the metronome of experience, which beats differently for each person. It differs from chronological time with its fixed intervals, and from social time with its emphasis on events and other people. It is time without obvious anchors. This is the preserve of the committed solitary.

Timetables and ritual: the seductions (and subversion) of structure

The prison timetable, while resented because it is inflexible and imposed, also offers a kind of refuge. The endlessly repeated cycle of doors being unlocked and locked, of mealtimes, of counts, of exercise periods, provides a skeleton to support each day. Because today is the same as yesterday and tomorrow will mirror today, life can be lived according to the rhythm of these repetitions, which start afresh each morning. Rather than moving forward the prisoner is static, spinning on the spot, the aim being nothing more grandiose than to spin on the same spot again the next day. Like his Victorian predecessor on the tread wheel, much effort is expended to no net effect, but too little effort will be harmful. Breytenbach (1984: 143) commented on the value of routine in the following terms: 'the same events coming around again, the rhythms being repeated, the familiarity of your situation—these deaden you to the passing of time'.

Timetables are important because they allow prisoners to avert their gaze from the future. They offer certainty when much is uncertain and give a direction, however monotonous and unwelcome, to the day. They provide staging points for the prisoner who might otherwise flounder and so offer a deadening solace. Breytenbach captured the sense of how the rigid structure afforded by the timetable can threaten to smother those upon whom it acts while simultaneously offering protection and support: 'Rhythms, routines, elements of your understanding and experiencing the self and the environment; fetters which make you weaker: but, as always, within the weakness the strength already lies—and so they become the ways in which you destroy time' (p. 150). By reducing uncertainty, the structuring of time helps prisoners to navigate their sentences. But there are dangers. As Zeldin (1995: 356) expressed it, 'Habits are comfortable, but when they fossilise, the humanity is gradually drained out of human beings.'

A detailed daily schedule serves four purposes. First of all it breaks the monotony and coordinates activities across the institution. Secondly, it allows for staff rosters to be drawn up and for staff time to be planned and paid for. Thirdly, it contributes to the imperative of security by ensuring that the whereabouts of each prisoner can always be ascertained; the timetable is as much a device for pinpointing prisoners' locations as it is for scheduling their activities. Fourthly, it emphasizes where the balance of power lies—namely with those who determine how time is allocated and for what purposes. The subversive possibilities offered by sloth and deliberate delay which are open to those occupying low social strata in the world at large do not exist to any great extent for the prisoner (or, on the occasions where they might, the punitive consequences of availing of them are disproportionately large). The timetable is the regulatory device par excellence.

Martel (2006) shows how the prison timetable becomes vital to prisoners as a framework within which they can express a measure of agency. While fixed schedules are alienating in the sense that they constrain human activity, those subjected to them always retain some decision-making potential, even if this is no more than deciding not to avail of recreation when it is offered, forgoing visits, or declining to eat at prison mealtimes, preferring instead to buy food for consumption when desired. According to Martel, 'However rigid, dominating and time-consuming it may be, the carceral schedule becomes vital to prisoners, as it gradually becomes familiar and provides much needed reference points to those estranged from their habitual environment in the community' (p. 597).

One of the prisoners interviewed by Medlicott (1999: 223) gave a good illustration of how he strove to bring outside life into synchrony (even harmony) with life inside, as to attempt the opposite would have been futile: 'I telephone the wife every day, and twice at weekends. We get up at 5 a.m. and write to each other. Then we have a cup of tea together at about 8 o'clock. She's changed her meal times, so that we eat together at lunch and tea.' Both husband and wife derived comfort from the fact that although forced to live apart they could create a common life (or at least an imitation of one) by sharing a schedule. Echols (2013) came up with a similar scheme during his time in solitary confinement on death row in Arkansas. On the night of every full moon he positioned a container full of water in his cell so that it caught the moon's reflection. Before sunrise he moved it to another location in the cell where direct sunlight would never reach it. His wife followed the same procedure and at the same time each night they would take a sip of 'moon water' while thinking of each other: 'In that moment we were united, no matter how far apart we might be' (p. 391).

One clear advantage of routinization is that time passes more quickly. Predictability, stability, and sameness speed time along. According to Serge (1970: 116), 'The mechanical rhythm of each day, repeated *ad infinitum*, leads to an almost painlessly automatized existence.' This emotional numbness is welcomed because it makes life bearable, but feared at the same time at because it might usher in a form of passivity and institutionalization that proves difficult to shake off.

9

Critical Fractions:
Life Lived and Life Left

The balance between time spent at liberty and time spent in custody is important. As it shifts in favour of the latter the prisoner must increasingly draw sustenance from prison experience and living in the present becomes inevitable. Other than a foolish or frustrating forward-looking stance there is nowhere for the gaze to rest; the past has receded so far that it is out of view. Many prisoners will have effected this temporal shift long before they arrive at this tipping point, either because they see the adaptive value of so doing or have exhausted the stock of non-prison memories. This is an acute problem for the prisoner serving a sentence of life without parole, whose relationship to the external world becomes so tenuous over time that it ceases to hold out any meaning. Often these men and women continue to hope that they will again experience life outside the prison before they die. This is part self-delusion, part irrepressible optimism, and it remains inchoate; were it to have concrete plans attached it would serve as a seedbed for despair.

The Pain Quotient

While the magnitude of the challenge is significant, the burden of prison time can be borne. What I term the 'pain quotient' (PQ) is the hurdle that must be overcome to make life bearable. This is offered as a device for thinking about the interplay between time and imprisonment in general terms. But in line with the analysis presented throughout this book, it applies with particular force to the experience of the man or woman held apart, for whom the dilemma of time comes into sharper focus. The two key variables involved in estimating the PQ are time to be served (this takes account of sentence length and point in sentence) and life to be lived (this takes account of chronological age and life expectancy). The sentence itself, or the amount of time served, or the prisoner's age tell us little when considered independently. They are merely numbers in the penal lottery. It is only when they are viewed dynamically, and interactively, that these factors can be used to sketch out the temporal parameters of pain. As the ratio of 'time to be served' and 'life to be lived' changes, so too does the challenge to be resolved in terms of making sense of prison time.

The PQ is smallest for a prisoner who has a lot of life to live and a short period of time left to serve. For such an individual, time orientation is relatively unimportant. It is greatest for the prisoner whose life expectancy is shorter than his prison term and for whom the absence of a non-prison future must be confronted. Given how skilful humans are at adapting to extreme environments, the state of suspended animation in which prisoners exist—described by Johnson and McGunigall-Smith (2008: 339) as 'the social equivalent of a coma'—can be continued as long as there is a possible future to exclude from consideration. When there clearly is not—impending old age may bring this into focus—then significant adjustments are required and it is crucial to devise a strategy for negotiating the temporal landscape of imprisonment.

Any prisoner's PQ can be ascertained objectively. This is the first of two steps required to identify the salience of time orientation. While the PQ indicates the scale of the challenge, it says little about how likely it is to be overcome. The second step requires the integration of this measurement with individual perceptions and preconceptions, the most important of which revolve around assessments of legitimacy. For example, consider two prisoners of equal age and health status, who have arrived at the same point in sentences of identical length; the PQ will be the same in each case. However, if one believes that the sentence received was comparatively light for the crime committed, and the other feels that their treatment was excessively harsh, the burden will be heavier for the latter individual. In tandem these steps provide a conceptual framework that helps us to understand the magnitude of the challenge presented by time.

Farber (1944) explored how attitudes, behaviour, and emotions were influenced by the amount of time a prisoner had served and how much more he expected to serve, and also what factors shaped time perspectives. Interviews conducted at Iowa State Penitentiary suggested that the extent to which prisoners suffered (or did 'harder time') was unrelated to sentence length or to time served but was influenced by the extent to which they felt their sentence was deserved or that they had been held, unfairly, beyond the point at which they should have been released. This research was carried out at a time when there was much more discretion associated with the release process. Few prisoners knew with any certainty how long they would serve and this calculation depended on the vagaries (as they saw it) of the parole board. This ambiguity was a source of considerable stress and whenever a request for clemency was rejected prisoners had to repack their hopes, reset their horizons, and get on with their sentences.

Farber found a curvilinear relationship between age and suffering, with young men being relatively sanguine—there is plenty of time ahead, they will still be fit and capable when released and imprisonment is a not overly bothersome interlude. Old men, whose lives were mostly lived, were similarly unperturbed. (While the PQ might have been high for members of the older group they possessed the skills required to soften its impact.) It was the group in the middle who exhibited most signs of desperation—while they stagnated in prison the best years of their lives slipped by and there would be too much ground to be made up on release. The relationship between suffering and time expected to be served was curvilinear too. Those prisoners who expected to be released soon (defined as within two years) and those who expected their release to be some way distant (at least five years) were less troubled than the intermediate group. Temporal orientation was more important than sentence length and time served. Where the release date was uncertain, but in the middle distance, and the prisoner was not too young to be careless about time (there is plenty more left) or too old to care (life has been lived already), the suffering was likely to be greatest. It was exacerbated if the individual felt their sentence was excessive or that they had been kept inside for too long.

Like Farber's model, the concept of PQ stresses the importance of the relationship between time served and time left to serve, but the uncertainty that was associated with the latter calculation in Iowa in the 1940s is less pressing in the early twenty-first century given the erosion or, in some jurisdictions, elimination, of parole discretion. As the reduction in indefiniteness has been accompanied by a significant increase in sentence lengths, the pain of uncertainty has been replaced in many cases by a distancing of release to a point beyond a prisoner's life expectancy; what is certain now is that they will never be released (on the challenges faced by the elderly prisoner see Crawley and Sparks 2005). Two of the three most significant predictors of suffering for Farber's prisoners—not knowing when they would get out and feeling that they had been held for too long—had diminished in significance for their counterparts 70 years later. The third factor—a perception that the sentence itself was unjust—may still have applied, although perhaps with less force given the standardization that has accompanied sentencing reforms; disproportionately severe sentences are less personal today.

Farber's work made a useful contribution in its shift away from an emphasis on single variables, such as sentence length or time served, as predictors of prisoner adjustment, and towards an elaboration of the experience of prison time that stressed perception, interaction, and flux. These insights are incorporated, and built upon, in the estimation of PQ which addresses a situation where there is more clarity about factors which varied greatly in the past. Indeed, its utility is dependent upon an ability to specify, with some precision, certain key durations and the relationships between them. Not many prisoners have written about how such a calculus might be applied to their lives. Indeed, the ability to predict life expectancy with a reasonable degree of accuracy presupposes a level of rational calculation that might not be found in many prisoners (or, for that matter, free citizens). Zeno (1968: 65) is an exception: 'I was thirty-eight when I was convicted, and if I serve twelve years I shall be fifty when I get out. With an expectation of seventy years I shall have twenty left to me. Can the first dozen be worth enduring for the marginal and problematic benefits of the remaining score?' Zeno decided that the anticipated benefits outweighed the costs, serving nine years of a life sentence before he was released. While his estimate of 'time to be served' proved to be exaggerated, so, too, did his estimate of 'life to be lived' as he died eleven years after regaining his liberty, aged 58 (Morgan 1998: 25).

The PQ takes account of how objective indices such as the fraction of life left to be lived, even if approximate, can (and must) be integrated with subjective interpretations around the purpose and fairness of one's confinement, and choices about how to influence the perception of time's passing. It is relevant to all prisoners regardless of where, with whom, or for how long they are incarcerated. There is a biological dimension here in that the female prisoner must contend with the diminution of her reproductive capacity and the possibility that incarceration may remove the opportunity for future motherhood. Prisoners play an active role in determining whether, and when, the PQ is felt as overwhelming. There are differing degrees of proficiency to be observed in this regard, with some individuals demonstrating an almost serene accomplishment and others struggling daily. The approaches that have been found most effective among the subgroup of prisoners who must grapple with time in the absence of company are set out in Chapter 10. In what follows the overall pattern of prisoner adjustment is reconceptualized, and reconfigured, to take account of shifting temporal orientation.

An Adjustment Curve

In a review of the subjective effects of punishment, Bronsteen et al. (2009: 1047) suggested that 'incarceration appears to result in substantial psychological distress upon imprisonment followed by gains in well-being as the prison term progresses'. The pains of confinement are most intense early on in a sentence and diminish somewhat thereafter before resurfacing as release approaches. The U-shaped adjustment curve described by Wheeler (1961) relates time spent, and time remaining, in custody to prisoner behaviour. Wheeler found that during the first six months and the last six months of their terms prisoners were likely to conform to conventional values and to the demands of the authorities, whereas in the intervening period they were guided by the norms of other prisoners; they underwent a process of 'prisonization' to use the term coined by Clemmer (1940: 299). The impact is marked for those isolated in the initial period of their imprisonment when the risk of suicide and self-harm is elevated. This is a particular problem in some Scandinavian countries when prisoners on remand are isolated and the uncertainty about how long they will spend there, and whether they will be convicted, adds to the pressure (Shalev 2008: 29–30; Smith 2006: 497–500).

In other words, when the individual's time perspective has not yet been recalibrated to take account of the demands of imprisonment, or when they are reorienting themselves for life after release, they are more likely to conform to conventional standards. In between it is the inmate code to which they subscribe and the values of the institution and the wider community are rejected. There are variations according to sentence length with some short-term prisoners never resetting their time horizons. Wheeler's model suggests that a growing number of prisoners without release dates augurs badly for prison managers as there is less chance that the prisonization process will go into reverse: prisoners who do not anticipate release will not feel pressure to realign their values with those of the wider community. Wheeler's empirical findings and the associated hypotheses have found, at best, qualified support (e.g. Akers et al. 1977; Atchley and McCabe 1968; Garabedian 1963). Nonetheless, his central message remains valid: introducing a temporal dimension to the analysis of prison life adds to our understanding of prison culture and prisoner conduct. Wheeler was keen to shift the emphasis away from a preoccupation with how long prisoners had served and towards how long they had left to serve. The latter interval, he argued, was potentially of greater significance in terms of determining attitudes and behaviour.

The U-shaped pattern of prisoner adaptation is closely related to the temporal perspective adopted by prisoners where tedium follows tumult and gives way to trepidation (see Table 9.1). Jones and Schmid (2000: 31), whose account of the phenomenology of imprisonment is informed by the prison experience of the first author, noted that, 'the problem posed by their imprisonment shifts from an outsider's fixation on physical survival to an insider's focus on enduring prison boredom'. First of all, newcomers are concerned with the protection of their bodily integrity and dealing with preconceived notions of what prison is likely to involve. Then they become preoccupied with boredom and how to mitigate its effects. Life is about fending off boredom rather than fending off other prisoners. The challenge is to deal with a tedious existence through adaptation and diversion.

What disturbs tranquillity is the collision of different time perspectives. At the point of entry to prison, 'now' competes with what was and generally loses out. At the point of departure from prison, 'now' competes with what might be, and again ends up the loser. In each case the current orientation becomes the focus of

Table 9.1 The three Ts of temporal adjustment

Tumult	The initial phase of imprisonment is chaotic because the present is contrasted (unfavourably) with an immediate past that still resonates strongly. When combined with remorse and withdrawal from drugs and alcohol (factors that independently interfere with clarity of thought) as well as from society, the first few days and weeks of incarceration can be especially painful. The individual is in a liminal state, betwixt and between the 'real' world and the convict society. There is much to learn and many new experiences are consigned to memory.
Tedium	After the initial period, the immediate past, which is now a prison past, becomes part of an extended present which the prisoner inhabits in a kind of suspended animation. Yesterday, today, and tomorrow are melded into an indistinguishable and timeless banality. Increasing effort is required to keep the past alive. Memories fade, significant events lose their lustre unless they are revivified through retelling, and the reservoir of meaningful personal narratives runs dry. An equilibrium is found where the focus is on managing the present rather than examining the past or planning the future.
Trepidation	When a release date looms, a future, and the possibilities it offers (even if fantastical), must be juxtaposed against the unremitting sameness that has defined life hitherto. It becomes increasingly difficult to suppress thoughts of an alternative, non-prison, life. An extended time horizon takes on a new salience. This contrast causes renewed turbulence.

dissatisfaction and angst. Prisoners seem to cope best when they reduce their dependence on external points of reference. Over the course of a prison sentence there is a shift in emphasis from variety and novelty to monotony. Early in their sentences prisoners struggle to come to terms with a threatening new environment where time is elongated and the perspective is on the past and towards an uncertain future. This is followed by a period when the focus is on the present, they have become habituated to the regime and, when viewed retrospectively, time appears to have sped by. Now they are in the 'long, mindless lope' that Schroeder (1976: 136) described. This is the rut into which prisoners settle to ease the passage of time. As the finishing line comes into view—either the prospect of release or a return to congregate living—there is a change of temporal pace and this allows old anxieties and new uncertainties to become influential again, causing destabilization.

Schroeder described how prisoners 'live by ontological rather than chronological time' (p. 184). He argued that during the initial period of confinement, time was stretched as the individual learned to come to terms with a plethora of new experiences and anxieties and to acquire the requisite life skills. Beyond this point 'the repetitions begin to occur so regularly that that's normally the point at which a long-timer draws in his horns, lets himself go numb and settles in for the ride, developing a steady, almost drugged rhythm that most effectively kills the time' (p. 184). As release approaches, anxieties resurface and there is a sense of trepidation about what lies ahead. This progression is very consistently reported. For example, Zietz (1961: 51) described how 'It is only at the beginning of his sentence and when he feels his time for release is near that time becomes an important factor.' In the intervening period it is 'practically meaningless' (p. 51). Molineux (1903: 23) recalled how, as he awaited execution, normal relationships with time were ruptured and his life was characterized by 'an endless waiting without expectancy'.

Most long-term prisoners arrive at a point where what they desire is simply to serve their time without tumult. As Zeno (1968) put it, the goal was to avoid peaks and troughs. Drawing upon a nautical image he described his plan as follows, 'I might well find a way of oiling the waters and creating an artificial calm. I might sail equably through the years, steering a middle course which avoids the rocks of authority, and keeps me in the lee of the bitter wind which blows continually out from my fellows' (p. 65). It takes considerable prison experience to render these waters tranquil and to navigate them successfully, but with maturity and effort, many prisoners manage to do so. For the prisoner who can choose a travelling companion—an option denied to those in solitary confinement—it is often someone with a similar PQ who fits the bill. Zeno described a process of sliding 'more or less painlessly through the years' once he had made a bearable 'groove' for himself (p. 179). When in the groove his direction of travel was virtually guaranteed. This is a popular and long-established analogy. Eighty years before Zeno committed his reflections to paper, George Bidwell (1888: 407) had written of 'running smoothly in the even groove of prison life'.

Two pacifists who were imprisoned during the First World War charted the stages through which the political prisoner passed, ranging from 'excitation', where there was a heightened awareness of the new environment and how it contrasted with what had been left behind, to 'apathy' (Hobhouse and Brockway 1922: 488, 490). The final stage was characterized by 'settled apathy and torpor. It seems to be a state of relative "non-desire," in which all vital functions are performed with an absence of energy or tone. The routine goes on mechanically and the passage of time is no longer noticed. Externally the prisoner appears to be calm and free from suffering' (pp. 490–1). This is a good description of how one can slip into the rut of prison life and ease through time without too much unnecessary friction. It accords with accounts that describe how the highs and lows of life are evened out, leaving a more constant, and more bearable, emotional trajectory.

Structuring Prison Time

For Meisenhelder (1985: 42) human activity is characterized by 'a casting of oneself toward the future'. Phenomenologically speaking, 'there is the future world of the not-yet that provides meaning to human existence' (p. 42) and this impacts on temporal orientation. The structure of prison time differs in that 'the prison life-world is without a meaningful zone of the future' (p. 46). The two essential characteristics of prison time, according to Meisenhelder, are 'a feeling of waiting and a sense of time as a burden' (p. 44). (In truth, these go hand in hand rather than being conceptually distinct.) The lack of meaningful activity and the unvarying repetition of routine activities contribute to a sense of boredom—always situational, sometimes existential—on the part of men and women whose futures have been deferred, sometimes indefinitely, and whose presents must be lived according to the dictates of others. For these reasons time is felt as burdensome rather than as a resource to be strategically deployed in pursuit of individual goals. It no longer has value because it is scarce but becomes a hyper-inflated currency, vast quantities of which must be disposed of in the face of an ever-diminishing return.

According to Meisenhelder (1985) there are two primary modes of adjustment to the new temporal arrangements. First, the prisoner 'creates time' by disrupting the pattern of prison activities. This is 'most frequently accomplished by creating dramatic incidents to which others must of necessity respond' (p. 47; this is akin to the style of 'killing time' in the scheme outlined by Calkins (1970) and reviewed in Chapter 8). The novelty of the situation and the prisoner's attentiveness to it mean that time is felt to pass more quickly. Examples of how time is created, according to Meisenhelder, include fights, riots, and escape attempts as well as more mundane activities such as mutual verbal abuse and visits to the prison shop. By this analysis, 'Risk-taking and adventure, thus, are acts of resistance through which inmates create time rather than passively serve it' (p. 48).

This argument had previously been made by Galtung (1961) who, drawing on his own experience of imprisonment as a conscientious objector in Norway, noted that anything that disturbs the regularity of the prison has the effect of altering the time perspective of the prisoner until order is restored. Spontaneity and unpredictability can soften the corrosive effects of a rigid regime. This leads to 'conscious interference with prison routines, especially by infractions of the rules and by conscious or unconscious provocation of illness' (p. 117). While feigning illness has a long history, breaking rules to pass the time is less common, although some prisoners incorporate occasional acts of resistance into their repertoire of survival stratagems (see Chapter 10).

The claim that chaos is introduced to speed up time does not fit neatly with the empirical reality, especially when it comes to the long-term prisoners for whom the demands of temporal reorientation are most pressing. Generally speaking this is a group that favours a predictable life, without highs and lows, where a course can be charted, and followed, with minimal deviation. Disruptive behaviour, and the undesirable consequences of disciplinary infractions that may follow, are at odds with this lifestyle. Prisoners whose PQ is high, such as those serving life without parole, tend to form stable and pacific prison communities. The reasons why prisoners become involved in conflicts and violence have been set out in some detail (e.g. Edgar et al. 2012) and the extent to which such behaviour is an attempt to break the monotony should not be exaggerated.

Also, the attention demanded by a crisis leads to a sense of 'protracted duration', with time seeming to pass more slowly, not a state of affairs that the experienced prisoner would wish to create. In a thought experiment about how prison life would feel if activities varied by chance each day rather than following a rigid timetable, Galtung (1961: 120) conceded that, while the accompanying unpredictability would no doubt relieve tedium and alter time perspectives and 'might prepare the prisoners for the capriciousness of real life', it would carry its own disadvantages: 'Inability to predict might be added punishment, and if this were true, prisoners might ask for a little institutionalized certainty, for the one certain "yes" or "no" they could use as a basis for orientation in prison life.' Penal institutions need clear routines with a fixed temporal order. Indeed, if prisoners are to succeed in subverting the timetable they must be confident that they can anticipate its orderly unfolding.

There is one major drawback associated with establishing a rhythm to prison life that allows time to pass unnoticed. It is that the prisoner who gets into a rut may worry that they have become institutionalized, that by sacrificing autonomy on the altar of convenience they are courting mental deterioration. For experienced prisoners, especially those who have survived prolonged isolation, there is an ever-present fear of becoming a 'docile body'. They are conscious of the possibility that 'Time penetrates the body and with it all the meticulous controls of power' (Foucault 1991: 152). In other words, this is a survival strategy with a barb.

The second style of adjustment is what Meisenhelder (1985: 49) terms 'marking time'. This involves using the institution's schedule as the framework for distinguishing one part of the day from the next, or one day from the succeeding or preceding one and it maps onto the styles of passing, doing and filling time described by Calkins (1970). The rigidity of the schedule and the pointlessness of many of the activities mean that this is not generally an effective way of speeding the passage of time. As a result it is supplemented with subjective markers of time such as leisure or educational activities (which individuals can calibrate according to their interests and abilities and which can be punctuated with targets such as the completion of a particular curriculum or the passing of an examination); the flow of prisoners in and out of the institution and the recruitment or replacement of staff (which act as temporal reference points—what I call 'time anchors'—as well as providing material for debate and speculation); and media engagement (especially television viewing, where personal preferences can allow a measure of control over the content of one's hours).

Time anchors are important because they allow for events to be organized and for time periods to be differentiated in a way that makes sense to observers, and creates shared understandings and memories, even if the relationship to calendric time is imprecise. During the ninth year of his captivity, when receiving

attention for a knee injury, Albert Speer, Hitler's favourite architect, told the medical aide that he had experienced a similar problem about two years earlier. However, the clinical notes revealed
that five years had in fact elapsed since the last treatment. Speer
(2010: 258) noted the reason for this temporal distortion in his
diary thus: 'where there are no events, there is no time'. For fertile
women in prison the menstrual cycle, and its disruption, together
with the advent of the menopause, act as additional time anchors
(see Wahidin and Tate 2005).

By Meisenhelder's (1985: 51) account, prisoners feel that time
passes more slowly during the initial and final phases of their sentences, while it speeds up during the middle phase (Leal 2001: 57
offers a similar view). This would seem to be at odds with what
prisoner accounts suggest, namely, that the intense activity and
excitement of the early phase mean that days are full and varied,
time rushes past, and a focus remains on the past and is tinged
with regret, remorse, anger and occasionally relief. The framework provided by Flaherty (1999) reconciles these two apparently
competing perspectives. During the early phase there is much
to learn and absorb and the extent that this experience is novel
determines whether time seems to pass quickly or slowly. During
the middle phase when the focus is on the present and the passing days are largely indistinguishable one from the other, time
drags as it is experienced—unless it can be rendered full of 'routine complexity'—but seems to have flown in retrospect. The final
phase involves enhanced activity as release preparations are made
and time perspectives are readjusted towards the future. But the
speedier passage of these fuller days is cancelled out by the sense
that as the release date approaches and is looked forward to with
increasing anticipation, time begins to crawl; by attending to time,
its passage is slowed. Meisenhelder's model is flawed because it
does not take sufficient account of the interplay between temporal
orientation at different points in a sentence, the development of a
prisoner's expertise when it comes to taming time, and the difference between how time is experienced as it passes compared with
how its passage is viewed in retrospect.

Threats to the Self

The long-term prisoners who spoke with Cohen and Taylor
(1972: 104–11) articulated a fear of deterioration (both mental

and physical) as they attempted to navigate a temporal landscape that offered few meaningful signposts apart from a release date that was either unbearably distant or, for those serving life sentences, enervatingly uncertain. To avoid the pain associated with the dashing of dreams that might not be realized these men tried to eschew thinking about the future. But at the same time they clung tenaciously to a belief that their incarceration was a hiatus that would eventually conclude with the resumption of normal social activities, carried out on their terms. They were in a liminal state, adamant that what they were experiencing behind bars was not life, but an anaemic substitute for it, and that full-blooded living would resume upon release.

What prisoners describe as a fear of mental deterioration may be better thought of as a fear of being unable to revive their pre-prison identities after adapting to an abnormal environment. They are anxious that they will lose the sense of their identity enduring over time. Perhaps it is not so much a concern about being psychologically impaired as one about being changed beyond recognition and, possibly, beyond repair. (Some, of course, work hard to drive this change process in an effort to distance themselves from the misdeeds and regrets of the past. They desire to be different and to cast off their pre-prison identities.) They may emerge fortified, but different, and whether this difference will interfere with their ability to lead fully social lives is a cause of anxiety. Psychological survival may require irreversible change and it is this prospect that alarms.

These fears are well grounded as the conditions of solitary confinement increase the likelihood of what Turner (1978: 1) described as a 'role-person merger'. Long-term solitaries are afraid that the role of prisoner will come to define them so completely that their previous identity is overwritten. As time passes the person and the role come into increasingly close alignment and they fear a complete merger such that they will end up being no more than their prison identity. Prisoners who withstand time through withdrawal fear that they will forever be withdrawn. Those who become self-sufficient worry they will lose the capacity for intimacy. It is not only psychological unravelling that prisoners fear. They are also anxious about not being able to return to the core of who they were before they entered prison. They are afraid that the identity changes wrought to play the role of prisoner will acquire an irrevocable quality and are concerned to remain identifiably the same to themselves and to others despite the erosion of character caused by an unyielding environment.

The challenge of survival was described by Bettelheim (1960: 127), reflecting on a year spent in Dachau and Buchenwald, as 'to protect my inner self in such a way that if, by any good fortune, I should regain liberty, I would be approximately the same person I was when deprived of liberty'. To achieve this approximate result—the best that any prisoner can hope for, even in far less aversive circumstances than a concentration camp—required splitting off a core self that might retain its integrity from the rest of the personality that would have to be remoulded to adapt to the new circumstances. The prisoner's fear, as captured by Bettelheim, is that in the process they will lose something important and they must strive to ensure that this is not their mind. The degree of identity transformation required to deal with lengthy isolation is so far-reaching that it is understandable why those who do this work worry greatly about the extent to which it can be undone. When life is stripped of intimacy (or the possibility of same) it loses much of its meaning and the individual so deprived sees their emotional range reduced and fears that their capacity for full-blooded engagement will be forever limited (on the pathological consequences of dividing the self to cope with a sense of ontological insecurity see Laing 1960).

Prisoners are bracketed off from family and community and while they continue to age, in many ways their opportunities for growth are suspended. Sapsford (1983: 76) found that prison time was viewed as 'an interruption of life, not a part of it, like a form of cryogenic suspension through which the patient remains fully conscious'. This idea has lengthy antecedents. In 1922, Mary Gordon, the first female prison inspector in Great Britain, described the prison as 'a place of suspended animation' (cited in Brown 2003: 24). Seventy-one years later, one of her successors, Stephen Tumim (1993: 2), recapitulated this theme, when he remarked that 'if prisons are essentially inactive places, those contained in them are locked in a time capsule until release'. For the prisoner in solitary confinement who is further denied opportunities for meaningful engagement with his or her fellows this suspension is more profound.

Dostoyevsky (2004: 79; emphasis in original) described a similar process when he observed that while a free man is enmeshed in the web of life, the convict is in a sort of limbo where reality is temporarily suspended, believing 'that he is, so to speak, *not at home*, but on a visit'. Betancourt (2010: 439) described her six years as a hostage in the Colombian jungle as a 'space of life outside time'. For prisoners who know they will never be released their status is not liminal, they are no longer betwixt and between two worlds but immured in a new one that has drawn permanent borders around their existence (see Jewkes 2005). They face a different challenge in temporal terms. So too the prisoner who faces execution, for whom there exists an unusual degree of clarity around when time will cease to be of significance. Drawing on his personal experience of death row, Zietz (1961: 51) observed that the conception of time for the condemned man is unique as, 'The scheduled date of execution becomes the known end of time.'

It is important to note that while the fear of deterioration is a perennial concern among prisoners it may be exaggerated. As Taylor (1961: 373) put it: 'The mental vacuity, dwindling memory, and inability to concentrate are all elements of the bogey of deterioration that forms one of the constantly recurring themes about men in captivity.' (The bogeyman, of course, is feared because of what he represents even when he is known not to exist.) While long-term prisoners worry about mental deterioration the reality is that in the main they learn to develop effective coping strategies. They work hard to maintain a level of mental energy that is ebbing away more slowly than they may think. Based on prisoner self-reports, Flanagan (1980: 155) concluded that 'most inmates do not report that imprisonment has seriously threatened their emotional well-being' (adding the caveat that a desire to project an image of strength and self-reliance may have exercised a dampening effect on the acknowledgement of such frailties). Similarly, in a study of life sentenced prisoners, Sapsford (1983: 22–3, 60) found that they were fearful of mental decline but usually managed to stave it off and that the deleterious consequences of prolonged confinement were sometimes exaggerated, the research evidence being, at best, 'patchy, inconclusive and on occasions contradictory' with the result that there was 'no evidence whatsoever for a general syndrome of "institutionalization" or "deterioration"'.

The finding that prisoners tend to adapt successfully to confinement, after an initially stressful period, mirrors a pattern more widely found in human society. Many life events, whatever their magnitude and whether negative or positive, do not have a lasting effect on the well-being of the parties concerned. In a review of the field of 'hedonic adaptation', Bronsteen et al. (2009: 1049–54) made the important point that while prisoners may adapt to many of the vagaries of incarceration, they are less well equipped to deal with its post-release legacy, particularly when this involves chronic illness, reduced employment prospects, defunct family ties, and community rejection; such life changes often prove stubbornly resistant to adaptation.

It might be argued that prisoners have a disproportionate fear of decomposition that is highlighted by their incarceration in an environment where time has a circular quality and where they watch the outside world speed by, afraid that they will be left behind. As they complete lap after monotonous lap of life according to the dictates of others and against an inflexible schedule, their families and friends at liberty surge ahead on a tide of time. People in the free world are carried forward in time regardless of their desires while prisoners feel that they cannot advance, however much they might like to. When there are so few changes in routine, so few milestones and major events, things seem to progress hardly at all. As Koestler (1942: 186) expressed it: 'Life in prison is a constant repetition of the same situations, the same thoughts and schemes. One lives and thinks in a vicious circle. The mind is made giddy by it; there is no escape. There is no progress, even time does not move forward in a straight line; it reappears in the same form.'

Cohen and Taylor's finding that prisoners feared mental deterioration has been widely replicated. Suedfeld et al. (1982: 330) found that when prisoners were first placed in solitary 'they were afraid that serious mental or physical deterioration would occur' but that 'in general this expectation was not borne out'. Similarly their anxiety about not being able to adjust was usually groundless and after a difficult few days, most adapted successfully. Koestler (1942: 116), awaiting execution in a Spanish prison in 1937, described how: 'The daily routine of life, even of life in a condemned cell, cannot sustain for long the melodrama of despair.' He found that he could draw upon unexpected resources to fortify his spirit, observing that: 'This is why situations lived through are never so bad in reality as in imagination. Nature sees to it that trees do not grow beyond a certain height, not even the trees of suffering' (p. 118).

Breytenbach (1984: 143) also commented on the individual's capacity to endure, relating time (as it is felt and remembered) to the process of adaptation thus:

Some periods are far longer than others. The first days...are interminable. You never expect to survive the first month. The first year...rears up in front of you like an unclimbable mountain—and you say to yourself: if one year is as bad as this, how in the name of King Kong and I am I going to survive the other eight?...Still, the same events coming around again, the rhythms being repeated, the familiarity of your situation—these deaden you to the passing of time. You look down from the bridge and you don't remember any water having passed under it. The past has the taste of water and you can't imagine now why it was so traumatic then. You haven't aged: the years were empty.

The same process is described by many: the unbearable is borne, the future recedes, and the lack of novelty compresses time so that the tedium of years has an amnesic quality. Returning to Koestler (1942: 119): 'The astonishing thing, the puzzling thing, the consoling thing about this time was that it passed.' Even under the most arduous of circumstances when each minute seems unbearably attenuated, it passes and another one follows. In other words, the gradient of decline turns out to be less steep than first imagined.

The struggle against time is given added impetus when the prisoner runs out of memories.

The Erosion of Memory

Salman Rushdie (2010: 8) described memory as 'the fuel that takes you back up the river of Time.' When the supply has been fully depleted the journey can no longer be attempted. The prisoner in solitary confinement is acutely aware of the finite nature of this fuel reserve. Wilbert Rideau (2011: 63) realized that a point arrives in a long sentence when one can no longer look to the past for memories to sustain one in the present. He captured this with his observation that 'old memories no longer bridge the gap'. The outside world has become so distant that it cannot be related to, or conjured up, in a meaningful way. Foote (1886: 116) noted how 'as the senses were unexercised, thought worked on memory until the brain seemed gnawing itself, as a shipwrecked man might assuage his thirst at his own veins'.

Christopher Burney (1962) was held in solitary confinement in Occupied France during the Second World War. He cultivated an energetic life of the mind to pass the time and this is humorously and self-deprecatingly described in his book, where he recounts 'holding the most absurd internal dialogues and believing them of great importance' (p. 127). These soliloquies were an effective diversion, keeping his mind off the cold and hunger and uncertain future and providing a sense of ontological security: 'I enjoyed the pastime and valued it, perhaps inordinately. For I viewed myself as a free man, waiting for the door to open on a new life' (p. 127). It goes without saying that such pursuits require a capacious and curious mind, which Burney, a bilingual army officer, clearly possessed. He drew great sustenance from the pieces of torn newspaper and pages ripped from books that were provided for use as toilet paper, or as he puts it, with characteristically dry humour: 'if I was lucky, I might have been given a new supply of paper—for a purpose quite unconnected with literature—and if I had not already learned its contents by heart, I could read it through and through until I had' (p. 21). From these scraps he derived much intellectual satisfaction.

Even the most talented and imaginative individual will run out of raw material for the mental furnace at some point and Burney knew that after an 18-month stay in solitary he was exhausting the internal resources required for continued sanity. The metronome was beginning to change tempo, signalling a potential loss of control. Beyond it further cogitation would rapidly descend into unproductive and damaging rumination. 'As long as my brain worked, solitude served a purpose, but I could see that it was slowly exhausting the fuel with which it had started, and if it stopped from inanition I would have nothing left but cold and hunger, which would make short work of me' (pp. 169–70). As Abbott (1981: 46–7) described this process, 'Memory is arrested in the hole [segregation unit]...Memory is not enriched by any further experience...As life in the hole, in the pure terrain of time, continues, your passions are aroused less and less with the help of memories and more and more by your ideals.' Clinging to a belief in justice or peace or politics or truth provides the weary traveller with sustenance for a few more furlongs of the journey. But because these ideals are so difficult to live up to in a life that has been deliberately stripped of external markers of meaning, they can become too slender to support the burden of prisoner expectation or, worse still, morph into empty mocking slogans, reminders of what cannot be.

The Irish republican Thomas Clarke (1922: 93), who served 15 years penal servitude in British prisons during the 1880s and

1890s, acknowledged that some prisoners were better able to bear their situation than others, but given enough time the system would win out regardless, in that

the person who goes into prison with a mind well stocked with healthy ideas will take longer to break down than the person ill-educated, or who carries in with him comparatively few ideas. While the man with a well-stored mind stands a better chance when 'up against' the silent system, yet no matter how well he may be equipped in this respect the system will win against him in the end.

Clarke described how, over time, the nourishment was gradually extracted from memories until all that remained was a bitter husk:

In the early years of the imprisonment he may be safe enough whilst his memory furnishes him with subject after subject to give the mind pleasurable occupation as he turns them over. In this way thoughts and ideas one after the other are turned over and examined until finally the whole stock has been under review. Commencing again, idea after idea is examined afresh, but with far less interest than the first time ... Finally there comes a time when by this process of elimination there remains not a single idea of the original stock that has not been quite 'played out' and has now become hateful. The silent system then wins, for the mind, though more or less enfeebled by this time, must occupy itself with something, and the dreary wretchedness and misery of the convict prison that have been kept at arm's length during the struggle now get their innings, while the spectre of insanity hovers close by waiting to take charge and complete the work of the silent system. (pp. 93–4)

Writing about the inherently social nature of the self, Mead (1934) recognized that the dialogue with the self requires renewal and refreshment through interaction. In the absence of social intercourse it atrophies:

But it is impossible to conceive of a self arising outside of social experience. When it has arisen we can think of a person in solitary confinement for the rest of his life, but who still has himself as a companion, and is able to think and to converse with himself as he had communicated with others ... This process of abstraction cannot be carried on indefinitely. One inevitably seeks an audience, has to pour himself out to somebody. (pp. 140–1)

Anderson (1994) recalled how he felt that he was beginning to fragment psychologically and that central to this process was the absence of meaningful human company. Without other people against whom he could make sense of himself he began to experience discomfiting insecurity: 'I'm afraid I'm beginning to lose my mind, to lose control completely. This solitary confinement is killing me. There is nothing to hold on to, no way to anchor my mind.... I never realized how dependent I was on other people, how much I needed to be around others, to feed off them mentally. Do I have anything of my own inside me? Is there any core there? Is everything I thought I was just based on a reflection of others?' (p. 219).

A self that frays in isolation can be more difficult to reconstruct. The process is insidious because there are no appropriate points of reference, no benchmarks of sanity. For those with occasional opportunities to talk, or who occupy themselves attempting to subvert the institution's strictures, or who are allowed a book, writing materials, radio, television, or opportunities to labour, it takes longer to arrive at this limit. Nevertheless, with time they will arrive there, especially as the balance between time lived outside and time lived inside flips in favour of the latter and the pain quotient increases. This is another reason why it is adaptive for the prisoner to root his or her thoughts in the present.

What is crucial to sustain psychological integrity is an occasional opportunity to replenish intellectual reservoirs so that the internal dialogue continues to flow. If it ceases there is a danger that the personality will collapse as there is no other source of stimulation to prop it up. These are more than just conversations. They are survival soliloquies. But they deteriorate in the retelling. As Koestler (1942: 118) put it: 'Just as the bear, hibernating, feeds on his own fat, so did I, in my head, feed from the dishes of thirty years of reading, learning and living. But my brain was drained dry and the few drops of thought that I squeezed out of it were pale, like thrice-brewed tea.'

After eight months of incarceration Bonhoeffer (2001: 42) described how his thoughts 'had grown rusty and tired' on account of being 'forced to live from the past', but that a letter from his best friend was a source of mental rejuvenation: 'When I read your letter yesterday, I felt as though a spring, without which my intellectual life was beginning to dry up, had begun once again to produce the first drops of water for a long, long time.' The fear that the pool of memories that nourishes the mind will evaporate is a perennial concern for prisoners. Bonhoeffer termed this his 'dialogue with the past' and wrote that his 'attempt to hold on to it and recover it, and above all, the fear of losing it, is the almost daily accompaniment of my life' (p. 113). His fear was that this dialogue would become too one-sided to sustain, that it would come to a stuttering halt, and that any attempt to resuscitate it might seem trite and, ultimately, futile. This would deprive him of an important existential plank.

Similarly, Echols (2013: 298), who spent 10 of his 18 years in prison in solitary confinement, recalled how:

You don't make many memories in prison—at least none you'd want to keep, or look back on fondly...The ones you came in with are the only ones you'll ever have. I would revisit mine constantly, trying desperately to wring every ounce of nourishment out of them that I possibly could. I was like a vampire, sucking them dry and then sifting through the dust in hopes of finding a drop I'd overlooked the previous hundred times.

The shrewd prisoner knows that the erosion of memory cannot be prevented and redoubles his or her efforts to live in the present and to devise a routine that keeps loneliness at bay and softens the impact of time. Describing the behaviour of a group of prisoners held in Occupied France during the Second World War in his novel *The Tenth Man*, Graham Greene (1986: 33) noted that 'there were as many times as there were prisoners'. While there is certainly some individual variation in how time is measured, experienced and combated, the response is not entirely idiosyncratic and a number of common approaches are presented in the next chapter.

10

Taming Time and Reframing Isolation

Scarce (2002: 304) described tussling with time thus: 'we inmates negotiated with time quite directly, attempting to make it do our will and refusing to bend to its heavy omnipresent hand'. But what does this entail in practical terms? 'Do your time and don't let the time do you', or a variation on this theme, is often heard in prisons, but what does it mean? The purpose of this chapter is to present a schema built from prisoner accounts to illustrate the most popular methods of taming time and thereby easing the burden of isolation. This analytical framework encapsulates seven stratagems that prisoners use to mitigate the harmful effects of time, alone, in a place not of their choosing and to a timetable not of their design. The emphasis is not on general patterns of adaptation to imprisonment but on how individuals respond to the specific exigencies of enforced solitude and the passing of long stretches of time. 'Surviving imprisonment compels the prisoner to develop new temporal competencies' according to Freeman (1997: ix). These involve making time bearable by speeding its passage, the sooner to return to the real world where life's arrow can resume its course.

Prisoners cannot avoid serving time in the sense of allowing it pass in an environment that they might rather exist outside of, but they struggle to avoid serving it as a slave would a master. While the need to tame time is most pronounced for prisoners whose pain quotient is high, the approaches they take may be used with profit by their peers for whom the relationship between 'time to be served' and 'life to be lived' is more favourable. Flaherty (2002: 380) commented that, 'Regrettably, the micromanagement of temporal experience has not been a topic of central concern in the sociology of time.' What follows is an attempt to make good this deficit by showing the steps that solitary prisoners have taken to modify the quality of their temporal experience. In the free world such modifications can have a playful quality. In prison this is a very serious business.

Some prisoners exacerbate their isolation as part of a deliberate survival strategy. Over the course of a long sentence family ties are difficult to maintain, and the trials and tribulations of those outside, which the prisoner is impotent to influence, can have an erosive effect on even the most committed relationships. Visits can make time harder to serve because they refocus time orientation and jolt the prisoner back to an alternative reality that is often an unhappy reminder of their predicament. Contacts with the outside world are painful reminders that while people they care about are changing, the prisoner is not. As Schroeder (1976: 135) put it in his memoir, 'The trouble with visits is that they won't let you forget.'

It was ever thus. Writing about his time in Holloway Gaol in London, Foote (1886) described how loved ones outside the prison were called to mind but their remembrance only served to reinforce their unavailability. As this prisoner recalled, the effects of the wandering mind were 'lovely in weal but terrible in woe' (p. 117). To avoid the inevitable frustration and distress, some prisoners sever these ties before time can corrode them. The attractions of disconnection are obvious but not unequivocal. As Flanagan (1980: 155) put it:

Some long-term inmates cauterise these relationships as a means of avoiding the anxiety and despair that accompany the separation. For the majority of prisoners who do not attempt this strategy, however, family ties become a two-edged sword over the years, providing encouragement and support and at the same time making it more difficult to do time.

In a later paper, Flanagan (1982: 118) captured this ambivalence when he observed that, 'The prisoner desperately seeks to keep contacts with the outside world salient, but adds to the stress of confinement by doing so.' While prisoners may declare that they would be better off without outside contacts, they also acknowledge that if their studied indifference to the outside world is fully reciprocated, then their prospects become bleaker still.

Toch (1992: 386) referred to the strategy of pre-emptively severing connections as the 'de-cathexis of relationships'. He described it as involving the suppression of thoughts of the outside world and the minimization of contact with lovers, families, and friends so that there can be an exclusive focus on coping with the tribulations of imprisonment. He added that while such a stance was widely recognized it was not always translated into action because it 'entails sacrifice of other coping options, which are those that call for outside support' (p. 387). Outside distractions give life meaning even if they make it more turbulent, and there are individual differences in the extent to which prisoners are prepared to make space in their lives for disruption over which they have no control, problems which they cannot ameliorate, and joy which is only ever partially shared. Given that female prisoners are more likely than their male counterparts to have children who depend on them, they may find the process of cutting ties to be more painful still.

After 40 days of isolation and cruel treatment at the hands of the Argentine army Timerman (1988) received a short letter from his wife. It had been written on the occasion of their twenty-seventh wedding anniversary and was accompanied by two candies. Furious and resentful he threw the letter into the latrine as soon as he had read it. The heartfelt missive had destroyed a protective shell he had painstakingly built around himself, which for its integrity required complete detachment from any reminder of the real world. This edifice, 'so heavily armored, so solid and irreplaceable, without cracks, has been penetrated by a letter and two candies...the structure collapses' (p. 85). The contrast between what he has left behind and what he must continue to endure becomes vivid and threatens to overwhelm. The prospect of once again stiffening his resolve becomes as colossal as it is essential. Should there be any doubt about the magnitude of this challenge Timerman dismisses it with his comment that, 'the chief enemy is not the electric shocks, but penetration from the outside world, with all its memories' (p. 85).

Prisoners who choose to deal with potential pain by cutting away the source and living the desiccated life that remains conspire (reluctantly) with the prison apparatus in dismantling their own humanity. When the view of self is restricted to what a prison setting reflects, this is life as beheld in a distorting mirror. Others manage a feat of compartmentalization whereby what is important to them outside is not terminated, but remains in aspic until release; before and after are thought of parenthetically. The danger of such an approach is obvious—that things will have changed irrevocably by this stage—but confronting this reality is deferred until it can be addressed at liberty; until then the notion of connection is enough. Still others continue to engage, but over the course of a long sentence, this is a strategy that requires a degree of confidence in the sturdiness of human relationships that few possess. According to a prisoner in Iowa State Penitentiary: 'A man is better off to break clear away [from outside contacts], but of his own and his people's accord, not because he's forced by authority. It shouldn't be done too sharply, though. The same thing holds for letters. A man could do better time that way' (Farber 1944: 223). This is a good expression of how it can be important to keep in touch during the tumultuous initial phase of adaptation but then to cope with the rest of the sentence it is easier to let go. Either no ties at all, or the strong and enduring bonds enjoyed by the fortunate few, are preferable to the vicissitudes of ordinary relationships.

In a book about imprisonment and prisoners' rights Fitzgerald (1977: 84) reported the following prisoner account: 'The value of an hour changes, and all the apparatus built up over the years for dealing with the passage of time suddenly becomes obsolete... It is not that time becomes irrelevant... No. It is merely that measured as the outside world measures it, time becomes intolerable. The prisoner has to learn how to deal with the passage of time in a different way.' Time in prison can have a tsunami-like quality with another wave of minutes and hours threatening to drown the prisoner every day. To avoid this fate many prisoners learn to tread water and some become adept at swimming against the tide.

A medley of their survival strokes, as revealed by their personal accounts, is summarized in Table 10.1. These are what I term the seven Rs of survival: Rescheduling, Removal, Reduction, Reorientation, Resistance, Raptness, and Reinterpretation. They lie within the prisoner's control and betoken a creative engagement with temporality which ranges along a continuum from passive withdrawal to frenetic activity. There are echoes here of the styles of time usage described by Calkins (1970) and reviewed in Chapter 8, but the intensity of the carceral experience evokes responses that are more varied, more situation-specific, and more deeply contoured. According to Rifkin (1987: 9), 'Every culture has its own unique set of temporal fingerprints. To know a people is to know the time values they live by.' Pursuing this analogy, the aim of this chapter is to present some of the arches, loops and whorls that characterize the prisoner society.

There is an eighth 'R', which is omitted from Table 10.1, because prisoners fear that once it becomes established it may herald psychological collapse. When observed in others it speaks not of survival, but of capitulation. This is reverie, which can be a welcome

Table 10.1 Stratagems for reducing time's abrasion: The seven Rs of survival

Rescheduling	Using different intervals to gauge the passage of time.
Removal	Routine work and exercise, busyness as an end in itself; all serve to alleviate the sources of stress, anxiety or discomfort that can protract duration.
Reduction	The burden of prison time is lightened by ensuring that there is less of it to deal with. This can be done by sleeping more and through the soporific effects of drug use.
Reorientation	Temporal horizons are reset so that the focus is emphatically on the present.
Resistance	'Beating the man', holding fast against the system, litigating, accentuating the absurd.
Raptness	Absorption in an activity like creative writing, craftwork, painting, or advanced study brings the benefits associated with 'routine complexity'.
Reinterpretation	For prisoners who can re-imagine and re-cast their predicament the potential rewards are substantial.

diversion in small doses, but is kept at bay by the wily prisoner for fear of not being able to refocus a wandering mind. In his classic account of prison life, Clemmer (1940: 244) wrote of 'reverie-plus', by which he meant a retreat to an interior world that is created to neutralize the deadening effects of a dreary, monotonous, and understimulating external world. The substitution of sparkling fantasy for humdrum reality can have damaging psychological effects for the prisoner if it is carried too far, as Nelson (1933a) noted when he wrote about the prevalence and potential harms of 'prison stupor'.

The stratagems in Table 10.1 are listed in ascending order of importance and in descending order of popularity. Rescheduling, Removal, Reduction, and Reorientation are commonly used and moderately effective. Resistance is less common but can sustain a prisoner for quite some time (although belligerence is fatiguing). Raptness, when mastered, is an effective way of truncating duration and investing time with meaning. Reinterpretation is rare but potent. Some prisoners master none of these techniques and their solitary time results in withdrawal, destructive rumination, and perhaps even psychosis.

Irvin Moore began serving a sentence of life without parole at the age of 22. Twenty-four years later, in an interview with Zehr (1996: 11) he reflected on his experience in the following terms:

A life sentence is like an insect encased in amber. Amber at one point is a fluid. As it is exposed to air, it becomes more viscous. Sometimes insects may get trapped in it. As it hardens, you see the insect's movements become slower. When it solidifies, he's just there. Thank God that I have been able to move enough to keep the liquid around me from solidifying.

The stratagems set out in this chapter constitute a variety of ways that prisoners have found useful to keep the liquid from solidifying.

Rescheduling

Some shape must be imposed on a sentence if its weight is not to become oppressive. A good example of one technique for so doing is given by Cohen and Taylor (1972: 97) in their account of how a recent arrival to Durham prison sought advice on how to structure a 20-year sentence to be told, 'It's easy, do it five years at a time.' While there is obviously a measure of bravado associated with the idea that there could be anything easy about this process other than verbalizing it, there is an important insight here, namely, that a schedule broken down into meaningful chunks seems more manageable. There are few individuals who measure their lives in units of 20 years, but a five-year term can be grasped. This is the around the length of time spent in secondary school and a little more than the interval between football world cups (rugby and soccer).

As part of the treatment of chronophobia, Russo (1943) recommended that prisoners divide their time into manageable chunks rather than allowing themselves to become overwhelmed by an undifferentiated long stretch yawning ahead; what Timerman (1988: 5) described as 'that elongated time which hovers over me oppressively in the cell'. The size of the unit of future time chosen is important. If it is too small, this can be destabilizing. Doodling with his pencil, Berkman (1970) absent-mindedly totted up the number of days, hours, minutes, and seconds he would serve if he completed his 22-year sentence. The total—in seconds—was 684,288,000. As if this was not a daunting enough prospect, Berkman then realized to his consternation that he had undercounted the number of days in the year by five, basing his arithmetic on 12 months of 30 days each, and that neither had he allowed for leap years. Recalculation brought him closer to 700,000,000 seconds in solitary. Startled he began again, this time allowing for time remitted for good conduct. On this occasion he went no further than the number of days which, at 5,170, was enough to horrify him. 'Appalled by the figures, I pace the cell in agitation. It is hopeless! It is folly to expect to survive such a sentence' (p. 230).

The narrator of *The House of the Dead* describes the point in his ten-year sentence when he called time to account: 'I remember that all those years, which were so much alike, passed drearily, miserably...And at last I mastered myself; I looked forward, and I reckoned off every day, and although a thousand remained, I took pleasure in ticking them off one by one. I saw the day off; I buried it, and I rejoiced at the coming of another day, because there were not a thousand left but nine hundred and ninety-nine days' (Dostoyevsky 2004: 234). What is significant here is when the countdown begins (only after two-thirds of the sentence has been served) and how it allows a feeling of control over the time remaining (not a thousand more days stretching into the distance, but a relentlessly diminishing tally, an irreversible downward trend which accrues increasingly to the prisoner's benefit). Speer (2010: 390) measured the progression of his sentence against the movement of the hands on what he called his 'Spandau Clock'. With three and a half years left to serve he equated his 21 years in custody (including one before he was sentenced) to a single day. By this reckoning it was almost 8 p.m. and another 11 seconds would pass each day until his release at the stroke of midnight. 'The smallest unit of time, a second, corresponds to two hours and ten minutes in Spandau' (p. 410).

Sometimes fixed periods of time are marked off, every cross on the calendar or mark on the cell wall representing another day or week or month's survival. While the image of the prisoner dispatching time like this is not uncommonly found in dramatic representations of prison life, it is not a technique popular with prisoners, as each scoring of the page or the paint is a very physical reminder of what has been lost and how this loss is accumulating. Every mark is another small victory for the clock. For long-sentence prisoners the destruction—by pen—of days, weeks, months, and years yields little more than a fleeting sense of satisfaction that is soon dwarfed by the realization that what is being recorded is the loss of another fragment of life, lived according to the rules of others. It seems to be the neophyte prisoner who marks a surface in order to keep track of time. With experience comes the realization that deflecting attention away from this kind of recording better serves the interests of the individual for whom time extends to a distant horizon.

Writing about prison life in Colombia, Leal (2001) described how the recent arrival scratched the wall to mark the end of each day but, when the scratches became too numerous, shifted the unit of measurement to the month. As the tally of months grew the unit became the year. He compared this to the way a child's age is counted—first in days, then months and finally years. The sequence is put into reverse as the end of the sentence approaches and the prisoner begins to count downwards: 'a year to go, 10 months, 9, 8,... until you reach about 100 days, then you start counting down the days 98, 97...' (p. 57). This is a process that seems to recognize no territorial distinctions. As Martel (2006: 596) described this shifting trajectory in her study of segregation in Canadian prisons: 'Suspended, time only resumes its relevance for a prisoner when release is in sight. At that point, the sentence is counted again, only this time it is counted backwards—one year to serve, then a few months, finally a few days.' A pre-release countdown signifies the impending restoration of liberty and of dominion over time. The associated danger is that a constant reminder of what might lie ahead can bring in its wake disorientating anxiety at just the time when the prisoner needs to marshal resources for the challenges ahead.

For the person serving an indefinite period of imprisonment, or a determinate sentence that exceeds their life expectancy, a countdown to an eventual release date may not be possible, so the temporal focus must be on other benchmarks such as parole reviews or a forthcoming court case. If all possibilities of eventual release have been extinguished, the internal deadlines of the prison assume even greater significance and the choice is between allowing them to dominate completely (the route to institutionalization) or attempting to maintain a parallel focus on the outside world (a route fraught with difficulty). Intriguingly, when prisoners in Pelican Bay SHU went on hunger strike in July 2011 one of their demands, to which the authorities acceded, was to be allowed have wall calendars for their cells (*New York Times*, 1 August 2011). It is likely that this was with a view to creating a more normal domestic environment in the bleakness of supermax confinement, rather than out of a wish to have a device to track time. It is also possible, of course, that however painful a focus on the future can be, this is trumped *in extremis* by a desire for connection with the outside world, even if this connection is no more than an acknowledgment that the days are passed in the same order, the months unfold in an identical sequence, and copies of similar calendars are pinned to the walls of offices and kitchens whose occupants are free to come and go as they please.

Removal

Goffman (1961: 63) defined 'removal activities' broadly, to include a wide range of 'voluntary unserious pursuits which are sufficiently engrossing and exciting to lift the participant out of himself, making him oblivious for the time to his actual situation. If the ordinary activities in total institutions can be said to torture time, these activities mercifully kill it.' The term is used very differently here. First of all, not every prisoner would agree that these pursuits are 'unserious'. Indeed, in many cases they are anything but. Also, it is ambitious to think that they kill time, the best that can be hoped for is that they anaesthetize the inmate to it. Finally, Goffman's use of the term collapses many of the categories that are enumerated in Table 10.1, and as such loses analytical precision. Removal, as used here, is about busyness as an end in itself, about easing oneself into the groove of prison life and alleviating the sources of stress, anxiety, and discomfort that can protract duration. These are the kinds of activities that virtually any prisoner can pursue.

One of the best ways of speeding the passage of time is to become absorbed in an activity. Edith Bone (1957) was held in solitary confinement in Hungary for seven years, several months of which were spent in total darkness in a filthy, freezing dungeon. Aged 61, she had been charged (wrongfully) with espionage for Britain. Bone came up with numerous ways to keep her mind and body active. Recalling something she had read in a story by Tolstoy, about a man who (like her) was kept in solitary confinement for seven years and occupied himself by taking imaginary walks in cities with which he was familiar, she embarked on similar peregrinations, wandering around London, Paris, Berlin, Vienna and many other places with which she was familiar. These mental meanderings led her to pace out her journeys back and forth along the floor of her narrow cell (10 feet long and four feet nine inches wide, most of the width being taken up by the bed). She decided to walk home to England and each day completed a certain distance (recorded on an abacus that she had made from bread), remembering the place she had reached, and resuming her journey from there the following day. Forward and back she strode until she had covered the distance to the Hungarian border, then onward to Vienna and Paris until she reached the Channel, beyond which lay England. 'I made this journey four times, using two different routes, once through Switzerland and once through Germany' (p. 107).

There is an interesting connection between Bone and another spirited prisoner. In Petrograd in 1919 Bone met Victor Lvovich Kibalchich—to whom she referred by his pen name of Victor Serge—who offered her a job as editor of the English edition of the *Communist International*, which she accepted. The chief editor under whom she worked, Vladimir Osipovich Mazin, had served 11 years of a life sentence and she remembered him as: 'the gentlest, kindest of men' (p. 19). Perhaps at this stage in her life she formed an impression of how men can triumph over brutal prison conditions, an understanding that stood her in good stead 30 years later?

Toohey (2011: 71) describes how boredom can be related to dromomania, which he characterizes as 'an uncontrollable and persistent desire to hurry off to some other distant place'. For obvious reasons, prisoners can only realize this desire imaginatively. Speer (2010) was perhaps the greatest make-believe dromomaniac. He marked out a circuit measuring 270 metres in the Spandau prison garden and between September 1954 and his release 12 years later he walked around this circuit more than 118,000 times covering a distance of 31,936 km. Speer's walking had a very specific purpose. He began by covering the 626 km from Berlin to Heidelberg, a journey that he completed on his fiftieth birthday. He then struck out on a world tour arriving at the Imperial Palace in Peking on 13 July 1959 and continuing across Asia to arrive at the Bering Strait in late February 1963. He had learned that the Bering Strait would be frozen at this time, thereby enabling him to walk across to Alaska and continue his journey through the US and to its conclusion near Guadalajara, Mexico. Each segment of the journey was researched in advance so that Speer could enjoy the landscape, the climate, the people and the way of life as he tramped along. He regretted that he had 'lost' the distance walked in Spandau from his arrival there in July 1947 until he embarked on his epic adventure seven years later. By his reckoning this amounted to more than 17,000 km and if added to the distance he had already completed, and planned to cover before his release, would have been equivalent to circling the globe at the equator, a distance which he estimated (incorrectly) at 47,000 km (p. 389).

Bone (1957: 131) was so busy, and engaged in so many different activities, that time passed quickly for her: 'What with writing a diary, learning Greek, walking the requisite number of miles every day, and reading books from the library, the time passed very quickly. In many prison memoirs I had read that time dragged in prison—I did not find it so, on the contrary it flew away too fast. The guards often looked at me wonderingly when I got the evening meal mixed up with the midday one and thought supper was lunch'. She replaced the burden of empty time with a regime that was tyrannous in its demands but had the virtue of being self-imposed.

Similarly, Bonhoeffer (2001) kept busy reading, writing, and reflecting on matters theological. In a letter from prison dated September 1943 he noted that: 'I've never had a moment's boredom in the five months and more that I've been here. My time is always fully occupied' (p. 18). In an epistle written the following month he described a day crowded with intellectual pursuits: 'for the work that I have set myself to do, the day is often too short, so that sometimes, comically enough, I even feel that I have "no time" here for this or that less important matter!' (p. 20). Grey (1988: 247) became a cruciverbalist in captivity, compiling a crossword each day for a period, with a view to having a stock ready for sale to newspapers and magazines when he was released. This helped him to remain mentally alert as well as keeping alive the prospect that a time would come when he was restored to normal life.

Austin Bidwell (1897: 454) made daily Bible study an integral part of his fight for psychological survival, learning many passages by heart, and declaring that 'It saved my life and reason.' He recalled that after 'ten or twelve' years he began to tire of the Bible and craved an alternative form of intellectual satisfaction: 'I was hungry, starving for mental food. Never had books appeared so attractive, never was kingdom so cheerfully offered for a horse as I would have offered mine for an octavo' (p. 454). In her history of the role of books, reading, and libraries in prison reform Fyfe (1992: 145) observed that, 'In separate confinement, books were part of the reforming apparatus.' Whatever about their role in effecting reformation they certainly provide a vital avenue for distraction and diversion.

Korn (1988a) described how prisoners held in administrative segregation at the High Security Unit in Lexington penitentiary, had strict limitations placed on the number of books allowed in their possession. Their personal libraries were capped at five titles, which Korn decried as, 'a mind-numbing limitation for the intelligent and studious women, whose only legitimate escape from confinement must be by means of the vigorous and varied exercise of their minds' (p. 11). Most of these women were well educated and politically motivated and their identification with their books went deep. What they read indicated their ideological preferences and bolstered their commitment to the ideas that had led to their incarceration; they provided a source of constancy in an uncertain and threatening environment.

Reading is a popular way for the literate prisoner to cope with what Nelson (1933b: 225) described as 'the leaden-footed hours of solitude'. The challenge for the prisoner held in isolation for a prolonged period is to find ways of ensuring that the weight does not bring them entirely to a halt; taming time means beating boredom. Many prisoners describe the delights of in-cell reading and the consequent precaution of rationing their supply so that the pleasure can be prolonged. *One Who Has Endured It* (1878: 100) described reading as 'an inestimable blessing', a sentiment shared by numerous prisoners then and since. Macartney (1936) spent much of his time struggling against the pettiness of the prison rules governing book borrowing and possession, and the poor stock of the Parkhurst prison library.

Reading is more than just a way of passing time or escaping from the pains of the present, although it can serve these twin purposes well. It can be cathartic and transformative. For an isolated prisoner it accomplishes several goals simultaneously, restocking the mind, allowing imaginative engagement with a text and its characters, and making the prisoner part of a community of readers. However insubstantial membership of this community may be it is not trivial; by consuming the printed word, diaphanous bonds are created. Sometimes reading is not just for pleasant absorption and distraction, but it is part of striving towards a clear goal. Under these circumstances it can be considered under Raptness (see below).

For those without literacy skills, despair and madness beckon. Unless, of course, they are prepared to test the physical limits of their endurance. Anderson (1994: 112) appreciated the value of exercise, recalling: 'I do sit-ups and push-ups in sets of twenty and twenty-five throughout the day, using the physical exertion as a kind of tranquilizer, whenever my spirits drop too low or my mind spins too fast.' The dosage of exercise could be adjusted according to the prevailing psychological conditions. Some prisoners have taken this to an extreme degree. One of the best known is Charles Bronson, who by 2010 had spent 36 years in prison, around 32 of them in solitary confinement. Bronson's strength is legendary throughout the prison system of England and Wales and he has devised an elaborate series of routines that can be followed, without the need for any equipment or a training partner, in the most cramped conditions. At 54 years of age he could complete 132 press-ups in 60 seconds and sometimes in the course of a day he would do up to 6,000 press-ups in his cell: 'It sounds inhuman, amazing, but remember, it's killing time for me; it's my buzz!' (Bronson and Richards 2007: 4) He is probably the only prisoner to have published a book—*Solitary Fitness*—drawing together his experiences in solitary confinement and his search for strength. Over a long prison career Bronson has been concerned to ensure that whenever physical confrontations arose with staff or other prisoners, he would not be found wanting.

Physical activity is more than just a way of adding musculature in the belief that this will either deter potential antagonists or be of assistance in overcoming them. It is also a way of filling the day, imposing order on an unruly mind, achieving the kind of bone tiredness that makes sleep possible however feverish the imagination, however pressing the thoughts of home.

Find a non-human companion

Many prisoners have found diversion and pleasure in the ants, spiders, mice, birds, and other creatures that become welcome companions. They are often ascribed human characteristics and the process of anthropomorphism allows a form of substitutive engagement for the person in solitude. Relatedness is a human need and when meaningful contact with other human beings is impossible, the personification of even the most humble animal is understandable. Davitt (1885: vi) 'affectionately dedicated' his prison diary to the memory of his pet blackbird, 'Joe', described as 'the little confiding friend whose playful moods and loving familiarity helped to cheer the solitude of a convict cell'.

George Bidwell (1888: 509) described how: 'the long years of solitude had produced in me such an unutterable longing for the companionship of something which had life, that I never destroyed any kind of insect which found its way into my cell—even when mosquitoes lit on my face I always let them have their fill undisturbed, and felt well repaid by getting a glimpse of them as they flew, and with the music of their buzzing'. What would have been a source of irritation and discomfort elsewhere became a welcome distraction in solitude; one could feel something that was not self-inflicted. George's brother Austin expressed identical sentiments when it came to the insects and mice that he befriended, even to the extent that he left the thirsty mosquito undisturbed on his face. Closer reading reveals that there was more than shared filial sentiment at work here. Austin shamelessly plagiarized these sections of his brother's book (see A. Bidwell 1897: 410–17 and G. Bidwell 1888: 505–9), casting some doubt upon his true credentials as a lover of the humblest creatures, and indeed, perhaps, on the originality and veracity of some of his other observations.

Cheng (1995) became an arachnophile. Watching a spider spin its web she was fascinated by the beauty and intricacy of the finished product. The joy and perfection of the natural world placed her mean-spirited captors in a different light: 'A miracle of life had been shown me…Mao Tze-tung and his Revolutionaries seemed much less menacing. I felt a renewal of hope and confidence…The tiny spider became my companion. My spirits lightened. The depressing feeling of complete isolation was broken by having another living thing near me, even though it was so tiny and incapable of response' (pp. 131–2). She drew inspiration from the spider's tireless efforts to make and remake its web deciding that she too would obey the natural instinct for survival: 'As long as I was in the No. 1 Detention House I would fight on resolutely and seriously to the best of my ability' (pp. 142–3).

A century earlier Sheehy (1888: 48) had arrived at the same conclusion: 'How deprivations may be endured, how miseries might be mitigated, what indomitable patient perseverance the most fragile are capable of, were some of the lessons read to me by the unflinching energy of a blind fly'. Similar sentiments were expressed by Grey (1988: 115–17) when he described the emotional and intellectual investment that he made in the ants whose antics became the object of his close attention during his solitary confinement in Peking. Whether a parliamentarian in custody in Ireland in the nineteenth century (Sheehy) or a journalist in detention in China in the twentieth century (Grey), there was comfort to be found in the presence of other living creatures, however tiny. This would seem to be a universal human characteristic according to Koch (1994: 62) who wrote that, 'Almost everyone personifies pets, especially in solitude.' When relationships with human beings cannot be formed they are forged with other creatures instead, who offer an outlet for humanity's innate sociability.

Reduction

One way of reducing the burden of lived time is to sleep through as much of it as possible. Some prisoners learn to turn off and tune out. As Shachak (1986: 226) put it: 'Not being aware of the passage of time through sleeping becomes a "gain" and not a loss of time.' Speer (2010: 43) took a similar approach during his long confinement, noting in his diary on 24 March 1947 that: 'Now I have reached twelve hours of sleep daily. If I can keep that up I shall be cutting my imprisonment by a full five years—by comparison with my normal sleeping time of six hours.' Fantasy and daydreaming are other elements of Reduction but, as noted above, if it is allowed to wander too freely in reverie the mind may prove difficult to bring back on track.

Not every prisoner can locate within themselves the resources required to carry on and a small number decide to conquer time by ending it. Medlicott (1999) described how some prisoners find the present unbearable, see time as the 'enemy' and have come up with what they perceive to be the ultimate way of routing it. By asserting control in this way—determining the mode and timing of their exit—they seek victory through capitulation. The prisoner who rushes to embrace death may feel that seizing dominion over the likely course of their life is a form of self-empowerment. For some, self-harming behaviour and the response that it evokes can become a survival strategy of sorts. Medlicott (2001: 142) reported how one prisoner, 'purposively filled his time, mostly by making his greeting cards or by laborious self-injury'. He was cutting to cope. This is a demonstration of how maladaptive practices can serve an important purpose for the person engaging in them.

It is not surprising that suicide rates are elevated among prisoners in the tumultuous early days of incarceration. In addition to whatever difficulties these groups face in terms of mental illness, drug withdrawal and fears for their bodily integrity, they are confronted with a major problem of time. Persons on remand cannot avoid contemplating a future which for them remains unsettled. As a result their lives are full of painful what-if scenarios and their gaze is directed outside the prison, with all of the associated psychic discomfort. Persons in the first phase of custody have an eye on the past, which is close, and feelings of regret, remorse or indignation—if only they could turn the clock back!—impinge on them as they try to wrestle their focus to the present.

The prisoners with whom Medlicott (1999) spoke, who were considered to be at risk of suicide, were characterized by a low level of ability to reframe time in a way that made it seem less empty, less immense, less threatening. Even those who were serving relatively short sentences felt that what lay ahead was unbearably burdensome. Prison time bore down heavily upon them and they could not see how to shake it off. They had not yet discovered the importance of shifting their focus away from what had been and what might be. Nor had they come up with a methodology for oiling the cogs of their internal time machine so that they became unaware of its every revolution. Some had a history of suicide attempts outside prison indicating that criminal justice factors were not always of overwhelming significance and that time was a pressure regardless of the spatial context.

Medlicott's informants found it virtually impossible to fill the large swathes of empty time with any sort of meaningful activity. They had not learned to truncate duration or to keep loneliness at bay. They were unable to resolve the paradox that emptier time felt heavier. This left them vulnerable to the intrusion of unwelcome thoughts or at risk of a retreat into fantasy and passivity. Medlicott described these prisoners as 'not now coping' as compared to the others in her sample who were 'now coping' (p. 216). This is a useful terminological refinement as it leaves open the possibility that some among the former group will learn to cope with the challenge of time while some among the latter group, who currently have the upper hand, may later find the tables turned against them. Medlicott found that the non-suicidal prisoners she spoke to had less to say about the phenomenon of time, they were not 'helplessly immured in the agonies of present time' (p. 223). There is a tragic irony here: to survive prisoners need to focus on the present, but for some this focus threatens to submerge them because they lack the skills required to speed up, or to ignore, or simply to bear, time's passage.

Perhaps the idea that one's destiny can ultimately be seized through suicide offers something for the desperate to cling to. The idea of suicide as a last resort can be a comfort when other options are dwindling. While it may be a temptation for many it becomes a concrete plan for few, especially in an environment where the opportunities for effective self-destruction are limited. Blindfolded and with his hands bound behind him, Timerman (1988: 88–9) would have found it highly problematic to make an attempt on his own life but he ruminated at length on the possibility:

suicide was the only thing that could share the long endless stretch of time, made up of time and more time, of interrogation and time, of cold and time, of hunger and time, of tears and time. How to fill those orifices of time if not with the preserved fruit of suicide? How to modify the rigid endless structure of time if not with the unforeseen originality of suicide?

While he continued to ponder the possibility, the days passed, the situation improved and Timerman lived: 'I was unable to tame the beautiful bull of suicide, nor did I fling myself on its horns or drench its back with my blood' (p. 92).

A more popular strategy for tuning out and deadening the impact of time passing involves drug use. Prisoners are often poly-drug users when at liberty but during periods of incarceration they are much more discriminating, generally limiting their choices to heroin and cannabis. These are the drugs of choice because they blunt the pains of captivity; they soothe and cosset, however temporarily. Drugs are used as an emotional emollient. They are also attractive in that they act as reminders of the pleasures of liberty and their illicit consumption in the custodial environment is a demonstration of the user's capacity to thwart the system, itself a source of private contentment. In addition, they may act to reconfigure temporality as cannabis, especially when consumed alone, slows down time (Ogden and Montgomery 2012).

While the experience of extended duration is usually avoided by prisoners it is likely that the quantity and quality of cannabis available to them is seldom sufficient to make this effect pronounced and that, on balance, the perceived advantages outweigh this possible drawback. Also, it is not necessarily a drawback if what is extended is a pleasant experience; the lengthening of a period of satisfied intoxication during which a painful reality is de-emphasized, can be viewed as an occasional treat. Substances such as LSD, amphetamines and Ecstasy, which act to heighten or intensify experiences are popular outside but rejected inside. The prisoner's time perspective, of necessity, is on the present, but this is a present to be neutralized rather than viewed in technicolor.

Using drugs to numb the pains of confinement can lead to seg-regation, whether for protection at the request of a prisoner who has accumulated debts that cannot be repaid, or as punishment for a prisoner who is involved on the supply side. Thus, the desire to deaden the effects of imprisonment can lead to their accentuation through removal from the main prisoner body to a place where the environment is less stimulating and the opportunities to escape it are greatly reduced. Drugs are a double-edged sword in another sense too. By causing some of the bonds of prisoner solidarity to dissolve, they weaken the foundations of support that could pre-viously have been relied upon. They can add to the volatility of prison life by introducing a new range of temptations to a group only too willing to yield to them. Finally, drugs (including those prescribed by prison doctors) allow a measure of escape from the probing self-reflection that can sometimes yield valued benefits and may further impede meaningful social engagement should the opportunity for same arise.

Another popular Reduction activity is television viewing. Watching television alone in-cell provides an effortless form of diversion. It is absorbing but too passive to be included under Removal. Klein (2006: 130; emphasis in original) observed that television offers 'nearly perfect ways to kill time in the present *and* in our memory in one fell swoop'. This is because the images that flicker on the screen engage the viewer's senses and grab their atten-tion so that intervals of time pass unnoticed. But the content is so inconsequential that it is not retained. It has the added attraction of allowing prisoners to keep something in common with those outside by following the same programmes, if they are allowed access to non-prison channels.

Reorientation

As discussed in Chapter 8, prisoners have long appreciated the benefits of living in an extended present. To survive they need to wade into the 'eternity of the instant' (Serge 1970: 160) without being drowned by it. If they can learn to tread water here they will look back with surprise at how rapidly the tide of time has ebbed. But there is a price to be paid; by bringing time horizons close they become wilfully blind to the joys and pains that lie beyond, the colour that makes life worth living. When the present is stretched in this way the past becomes a shrivelled husk and the future remains inchoate; while more than suspended animation, this is less than full-blooded living. For prisoners to survive psychologically it is important that they shift their time orientation. Dwelling on the past and any associated remorse or regret, or obsessing about a future life which is unlikely to arrive in the wished-for format, introduces a degree of fretfulness that is inimical to successful navigation of the temporal landscape. It takes time for this realization to dawn. To cope with the 'massive disordering of temporality' that accompanies imprisonment prisoners must devise suitable 'anti-memory devices' (Timerman 1988: 36).

The diametric opposite of the undeviating focus on the present is what Maybrick (1905: 74–5) described as 'the long vista of to-morrow, to-morrow, to-morrow . . . all filled with desolation and despair'. Realizing that she could not attend simultaneously to life outside prison and life inside, and that a retrospective focus would make her vulnerable to mental instability, she shut out the past and pushed thoughts of an alternative existence to the margins: 'My safety lay, as I found, in compressing my thoughts to the smallest compass of mental existence, and no sooner did worldly visions or memories intrude themselves, as they necessarily would, than I immediately and resolutely shut them out as one draws the blind to exclude the light' (p. 105). One of the reasons that Berkman's incarceration exacted such a huge personal toll was that he allowed his thoughts to wander to the outside world and the behaviour of his comrades. He learned that, 'The memory of the life "outside" intensifies the misery of the solitary' (Berkman 1970: 238). Perhaps because of his commitment to praxis he found it more difficult to effect the kind of disconnection from the wider world that makes the prison present more bearable. Also, to cease thinking about the progress of the political struggle for which he had sacrificed his liberty would have called into question not so much the ideological purity of his actions but the point of them. To acknowledge that his violence had been for naught would have been to invite a sense of futility and despair.

Zimbardo and Boyd (2008: 26) see the route to self-fulfilment as the development of 'a balanced time perspective in place of a narrowly focused single time zone. A balanced time perspective will allow you to flexibly shift from past to present to future in response to the demands of the situation facing you so that you can make optimal decisions.' This is an almost impossible aspiration for the solitary prisoner for two reasons. First, psychological survival demands a disproportionate focus on the present and a 'knifing-off of past experience', to borrow a phrase from the account of adjustment to military life provided by Brotz and Wilson (1946: 374). For soldiers undergoing induction training, past experiences were irrelevant, and even unhelpful, and future prospects lay beyond their direct control, with the result that, 'Time had only a present phase' (p. 375). Secondly, the situational context is, by definition, inflexible and unyielding and the kinds of decisions it allows are generally sub-optimal.

Resistance

A simple way of subverting the system of solitary confinement is to undermine its desire to prohibit social intercourse, something prisoners have been adept at doing since the first attempts were made to isolate them. Burt (1852: 272) described the method of communicating by knocking on walls as 'the prisoners' electric telegraph'. This was a simple and cumbersome method involving one knock for A, two for B and so forth. Three quick taps indicated that a word had been completed. With practice, messages could be transmitted and received swiftly and a conversation of sorts could take place between prisoners in contiguous cells. One wonders given low levels of literacy, whether this tedious practice did much more than give prisoners the comfort of knowing that meaningful contact was possible, even if the provision of detailed information was necessarily limited. There must also have been a concern that, given its simplicity, any tapping heard by staff could very easily be deciphered.

Despite the tiresome nature of the practice and the danger of being overheard, the simplicity of the system meant that it remained popular and some prisoners became adept at keeping in touch this way. Paul Ignotus (1959: 141) described how during six and a half years as a political prisoner in Hungary he developed a passionate relationship with a woman whose facility at rapping the wall allowed her to chat 'with unremitting élan' and whose tech-nique 'was fast and astoundingly self-confident. She would inter-rupt any sentence by fast knocks suggesting that she knew what the end of it was to be...I was just dumbfounded by the shower of her knocks...Her proximity permeated me.' The bond they estab-lished was such that they became betrothed before they met in person and were married after they were released. In his words, 'It was love at first lack of sight' (p. 143). For the skilled practitioner, then, a friendly barrage of knocks can be a welcome relief from solitude as well as a way of killing time.

More sophisticated prisoners could have used Morse code to transmit their thoughts (e.g. Clarke 1922: 11–12), but while easier on the knuckles they still ran the risk of having their messages unscrambled by those for whom they were not intended. Those who were yet more ingenious developed ciphers which reduced the number of knocks (or hand signals or flashes of a light) required to indicate a particular letter by referring to its coordinates on a predetermined grid, and made interpretation difficult for those who lacked the key (for an example of such a system, see Wines 1895: 158–9).

When tapping is not possible there are other ways of com-municating as shown by the POWs who dragged their san-dals so that the flapping was communicative or who, when sweeping the compound, used the sequencing of brush strokes to send messages (Deaton et al. 1977: 249). Breytenbach (1984: 227) described how enterprising prisoners sometimes used a mouse that they had tamed to act as a messenger by training it to go from one cell to another with, for example, some tobacco strapped to its body. The mouse's reward was a morsel of bread and the prisoner's was a smoke that was all the more sweet for its illicit origins. All of these practices serve to frustrate the interests of those who wish for isolation to be complete. For the prisoner they allow communication (however patchy and infrequent), a sense of triumphing over the author-ities by expressing a measure of personal autonomy and initia-tive (however limited in effect), and a welcome distraction from time's otherwise sluggish passage.

Nineteenth-century prisoners sometimes scratched messages on the tins in which food was delivered to their cells. These were collected afterwards for redistribution with the next meal which meant that inscribers could not know who would be exposed to

their handiwork, but must have drawn comfort from the knowledge that their words had a potential audience. Sometimes the
inscriptions were no more than a name. On other occasions they
were humorous, such as, 'Wouldn't you like a pork pie?' (Priestley
1999: 47). *One Who Has Endured It* (1878: 108) described how
even the cutlery told a tale: 'Some men amused themselves with
scratching, not only their names, but a short history of their case
and supposed grievances on the tin knives. Some, again, chose this
method to give vent to expletives and anathemas against the prison
authorities, that they did not dare to speak. I need hardly say that
these latter did not bear either signature or official numbers.'
Surreptitiously scrawling graffiti on the walls of the exercise yard
was another one-way mode of communicating and O'Donovan
Rossa (1899: 91) recalled of his time in Pentonville in the mid
1860s that:

'Twas a recreation in solitude to read the evidence of live beings being
around, even though you did not see them, it was the dead wall speaking
to you, and though the language had not the chastity of death about it,
still it brought you more cheer than if there were no traces of life to be
seen. You came to read 'cheer up'—'cheer up,' so often, or, at least, I came
to read it, that I felt myself growing sympathetic towards the writers.

Rosenberg (2011) described the messages carved into the wall
in a holding cell that she briefly occupied in New York in 1984.
The content was varied, ranging from names and expletives to
political slogans, but she immediately grasped the underlying
motivation, which had not changed since the time of O'Donovan
Rossa: 'I understood the need to make a mark, to leave a message,
to scream out loud in this disembodied hole, "I was here. Don't
let me disappear" ' (p. 22). However untidy the scrawl and cryp-
tic the message, it signifies resistance, a refusal to be effaced, a
desire to be noticed. Perhaps the most elaborate strategy devised
by a prisoner to subvert the rule of silence was a newssheet, *The
Irish Felon*, ingeniously and surreptitiously typeset and printed
by Clarke (1922: 37–41) during his time at Chatham Prison
in the 1880s. Molineux (1903: 34–53) described a handwrit-
ten newspaper, *The Murderers' Home Journal*, which appeared
complete with advertisements, poetry, illustrations, local news,
editorials and readers' letters, that he produced for the enter-
tainment and edification of the prisoners who shared death row
with him.

'Beat the man' or rage against the machine

Some prisoners who spent many years in isolation described how the best way to do time was to outmanoeuvre the authorities, an approach known as 'beating the man'. These small, and sometimes pyrrhic, victories could take many forms. When he discussed survival techniques with maximum security prisoners in Leavenworth, Earley (1992: 282–3) was given a variety of examples:

Pour breakfast cereal in the sink in your cell, add water, and let it curdle for several days. It will become potent enough to get you drunk. You've just beat the man. Remove the thin steel wire from inside an eyeglass case and rub it against the bars. It will saw through them. You've just beat the man. . . . Every day that an inmate survived in prison without breaking, he had won a silent victory. He had beat the man.

Thomas Silverstein, who has been denied human contact for longer than any other prisoner in the US federal system, considered suicide on occasion but ruled it out because of his belief that his demise would be welcomed by the Bureau of Prisons and he wished to deny them this pleasure, and also because if he took his own life he felt that this would send a message to other prisoners that 'fighting back is useless' (Earley 1992: 436). His decision to stay alive is a strategy of stubborn resistance ('beating the man') as well as a gesture of inmate solidarity.

Some prisoners feed off the hate that solitary confinement incites and believe that this strengthens them. By raging against the machine they subscribe to the Nietzschean view that what does not kill one makes one stronger. 'Pure, unadulterated hate could sustain a man for years' according to Earley (1992: 283). Hate and the desire for revenge gave the prisoner options in the face of overwhelming odds. But constant enragement is incompatible with long-term mental health and the experience of most prisoners seems to be to replace explosive rage with simmering anger or resigned acceptance. The energy needed to hate depletes an individual's resources so that what is left for self-preservation may be insufficient. The loss of physical strength is no doubt a factor here along with the obvious inequality of arms; even the strongest prisoner at the peak of his powers is no match for a team of well-equipped guards.

In addition to individual prisoners who are sustained for a time by fury and whose strategy for tackling time is to interrupt its flow with violence and disorder (a road seldom taken for reasons discussed in Chapter 9) prisoners who espouse a common cause adopt strategies of Resistance. These are designed to promote camaraderie and maintain discipline as well as to buck the smooth operation of the prison machine. Some find a measure of satisfaction in highlighting the absurdity of their situation or the incompetence of their captors. Resistance of this kind can have a haughty, mocking quality and risks arousing the ire of those against whom it is directed. For politically motivated prisoners whose crime is their pacifism, Resistance can involve challenges that proceed along legal and administrative routes as well as direct confrontation of staff (see Levy and Miller 1971: 165–97). Activities of this kind have an avowedly educational dimension: they contribute to the intellectual and political development of the prisoner. They also serve to uphold morale, to generate publicity, and to undermine the criminal justice system. For the political prisoner who is engaged with these possibilities, the sentence can be rendered meaningful and potentially transformative.

It could be argued that political prisoners rage against the machine, while their otherwise motivated peers try to beat the man. The desire for the first group is a victory over the system, even if they lose out personally, while for others beating the man is a purely personal achievement. Defeating the system implies beating the man but not vice versa. For the political prisoner individual staff may be targeted but this is not necessarily personal; they are collateral damage in a bigger battle. For others, vanquishing a particular staff member might be the objective, regardless of any wider ramifications.

No matter how strenuously the prison system attempts to shut down the prisoner's ability to resist, this process will inevitably be incomplete. A measure of negotiation is always possible between an individual (however oppressed) and their environment (however apparently unyielding). Shalev (2009a: 73) described a practice known as 'gassing' whereby prisoners throw a mixture of urine and faeces at officers. Even when denied access to anything that could be made into a weapon and when rarely allowed within a shackled arm's reach of a guard, prisoners can still use their body products offensively. A well-aimed handful of human waste hurled from within a cell is a statement of dissatisfaction that is as emphatic as it is obnoxious. While contrary to the thrower's interests, such behaviour is a pungent declaration of autonomy in a setting where most routes to self-expression have been extinguished.

Prison officers are well equipped to respond, of course, and prisoners who 'gas' them risk being gassed in return as chemical agents are regularly used to facilitate cell extractions.

Rhodes (2004) described how staff in maximum security prisons in Washington State sometimes dressed in waterproof jumpsuits when delivering meals as a precaution against an inmate hurling bodily waste in their direction when the cuff port was opened to allow a tray to be handed in. She explained the significance of this act in the following terms: 'The prisoner who sees himself defined as a piece of shit hurls into the faces of his keepers the very aspect of himself that most intensely represents his contaminated status in their eyes' (p. 45). A suspected al-Qaida terrorist detained by the US Army in highly restrictive conditions at Guantanamo Bay recalled how, 'We started to throw buckets of shit on the guards through the fence...I pissed on their faces too' (el Gorani and Tubiana 2011: 34). Carlton (2007: 128) described a variation on this theme, known as 'bronzing up', practised by prisoners in Australia. Rather than hurling their excrement at prison officers they smeared it on the walls of their cells, causing revulsion among the staff whose job it was to restore the walls to their original condition. The appeal for the prisoners, once they overcame the feeling of nausea associated with this practice, was that they could express their dissatisfaction using a substance the supply of which the authorities could not control.

The subversive use of waste in dirty protests—sometimes including menstrual blood (O'Keefe 2006)—while confirming the staff view of prisoners as subhuman and unfathomable, can be viewed by its practitioners as a gesture that is rational, deliberate, proactive, provocative, and even political. Paradoxically, it may serve to bolster pride and re-affirm individual self-control. Desperate situations evoke desperate acts of Resistance.

Another way to resist is through litigation. As James (2009: 24) put it in an introductory note to a book about jailhouse lawyers in the US: '[They] learn the law, the precedents, the jargon, and mount a legal defense, often formidable...In the process they carve out a life for themselves, a victory in itself.' (In a previous era, and illustrating shifting conceptions of mental illness, this kind of activity might have been seen as symptomatic of an underlying disorder. In their review of the history of prison psychoses, Nitsche and Wilmanns (1912: 46) described pathological conditions known as 'litigious paranoia' and 'delirium of innocence'.

Pity the wrongfully convicted prisoner who attempted to effect his release through the courts but by so doing confirmed his madness.) The legal process grinds slowly, and prisoners in the US can still be embroiled in court proceedings a decade and more after conviction. Thus, prisoners who resist through litigation can find themselves on a long journey during which hope is never fully extinguished. Those who become skilled in legal matters can put their talents at the service of others, even from the remove of their solitary cells, and thereby rise in status.

Every prisoner can resist but not all can achieve Raptness, which is discussed next.

Raptness

Raptness relates to specific pursuits over which it takes time to achieve mastery. It is about a state of focused absorption in a goal-directed activity like creative writing, study, craftwork, or painting that, once mastered, brings the benefits associated with 'routine complexity'. The activity is one that is important to the individual, and may become a key part of their identity. Raptness is distinguished from Removal because it is more specialized, purposive, and individualized. Removal involves the release and stress-busting aspects of keeping busy, often through physical work (of whatever kind) and exercise (however varied). Generally speaking this is not the kind of activity that requires mastery in the way that Raptness does. As well as speeding the passage of time Raptness results in a product that may enhance the self-respect and status of the person who produced it, setting them apart in terms of accomplishment. This distinguishes it from involvement in prison work more generally, in which the individual may invest no particular significance beyond its value as a Removal activity. Raptness is about following pursuits that are meaningful and individuating. As well as helping time to pass, such pursuits invest it with purpose and this further reduces its weight.

Writing helps prisoners to come to terms with the time they have lost as well as what remains for them. There is the possibility of communing with people outside prison in a direct and personal way as well as the chance of freedom by instalments: 'Whenever I get published outside these walls, it is as though a piece of me gets out' (David Wood, cited in Chevigny 1999: 348). Similarly, and poignantly, William Orlando: 'Writing is all I have, a lament and a boast' (cited in Chevigny 1999: 341). For intellectual stimulation Waite (1994: 370) composed his autobiography in his head. As a diversion on one occasion he began a comic novel, an enterprise that became so engrossing he worked on it continuously for 36 hours, foregoing sleep so that he could allow his characters to become fully developed. He was worn out by the end. This is a good example of how the creative process can energize but then exhaust.

Denied any human contact, Thomas Silverstein became dependent on his artistic endeavours to maintain a sense of self. 'In the absence of human contact, my art had become central to my identity. It was almost the only way I knew I was alive, that I existed. No one spoke to me, but I felt that I was able to communicate that I was a living human being by making art. Without it I felt like a part of my soul had been taken from me' (Silverstein 2011: para. 123; relatedly, see O'Donnell 2014).

Writing is not always carried out with a view to preserving a record of experience or in the hope of future publication or for the edification of another. Sometimes the movement of pen across paper, and the translation of ideas and moods into words and sentences, is reward enough. By reading what they have written, scribes can achieve a deeper understanding of their situation. There is a concreteness, a physicality, about the written word that demands it is taken seriously. Reading what one has written adds quality to one's internal dialogue by creating an account of one's environment which can then act as a prompt to reflection.

The act of writing is itself important. The scratching of a pencil on a page, the reviewing and revising, the deletions and annotations, the marginalia; all force clarity on thoughts that might otherwise have continued to careen across an anxious mind, with potentially ruinous consequences. The discipline required to bring words together into sentences which can be enjoined into paragraphs helps to draw coherence from chaos and offers some clear reference points in a new and bewildering territory. As Speer (2010: 24) wrote in his prison diary, 'What has been written down, formulated with some care, takes on a certain stamp of definiteness.' This is true even if the text is not retained. Betancourt (2010: 434) wrote regularly during her captivity but burned everything for fear that it would fall into the wrong hands. The act of writing was cathartic and self-sustaining, but also fraught with danger. However, the risk was worth taking because of the psychological benefits. If what is written is read by others there is the possibility that a shared universe of meaning will emerge and that words will become bonds. The solitary who writes for an imagined reader is no longer completely alone.

Honest writing requires ruthless self-examination and when the task has been completed it demands attention. It is more difficult to avoid words on a page than to push away a troubling thought. Breytenbach (1984: 155) described how, 'it is unbalancing something very deeply embedded in yourself when you in reality construct, through your scribblings, your own mirror. Because in this mirror you write hair by hair and pore by pore your own face, and you don't like what you see.' The prison becomes a crucible for rewriting (and, perhaps, remaking) the self. While few prisoners will share Breytenbach's talent his argument holds true in general; anyone who commits their thoughts to paper is then faced with the raw materials for cogitation, anguish, and possibly relief.

Literature can absorb the attention of the prisoner but this is not Raptness because it does not involve the creation of something new. Sometimes reading is Raptness when it is part of a programme of study, but reading for pleasure falls outside of this and is better considered as Removal. While reading is welcomed as a way of passing the time, breaking the monotony, and either absorbing information or stimulating the imagination, writing serves a higher purpose by becoming a passion that infiltrates the person and initiates a journey to destinations that may be unknown at the outset; this is true escapism.

Reinterpretation

Those who can devise, or adopt, a frame of reference that puts their pain in context seem to draw succour from their predicament. Things no longer appear frighteningly random; there is an order to them, a pattern to be revealed. This can happen in a variety of ways. Some find comfort in organized religion and cast themselves as participants in a drama where worldly suffering is of little consequence when compared with the joys of paradise. Others find common purpose with those who share a perspective, or an enemy. This ranges from the hate-filled solidarity of the Aryan Brotherhood, to the neighbourhood allegiances that define street gang membership, to the seductions of the political creed *du jour*.

Seeing oneself as part of something larger, as more than a cipher, eases the pain of confinement.

However, the value of such a sense of belonging can have shallow roots. The gang member may become disaffected and find himself at risk from former friends; the tattoos that once displayed fealty now serving as inky targets for another's shank. The racist may find himself becoming poisoned by his own venom. The attractiveness of political agitation can wax and wane. Rhetorical posturing may not give way to deeper change. It is those few prisoners who develop a coherent *Weltanschauung* that is not affected by the shifting preferences of their peers who best survive the vagaries of imprisonment. Writing of the aftermath of apartheid, Nelson Mandela (1994: 748) commented that one of the unintended effects of decades of brutal treatment in South Africa was that it had created a generation of extraordinarily courageous and wise leaders: 'Perhaps it requires such depths of oppression to create such heights of character.' There are also some individuals who seem to lack an overarching framework into which to locate their 'struggle' but possess an extraordinary capacity to develop an internal life that sustains them through rigours that, for most, would surely be intolerable.

Berkman (1970), despite unrelentingly harsh treatment, was sustained by the discipline of constant self-examination. His ideological purism kept him mentally intact no matter how dreadful the prevailing conditions. By his account there was some reward to be gained from his predicament. He learned that he could cope with terrible hardships and he found that his belief system was confirmed, that the ideas which had motivated the act that led to his incarceration provided the blueprint for an engaged and meaningful life. In anarchism he had found an unbreakable thread with which to stitch together a lifetime of experiences and to incorporate new ones as they occurred. Adhering to his principles helped him to stiffen his resolve, even in the direst circumstances. He knew that the coherence, and solidity, of his belief system set him apart from other prisoners and while he struggled to understand the reluctance on the part of his fellow convicts to subscribe to anarchism, he drew comfort from his own unwavering commitment.

For prisoners who can re-imagine and re-cast their predicament, the potential rewards are substantial. Some bring this perspective with them. Others develop it during their time inside. Erwin James (2003) described a fellow prisoner who one night made a ligature from his sheet, tied one end to a bar on the cell window and placed the noose around his neck, pulling it tight and preparing to drop from the end of the bed to his death. A dozen times he climbed onto the end of the bed and pulled the noose tight, until finally the crisis was over. As the prisoner recounted what happened on the twelfth occasion, 'I actually took one foot off the bed and it was in that instant that I realized I had a choice' (p. 86). He continued, 'So I made the choice to do the time. After that I felt in control, no longer helpless' (p. 86). This is an example of how individuals who wrest back control over their destinies or, at least, feel that it is within their power to do so, can survive. In his book on boredom and the religious imagination Raposa (1999: 74) captured this notion well when he wrote that

the theological literature about boredom displays less concern with how one came to feel bored than with what one proceeds to do in response to the feeling. What one decides to do itself presupposes an ability to discern the meaning of one's experience. My sense that 'nothing matters' can take the form of either a boredom close to despair or of a religious insight, powerful and liberating. So this business of discernment is hardly a trivial matter.

Interpretation is vital. In the closing lines of a poem that the journalist Terry Anderson (1994: 1) wrote about almost seven years spent in dreadful conditions as a hostage in Lebanon, he asks and answers a question of fundamental importance that captures the vital role of interpretation in psychological survival: 'Wasted, empty years? Not quite./No years are empty in a life;/and wasted— that depends on/what is made of them, and after.' When prisoners realize that their basic survival needs of shelter, food (however poor), and safety (even if threats to bodily integrity cannot be eradicated) will be met, the search to extract meaning from their circumstances begins in earnest.

Acceptance

Raposa (1999: 75) elaborated on the meaning of discernment by drawing on the spiritual exercises of St Ignatius of Loyola, which are underpinned by the prescription that 'we must make ourselves indifferent to all created things'. Strength is found in surrender, in ceasing to resist, in what Maybrick (1905: 103) described as 'the opiate of acquiescence'. In the words of Tolle (2005: 171; emphasis in original), 'Surrender is the simple but profound wisdom of *yielding to* rather than *opposing* the flow of life.' For the prisoner who can develop this Ignatian attitude, even if he has no God, the rewards of detachment are available.

Alternatives to resigned detachment are self-deception or a retreat into fantasy, both of which involve a kind of disengagement that is likely to impair relationships and impede reintegration. Grey (1988: 263) seemed to exhibit this kind of radical acceptance when he recorded in his diary that 'I suppose if it is to be, it is to be. I can only accept what comes.' Likewise, Bonhoeffer (2001: 4) concluded that: 'The great thing is to stick to what one still has and can do... and not to be dominated by the thought of what one cannot do.' What is required is a redefinition and reinterpretation of circumstances that are not amenable to change.

In her study of women held apart in Canadian prisons, Martel (2006) showed how segregation (which was generally of short duration) could be viewed by those subjected to it as a destructive interval or as a time for refreshing the spirit, for rebuilding and consolidating a fragile identity. The same place can serve several purposes and the meaning which is invested in the experience determines whether it is seen as pointless pain or a potential source of inner strength.

Keenan (1992: 31–2) was careful to distinguish between acceptance and capitulation, arguing that: 'acceptance should not be seen as a defeat of our powers of resistance and of maintaining the integrity of the self. It is simply that in a situation of total confinement one has to learn to unhook from the past in order to live for the present.' This entails a determination not to struggle in a futile fashion against that which cannot be overcome, matched by an equal determination not to give internal assent to unacceptable circumstances. An active mind and a lack of bitterness together with a healthy body are key ingredients of the survival strategy for many long-term isolates.

Reinterpretation is not sought by Christians alone although it is this faith tradition that has done most to shape the penitentiary experience in Europe and North America. In her account of how prisoners at Alabama's maximum-security Donaldson prison responded to a ten-day Vipassana meditation course, Phillips (2008: 14) described how participants were trained to experience and observe their misery 'with constancy and equanimity, looking at it squarely with patience and fortitude'. If an individual comes to accept the impermanence of their existence then any suffering that accompanies it is easier to bear. Mastery of the mind is one of the keys to contentment, whether it is found in the teachings of Jesus Christ or the Buddha. There is some evidence that mindfulness techniques can have a beneficial impact on psychosis and that they can be applied to good effect in correctional settings (Samson 2012; Shonin et al. 2013). These encouraging findings have practical implications for prisoners in solitary confinement among whom the seriously mentally ill are over-represented.

In letters written during his incarceration in England, E. Williamson Mason (1918: 140), a conscientious objector during the First World War, showed a clear grasp of the harms caused by imprisonment but found it easy to rise above them as he viewed his prison uniform not as a 'criminal's garb' but as a 'suit of honour'. Had it been the former he mused, he would have ended his prison term worse than he began it. This perspective on his confinement, together with the benefits of a good education and a commodious mind, combined to make his prison experience bearable. He saw himself as standing apart from other prisoners on account of the reason for his captivity and this is why he suffered less, despite identical deprivations, and quite possibly the added opprobrium heaped upon those who refused to go to the Front, where many had uncomplainingly laid down their lives when commanded to do so. Clearly Mason's principles buoyed his mood throughout his prison sentences and the upbeat nature of his epistles occasionally verges on the comical, as for example when he expounds on the prison as a place for rest, reflection and reinvigoration, concluding: 'I cannot believe the man exists who would not be better for a dose of prison' (p. 175).

Waite (1994: 64) also attempted to ease his burden by reconceptualizing it: 'Was it St Cyprian who said: "These are not chains, they are ornaments"?' The terrorists' manacles which he was forced to wear chafed the same, but menaced less, when they were thought of as baubles. Just as Mason rejected the notion that he was a criminal, Waite clung to an alternative definition of self: 'I am doing my level best to continue in my role as envoy and not change to that of hostage. I don't want to accept that I am a captive' (p. 98). Even in the face of seemingly overwhelming odds the self is not so brittle that it will inevitably disintegrate.

There is a distinction between 'inner silence (taciturnity) and outer, physical silence' (Belisle 2003: 19). Prisoners in solitary confinement have the latter imposed but may be raging inside. If they can find inner quietude—what Belisle described as 'the monk within' (p. 172)—without being overwhelmed by it, they will cope (and perhaps even thrive). Of course, there may be a secular equivalent to this process, but given the Christian origins of the penitentiary and the language used by prisoners which tends to reflect the narratives of redemption and resurrection with which they are familiar, the religious analogy is the one in which the literature is steeped. In an article that was published as the introduction to a reissue of Berkman's book, Goodman (1970: 370) observed that over a term of imprisonment, some prisoners make 'the philosophical discovery that wherever one is is a sample of all the reality that there is.' Berkman (1970: 415) himself had observed how, 'With maturity we become more universal'. If this realization dawns, the yearning for an alternative existence is quieted and the outside world intrudes less forcefully.

After five years of solitary confinement and having spent many more waiting for a death sentence to be overturned, Jacobs (2007: 122) came to realize the limits of the prison: 'They might be able to keep me here, take my time and circumscribe my space, but they can't have my mind or my heart or my spirit. Those are mine and no one can take them away from me... within these walls, it is up to me what kind of a world this will be—a joyous one, or a sad one, filled with peace and calm, or misery and fear.' This is the nub of the matter. If someone can formulate such a perspective they will endure. This realization was an epiphany for Jacobs and by her account when she could surrender the self and at the same time accept that much lay beyond her control she found 'an added dimension in the world' (p. 123). She began to meditate and introduced yoga to her daily routine: 'I was no longer a prisoner. I was a monk in a cave... The only way I was restricted was bodily. Except for that, I was as free, or more free, than I had ever been' (p. 124). Yoga became very important to Grey (1988: 181) during his solitary period for two reasons that he identified: 'It helped me to adjust mentally to the isolation and confinement and helped me to keep myself in as good a physical condition as the circumstances allowed.' Meditation and yoga promote orientation towards the present and that is part of why they are found helpful by prisoners who discover them.

There is always scope to redefine one's situation and to attempt to sculpt the social environment through interaction and negotiation with staff and other prisoners, should they occasionally hove into view. Even if such attempts fail, the very fact that they can be made is a reminder to the prisoner that not all of their personal autonomy has been stripped away and nor can it be. This is not to suggest that hardship can simply be imagined out of existence. Austin Bidwell (1897: 462) put it well when he remarked that: 'No man can make a bad thing good or trick himself into believing that suffering is pleasure. If pain be not an evil, it is an exceedingly good imitation, and the wisest philosopher is just as restless under the toothache as the most perfect idiot.'

Reinterpretation is the most elusive of the seven Rs of survival. Prisoners who master it create a bearable psychological environment where the tight confines within which they are forced to exist can be perceived and felt differently. Thoreau (1965: 67) exhorted his contemporaries to remove distractions from their lives and to strive for 'Simplicity, simplicity, simplicity.' This simplicity is forced upon the isolated prisoner and some manage to bend it to their purpose. They speak of becoming free, of maturity and growth, of unquenchable hope, of the importance of religion and spirituality, of redefining and undermining adversity so that it hurts less. These themes are picked up and fleshed out in the concluding chapter.

11

Withstanding Time's Abrasion

Not every prisoner conquers prolonged solitariness but those who do share certain characteristics. They believe that how they respond lies within their control. They swiftly determine that this is a challenge from which they will emerge victorious. Survivors have a context, a 'containing framework' (Koch 1994: 71) of some description; ideology and a sense of connection—however attenuated—provide solid foundations for endurance. They see themselves as cogs in a machine which must keep turning if the larger enterprise is to remain credible. As Nietzsche (1994: 468) put it in *Twilight of the Idols*, 'If we have our own why of life, we shall get along with almost any how.' (The version popularized by Frankl (2004: 84; emphasis in original) is pithier: 'He who has a *why* to live for can bear with almost any *how*.')

Prisoners who come to see themselves as part of something greater will find it easier to carry on. An overarching purpose lends coherence (and credence) to life events that might otherwise feel disjointed or confusing. To get through the day they endeavour to immerse themselves in the present and to derive profit from the immediate environment, however inhospitable. They devise effective stratagems for handling time (see Table 10.1), especially empty, unchanging time and may even become grateful for what they have managed to extract from their incarceration. They can withstand the rigours of self-examination, finding that the fruits of introspection are not poisonous. They become indifferent to their captors, learning that hatred is corrosive and that it will be to their ultimate disadvantage if they cannot achieve a degree of emotional distance. Rage, especially when impotent, is suffocating. They are inspired by their own behaviour. Prisoners who emerge unbroken from long periods of arduous solitude rise in their own esteem and in that of their fellows. They become the standards against which fortitude is measured.

Not everyone who satisfies these conditions will survive, but those who do seem to have done so. There are individuals who have emerged—strengthened—from the most horrendous stretches of isolation, whose defiant survival is awesome testimony to human resilience. Not many possess the qualities required, in the necessary measure, for such feats of endurance, but by studying the stories of those who do, there may be more general lessons to learn about 'how elastic the limits of what is bearable are' (Koestler 1942: 140). Finally, those who do better in solitude are often older. While they may lack the physical strength of youth they benefit from the emotional independence that accompanies ageing. As Storr (1988: 168) expressed it, older people 'are more content to be alone, and become more preoccupied with their own, internal concerns.' This developing independence softens the impact of isolation. There is another comfort associated with old age, namely, the perception that life is speeding up. As noted in Chapter 8, this makes time's passage less abrasive.

Solitary confinement in a prison cell severely compromises the occupant's ability to exercise mastery over the environment. The interaction between person and place is far less variegated than almost anywhere else and opportunities to make plans and then to see those plans through to satisfactory conclusions are drastically reduced. Choices are limited and the outcomes which remain within the individual's control tend to be aversive. Truculence will be repaid in kind, and swiftly; of this the prisoner can be fairly certain. The cell extraction team can be relied upon to respond to breaches of the rules, especially when they are persistent. But the creation of a beneficent environment through acts of individual will is a much more challenging proposition. It is a peculiar kind of control that cannot be wrested from the solitary prisoner, namely the capacity to cause a further deterioration of his or her situation. But, as shown in Chapter 7, this power is occasionally exercised to demonstrate that some vestiges of humanity are unextinguishable.

To survive it is important to set one's own limits, to define the parameters of one's existence—however narrowly—and to strive to remain within them. Recalling his time in solitary confinement as a POW in a Syrian prison in 1973 and 1974, Shachak (1986: 225) described how, 'I deliberately limited the boundaries of my world'. On one occasion he became ill and decided that to conserve his strength he would not reply when other prisoners called out to him. This caused consternation regarding his whereabouts. When he was ready to be sociable again he announced that he had been there all the time. His fellow prisoners found it difficult to understand why they had been ignored, but for Shachak the rationale was pellucid: 'My insistence in adhering to the decision to remain silent appeared ridiculous to them, but was essential to me as evidence that I was in control of my life circumstances' (p. 225).

Molineux (1903: 236–7) described how the isolation he experienced on death row in the opening years of the twentieth century allowed him to cultivate his imagination: 'No one could sentence my thoughts to imprisonment, they were free. I began to live mentally.' Despite the awfulness of his surroundings and the uncertainty about his future (he was acquitted following a retrial that took place three years after his original conviction) he turned the situation to his profit, concluding that, 'I "found *myself*" in the Death-Chamber' (p. 240; emphasis in original). Isolation, whether sought out or enforced, can be reinterpreted as an opportunity for identity work, as a time to supplant corrosive negativity with peace and calm. The feeling of being in control is important, even if largely illusory. Although the past cannot be changed, one's attitude towards it can be and every individual can rewrite their personal narrative. It is not uncommon for autobiography to become ought-to-biography. The prisoner's life, like anyone's, is a work in progress. (As noted in Chapter 8, the scope for such re-narration narrows as the period alone is prolonged.)

What is striking about so many prisoner accounts is the contrast between the extraordinary journeys taken by the mind and the close confinement of the body; when the latter is trapped the former can wander, unfettered. In this way the deprivation of liberty can never be total. The prisoner who decides to view his situation as one of reflective disengagement fares better in solitude. Ronnie Turner, a former police officer sentenced to 15 years for rape, experienced an intellectual epiphany after reading the work of Trappist monk, Thomas Merton. As Turner (2000: 216) recounted it:

Merton said that a monastery could be like a prison for a monk who thought he had to be there. It occurred to me that if a monastery could be like a prison, then a prison could be like a monastery. The only difference Thomas Merton's monks displayed was the difference in their attitude. I reasoned that I could change my prison into a monastery by changing my attitude about where I was and why I was there.

Similarly, a prisoner explained to Leder (2004: 59; emphasis in original) 'When you read the *Koran* and the *Bible*, you'll see that different prophets went to the *cave* for comfort and isolation. And the cell's like that cave.' There is an echo here of the words written in prison by Samuel Speed in 1677 and used by Throness (2008: 300) to bring to a close her book on the theological origins of the Penitentiary Act 1779: 'A Jayl's the centre of this Iron-age/ Yet not my Prison, but mine Hermitage.' (Speed was clearly inspired by Richard Lovelace's poem, 'To Althea, from Prison'.) That prisoners continued to express a similar sentiment more than 300 years later says something about how deeply embedded is the idea that the prisoner and the monk can be seen to share a similar spatio-temporal orientation. Each resides in an institution to which he is committed and where a large measure of personal autonomy is invariably foregone. Each is viewed as having the capacity to transcend his immediate environment and find spiritual rejuvenation. Each can fail in the process.

The idea that the experience of solitude has made the individual freer is found in many narratives. This is the realization of the dream of the nineteenth-century reformers that imprisonment would provide a springboard for spiritual rebirth. More often the prison sentence is seen as a time of limbo with any possibility of resurrection awaiting release. In a book that blends penal theory and literary criticism, Smith (2009: 133) observed that 'the poetics of personal escape' have exercised a lasting hold on the American imagination. As he elaborated, 'the image of an inviolable core of being—a selfhood deeper than skin and bone, eluding the assaults and degradations of punishment—is among the most common tropes in the writings of those living and dying inside prison walls' (p. 133).

Prisoners who see their imprisonment as an opportunity for their minds to travel in new directions create what Leder (2004: 59) termed 'a haven for thoughtful exploration'. If they succeed in decoupling their mental life from their physical environment, the rewards can be great. Cramped conditions become less oppressive: 'my space is supposed to be restricted, but my ideas don't have to be, and that's where I find all my freedom...When I was on the street, I had *less* space than I do in prison' (Tray Jones, cited in Leder 2004: 59; emphasis in original). Despite the odds, some prisoners manage to turn their incarceration to their advantage and to engage in a process of redefining and remoulding the self. Sometimes they are happy to cast off a pre-prison identity that was defined by a diminution of life prospects (both for themselves and others). A desire to be able to look back on a difficult situation and to feel that it was managed successfully helps too: 'I want in later years to look back on the time here, not with shame, but with a certain pride. That's the only thing that no one can take from me' (Bonhoeffer 2001: 45). Rideau (2011) felt that it would be beneath his dignity to evade the hardships of solitary confinement through drugs, self-harm or mental illness (whether real or feigned). For him the only authentic approach was to tackle the pain head on and not to relent:

I am stronger than the punishment. The only way to beat it, to rise above it, is to regard the punishment as a challenge and see my ability to endure it while others cannot as a victory. Whenever another man falls under the pressure, it's a triumph for me. Callous, some would call me. A man falls, broken, insane or dead, and I feel nothing but triumph. But this is no place for pity—not for the next man, nor for myself. It would break me. The hard truth about solitary is that each man must struggle and suffer alone. (p. 65)

Thus, the prisoner who resists the pressure draws strength from those who do not and the determination to endure is reinforced by the competitive advantage that is enjoyed over those who find themselves in similar circumstances but lack the wherewithal to cope.

Early Adapters

Those who triumph over penal adversity often show precocious adaptation to their predicament. Just as suicide and self-harm are most likely in the first phase of adjustment, before tumult has been displaced by tedium (see Table 9.1), so, too, would it appear that the resilient show their colours early on. A few are resolute from the beginning; they determine to live or to die come what may, insofar as they retain any capacity to guide events. The survivors are not as amazed by their courage as others may be; for them it is a matter of discipline, duty, or choosing life as the answer to the most significant existential question that they have been asked. The suicides are often identifiable in advance and their deaths cause less surprise. The risk factors are well known. There are too few ties to bind them securely to life. But these groups—those with a seemingly bottomless capacity to endure and those whose grip on life is so tenuous as to prove inadequate—define end points along a spectrum of adaptation. Most prisoners cope, more or less successfully (and more or less querulously) with the quotidian rigours of incarceration; they get by, however anguished. If meaningful social contact is prohibited, whether for disciplinary or administrative reasons, and this prohibition is prolonged, most will suffer. But again, a minority evince a striking capacity to endure. Prisoners have to challenge themselves to survive and their initial response to this challenge can be of lasting significance.

According to Serge (1970: 57): 'The first day in a cell contains, in miniature, the months, years, decades which will follow... The effects of living in a cell develop according to a constant curve: I tend to think that only their rhythm may vary among individuals.' The rhythm of successful adaptation can soon be discerned. Burney (1962: 14) lost no time coming to terms with his surroundings: 'But I became an anchorite with almost the ease of inborn talent, as puppies learn to swim, and in the earliest days I had already established the routine by which I was to live, with little variation, for five hundred and twenty-six days.' As she was being driven by the police to the No. 1 Detention House in Shanghai where she would spend six and a half years in solitary confinement Cheng (1995: 117) decided that she would not be cowed into submission: 'I realized that the preliminary period of my persecution was drawing to a close. Whatever lay ahead, I would have to redouble my efforts to frustrate my persecutors' attempt to incriminate me. As long as they did not kill me, I would not give up. So, while I sat in the jeep, my mood was not one of fear and defeat but one of resolution.' Despite gruelling hardship, repeated bouts of serious illness, a grossly inadequate diet, the threat of life imprisonment or execution, and the unrelieved grimness of her solitary cell, she clung unwaveringly to her innocence, to the angry bafflement of her persecutors.

The Bidwell brothers and their co-accused made an immediate decision to survive, come what may, and devised a strategy to make this more likely. Austin described how

in the very instant of our overwhelming defeat, standing in the dark mouth of the stone conduit leading from the Old Bailey to the dungeons of Newgate, by virtue of the high resolve we made, we conquered Fate at her worst, and by our act in establishing a secret bond of sympathy in our separation dropped the bad, disastrous, past, and starting on new things planted our feet on the bottom round of the ladder of success, feeling that, with plenty of faith and endurance, Fortune, frown as she might now, must in some distant way turn her wheel and smile again. (Bidwell 1897: 389)

So what was this clever, life-preserving plan, the measure that Austin Bidwell described as 'an invisible bond that no tyranny could break' (p. 478)? Quite simply it involved a degree of structured and coordinated reflection that took advantage of the limited materials that would be available for such:

we swore never to give in, however they might starve us, even grind us to powder, as we felt they would certainly try to do. We knew that in their anxiety about our souls they would be sure kindly to furnish each with a Bible, and we promised to read one chapter every day consecutively, and, while reading the same chapter at the same hour, think of the others. For twenty years we kept the promise. (p. 478)

Austin Bidwell recalled how on the fourth day of his life sentence, when despair and regret threatened to undo him, he 'sprang up, saying to myself the hour and minute had come for me to decide—either for madness and a convict's dishonored grave, or to keep the promise I had made to my friends—never to give in, but to live and conquer fate . . . From that hour I never despaired again' (p. 392). While this plan did not protect them from all of the harsh vicissitudes of penal servitude—George Bidwell (1888: 45–6, 470) planned suicide the night after he was sentenced and cut his throat much later; the timing of the first act reinforcing the point about the die being cast early—and allowing for a measure of retrospective self-aggrandizement, it certainly seemed to offer an additional layer of psychological shelter. With the bond in place, and reinforced every day through a feat of synchronized reading, the Bidwells felt connected; a connection that could not be sundered. When he arrived in Auschwitz, Frankl (2004: 31) decided that, despite the hopelessness of the situation and the very real danger of death, he would not take his own life: 'I made myself a firm promise, on my first evening in camp, that I would not "run into the wire". This was a phrase used in camp to describe the most popular method of suicide—touching the electrically charged barbed-wire fence.' He preserved the integrity of his self by finding meaning in suffering.

Waite (1994) knew before he travelled to Beirut that there was a possibility he would be seized and taken hostage. This did not make his captivity any more bearable; indeed he may have had cause to regret his attempts to intervene on behalf of other hostages given that he lost his own liberty as a result. Regardless of how he felt about his situation and his role in bringing it about, he was resolute from the start. To prepare himself for the ordeal ahead he refused all food for the first week; this fast was an act of strengthening the will. He also decided upon three resolutions that would act as lodestars throughout whatever lay ahead: 'no regrets, no sentimentality, no self-pity' (p. 9). Years later when the weight of his isolation threatened to become crippling he recalled these resolutions and drew strength from them: 'Ridiculous, pompous statements, yet they have some meaning for me' (p. 369). Deciding on a mantra when he entered the first of many makeshift cells, and adhering to it when exhausted, helped him to stave off the advent of a complete collapse. These words, even if they had become trite through repetition, offered a metaphorical crutch for a man with few other supports.

Speer's captivity was long—he was in custody for one year before the Nuremberg trials and served 20 years after his conviction—but it was never entirely solitary. He was transferred to Spandau prison in Berlin with six other war criminals but relations were strained and for the final ten years of his sentence he had only the company of Rudolf Hess and Baldur von Schirach, from each of whom he was more or less estranged. He too was an early adapter, noting in his diary on 8 December 1946 that: 'I am beginning to set up a program for myself, to organize my life as a convict. To be sure, I have only the experience of six weeks to go by, with more than one thousand and thirty weeks still before me. But I already know that a life plan is important if I am to keep going' (Speer 2010: 23). He took an unusually disciplined approach to his confinement, devising a ten-year programme of education and research, which would be broken up by periods of 'vacation' when he would desist from formal study. These structured intellectual pursuits were accompanied by hugely ambitious landscaping projects in the Spandau prison garden. As an architect, Speer must have been more profoundly aware than most prisoners of how the built environment shapes attitudes and behaviour. This may help to explain the nature of his response to confinement which entailed reimagining, and refashioning, the boundaries within which he was forced to exist. (Speer had toyed with the idea of suicide when he learned he was to be prosecuted at Nuremberg, but did so only fleetingly.)

This is not to say that those who find the early stages difficult will not overcome them, but their task is a more onerous one. Nor is it to say that those who find a rhythm to sustain themselves early on will be able to maintain it indefinitely. But a general pattern of early adaptation seems evident. There is a hint of this in the historical literature. One of the prisoners interviewed by Beaumont and Tocqueville (1833: 191) had experience of Walnut Street jail as well as the separate system enforced at Eastern State Penitentiary. While many prisoners preferred the opportunities for communication offered at the former establishment, this individual was more sanguine, commenting: 'If he takes solitary confinement bad, he falls into irritation and despair; if, on the contrary, he immediately sees the advantages which he can derive from it, it does not appear insupportable.' Those who identify, early on, a way to turn things to their benefit can render even the least favourable circumstances bearable.

Berkman (1970) is an interesting exception to the rule. Initially determined to commit suicide, he sharpened a tin spoon to shove into his heart but this implement was found and confiscated by a prison officer before he could carry out his plan. When thus frustrated he was convinced that he would not be able to survive. He saw 22 years in prison as a lifetime, which given his age (21 when sentenced) it certainly was. Contemplating his fate, Berkman commented that 'A strong man might live five years; I doubt it, though; perhaps a very strong man might. *I* couldn't; no, I know I couldn't; perhaps two or three years at most' (p. 108; emphasis in original). To add to his difficulties, he had no prior experience of custody, no benchmark of acceptable conditions, no strategies for coping with time, and was dismayed that the People (capitalized in his account), for whom he struck out and risked all, did not appreciate his actions. Compounding matters, he discovered that his fellow prisoners were a fairly brutal (and conservative) lot, who were unreceptive to the lures of anarchism. Berkman survived the rest of his prison sentence despite the consistently cruel treatment meted out to him, but 30 years after his release, in despondency, he took his own life.

There are parallels here with the life history of Philip Grosser, with whom Berkman corresponded. Grosser (2007) refused to enlist in the US Army in 1917 and was subjected to three years of harsh incarceration as a result. He survived chains, enforced standing, and solitary confinement in Alcatraz, but in 1933, aged 42, he committed suicide by jumping in front of a train in Boston. It is thought that extreme poverty and the associated despair drove him to his death. He was eventually crushed by the capitalist machine which, as an anarchist, he had devoted his life to undermining. Tragically, he could withstand the deprivations of imprisonment better than the indignity and penury of his life at liberty.

Given his youth, inexperience, naive idealism, long sentence, belief that he could not cope, and desire to die, how did Berkman manage to survive? There are several elements to the explanation. He was sustained by the notion that he might be able to escape and that there would be greater propaganda value associated with this than with suicide (a more selfish kind of escape, seen in this context). Despite his unpreparedness for prison life and the awfulness of his treatment he was tenacious because the Cause demanded it. His anarchist ideals made him steadfast in the face of what would otherwise have been unbeatable odds. As part of a movement, his travails, however personally difficult, were insignificant. Something else that kept Berkman alive was his determination to deny his captors, who for so long had taken a perverse interest in frustrating, humiliating and oppressing him, the ultimate satisfaction of his death: 'The thought of the enemy's triumph fans the embers of life. It engenders defiance, and strengthens stubborn resistance' (Berkman 1970: 400).

Davis (2001: 427) observed how, 'Working the interstices between confinement, surveillance, control, and brutality, a remarkable number of imprisoned men and women have managed to invent subversive spaces within which to nurture their knowledge and creativity.' When the wellsprings of inspiration are found in a place as barren as a solitary confinement cell the results are more striking still. Considering how isolation feels, over time, it is necessary to be cognizant of the variation in solitary confinement environments (see Table 6.2), and the extent to which a general process of adaptation renders the unbearable, bearable (Table 9.1). As Koestler (1942: 119) remarked of his time in the condemned cell: 'The astonishing thing, the puzzling thing, the consoling thing about this time was that it passed.' The previous chapter addressed what can be done to reduce the abrasive power of time and to lighten the burden of solitude. Table 10.1 summarized the survival secrets of successful solitaries and elucidated how prisoners make time tractable. Next the focus shifts to what we can learn about the interior lives of people who are forced into isolation, especially the repetitively expressed themes of redemption and hope.

Seeking Refuge in a Supreme Being

Not everyone manages Reinterpretation, but those who do try hard to share a sense of what this means to them, even if easy articulation is not possible. For those who possess, or discover, a religious sensibility, suffering can be accompanied by acceptance, self-actualization, and gratitude. God is company for prisoners who discover that they cannot go it alone. Commenting on Prisoner No. 20, interviewed during their visit to Eastern State Penitentiary, Beaumont and Tocqueville (1833: 190) noted the ubiquity of religious sentiment among the prisoners they met: 'The turn of ideas of this prisoner, is peculiarly grave and religious; it is a remark which we have had occasion to make upon almost all whom we have visited.'

One legacy of the role that religious ideals played in the origins of the penitentiary is that religion continues to be 'unusually salient' in prisons (Beckford 2001: 374). Prisoners are likely to come into contact with organized religion more regularly in prison than outside, whatever their personal proclivities in this regard. Furthermore, traditional modes of Christian religious practice dominate, notwithstanding the large number of conversions to Islam among prisoners in Western countries, especially the US (Hamm 2009; Pew Forum on Religion and Public Life 2012). This may shape the way that prisoners experience solitary confinement if religiosity becomes important to them. The growing number of US prisoners who will never be released face a substantial challenge. To make sense of a predicament where the usual temporal markers do not apply requires either myopic immersion in the present or a wistful gaze towards the hereafter. Both, in essence, amount to the same thing—a deliberate redirection of attention to cope with the effacement of a non-prison future.

According to Beckford (2001: 372), 'prisoners display unexpectedly high levels of public religious activity compared with people from similar social backgrounds outside prison'. A corollary of this may be that they remain receptive to the messages of redemption, reformation, and sacrifice to which the eighteenth- and nineteenth-century reformers were so attuned but which are some way distant from the concerns of many contemporary commentators on penal affairs. It is possible that John Howard would have more in common in this regard with many prisoners today than would his twenty-first century counterparts. He would know what they meant about being 'born again'.

This is not to say that prisons are full of happy believers, but that inmates find themselves in an environment where the religious influence is often part of the fabric of the buildings and where religious personnel are a significant presence. This means that should they be open to the language of repentance and salvation they will have no difficulty finding an interlocutor. The experience of a personal Calvary is often the stimulus for God-seeking among those who had previously found adequate refuge in worldly things. Such seeking can have positive repercussions. The reported effects of religious beliefs, practices, and rituals as well as more individual approaches to spirituality among prisoners include less frequent and less severe depression, and fewer rule violations (Eytan 2011).

It is probably fair to say that those whose political beliefs nourish them during their incarceration find themselves behind bars, to some extent at least, on account of those beliefs, and a term of imprisonment may have been envisaged as an occupational hazard of sorts. Often they are the beneficiaries of support networks outside the prison and the respect—however grudging—of other inmates who recognize a degree of selflessness associated with their conduct. While they can be broken, they have further to bend than prisoners devoid of an overarching purpose. Radicalization can occur during a prison sentence but the dynamic is different. It seems that what happens more often during imprisonment is that religious feelings are evoked and these are drawn upon for support. Those who believe that they contain within themselves a spark of the Divine can fan this into a flame that warms and sustains, no matter how grim the surroundings or how bleak the prospects. The comforts of faith are substantial when they provide insulation from both a regret-filled scrutiny of the past and a despairing glance towards the future. All one can do is follow the path that has been chosen, even if the destination remains unclear: 'I believe that nothing that happens to me is meaningless...As I see it, I'm here for some purpose, and I only hope I may fulfil it' (Bonhoeffer 2001: 97; see also Maruna et al. 2006).

Burney (1962: 89) reported a spiritual awakening which involved a reinterpretation of his place in the world and the sources of meaning that might comfort him: 'I was slowly and unconsciously coming to accept that my impotence and littleness could attract a support to which my erstwhile self-importance could never have aspired'. He continued: 'Having in this way relinquished my illusion of being the pivot and focus of all things, I found that the imminence of death was less oppressive than before' (p. 90). What Burney described resembles the kind of surrender aspired to by those in contemplative religious life, which asceticism and isolation sometimes bring close. He believed that his predicament caused him to attend to forces greater than himself, a dimension of life that he felt he stumbled into, but with a certain inevitability: 'I was quite content to accept that whatever came, came from God's wish that it should be so, and I had only a passing interest in the intermediate steps' (p. 134).

As a Christian pastor Richard Wurmbrand spent a total of 14 years in jail in Communist Romania for his beliefs, three years of this in solitary confinement in an underground cell. When he was taken from his cell it was usually to be interrogated or beaten. (In a Benthamite touch the prison guards who kept him under lock and key wore felt-soled shoes so that he could not hear their approach.) Wurmbrand is interesting for two reasons. First, because of the depth of his belief, which consoled him when he felt that he was almost at breaking point, and which allowed him to place his most abject suffering into a theological context where it could become a source of strength: 'I have had moments of knowing the victory of faith in prison. I have also had moments of despair. I thank God for both. The latter had some good in them, in that they showed me my limitations and taught me not to rely on my own victories, nor on my faith, but on the atoning blood of Jesus Christ' (Wurmbrand 1969: 9). Even the most awful circumstances could become inspirational when they were seen to contain elements of a Christian message.

Secondly, Wurmbrand's prodigious memory and self-discipline helped him to cope with beatings, hallucinations, depression, drugging, and sensory deprivation. During his time in solitary he slept by day and spent the night in prayer and carrying out spiritual exercises. Each night he composed, and delivered, a sermon. This was done without the aid of pen, paper, Bible or any other book as he was denied such luxuries. When a sermon was completed to his satisfaction he memorized it by reducing its key elements to a short rhyme which he learned by heart. These were so securely committed to memory through repetition that after release he could recall some 350 homilies. He emerged from prison with his own stigmata (the torturer's legacy) as well as an interpretation of his suffering that was to offer comfort to many whose beliefs were oppressed by a political system that would brook no dissent.

Storr (1988: 60) recalled a television debate involving Anthony Grey, who had been held in solitary confinement in China, and Arthur Koestler, who had the same experience in Spain:

Both felt that solitude enhanced their appreciation of, and sympathy with, their fellow men. Both had intense experiences of feeling that some kind of higher order of reality existed with which solitude put them in touch. Both felt that trying to put this experience into words tended to trivialize it, because words could not really express it. Although neither man subscribed to any orthodox religious belief, both agreed that they had felt the abstract existence of something which was indefinable or which could only be expressed in symbols.

These men felt that they had glimpsed a fragment of something that appeared to be beyond comprehension, that there existed a level of reality they could not begin to decipher. This insight was as rewarding as it was baffling. Such bafflement is not unusual according to Maitland (2008: 78) who reflected that: 'Repeatedly, in every historical period, from every imaginable terrain, in innumerable different languages and forms, people who go freely into silence come out with slightly garbled messages of intense *jouissance*, of some kind of encounter with nature, their self, their God, or some indescribable source of power.' As the above quote about Koestler and Grey shows, and as so many prisoner testimonies confirm, this experience is also found among those who do not go freely into silence and who may not possess any kind of religious faith. Silence forces a confrontation with the self that seems to open new possibilities.

Abu-Jamal (1997) described watching a lightning storm from his cell on death row. He believed that he had less than one month left to live but found himself rejuvenated by the knowledge that mankind was puny and insignificant when compared with the raw power of nature. The apprehension of universality restored his sovereignty over time. At this moment he felt that he would prevail:

I saw that there is a Power that makes man's power pale. It is the power of Love; the power of God; the power of Life. I felt it surging through every pore. Nature's power prevailed over the man-made, and I felt, that night, that I would prevail. I would overcome the State's efforts to silence and kill me. (p. 31)

This is an example of the kind of 'peak experience' described by Maslow (1970: 75), who believed that 'a single glimpse of heaven' can have a transformative impact, on occasion banishing a sense of meaninglessness and pointlessness from an individual's life. For Maslow intense feelings of awe, interconnectedness, revelation of a higher truth, and appreciation of the natural world are fundamentally non-religiously inspired. This would account for the atheists who have recounted that solitary confinement incorporated some of these elements but who eschewed a religious explanation. A characteristic shared by solitaries of all faiths and none is one of 'feeling vibrantly, often ecstatically, *alive* in a *living* world' (Kull 2008: 132; emphasis in original; see also McBride 2014).

A cynic might suggest that the religious fervour described by some of those who have endured awful experiences of captivity is itself a symptom of a break with reality that is elicited by loneliness, confusion, and possibly despair. But this would be a caricature. Those who have this experience can be uncomfortable with it and uncertain about it. It seems to be a sense of something profound but indescribable, of something bigger, of an appetite for meaning that cannot be sated. They often describe it using the language of Christian spirituality because this is a frame of reference with which they are familiar. Prisoners of other faiths would no doubt draw upon other resources to aid their descriptions. Also, this aspect of the experience unfolds over time in captivity. It is something that takes a while to be felt and to be acknowledged. Given the regularity of its appearance, and the awed tones in which it is described, we should be slow to dismiss this element of the solitary experience. Regardless of how it might appear to a neutral observer, it is invested with great meaning by those exposed to it, and if we are to remain true to their accounts this aspect should not be neglected.

This explains why some prisoners report being grateful for what they have been through. Doors have been opened for them (metaphorically) just as others have been shut (literally). It might be only the fortunate and literate few who are driven to acknowledge this experience in writing, and most solitary prisoners may not undergo this kind of transformation, but the fact that it is found in texts written far apart geographically and historically suggests it is of some importance. The lesson is clear: not all can bear prolonged isolation, but for some of those who can, the experience is fortifying and even, occasionally, uplifting.

In order to survive some prisoners develop an attentiveness to the 'now' that many of their peers at liberty are searching for (e.g. Tolle 2005). Having been wrenched from the world, they find themselves—at no inconsiderable cost—adopting a temporal orientation that is occasionally accompanied by deep feelings of universality, a kind of mindfulness that many seek, but few find. One does not wish to give the impression that prisoners are crypto-mystics, simply that their circumstances release potential that might otherwise have remained pent up. This may be why so many of them, despite the obvious hardships, feel they have been strengthened and enriched by their experience. They have learned to rise above the immediate environment by locating the transformative power of the present, when the distractions of past and future have been reduced to a minimum.

Isolation, therefore, would seem to lead to one of three outcomes: madness, muddling through, or mindfulness. Madness is most likely if the person is idle, there is no wider framework in which they can locate their experience, and they have not become adept at mitigating the harshness of solitary confinement and the expanses of time yawning to be filled. Under such circumstances profound boredom is felt as exceedingly painful and sometimes unendurable. These feelings are intensified in the event of pre-existing mental disorder and they are given a sharper edge if the isolation is seen as punitively intended and illegitimately imposed. For those who have mastered the seven Rs of survival, especially Raptness and Reinterpretation, the experience can be transformed into something rich and life-affirming at the same time as it is painful and destructive. For most solitary prisoners a middle course is negotiated. They muddle through, perturbed but not destroyed by their profound aloneness. They have learned Rescheduling, Removal, Reduction, and Reorientation and may, on occasion, offer Resistance.

When it comes to making sense of the impacts of isolation the role of voluntariness is important but not crucial. Some of those who welcome solitude are nonetheless overwhelmed. Others upon whom solitude is thrust triumph over it. There is more at play here than whether the confinement is imposed or invited. Critically significant is that the solitude is seen as purposeful; that it has a meaning beyond its immediate parameters. When this disinte-grated for the monk, accidie became an issue (see Chapter 4). When this is constructed for the prisoner, acceptance becomes possible. This perspective offers a bridge between a temporal orientation that becomes a necessity for prisoners and a high level of reporting of spiritual experiences. It could be hypothesized that prolonged solitary confinement makes the possibility of transcendence over time more likely.

The Buoyancy of Hope

If a prisoner is to survive prolonged solitude a window to a hypothetical future must remain open, however slightly. Davitt (1885: 180) described hope as the 'all-sustaining prison virtue'. He described prison as a 'paradise of castle-builders' by which he meant men who had become adept at 'hiding the worst features of the objective present behind a picture of a pleasant and happy, if imaginary, future' (p. 180). But it would seem that these prisoners were dreaming rather than planning and while they derived com-fort from the exercise they were aware that it involved a dollop of self-delusion. A future orientation of this kind does not cause pain because it is unreal and known to be so. Planning for the future which must be tempered with reality runs the risk of causing stress and anxiety and so is avoided. Dreaming of a life of riches, ease, and beauty does not because it is unlikely ever to happen.

The theme of hope runs through prisoner accounts. But this is hope decoupled from the future and unburdened by plans. It is a deep longing for an afterlife (whether temporal or spiritual), but is not anchored to specific people or events. Hoping to do particular things, at particular times, with particular people can be fraught, as planning often is. What prisoners express is the importance of a belief in hope rather than a hope for anything specific. This is hope without contingency, an amorphous hope that defies attachment to things. This is why it can coexist with a temporal orientation that is firmly on the present. Pinning hope to a set of circumstances is risky as the latter lie outside the control of the individual (espe-cially the imprisoned individual) and if they are dashed so, too, is hope. When prisoners talk about hope it is not freighted with the burden of expectation. It is unconditional hope; to place condi-tions on its realization is to invite anguish. Hope is a positive atti-tude to the future rather than the anticipation of any specific event coming to pass. It is defined by a yearning for change and progress, even if the objective circumstances suggest that positive developments are highly unlikely. Even if built on slender foundations—and ultimately thwarted—hope can sustain and inspire.

Marcel (1962: 36) observed that 'The truth is that there can strictly speaking be no hope except where the temptation to despair exists.' This inverse relationship seems strong. When the 'temptation to despair' is greatest then the triumph of hope is most spectacular. Hope, if invested in a deity, is accompanied by a set of precepts and principles that allow life to be lived with dignity. Recall Clayton Fountain wishing to wear the habit that would have symbolized a new-found purpose and acceptance but that simultaneously placed upon him an expectation of conduct that was in keeping with his new station in life; a man of God must strive for a Godlike existence. The solitary prisoner with faith is part of a community of believers, even if congregation is never possible. Strength can be drawn from devotional practice (or, indeed, from a deep commitment to art or politics) which can also act as the assertion of autonomy or, on occasion, the embodiment of resistance.

What comes through strongly in prisoner narratives is a need to believe in a future, but not to orientate oneself towards it or to make concrete plans for it; to accept what is and to hope for what might be. Clayton Fountain captured the importance of remaining hopeful even against enormous odds: 'I will certainly continue to hope that I will be paroled, yet at the same time I have also accepted that I will die in prison—that this is to be my "home" for the rest of my life. Yes, I know that this is a paradox, but it is true' (cited in Jones 2011: 93). Hope offers solace even if its object will never be realized. When it evaporates the consequences can be dramatic. As poet and playwright Michael Harding (2011) put it, 'there's no solitude to compare with the derelict sanctuary of a heart with no hope'.

Post-traumatic Growth

There is nothing positive about trauma. But the effort to make sense of adversity, to overcome the challenges that follow in its wake, and to create meaning out of altered circumstances, can serve as a platform for personal growth. Bronsteen et al. (2009: 1042) reviewed the effects of serious disability on subjective well-being and found a general pattern of successful adaptation, leading them to conclude that while the underlying mechanisms were not well understood: 'it seems as if people have a "psychological immune system" that helps them cope with the effects of many kinds of adverse events'.

Not everyone is affected by trauma in the same way. Some emerge emotionally unscathed, some recover without prolonged distress, some are impaired. It is the group who are changed but in the process move beyond their previous level of functioning that has experienced post-traumatic growth (Joseph 2012: 71–3). Those who report the most growth are not the individuals who easily slough off the effects of traumatic circumstances, but those who are shaken up (but not overwhelmed) by them. In their efforts to reconcile the tensions between the world as now revealed to them and their previous assumptions, they come to new understandings and accommodations. They learn more about their psychological boundaries and how far they can be pushed and redefined; they identify capacities to cope that had been hidden; they strike new terms of engagement with their life-worlds. They become accomplished reappraisers.

The seeds of some pine trees are stored in very durable resinous cones, sometimes for many years, until the heat of a forest fire opens them and allows new growth to occur. The destructive force of a major environmental hazard releases the growth potential within the cone's tough exterior. Without fire the seeds will not germinate. These cones are described by botanists as 'serotinous' meaning that they remain unopened for a long time. In other words, the desolation that is visible after a forest fire is essential for some species to thrive. This is a fitting metaphor for the traumatic growth that some prisoners write about.

According to Joseph (2012), a traumatic experience is often followed by a deeper appreciation of human relationships, an increased sense of compassion for others, and a longing for intimacy. People can change the way they see themselves, identifying new strengths and accepting limitations. They sometimes adopt a philosophy of life which places more emphasis on living in the present and less on material possessions. In a review of the evidence, Joseph (2012: 83) concluded that across a wide range of domains including transportation accidents, natural disasters, terrorist attacks, crime victimization, medical problems, and bereavement: 'between 30 and 70 per cent of trauma survivors report at least some form of benefit following the events in question.' The capacity for trauma to catalyse growth is reduced for prisoners in solitary confinement where the scope to deepen human relationships has largely been removed. But it is clear from the testimonies reviewed for this book that mature philosophical answers to existential questions are sometimes formulated. Difficult circumstances can be a launching pad for growth. Prisoners in solitary confinement can re-author their lives into tales of triumphant endurance, but the obstacles to so doing should not be underestimated.

The theory of post-traumatic growth is underpinned by the idea that striving to realize one's potential is a fundamental human characteristic. Joseph (2012: 120) proposed that post-traumatic growth occurs most readily when basic psychological needs are met. One of these needs—that of relatedness, which entails a sense of feeling accepted, respected, nurtured, belonging, connected— cannot easily be addressed by the prisoner in solitary confinement. According to Ryan and Deci (2000), upon whose work Joseph draws, competence and autonomy are the other innate psycho-logical needs that, if fulfilled, lead to enhanced self-motivation and mental health. Again, they are unlikely to be satisfied in soli-tary confinement. That some solitary prisoners manage to thrive despite these significant obstacles makes their achievement all the more extraordinary.

At issue here is what we can learn about our common human-ity from the experiences of those who have lived *in extremis*. The further one travels from everyday experience the more one learns about the elasticity of the self and the outer bounds of endur-ance. The capacities to resist, to reassess, to recalibrate, and to rejoice become clear only when they are severely tested. In the words of Brian Keenan (1992: xv), the paradox of extreme cap-tivity is 'how in the most inhuman of circumstances men grow and deepen in humanity. In the face of death but not because of it, they explode with passionate life.' After four and a half years as a hostage in the Lebanon, Keenan described himself as 'a cross between Humpty Dumpty and Rip Van Winkle—I have fallen off the wall and suddenly awake I find all the pieces of me, before me. There are more parts than I began with' (p. xi). There is an important point here: while fractured, he is not diminished. The challenge is to assemble a new—and stable—self that incor-porates the additional fragments; a mosaic that brings his life story up to date. This is like the metaphor of the shattered vase that Joseph (2012: 113–14) uses to illustrate how those who try to replicate their former selves after a traumatic event may find that the resulting structure is superficially intact but inherently fragile, while those who build something new out of the pieces are better able to accommodate the changes to their worlds.

Tragedy can be transformational. Some crumble but others—many others—find wisdom and strength in surviving trauma. The fact of survival sometimes pricks a slumbering consciousness into a new state of alertness. This is not to argue that stressful life experiences such as prolonged solitary confinement are ultimately rewarding, but simply to suggest that they might be, and that the literature is somewhat lopsided in this regard with little account taken of the positives that can emerge from a negative experience. Penal isolation can be seen as a (forced) march towards meaning that on rare occasions leads to suicidal despair or profound self-actualization. More typically it involves a blend of distress, reflection, and cognitive realignment that allows something meaningful to be wrought out of suffering. The focus is not so much on the suffering itself as on the transformation that can arise as a result of it. The gains of solitude are not confined to a small number of extraordinary individuals. They are part of a pattern; burdens can yield benefits.

Breytenbach (1984: 130) was unequivocal about the harmful nature of his prolonged solitary confinement: 'parts of you are destroyed and these parts will never again be revived...And this damage is permanent even though you learn to live with it, however well camouflaged.' But he also identified—to his surprise—a range of positive effects characterized by increased perceptual acuity and emotional depth:

by being forced to turn in upon yourself you discover, paradoxically, openings to the outside in yourself which you have not been aware of before. You grow rich with the richness of the very poor; the smallest sign of life from outside becomes a gift from heaven, to be cherished. You really see things for what they are, stripped of your own overbearing presence. A blanket really is a blanket, and though it is grey, it has a million colours in it...You roll and smoke a cigarette and its aroma is worth all the valleys of Turkey...No king was ever as blessed as you are. (pp. 130–1)

In the afterword to his account of nearly seven years as a hostage in the Middle East, Anderson (1994: 404) expressed a sense of gratitude for the changes captivity wrought in his life and that of his family:

While no one chooses the kind of terrible events that engulfed us, we have much to be thankful for out of those years of testing. We know ourselves, and each other, much better than we might have. We know the depth and strength of our love. And we have a deeper, stronger faith in God. 'That which does not destroy me, makes me stronger,' Nietzsche wrote. We are stronger, and our life is full of joy.

Anderson acknowledged that he was transformed by his experience as a hostage but argued at the same time that he was an active participant in the recasting of his identity, that despite the overwhelming environmental pressures he contributed in no small way to shaping his own destiny. Similarly, Cheng (1995: 120), whose health was almost ruined by her solitary confinement in a Chinese prison, looked back on her struggle for survival as an experience that made her 'a spiritually stronger and politically more mature person'. In acknowledging his tremendous good fortune in surviving the Lager, and notwithstanding how much suffering he experienced and witnessed, Levi (1987: 398) stated that, 'the sum total is clearly positive: in its totality, this past has made me richer and surer'. This is an emphatic affirmation of the possibility of post-traumatic growth.

The Art of Living

Frankl (2004: 75) discovered that when everything appears to have been removed, the freedom to choose one's attitude remains: 'everything can be taken from a man but one thing: the last of the human freedoms—to choose one's attitude in any given set of circumstances, to choose one's own way'. The misery of the concentration camp, the associated hopelessness, and the constant fear of impending death could not obliterate this fundamental freedom: 'any man can, even under such circumstances, decide what shall become of him—mentally and spiritually' (p. 75). While protecting his physical integrity and prolonging his life were almost always beyond his control, how he made sense of his suffering and with what degree of dignity he bore it, it fell to the individual to determine. This freedom gave life its meaning: 'there is also purpose in that life which is almost barren of both creation and enjoyment and which admits of but one possibility of high moral behaviour: namely in man's attitude to his existence, an existence restricted by external forces' (p. 76).

It was a rare person who could remain brave, generous, and serene in the milieu of the concentration camp, but some managed to do so and through their attitude to suffering they demonstrated the existence of the human capacity to make the critical decision that Frankl described. This courageous few showed how sense could be made of suffering and how a new layer of meaning could be added to a life that was almost certain to be further degraded and then snuffed out. Not many men or women have the fortitude to behave like this, but the fact that some do suggests that all might.

It is important not to exaggerate the extent to which prisoners in twenty-first-century solitary confinement cells will be able to triumph over extreme adversity but the message from Frankl is that this is not happenstance; those who win out have decided to do so and those who withdraw, take their own lives, prey on (or pray with) their comrades, or conspire with the authorities have also chosen their course of action. Frankl's insight is that life can be meaningful as well as desperately unhappy. To say that isolated prisoners can derive something positive from their situation does not imply that they must enjoy it. For long-term prisoners of a reflective bent, solitary confinement is sometimes seen as a catalyst for personal development. For those ready to accept the rewards that sobriety and critical reflection can bring, the cell can be redefined as a 'house of healing' (Casarjian 1995).

Frankl (2004: 139) defined 'tragic optimism' as the idea that meaning can be wrought from the direst circumstances and that persons who take responsibility for their decisions can strive to convert suffering into accomplishment. He suggested that the most powerful arguments in favour of this notion are those that can be made from individual cases. To this end, the methodology adopted for this book has been to present a wide range of accounts rather than to concentrate on a few. By a process of aggregation these personal testimonies of unlikely triumph over the least favourable conditions add weight to Frankl's idea. If some can achieve a demeanour of tragic optimism then why not others? Frankl's argument was not that suffering is essential to render life meaningful; far from it. His view was that if suffering could be avoided it should be and that it was only triumph over unavoidable suffering that was meaningful.

Bettelheim (1960), whose later contributions to psychology became mired in controversy, also wrote of the indefatigability of the human spirit under duress. Based on observation and introspection he concluded that however adverse the circumstances, the realm of personal choice could never be totally vanquished. Where life had been reduced to a largely futile struggle to subsist, the attitude one took to such circumstances remained a matter for the individual to determine:

> Prisoners who understood this fully, came to know that this, and only this, formed the crucial difference between retaining one's humanity (and often life itself) and accepting death as a human being (or perhaps physical death): whether one retained the freedom to choose autonomously one's attitude to extreme conditions even when they seemed totally beyond one's ability to influence them. (p. 158)

Bettelheim described the ability to determine one's own attitude to life's vicissitudes as 'the last, if not the greatest, of the human freedoms' (p. 158). The fact that these choices were brutally restricted did not diminish their significance. The prisoner who chose to spend an idle moment resting or talking or reading was demonstrating a capacity to make decisions that confirmed his or her humanity had not been, and could never be, entirely expunged.

Closing the Circle

There are four reasons why monastic history is a relevant distal consideration in this book. The first is that the idea of penitential incarceration originated with the monks. As Peters (1995: 29) put it, they were responsible for 'the first instances of confinement for specific periods and occasionally for life for the purpose of moral correction'. The second is the role of monks in emphasizing the importance of clock time. Indeed, clocks were invented so that the canonical hours could be marked punctually. Keeping track of time allowed the activities of men to be synchronized. As Foucault (1991: 150) remarked of the religious orders: 'they were the specialists of time, the great technicians of rhythm and regular activities'. The monk's timetable is tiring but not tiresome; the prisoner's is tiresome but not tiring. What is awesome for one can be irksome for the other. The third is the contribution to early prison architecture of the monk's cell. The fourth is the qualified endorsement of solitude, the realization that to be safe it must be tempered with engagement.

The wheel comes full circle with Clayton Fountain attempting to insert a Cistercian rhythm into a life lived in a maximum-security solitary confinement cell that he had redefined as a hermitage. While there is no element of voluntarism to his confinement, and while the schedule according to which he desired to live was in conflict with the schedule according to which he was required to organize his daily affairs, his strivings illustrate how far a person who has been stripped of almost everything can go to transform their life by reinterpreting it. The rules of monastic life stress the importance of relatedness to others; a context of meaning in which to make sense of everyday activities; structure; the availability of wise and supportive guides; wholesome food; and variety (mixing manual and intellectual pursuits). To a greater or lesser extent they embody five of the seven Rs of survival described in Table 10.1, including the most important one (Reinterpretation). Missing, for obvious reasons, are Resistance (the monk who fights the system is free to leave) and Reduction (the monk who wants to sleep away his vocation will not be able to do this within the confines of the monastery).

As a prisoner in long-term solitary confinement without any prospect of release and few interlocutors, the distance between Fountain's cellular life and that of a taciturn monk might appear easily bridgeable. But this is to downplay the profundity of what he accomplished. The decision to redefine his experience as monastic and sacrificial (in the sense of him offering up his suffering to his God) rather than punitive and sacrificial (in the sense of his treatment being used as a cautionary tale for other prisoners) is hugely significant. He seized control of his destiny and applied to his situation a frame of reference that it was beyond the power of officialdom to shift. His dialogues became internal ones that could not be interfered with, redirected, or stripped of meaning by any external authority. While his objective conditions of confinement may have remained the same, his subjective experience of them shifted radically. He had his own 'monastic schedule' (Jones 2011: 96), following the same seven daily offices as his Trappist brothers in Assumption Abbey. He had looked forward to wearing a monk's habit over his prison clothing, but his unexpected early death meant that he never had the opportunity to test the willingness of the prison authorities to allow him do so.

In his study of the spiritual regeneration of Clayton Fountain, Jones (2011) repeated a comment made to him by a member of the chaplain's staff. This individual, struggling to understand how anyone could have endured the degree of isolation and rejection that Fountain seemed to be coping with commented, 'The fact that he hasn't become unglued under such conditions only proves how crazy the man is. A sane person would have been a basket case long before this' (p. 2). This is interesting doublespeak: his sanity is offered as evidence of his insanity! It also shows how deeply rooted is the notion that people will invariably unravel in solitude. Fountain's story of survival and his quest for redemption is transformed into a narrative of madness and threat.

Another of the unremarked benefits of incarceration is that prisoners grow up more than others or, indeed, more than they would have done had they remained at liberty, where their chances of an early demise are higher. Given the dangers associated with life on the street, incarceration can extend life expectancy for a particularly vulnerable population. This is not to say that arrangements could not be made to provide individuals with similar life-extending opportunities in the community, but simply to acknowledge—as some prisoners do—that had they not been incarcerated they would have wreaked further havoc on their own lives and the lives of those around them. By taking them out of circulation and creating a situation which forces introspection, personal transformations can result that would not otherwise have become manifest. This not an argument for more prison, or even that prison exercises a beneficial effect overall, but simply an assertion, based on prisoner testimonies and research findings, that in some cases incarceration is life-preserving (and maybe life-enhancing) and to deny this possibility is to ignore the complexity of imprisonment and how it is felt.

The idea of life after prison as a rebirth of some kind runs deep. Berkman (1970) entitled the fourth and final part of his prison memoir 'The Resurrection'. After his civil death in Pittsburgh's Western Penitentiary, Berkman came back to life to continue the struggle. The realization that his task was incomplete filled him with vigour and determination and he closed his book with the following words to a friend who seemed alarmed by his renewed sense of purpose: 'My resurrection, dear friend. I have found work to do' (p. 512). There are echoes here of the final sentence of Dostoyevsky's *House of the Dead*, 'Freedom, new life, resurrection from the dead...What a glorious moment!' (2004: 247), and Austin Bidwell (1897: 481) closed his prison memoir with a not dissimilar ejaculation: 'I realized that I was free, with health and strength, with courage to begin again the battle of life, and in my irrepressible emotion I cried aloud, and my cry was like a prayer—"God is good." ' These three men had little in common biographically and their prison experiences varied greatly but they were united by the thrilling prospect of a return to company of their own choosing. They were energized by the idea that once among people again they could strive to be fully human.

Coda

To conclude, it is necessary to reiterate what this book is not. First, it is not an apologia for cruel treatment. It is not intended to offer a penal fig leaf to those who wish to impose more solitude on more people for more time. It is not an attempt to downplay the emotional toll exacted by isolation or to discount the profound and life-limiting personal changes that are required to manage the temporal dimension of imprisonment. The fact that some prisoners in solitary confinement can transcend the degradation and loneliness of their immediate circumstances does not mean that more of them should be given this opportunity. That people triumph over adversity is not a reason for more adversity. Above all, the book is not a paean to complacency. To read it in this way would be facile and disingenuous. The penal hawk who finds succour in these pages is guilty of heroic self-deception. So many people are being unnecessarily damaged by an approach to punishment (exemplified by the supermax) that has lost sight of the inherent dignity of the person that the only rational response is to challenge its continuation and to resist its expansion.

So what, then, is the book about? Well, there is an element of revisionism, of course, or at least an attempt to return to some areas where a settled view had been established (e.g. the unequivocally damaging nature of solitary confinement and its early historical manifestations), and to re-examine the evidence before offering an interpretation with a different set of emphases. There is also an attempt to focus scholarly attention on an aspect of the prison experience—time, its meanderings, measures and meanings—that seldom receives sustained attention. Fundamentally, imprisonment is about time and the importance of this factor has varied

with changing sentence lengths, life expectancies, penal philosophies, collective priorities, and individual cognitions. This book
makes an effort to insert the dimension of time into studies of
prison life, so that it becomes more than an externally imposed
marker of punitive intent and is seen as a factor that is actively
engaged with by prisoners. Out of this engagement emerges a set of
working hypotheses about how to respond to an existential challenge that demands an orientation towards the present, particularly in circumstances when the possibility of release, if it exists,
lies some way distant and is at the discretion of others.

Throughout these pages will be found an undercurrent of
admiration for the capacity of individuals to resist—however
imperfectly—the imposition of hardships that could crush them.
That some men and women flourish in hostile environments is an
acknowledgement that no matter how prison systems contrive to
add to the layers of misery imposed on those behind bars, there
will be triumphs as well as tragedies. There is no gainsaying that
some people derive rewards, however qualified, from penal isolation. They profit in two senses: their chances of premature, violent death are reduced, and they can unlock a self-understanding
that may otherwise have remained closed to them. Sometimes this
results in a degree of acceptance and serenity that eases the burden of captivity on a personal level; these are the 'tragic optimists'
described by Frankl (2004: 139), men and women who have mastered the art of living. Sometimes it results in the generation of
activities, such as peacemaking or solidarity building, which benefit the wider prison population. Sometimes it eventuates in poetry
and prose which can educate and enrich all literate people. These
individual success stories, in other words, redound to our collective advantage. In addition, they sound a note of hope—however
faint and faltering—in a context more often characterized by
resignation or despair. Finally, they reveal the scholarly rewards
that accompany scrutiny of the temporal lives of the most isolated
among our number, an endeavour to which it is hoped this book
will recruit new enthusiasts.

Appendix

The key prisoner writings drawn upon in this book are listed overleaf. The list does not pretend to be exhaustive of the genre. Its purpose is simply to indicate the range of source materials that, in conjunction with academic critiques, official publications, personal communications, interviews, field visits, newspaper articles, administrative statistics, the reports of campaigning bodies, and other data, inform the arguments advanced throughout the preceding pages. It is a sample of the most literate and stimulating works. As with all lists, this one will no doubt have its critics, but I have tried to include a chronologically and geographically diverse cross-section of accounts penned by men and women who survived enforced solitude for extended periods; these memoirists could not avoid grappling with the temporal dimension of their existence.

Nor is the table a complete tally of the prisoner writings referred to throughout the text. Other narratives are incorporated insofar as they shed light on the questions of time and solitude. For example, Brian Keenan and Terry Anderson, each of whom spent years as hostages in Beirut, have interesting things to say about their experiences of solitary confinement, but as they spent most of their time in close proximity with other captives, they are not included in the table. Similarly, the musings of Ingrid Betancourt in the Colombian jungle, Wilbert Rideau in an Angola prison, Damien Echols on death row in Arkansas, Bruno Bettelheim in Dachau and Buchenwald, Philip Grosser in Alcatraz, and the pseudonymous Zeno in England, offer much food for thought and are quoted on occasion. Sara Maitland and Robert Kull sought out solitude and provided nuanced accounts of its effects, but as voluntary isolates they are excluded from the list.

The books by Fyodor Dostoyevsky and Victor Serge (the pen name of Victor Lvovich Kibalchich) are best described as semi-autobiographical, but as they are deeply rooted in personal experiences of incarceration and full of important insights, as well as capturing many matters that continue to be of relevance to prisoners, it was deemed appropriate to include them. (Tolstoy said of Dostoyevsky's masterpiece, *The House of the Dead*, that: 'I know no better book in all modern literature.')

Albert Speer spent little time in isolation but for company he was limited to the same small group of men (never numbering more than six) with whom relations were distant and he was forced to draw heavily on his own resources for the duration of his 20-year prison term. Similarly, while Viktor Frankl was seldom alone in the concentration camp, his ability to recast his predicament is testament to the human capacity to triumph over appalling hardships. He demonstrates how, even in the most impoverished and hazardous of circumstances, the individual's freedom of choice can never be entirely obliterated. Also, like Dostoyevsky, he shows how the presence of others does not necessarily relieve the pain of isolation.

Breyten Breytenbach spent the first two of his seven years in South African prisons in solitary confinement and is included because this is a long enough period to merit consideration and also because of the profundity of some of his observations. Indeed, even when he was restored to company his freedom to communicate with other prisoners was severely curtailed. Arthur Koestler spent only two months in isolation during the Spanish Civil War, during which time he expected to be executed. While the period he spent incommunicado was relatively brief, his reflections on the passage of time—brought into sharp focus by his fear of impending death—combined with his literary prowess, make his account a richly rewarding one to read. First-person accounts from condemned men who are endowed with the ability to capture their experience in writing are rare indeed.

Stories of solitariness: a sampler

Author (Period of captivity)	Place	Title of Memoir
Jabez Balfour (1895–1906)	England	*My Prison Life*
Alexander Berkman (1892–1906)	USA	*Prison Memoirs of an Anarchist*
Austin Bidwell (1873–93)	England	*Bidwell's Travels, from Wall Street to London Prison – Fifteen Years in Solitude*
George Bidwell (1873–87)	England	*Forging His Chains*
Edith Bone (1949–56)	Hungary	*Seven Years Solitary*
Dietrich Bonhoeffer (1943–5)	Germany	*Letters and Papers from Prison*
Breyten Breytenbach (1975–82)	South Africa	*The True Confessions of an Albino Terrorist*
Christopher Burney (1942–3)	France	*Solitary Confinement: An Exercise in Liberty*
Nien Cheng (1966–73)	China	*Life and Death in Shanghai*
Michael Davitt (1870–7; 1881–2)	England	*Leaves from a Prison Diary, or Lectures to a Solitary Audience*

Author	Place	Title of Memoir
Fyodor Dostoyevsky	Russia	*The House of the Dead*
Viktor Frankl (1942–5)	Poland/Germany	*Man's Search for Meaning*
Anthony Grey (1967–9)	China	*Hostage in Peking*
Arthur Koestler (1937)	Spain	*Dialogue with Death*
Florence Maybrick (1889–1904)	England	*My Fifteen Lost Years*
Victor Serge	France	*Men in Prison*
Albert Speer (1946–66)	Germany	*Spandau: The Secret Diaries*
Jacobo Timerman (1977–9)	Argentina	*Prisoner Without a Name, Cell Without a Number*
Terry Waite (1987–91)	Lebanon	*Taken on Trust*
Richard Wurmbrand (1948–56; 1959–64)	Romania	*Sermons in Solitary Confinement*

References

A Carthusian (1975), *They Speak by Silences*, London: Darton, Longman and Todd. (Originally published in 1955 by Longmans, Green and Co. Ltd.)

Abbott, J. H. (1981), *In the Belly of the Beast: Letters from Prison*, London: Hutchinson.

Abu-Jamal, M. (1997), *Death Blossoms: Reflections from a Prisoner of Conscience*, Farmington, Pa: Plough Publishing House.

Adshead, J. (1845), *Prisons and Prisoners*, London: Longman, Brown, Green and Longman.

Akers, R. L., Hayner, N. and Gruninger, W. (1977), 'Time served, career phase, and prisonization: Findings in five countries', in R. G. Leger and J. R. Stratton (eds), *The Sociology of Corrections: A Book of Readings*, New York: John Wiley and Sons, pp. 216–27.

American Bar Association (2011), *ABA Standards for Criminal Justice (Third Edition): Treatment of Prisoners*, Washington DC: ABA.

Amnesty International (2011), *USA: 100 Years in Solitary: The 'Angola 3' and Their Fight for Justice*, London: Amnesty International.

Amnesty International (2012), *USA: The Edge of Endurance: Prison Conditions in California's Security Housing Units*, London: Amnesty International.

Anderson, T. (1994), *Den of Lions: Memoirs of Seven Years*, New York: Ballantine Books. (Originally published in 1993 by Crown)

Andrew, J. M. and Bentley, M. R. (1976), 'The quick minute: Delinquents, drugs and time', *Criminal Justice and Behavior*, 3: 179–86.

Anonymous (1871), 'Review of Mr. Tallack's paper on the prison system of Great Britain and the United States', *The Journal of Prison Discipline and Philanthropy*, New Series, 10: 36–49.

Anonymous (1883), 'Dickens's Dutchman out of jail: A queer old man who says he cannot lead an honest life', *New York Times*, 15 June.

Anonymous (1987), 'Introduction', *The Prison Journal*, 67: 1–37.

Atchley, R. C. and McCabe, M. P. (1968), 'Socialization in correctional communities: A replication', *American Sociological Review*, 33: 774–85.

Bacote v. Federal Bureau of Prisons, case 1:12–cv–01570, 18 June 2012, USDC Colorado.

Balfour, J. S. (1907), *My Prison Life*, London: Chapman and Hall.

Barnes, H. E. and Teeters, N. K. (1943), *New Horizons in Criminology*, New York: Prentice-Hall.

Barnes, H. E. and Teeters, N. K. (1959), *New Horizons in Criminology*, 3rd edn, Englewood Cliffs, NJ: Prentice-Hall.

Baxendale, A. S. (2011), *Before the Wars: Churchill as Reformer (1910–1911)*, Oxford: Peter Lang.

Baxter, C., Brown, W., Chatman-Bey, T. et al. (2005), 'Live from the panoptican: Architecture and power revisited', in J. James (ed.), *The New Abolitionists: (Neo)Slave Narratives and Contemporary Prison Writings*, Albany, NY: State University of New York Press, pp. 207–15.

Beckett, S. (2006), 'The Unnamable', in P. Auster (ed.) *Samuel Beckett: The Grove Centenary Edition*, Vol. II Novels, New York: Grove Press, pp. 283–407. (Originally published in 1953 by Les Editions de Minuit)

Beckford, J. A. (2001), 'Doing time: Space, time religious diversity and the sacred in prisons', *International Review of Sociology*, 11: 371–82.

Belisle, P. D. (2003), *The Language of Silence: The Changing Face of Monastic Solitude*, London: Darton, Longman and Todd.

Benjamin, T. B. and Lux, K. (1975), 'Constitutional and psychological implications of the use of solitary confinement: Experience at the Maine State prison', *New England Journal on Prison Law*, 2: 27–46.

Bentham, J. (1843), *The Works of Jeremy Bentham published under the Superintendence of his Executor, John Bowring*, Vol. 10 (Memoirs Part I and Correspondence), Edinburgh: William Tait.

Berkman, A. (1970), *Prison Memoirs of an Anarchist*, New York: Schocken Books. (Originally published in 1912 by Mother Earth Publishing Association)

Betancourt, I. (2010), *Even Silence Has an End: My Six Years of Captivity in the Colombian Jungle*, London: Virago.

Bettelheim, B. (1960), *The Informed Heart: Autonomy in a Mass Age*, Glencoe, Ill: The Free Press.

Bidwell, A. (1897), *Bidwell's Travels, from Wall Street to London Prison—Fifteen Years in Solitude*, Hartford, Conn: Bidwell Publishing Company.

Bidwell, G. (1888), *Forging his Chains: The Autobiography of George Bidwell*, Hartford, Conn: S. S. Scranton and Company.

Bone, E. (1957), *Seven Years Solitary*, London: Hamish Hamilton.

Bonhoeffer, D. (2001), *Letters and Papers from Prison: An Abridged Edition* (edited by E. Bethge), London: SCM Press. (Originally published in 1953 by SCM Press)

Bonsall, E. H., Sharpless, T., Lathrop, C.C. and Love, A. H. (1862), 'Report', *The Journal of Prison Discipline and Philanthropy*, New Series, 1: 3–57.

Breytenbach, B. (1984), *The True Confessions of an Albino Terrorist*, London: Faber and Faber.

Briggs, C. S., Sundt, J. L. and Castellano, T. C. (2003), 'The effect of supermaximum security prisons on aggregate levels of institutional violence', *Criminology*, 41: 1341–76.

Brodie, A., Croom, J. and Davies, J. O. (2002), *English Prisons: An Architectural History*, Swindon: English Heritage.

Brodsky, S. L. and Scogin, F. R. (1988), 'Inmates in protective custody: First data on emotional effects', *Forensic Reports*, 1: 267–80.

Bronson, C. and Richards, S. (2007), *Solitary Fitness*, London: John Blake.

Bronsteen, J., Buccafusco, C. and Masure, J. S. (2009), 'Happiness and punishment', *University of Chicago Law Review*, 76: 1037–81.

Bronstein, A.J. (1981), 'Legal and constitutional issues related to last-resort prisons', in D. A. Ward and K. F. Schoen (eds), *Confinement in Maximum Custody: New Last-Resort Prisons in the United States and Western Europe*, Lexington, Mass: D. C. Heath, pp. 71–8.

Brotz, H. and Wilson, E. (1946), 'Characteristics of military society', *American Journal of Sociology*, 51: 371–5.

Brown v. Plata 131, S Ct 1910 (2011).

Brown, A. (2003), *English Society and the Prison: Time, Culture and Politics in the Development of the Modern Prison 1850–1920*, Suffolk: The Boydell Press.

Bruscino v. Carlson 654, F Supp 609 (S D Ill 1987).

Bureau of Justice Statistics (2008), *Census of State and Federal Correctional Facilities 2005*, Washington DC: U.S. Department of Justice, Office of Justice Programs.

Burney, C. (1962), *Solitary Confinement: An Exercise in Liberty*, 2nd edn, London: The Reprint Society. (Originally published in 1952 by Clerke and Cockeran)

Burns, J. H. (1966), 'Bentham and the French Revolution', *Transactions of the Royal Historical Society*, 5th Series, 16: 95–114.

Burt, J. T. (1852), *Results of the System of Separate Confinement as Administered at the Pentonville Prison*, London: Longman, Brown, Green and Longmans.

Buxton, T. F. (1818), *An Inquiry, whether Crime and Misery are Produced or Prevented, by our Present System of Prison Discipline*, 3rd edn, London: Arch, Butterworth and Hatchard.

Cacioppo, J. and Patrick, W. (2008), *Loneliness: Human Nature and the Need for Social Connection*, NY: WW Norton and Co.

Cajani, L. (1996), 'Surveillance and redemption: The *Casa di Correzione* of San Michele a Ripa in Rome', in N. Finzsch and R. Jutte (eds), *Institutions of Confinement: Hospitals, Asylums and Prisons in Western Europe and North America, 1500–1950*, Cambridge: Cambridge University Press, pp. 301–24.

Calkins, K. (1970), 'Time: Perspectives, marking and styles of usage', *Social Problems*, 17: 487–501.

Carlton, B. (2007), *Imprisoning Resistance: Life and Death in an Australian Supermax*, Sydney: Institute of Criminology Press.

Casarjian, R. (1995), *Houses of Healing: A Prisoner's Guide to Inner Power and Freedom*, Boston, Mass: Lionheart Press.

Cheng, N. (1995), *Life and Death in Shanghai*, London: Flamingo. (Originally published in 1986 by Grafton)

Chevigny, B. G. (1999), *Doing Time: 25 Years of Prison Writing*, New York: Arcade Publishing.

Clare, E. and Bottomley, K. (2001), *Evaluation of Close Supervision Centres*, Home Office Research Study 219, London: Home Office Research, Development and Statistics Directorate.

Clark, E. (2007), *Still Life: Killing Time*, Stockport: Dewi Lewis.

Clarke, T. (1922), *Glimpses of an Irish Felon's Prison Life*, Dublin: Maunsel and Roberts. (Originally published in instalments in *Irish Freedom* in 1912–13)

Clay, W. L. (1861), *The Prison Chaplain: A Memoir of the Rev. John Clay, Late Chaplain of the Preston Gaol by His Son, the Rev. Walter Lowe Clay*, Cambridge: Macmillan and Co.

Clemmer, D. (1940), *The Prison Community*, New York: Holt, Rinehart and Winston.

Cobb, E. (1977), *The Ecology of Imagination in Childhood*, New York: Columbia University Press.

Cohen, A. (2012), 'Death, yes, but torture at Supermax?', *The Atlantic*, 4 June.

Cohen, F. (2008), 'Penal isolation: Beyond the seriously mentally ill', *Criminal Justice and Behavior*, 35: 1017–47.

Cohen, S. and Taylor, L. (1972), *Psychological Survival: The Experience of Long-term Imprisonment*, Harmondsworth: Penguin.

Coid, J. W. (2001), 'The Federal Administrative Maximum Penitentiary, Florence, Colorado', *Medicine, Science and the Law*, 41: 287–97.

Collins, P. (1994), *Dickens and Crime*, 3rd edn, New York: St. Martin's Press.

Collins, W. C. (2004), *Supermax Prisons and the Constitution: Liability Concerns in the Extended Control Unit*, Washington DC: US Department of Justice National Institute of Corrections.

Commission on Safety and Abuse in America's Prisons (2006), *Confronting Confinement*, New York: Vera Institute of Justice.

Commission on Transportation and Penal Servitude (1863), *Report*, London: HMSO.

Commissioners for the Government of the Pentonville Prison (1844), *Second Report*, London: HMSO.

Commissioners for the Government of the Pentonville Prison (1845), *Third Report*, London: HMSO.

Commissioners for the Government of the Pentonville Prison (1846), *Fourth Report*, London: HMSO.

Commissioners for the Government of the Pentonville Prison (1847), *Fifth Report*, London: HMSO.

Commissioners for the Government of the Pentonville Prison (1848), *Sixth Report*, London: HMSO.

Cooley, C. H. (1902), *Human Nature and the Social Order*, New York: Charles Scribner's Sons.

Council of Europe (2003), 'Management by Prison Administrations of Life Sentence and Other Long-Term Prisoners', Recommendation (2003) 23 of the Committee of Ministers to Member States, Strasbourg: Council of Europe.

Crawford, W. (1834), *Report on the Penitentiaries of the United States*, London: House of Commons.

Crawley, E. and Sparks, R. (2005), 'Older men in prison: Survival, coping and identity', in A. Liebling and S. Maruna (eds), *The Effects of Imprisonment*, Cullompton: Willan, pp. 343–65.

Crewe, B. (2011), 'Depth, weight, tightness: Revisiting the pains of imprisonment', *Punishment & Society*, 13: 509–29.

Davis, A. (2001), 'Writing on the wall: Prisoners on punishment', *Punishment & Society*, 3: 427–31.

Davitt, M. (1882), *The Prison Life of Michael Davitt, related by Himself, together with his Evidence before the House of Lords Commission on Convict Prison Life*, Dublin: J. J. Lalor.

Davitt, M. (1885), *Leaves from a Prison Diary, or Lectures to a Solitary Audience*, Vol. 1, London: Chapman and Hall.

Dayan, C. (2011), 'Barbarous confinement', *New York Times*, 17 July.

de Beaumont, G. and de Tocqueville, A. (1833), *On the Penitentiary System in the United States and its Application in France; with an Appendix on Penal Colonies, and also, Statistical Notes* (translated by F. Lieber), Philadelphia, Pa: Carey, Lea and Blanchard.

Deaton, J. E., Berg, S. W., Richlin, M. and Litrownik, A. J. (1977), 'Coping activities in solitary confinement of U.S. Navy POWs in Vietnam', *Journal of Applied Social Psychology*, 7: 239–57.

Del Raine, R. (1993), 'USP Marion's version of Orwell's 1984 and beyond', *Journal of Prisoners on Prisons*, 4: 1–11. (Formatted online version 2006)

Department of the Interior, Census Office (1896), *Report on Crime, Pauperism, and Benevolence in the United States at the Eleventh Census: 1890*, Part I Analysis, Washington DC: Government Printing Office.

Departmental Committee on Prisons [Gladstone Committee] (1895a), *Report*, London: HMSO (C (Second Series) 7702).

Departmental Committee on Prisons [Gladstone Committee] (1895b), *Minutes of Evidence Taken*, London: HMSO.

Dickens, C. (1850), 'Pet prisoners', *Household Words: A Weekly Journal*, 27 April, 97–103.

Dickens, C. (2000), *American Notes for General Circulation*, London: Penguin Classics. (Originally published in 1842 by Chapman and Hall)

Dolan, J. (2010), 'Objections raised to caging inmates during therapy', *Los Angeles Times*, 28 December.

Dostoyevsky, F. (2004), *The House of the Dead* (translated by C. Garnett), Mineola, New York: Dover Publications. (Originally published in 1862 by V tip. Iosafata Ogrizko)

Downes, D. (1988), *Contrasts in Tolerance: Post-war Penal Policy in the Netherlands and England and Wales*, Oxford: Clarendon Press.

Draaisma, D. (2004), *Why Life Speeds Up As You Get Older: How Memory Shapes our Past*, Cambridge: Cambridge University Press.

Earley, P. (1992), *The Hot House: Life Inside Leavenworth Prison*, New York: Bantam.

Eastern State Penitentiary Task Force (1994), *Eastern State Penitentiary Historic Structures Report*, Vol. 1, City of Philadelphia: Philadelphia Historical Commission.

Echols, D. (2013), *Life After Death: Eighteen Years on Death Row*, London: Atlantic Books. (Originally published in 2012 by Blue Rider Press)

Edgar, K., O'Donnell, I. and Martin, C. (2012), *Prison Violence: The Dynamics of Conflict, Fear and Power*, London: Routledge. (Originally published in 2003 by Willan)

Eisenman, S. F. (2009), 'The resistable rise and predictable fall of the U.S. supermax', *Monthly Review: An Independent Socialist Magazine*, November, 31–45.

el Gorani, M. and Tubiana, J. (2011), 'Diary', *London Review of Books*, 15 December, 33–5.

Epps, C. (2012), 'Reassessing solitary confinement: The human rights, fiscal, and public safety consequences', US Senate Committee on the Judiciary, Subcommittee on the Constitution, Civil Rights, and Human Rights, Hearing on Solitary Confinement, 19 June.

Evans, M. and Morgan, R. (1998), *Preventing Torture: A Study of the European Convention for the Prevention of Torture and Inhuman or Degrading Treatment or Punishment*, Oxford: Oxford University Press.

Evans, R. (2010), *The Fabrication of Virtue: English Prison Architecture 1750–1840*, New York: Cambridge University Press. (Originally published in 1982 by Cambridge University Press)

Eytan, E. (2011), 'Religion and mental health during incarceration: A systematic literature review', *Psychiatric Quarterly*, 82: 287–95.

Farber, M. L. (1944), 'Suffering and the time perspective of the prisoner', *University of Iowa Studies: Studies in Child Welfare*, 20: 155–227.

Fazel, S. and Baillargeon J. (2011), 'The health of prisoners', *The Lancet*, 377: 956–65.

Fellner, J. (2011), 'What should we think about the study on the psychological impact of confinement at Colorado State Penitentiary? A human rights perspective', *Correctional Mental Health Report*, 13: 5–6, 15–16.

Fiddler, M. (2010), 'Four walls and what lies within: The meaning of space and place in prisons', *Prison Service Journal*, 187: 3–8.

Field, J. (1848), *Prison Discipline and the Advantages of the Separate System of Imprisonment with a Detailed Account of the Discipline Now Pursued in the New County Gaol, Reading*. Vol. 1, 2nd edn, London: Longman, Brown, Green and Longmans.

Fitzgerald, M. (1977), *Prisoners in Revolt*, London: Penguin.

Flaherty, M. G. (1999), *A Watched Pot: How We Experience Time*, New York: New York University Press.

Flaherty, M. G. (2002), 'Making time: Agency and the construction of temporal experience', *Symbolic Interaction,* 25: 379–88.

Flaherty, M. G. (2011), *The Textures of Time: Agency and Temporal Experience*, Philadelphia, Pa: Temple University Press.

Flanagan, T. J. (1980), 'The pains of long-term imprisonment', *British Journal of Criminology*, 20: 148–56.

Flanagan, T. J. (1982), 'Lifers and long-termers: Doing big time', in R. Johnson and H. Toch (eds), *The Pains of Imprisonment*, Beverly Hills, Calif: Sage, pp. 115–28.

Foote, G. W. (1886), *Prisoner for Blasphemy*, London: Progressive Publishing.

Forsythe, B. (2004), 'Loneliness and cellular confinement in British prisons 1878–1921', *British Journal of Criminology*, 44: 759–70.

Foucault, M. (1991), *Discipline and Punish: The Birth of the Prison* (translated by Alan Sheridan), London: Penguin. (Originally published in 1977 by Allen Lane)

Franke, H. (1995), *The Emancipation of Prisoners*, Edinburgh: Edinburgh University Press.

Frankl, V. E. (2004), *Man's Search for Meaning* (translated by Ilse Lasch), London: Rider Books. (Originally published in 1946 by Verlag für Jugend und Volk)

Franzen, J. (2004), *How to Be Alone*, London: HarperPerennial.

Freeman, C. B. (1997), *Doing Time: An Ethnomethodological Investigation of Time in a Prison*, MA Thesis, Department of Anthropology, University of Calgary.

Freeman, A. and Aiyetoro, A. A. (1988), 'Report on the High Security Unit for Women, Federal Correctional Institution, Lexington, Kentucky', *Social Justice*, 15: 1–7.

Fyfe, J. (1992), *Books Behind Bars: The Role of Books, Reading, and Libraries in British Prison Reform, 1701–1911*, Westport, Conn: Greenwood Press.

Gaddis, T. E. (1962), *Birdman of Alcatraz*, Sydney: Horwitz Publications. (Originally published in 1955 by Victor Gollancz)

Galtung, J. (1961), 'Prison: The organization of dilemma', in D. R. Cressey (ed.), *The Prison: Studies in Institutional Organization and Change,* New York: Holt, Rinehart and Winston, pp. 107–45.

Gann, K. (2010), *No Such Thing as Silence: John Cage's 4'33",* New Haven, Conn: Yale University Press.

Garabedian, P. G. (1963), 'Social roles and processes of socialization in the prison community', *Social Problems,* 11: 139–52.

Gawande, A. (2009), 'Hellhole: The United States holds tens of thousands of inmates in long-term solitary confinement. Is this torture?', *The New Yorker,* 30 March, 36–45.

Gendreau, P. and Bonta, J. (1984), 'Solitary confinement is not cruel and unusual punishment: People sometimes are!', *Canadian Journal of Criminology,* 26: 467–78.

Gibbens, T. C. N. (1961), 'The prisoner's view of time—by a former POW', *The Prison Journal,* 41: 46–9.

Gibson, M. (2011), 'Review essay: Global perspectives on the birth of the prison', *American Historical Review,* 116: 1040–63.

Gluzman, S. (1982), 'Fear of freedom: Psychological decompensation or existentialist phenomenon?', *American Journal of Psychiatry,* 139: 57–61.

Goffman, E. (1961), 'On the characteristics of total institutions: The inmate world', in D. R. Cressey (ed.), *The Prison: Studies in Institutional Organization and Change,* New York: Holt, Rinehart and Winston, pp. 15–67.

Gomez, A. E. (2006), 'Resisting living death at Marion penitentiary, 1972', *Radical History Review,* 96: 58–86.

Goode, E. (2012), 'Prisons rethink isolation, saving money, lives and sanity', *New York Times,* 10 March.

Goodman, P. (1970), 'Memoirs from prison', *Dissent,* 1 July: 368–71.

Graber, J. (2011), *The Furnace of Affliction: Prisons & Religion in Antebellum America,* Chapel Hill, NC: University of North Carolina Press.

Grann, D. (2004), 'The Brand: How the Aryan Brotherhood became the most murderous prison gang in America', *The New Yorker,* 16 and 23 February, 156–71.

Grass, S. (2003), *The Self in the Cell: Narrating the Victorian Prisoner,* London: Routledge.

Grassian, S. (1983), 'Psychopathological effects of solitary confinement', *American Journal of Psychiatry,* 140: 1450–4.

Grassian, S. (2006), 'Psychiatric effects of solitary confinement', *Washington University Journal of Law and Policy,* 22: 325–83.

Grassian, S. and Friedman, N. (1986), 'Effects of sensory deprivation in psychiatric seclusion and solitary confinement', *International Journal of Law and Psychiatry,* 8: 49–65.

Grassian, S. and Kupers, T. (2011), 'The Colorado study vs. the reality of supermax confinement', *Correctional Mental Health Report,* 13: 1, 9–11.

Gray, F. C. (1847), *Prison Discipline in America*, Boston: Little and Brown.

Greco, J. M (2003), 'Staffing a supermax prison', in D. Neal (ed.), *Supermax Prisons: Beyond the Rock*, Lanham, Md: American Correctional Association, pp. 37–51.

Greene, G. (1986), *The Tenth Man*, London: Penguin. (Originally published in 1985 by The Bodley Head)

Grey, A. (1988), *Hostage in Peking*, London: Weidenfeld and Nicolson. (Originally published in 1970 by Michael Joseph)

Griffin, E. (1993), 'Breaking men's minds: Behavior control and human experimentation at the federal prison in Marion', *Journal of Prisoners on Prisons*, 4: 1–8. (Formatted online version 2006)

Grosser, P. (2007), *Alcatraz: Uncle Sam's Devil's Island: Experiences of a Conscientious Objector in America During the First World War*, Berkeley, Calif: Kate Sharpley Library. (Originally published *c.* 1933 by The Excelsior Press)

Halpern, S. (1993), *Migrations to Solitude: The Quest for Privacy in a Crowded World*, New York: Vintage Books.

Hamm, M. S. (2009), 'Prison Islam in the age of sacred terror', *British Journal of Criminology*, 49: 667–85.

Haney, C. (2003), 'Mental health issues in long-term solitary and "supermax" confinement', *Crime and Delinquency*, 49: 124–56.

Haney, C. (2008), 'A culture of harm: Taming the dynamics of cruelty in supermax prisons', *Criminal Justice and Behavior*, 35: 956–84.

Haney, C. (2009), 'The social psychology of isolation: Why solitary confinement is psychologically harmful', *Prison Service Journal*, 181: 12–20.

Haney, C. (2011), 'Declaration', Exhibit 17, *Silverstein v. Federal Bureau of Prisons*, Civil Action No. 07–cv-02471–PAB–KMT, USDC Colorado, 27 February.

Haney, C. (2012), 'Testimony', US Senate Committee on the Judiciary, Subcommittee on the Constitution, Civil Rights, and Human Rights, Hearing on Solitary Confinement, 19 June.

Haney, C. and Lynch, M. (1997), 'Regulating prisons of the future: A psychological analysis of supermax and solitary confinement', *New York University Review of Law and Social Change*, 23: 477–570.

Hanway, J. (1776), *Solitude in Imprisonment*, London: J. Bew.

Harding, C. (1988), '"The inevitable end of a discredited system"? The origins of the Gladstone Committee report on prisons', *The Historical Journal*, 31: 591–608.

Harding, M. (2011), 'They say men ought not to cry', *The Irish Times*, 7 January.

Hartman, K. E. (2008), 'Supermax prisons in the consciousness of prisoners', *The Prison Journal*, 88: 169–76.

Hemming, H. (2008), *In Search of the English Eccentric*, London: John Murray.

Henriques, U. R. Q. (1972), 'The rise and decline of the separate system of prison discipline', *Past and Present*, 54: 61–93.

Hinkle, L. E. and Wolff, H. G. (1956), 'Communist interrogation and indoctrination of "enemies of the states": Analysis of methods used by the Communist State Police (a special report)', *AMA Archives of Neurology and Psychiatry*, 76: 115–74.

H.M. Inspectorate of Prisons (2006), *Extreme Custody: A Thematic Inspection of Close Supervision Centres and High Security Segregation*, London: HMIP.

Hobhouse, S. and Brockway, A. F. (1922), *English Prisons To-Day: Being the Report of the Prison System Enquiry Committee*, London: Longmans, Green and Co.

Home Department (1851), *England and Wales: Tables Showing the Number of Criminal Offenders Committed for Trial or Bailed for Appearance at the Assizes and Sessions in Each County, in the Year 1850, and the Result of the Proceedings*, London: HMSO.

Home Department (1861), *Judicial Statistics 1860—England and Wales*, London: HMSO.

Howard, J. (1777), *The State of the Prisons in England and Wales with Preliminary Observations and an Account of Some Foreign Prisons*, Warrington: William Eyres.

Human Rights Watch (1991), *Prison Conditions in the United States*, New York: Human Rights Watch.

Hunt, A. (1998), 'The great masturbation panic and the discourses of moral regulation in nineteenth- and early twentieth-century Britain', *Journal of the History of Sexuality*, 8: 575–615.

Huxley, A. (1923), *On the Margin: Notes and Essays*, London: Chatto and Windus.

Ignatieff, M. (1989), *A Just Measure of Pain: The Penitentiary in the Industrial Revolution 1750–1850*, London: Penguin. (Originally published in 1978 by Pantheon)

Ignotus, P. (1959), *Political Prisoner*, London: Routledge and Kegan Paul.

Immarigeon, R. (1992), 'The "Marionization" of American prisons', *National Prison Project Journal*, 7: 1–5.

Inspectors General of the Prisons of Ireland (1840), *Eighteenth Report on the General State of the Prisons of Ireland, 1839*, Dublin: HMSO.

Jackson, M. (1983), *Prisoners of Isolation: Solitary Confinement in Canada*, Toronto: University of Toronto Press.

Jacobs, S. (2007), *Stolen Time: The Inspiring Story of an Innocent Woman Condemned to Death*, New York: Doubleday.

James, E. (2003), *A Life Inside: A Prisoner's Notebook*, London: Atlantic Books.

James, S. (2009), 'Note from the UK publisher', in M. Abu-Jamal (ed.), *Jailhouse Lawyers: Prisoners Defending Prisoners v. The USA*, San Francisco, Calif: City Lights Books, pp. 21–6.

James, W. (1890), *The Principles of Psychology*, Vol. 1, New York: Henry Holt.

Jeffreys, D. S. (2013), *Spirituality in Dark Places: The Ethics of Solitary Confinement*, New York: Palgrave Macmillan.

Jewkes, Y. (2005), 'Loss, liminality and the life sentence: Managing identity through a disrupted lifecourse', in A. Liebling and S. Maruna (eds), *The Effects of Imprisonment*, Cullompton: Willan, pp. 366–88.

Jewkes, Y. (2012), 'Aesthetics and an-aesthetics: The architecture of incarceration', in L. Cheliotis (ed.), *The Arts of Imprisonment: Control, Resistance and Empowerment*, Surrey: Ashgate, pp. 27–45.

Jewkes, Y. and Johnston, H. (2007), 'The evolution of prison architecture', in Y. Jewkes (ed.) *Handbook on Prisons*, Cullompton: Willan, pp. 174–96.

Johnson, R. (2005), 'Brave new prisons: The growing social isolation of modern penal institutions', in A. Liebling and S. Maruna (eds), *The Effects of Imprisonment*, Cullompton: Willan, pp. 255–84.

Johnson, R. and McGunigall-Smith, S. (2008), 'Life without parole, America's other death penalty: Notes on life under sentence of death by incarceration', *The Prison Journal*, 88: 328–46.

Johnston, N. (2000), *Forms of Constraint: A History of Prison Architecture*, Urbana and Chicago: University of Illinois Press.

Johnston, N. (2004), 'The world's most influential prison: Success or failure?', *The Prison Journal*, 84: 20S–40S.

Johnston, N., Finkel, K. and Cohen, J. A. (1994), *Eastern State Penitentiary: Crucible of Good Intentions*, Philadelphia, Pa: Philadelphia Museum of Art.

Jones 'El v. Berge 164, F Supp 2d 1096 (WD Wis, 2001).

Jones, R. S. and Schmid, T. J. (2000), *Doing Time: Prison Experience and Identity among First-Time Inmates*, Stanford, Conn: JAI Press.

Jones, W. P. (2011), *A Different Kind of Cell: The Story of a Murderer who Became a Monk*, Grand Rapids, Mich: Eerdmans.

Joseph, H. S. (1853), *Memoirs of Convicted Prisoners Accompanied by Remarks on the Causes and Prevention of Crime*, London: Wertheim and Co.

Joseph, S. (2012), *What Doesn't Kill Us: The New Psychology of Posttraumatic Growth*, London: Piatkus. (Originally published in 2011 by Basic Books)

Kahan, P. (2008), *Eastern State Penitentiary: A History*, Charleston, SC: The History Press.

Kaiser, D. and Stannow, L. (2013), 'The shame of our prisons: New evidence', *New York Review of Books*, 24 October, 57–9.

Kanas, N., Sandal, G., Boyd, J. E., Gushin, V. I., Manzey, D., North, R. et al. (2009), 'Psychology and culture during long-duration space missions', *Acta Astronautica*, 64: 659–77.

Keenan, B. (1992), *An Evil Cradling*, London: Hutchinson.

Kenny, C. (2011), *The Power of Silence: Silent Communication in Daily Life*, London: Karnac Books.

Keve, P. W. (1983), 'The quicksand prison', *The Prison Journal*, 63: 47–58.

King, K., Steiner, B. and Breach, S. B. (2008), 'Violence in the supermax: A self-fulfilling prophecy', *The Prison Journal*, 88: 144–68.

King, R. D. (1999), 'The rise and rise of supermax: An American solution in search of a problem?', *Punishment & Society*, 1: 163–86.

King, R. D. (2005), 'The effects of supermax custody', in A. Liebling and S. Maruna (eds), *The Effects of Imprisonment*, Cullompton: Willan, pp. 118–45.

King, R. D. and McDermott, K. (1995), *The State of Our Prisons*, Oxford: Oxford University Press.

Klein, S. (2006), *Time: A User's Guide Making Sense of Life's Scarcest Commodity* (translated by Shelley Frisch), London: Penguin.

Koch, P. (1994), *Solitude: A Philosophical Encounter*, Chicago: Open Court.

Koestler, A. (1942), *Dialogue with Death* (translated by Trevor and Phyllis Blewitt), New York: Macmillan.

Korn, R. (1988a), 'The effects of confinement in the High Security Unit at Lexington', *Social Justice*, 15: 8–19.

Korn, R. (1988b), 'Follow-up report on the effects of confinement in the High Security Unit at Lexington', *Social Justice*, 15: 20–9.

Krakauer, J. (2007), *Into the Wild*, London: Pan Books. (Originally published in 1996 by Random House)

Kull, R. (2008), *Solitude: Seeking Wisdom in Extremes: A Year Alone in the Patagonia Wilderness*, Novato, Calif: New World Library.

Kuntz, W. F. (1988), *Criminal Sentencing in Three Nineteenth-Century Cities: Social History of Punishment in New York, Boston, and Philadelphia 1830–1880*, New York: Garland.

Kunzel, R. (2008), *Criminal Intimacy: Prison and the Uneven History of Modern American Sexuality*, Chicago, Ill: University of Chicago Press.

Kupers, T. A. (2008), 'What to do with the survivors? Coping with the long-term effects of isolated confinement', *Criminal Justice and Behavior*, 35: 1005–16.

Kupers, T. A., Dronet, T., Winter, M., Austin, J., Kelly, L., Cartier, W. et al., (2009), 'Beyond supermax administrative segregation: Mississippi's experience rethinking prison classification and creating alternative mental health programs', *Criminal Justice and Behavior*, 36: 1037–50.

Kurki, L. and Morris, N. (2001), 'The purposes, practices, and problems of supermax prisons', in M. Tonry (ed.), *Crime and Justice: A Review of Research*, Vol. 28, Chicago, Ill: University of Chicago Press, pp. 385–424.

La Guer, B. (2000), 'Notes from life and death', in J. Evans (ed.), *Undoing Time: American Prisoners in their Own Words*, Boston: Northeastern University Press, pp. 163–7.

Laing, J. and Crouch, G. (2009), 'Lone wolves? Isolation and solitude within the frontier travel experience', *Geografiska Annaler: Series B, Human Geography*, 91: 325–42.

Laing, R. D. (1960), *The Divided Self: An Existential Study in Sanity and Madness*, London: Tavistock Publications.

Lane, H. (1835), *Five Years in State's Prison, or, Interesting Truths showing the Manner of Discipline in the State Prisons at Singsing and Auburn*, 4th edn, New York: Luther Pratt and Son.

Lauer, R. H. (1981), *Temporal Man: The Meaning and Uses of Social Time*, New York: Praeger.

Leal, W. C. (2001), 'From my prison cell' (translated by D. Mond), *Latin American Perspectives*, 28: 149–64.

Leder, D. (2004), 'Imprisoned bodies: The life-world of the incarcerated', *Social Justice*, 31: 51–66.

Leigh Fermor, P. (2004), *A Time to Keep Silence*, London: John Murray. (Originally published in 1957 by John Murray)

Levi, P. (1987), *If This is a Man* and *The Truce* (combined volume, translated by S. Woolf), London: Abacus. (Originally published in 1979 by Penguin)

Levy, H. and Miller, D. (*c.* 1971), *Going to Jail: The Political Prisoner*, New York: Grove Press.

Lieber, F. (1838), *A Popular Essay on Subjects of Penal Law, and on Uninterrupted Solitary Confinement at Labor, as Contradistinguished to Solitary Confinement at Night and Joint Labor by Day*, Philadelphia, Pa: Philadelphia Society for Alleviating the Miseries of Public Prisons.

Liebling, A. (1999), 'Prison suicide and prisoner coping', in M. Tonry and J. Petersilia (eds), *Crime and Justice: A Review of Research*, Vol. 26, Chicago, Ill: University of Chicago Press, pp. 283–359.

Liebling, A., Arnold, H. and Straub, C. (2011), *An Exploration of Staff–Prisoner Relationships at HMP Whitemoor: 12 Years On*, Revised Final Report, London: Ministry of Justice, National Offender Management Service.

LIS Inc. (1997), 'Supermax housing: A survey of current practice', *Special Issues in Corrections*, March, Longmont, Colo: US Department of Justice, National Institute of Corrections Information Center.

Long, C. and Averill, J. (2003), 'Solitude: An exploration of benefits of being alone', *Journal for the Theory of Social Behaviour*, 33: 21–44.

Long C. R., Seburn M., Averill J. R. and More T. A. (2003), 'Solitude experiences: Varieties, settings, and individual differences', *Personality and Social Psychology Bulletin*, 29: 578–83.

Lovell, D., Johnson, L. C. and Cain, K. C. (2007), 'Recidivism of supermax prisoners in Washington State', *Crime and Delinquency*, 53: 633–56.

Lovell, D. and Toch, H. (2011), 'Some observations about the Colorado segregation study', *Correctional Mental Health Report*, 13: 3–4, 14–15.

Lucas, W. E. (1976), 'Solitary confinement: Isolation as coercion to conform', *Australian and New Zealand Journal of Criminology*, 9: 153–67.

Lynch, M. (2002), 'Selling "securityware": Transformations in prison commodities advertising, 1949–99', *Punishment & Society*, 4: 305–19.

Lynch, M. (2010), *Sunbelt Justice: Arizona and the Transformation of American Punishment*, Stanford, Calif: Stanford University Press.

Macartney, W. (1936), *Walls Have Mouths: A Record of Ten Years' Penal Servitude*, London: Victor Gollancz.

Mackenzie, V. (1998), *Cave in the Snow: A Western Woman's Quest for Enlightenment*, London: Bloomsbury.

Madrid v. Gomez 889, F Supp 1146 (ND Cal, 1995).

Maguire, N. K. (2006), *An Infinity of Little Hours: The Trial of Faith of Five Young Men in the Western World's Most Austere Monastic Order*, Jackson, Tenn: Public Affairs.

Maitland, S. (2008), *A Book of Silence: A Journey in Search of the Pleasures and Powers of Silence*, London: Granta.

Mandela, N. (1994), *Long Walk to Freedom*, London: Little, Brown and Company.

Mann, T. (1996), *The Magic Mountain* (translated by H. T. Lowe-Porter), London: Minerva. (Originally published in 1924 by S. Fischer Verlag)

Marcel, G. (1962), *Homo Viator: Introduction to a Metaphysic of Hope* (translated by Emma Craufurd), New York: Harper and Row. (Originally published in 1951 by Victor Gollancz)

Martel, J. (2006), 'To be, one has to be somewhere: Spatio–temporality in prison segregation', *British Journal of Criminology*, 46: 587–612.

Maruna, S., Wilson, L. and Curran, K. (2006), 'Why God is often found behind bars: Prison conversions and the crisis of self-narrative', *Research in Human Development*, 3: 161–84.

Maslow, A. H. (1970), *Religions, Values, and Peak Experiences*, New York: Viking Compass. (Originally published in 1964 by Kappa Delta Pi Publications)

Mason, E. W. (1918), *Made Free in Prison*, London: Allen and Unwin.

Maybrick, F. E. (1905), *My Fifteen Lost Years*, New York: Funk and Wagnalls.

McBride, R. (2014), 'Secular ecstasies', *The Psychologist*, 27: 168–70.

McCleery, R. (1961), 'Authoritarianism and the belief system of incorrigibles', in D. Cressey (ed.) *The Prison*, New York: Holt, Rinehart and Winston, pp. 260–306.

McConville, S. (1981), *A History of English Prison Administration: Volume I 1750–1877*, London: Routledge and Kegan Paul.

McCoy, A. W. (2006), *A Question of Torture: CIA Interrogation, from the Cold War to the War on Terror*, New York: Metropolitan Books.

McElwee, T. B. (1835), *A Concise History of the Eastern Penitentiary of Pennsylvania together with a Detailed Statement of the Proceedings of the Committee*, Vol. 2, Philadelphia, Penn: Neall and Massey.

McNeill, D. (2014), 'Japanese authorities free world's longest-serving death row prisoner', *The Irish Times*, 28 March.

Mead, G. H. (1934), 'The self and the organism', in *Mind, Self, & Society From the Standpoint of a Social Behaviorist* (edited by Charles W. Morris), Chicago, Ill: University of Chicago Press, pp. 135–44.

Mears, D. P. (2006), *Evaluating the Effectiveness of Supermax Prisons*, Research Report, Washington DC: Urban Institute Justice Policy Center.

Mears, D. P. (2008), 'An assessment of supermax prisons using an evaluation research framework', *The Prison Journal*, 88: 43–68.

Mears, D. P. and Bales, W. (2009), 'Supermax incarceration and recidivism', *Criminology*, 47: 1131–66.

Medlicott, D. (1999), 'Surviving in the time machine: Suicidal prisoners and the pains of prison time', *Time & Society*, 8: 211–30.

Medlicott, D. (2001), *Surviving the Prison Place: Narratives of Suicidal Prisoners*, Aldershot: Ashgate.

Medlicott, D. (2004), 'Narratives of memory, identity and place in male prisoners', in D. Robinson, C. Horrocks, N. Kelly and B. Roberts (eds), *Narrative, Memory and Identity: Theoretical and Methodological Issues*, Huddersfield: University of Huddersfield, pp. 105–17.

Meisenhelder, T. (1985), 'An essay on time and the phenomenology of imprisonment', *Deviant Behavior*, 6: 39–56.

Melges, F. T. (1982), *Time and the Inner Future: A Temporal Approach to Psychiatric Disorders*, New York: John Wiley and Sons.

Meranze, M. (2000), 'A criminal is being beaten: The politics of punishment and the history of the body', in R. B. St George (ed.), *Possible Pasts: Becoming Colonial in Early America*, Ithaca, NY: Cornell University Press, pp. 302–23.

Metcalf, H., Morgan, J., Oliker-Friedland, S., Resnik, J., Spiegel, J., Tae, H. et al. (2013), *Administrative Segregation, Degrees of Isolation, and Incarceration: A National Overview of State and Federal Correctional Policies*, A Project of the Liman Public Interest Program at Yale Law School, June.

Metzner, J. L. and Fellner, J. (2010), 'Solitary confinement and mental illness in U.S. prisons: A challenge for medical ethics', *Journal of the American Academy of Psychiatry and the Law*, 38: 104–8.

Metzner, J. L. and O'Keefe, M. L. (2011), 'Psychological effects of administrative segregation: The Colorado study', *Correctional Mental Health Report*, 13: 1–2, 12–14.

Molineux, R. B. (1903), *The Room with the Little Door*, New York: G. W. Dillingham.

Moody, T. W. (1941), 'Michael Davitt in penal servitude 1870–1877', *Studies: An Irish Quarterly Review*, 30: 517–30.

Morgan, J. P. (1998), 'Zeno: Solving a 30-year-old literary mystery', *Punch*, 15 August, 23–25.

Mumola, C. J. (2005), *Suicide and Homicide in State Prisons and Local Jails*, Bureau of Justice Statistics Special Report, Washington DC: US Department of Justice.

Mushlin, M. B. (2012), 'Unlocking the courthouse door: Removing the barrier of the PLRA's physical injury requirement to permit meaningful judicial oversight of abuses in supermax prisons and isolation units', *Federal Sentencing Reporter*, 24: 268–75.

Naday, A., Freilich, J. D. and Mellow, J. (2008), 'The elusive data on supermax confinement', *The Prison Journal*, 88: 69–93.

Nardini, J. E. (1952), 'Survival factors in American prisoners of war of the Japanese', *American Journal of Psychiatry*, 109: 241–8.

Nellis, A. and King, R. S. (2009), *No Exit: The Expanding Use of Life Sentences in America*, Washington DC: The Sentencing Project.

Nelson, V. F. (1933a), 'Prison stupor', *The American Mercury*, 28: 339–44.

Nelson, V. F. (1933b), *Prison Days and Nights*, Boston: Little, Brown.

Nietzsche, F. (1994), *The Portable Nietzsche* (edited and translated by Walter Kaufmann), New York, Penguin Classic. (Originally published in 1954 by Viking Penguin)

Nitsche, P. and Wilmanns, K. (1912), *The History of the Prison Psychoses* (translated by F. M. Barnes and B. Glueck), Nervous and Mental Disease Monograph Series No. 13, New York: Journal of Nervous and Mental Disease Publishing Company.

No. 7. (1903), *Twenty-five Years in Seventeen Prisons: The Life Story of an Ex-Convict with his Impressions of our Prison System*, London: F. E. Robinson.

Noonan, M. E. (2012), *Mortality in Local Jails and State Prisons, 2000–2010: Statistical Tables*, Washington DC: US Department of Justice, Office of Justice Programs, Bureau of Justice Statistics.

Norris, K. (2008), *Acedia & Me: A Marriage, Monks and a Writer's Life*, New York: Riverhead Books.

O'Donnell, I. (2014), 'Time and isolation as performance art: A note', *Crime, Media, Culture*, 10: 81–6.

O'Donovan Rossa, J. (1899), *Irish Rebels in English Prisons: A Record of Prison Life*, with supplementary chapter, New York: P. J. Kenedy. (Originally published in 1874 by P. J. Kenedy)

O'Keefe, M. L., Klebe, K. J., Stucker, A., Sturm, K. and Leggett, W. (2010), *One Year Longitudinal Study of the Psychological Effects of Administrative Segregation*, Report to the National Institute of Justice, Colorado: Department of Corrections and University of Colorado, Colorado Springs.

O'Keefe, T. (2006), 'Menstrual blood as a weapon of resistance', *International Feminist Journal of Politics*, 8: 535–56.

Ogden, R. and Montgomery, C. (2012), 'High time', *The Psychologist*, 25: 590–2.

Olivero, J. M. and Roberts, J. B. (1990), 'The US federal penitentiary at Marion, Illinois: Alcatraz revisited', *New England Journal on Criminal and Civil Confinement*, 16: 21–51.

One Who Has Endured It. (1878), *Five Years' Penal Servitude*, 3rd edn, London: Richard Bentley and Son.

Pasternak, B. (1991), *Doctor Zhivago* (translated by Max Hayward and Manya Harari), London: Collins Harvill. (Originally published in 1958 by Collins and The Harvill Press)

Patten, R. L. (1978), *Charles Dickens and his Publishers*, Oxford: Clarendon Press.

Perkinson, R. (1994), 'Shackled justice: Florence federal penitentiary and the new politics of punishment', *Social Justice*, 21: 117–32.

Peter, W. (1845), 'Letter to Job R. Tyson, Esq., 25 January 1845', *Pennsylvania Journal of Prison Discipline and Philanthropy*, 1: 86–8.

Peters, E. M. (1995), 'Prison before the prison: The ancient and medieval worlds', in N. Morris and D. J. Rothman (eds), *The Oxford History of the Prison: The Practice of Punishment in Western Society*, New York: Oxford University Press, pp. 3–47.

Pew Forum on Religion and Public Life (2012), *Religion in Prisons: A 50-State Survey of Prison Chaplains*, Washington DC: Pew Research Center.

Phillips, J. (2008), *Letters from the Dhamma Brothers: Meditation Behind Bars*, Onalaska, Wash: Pariyatti Press.

Playfair, G. (1971), *The Punitive Obsession: An Unvarnished History of the English Prison System*, London: Victor Gollancz.

Power, E. (1964), *Medieval English Nunneries*, New York: Biblo and Tannen. (Originally published in 1922 by Cambridge University Press)

Prendergast, A. (2007), 'The caged life: Is Thomas Silverstein a prisoner of his own deadly past—or the first in a new wave of locked-down lifers?', *Denver Westword News*, 16 August. (http://www.westword.com/2007-08-16/news/the-caged-life/, accessed 26 February 2014)

Priestley, P. (1999), *Victorian Prison Lives: English Prison Biography 1830–1914*, London: Pimlico. (Originally published in 1985 by Methuen and Co.)

Prison Association of New York (1845), 'First report, December 1844', *Pennsylvania Journal of Prison Discipline and Philanthropy*, 1: 31–51.

Prison Discipline Society, Boston (1843), *Eighteenth Annual Report of the Board of Managers*, Boston: Prison Discipline Society.

Prochnik, G. (2010), *In Pursuit of Silence: Listening for Meaning in a World of Noise*, New York: Doubleday.

Radic, R. (2011), 'Thomas Silverstein: The most feared convict in the USA', in R. Barratt (ed.), *The Mammoth Book of Hard Bastards*, London: Constable and Robinson, pp. 18–39.

Raposa, M. L. (1999), *Boredom and the Religious Imagination*, Charlottesville, Va: University Press of Virginia.

Reiter, K. (2012), 'Parole, snitch, or die: California's supermax prisons and prisoners, 1997–2007', *Punishment & Society*, 14: 530–63.

Reyes, H. (2007), 'The worst scars are in the mind: Psychological torture', *International Review of the Red Cross*, 89: 591–617.

Rhodes, L. A. (2002), 'Psychopathy and the face of control in supermax', *Ethnography*, 3: 442–66.

Rhodes, L. A. (2004), *Total Confinement: Madness and Reason in the Maximum Security Prison*, Berkeley, Calif: University of California Press.

Rhodes, L. A. (2005), 'Changing the subject: Conversation in supermax', *Cultural Anthropology*, 20: 388–411.

Richards, S. C. (2008), 'USP Marion: The first federal supermax', *The Prison Journal*, 88: 6–22.

Rideau, W. (2011), *In the Place of Justice: A Story of Punishment and Deliverance*, London: Profile Books.

Ridgeway, J. (2011), 'God's own warden', *Mother Jones*, July/August, 44–51.

Rifkin, J. (1987), *Time Wars: The Primary Conflict in Human History*, New York: Touchstone.

Riveland, C. (1999), *Supermax Prisons: Overview and General Considerations*, Washington DC: US Department of Justice National Institute of Corrections.

Rosenberg, S. (2011), *An American Radical: Political Prisoner in My Own Country*, New York: Citadel Press.

Rosenfeld, R. (2000), 'Patterns in adult homicide: 1980–1995', in A. Blumstein and J. Wallman (eds), *The Crime Drop in America*. New York: Cambridge University Press, pp. 130–63.

Rothman, D. J. (1971), *The Discovery of the Asylum: Social Order and Disorder in the New Republic*, Boston: Little, Brown and Company.

Rothman, D. J. (2002), *Conscience and Convenience: The Asylum and Its Alternatives in Progressive America*, Revised Edition, New York: Aldine de Gruyter. (Originally published in 1980 by Little, Brown and Company)

Royal Commission on Capital Punishment 1949–1953 (1953), *Report*, London: Stationery Office (Cmd 8932).

Ruiz v. Brown, case 4:09–cv–05796–CW 2012, 31 May 2012, USDC ND California.

Ruiz v. Johnson 37, F Supp 2d 855 (SD Tex, 1999).

Rush, B. (1812), *Medical Inquiries and Observations, upon the Diseases of the Mind*, Philadelphia, Pa: Kimber and Richardson.

Rushdie, S. (2010), 'Interview', *Time Magazine*, 22 November, 8.

Russo, S. (1943), 'Chronophobia: A prison neurosis', *Mental Hygiene*, 27: 581–91.

Ryan, R. M. and Deci, E. L. (2000), 'Self-determination theory and the facilitation of intrinsic motivation, social development, and well-being', *American Psychologist*, 55: 68–78.

Samson, C. (2012), 'Should we be more mindful of psychosis?', *The Psychologist*, 25: 942–3.

Sapsford, R. J. (1983), *Life Sentence Prisoners: Reaction, Response and Change*, Milton Keynes: Open University Press.

Sartre, J. P. (1947), *Huis Clos*, Paris: Éditions Gallimard. (First performed in May 1944)

Scarce, R. (2002), 'Doing time as an act of survival', *Symbolic Interaction*, 25: 303–21.

Schreiner, E. (2000), *Time Stretching Fear: The Detention and Solitary Confinement of 14 Anti-Apartheid Trialists 1987–1991*, Cape Town: Robben Island Museum.

Schroeder, A. (1976), *Shaking it Rough: A Prison Memoir*, Toronto, Ontario: Doubleday.

Select Committee of the House of Lords [Carnarvon Committee] (1863), *Report on the Present State of Discipline in Gaols and Houses of Correction*, British Parliamentary Papers (499), IX.

Sellin, T. (1927), 'Dom Jean Mabillon: A prison reformer of the seventeenth century', *Journal of the American Institute of Criminal Law and Criminology*, 17: 581–602.

Serge, V. (1970), *Men in Prison* (translated by Richard Greeman), London: Victor Gollancz.

Shachak, O. (1986), 'Componentiality as a survival strategy in a total institution: Case study of a POW in solitary confinement in a Syrian prison', in N. A. Milgram (ed.), *Stress and Coping in Time of War: Generalizations from the Israeli Experience*, New York: Brunner/Mazel, pp. 216–29.

Shalev, S. (2008), *A Sourcebook on Solitary Confinement*, London School of Economics: Mannheim Centre for Criminology.

Shalev, S. (2009a), *Supermax: Controlling Risk through Solitary Confinement*, Cullompton: Willan.

Shalev, S. (2009b), 'Inside a supermax', *Prison Service Journal*, 181: 21–5.

Shalev, S. and Lloyd, M. (2011), 'Though this be method, yet there is madness in't: Commentary on one year longitudinal study of the psychological effects of administrative segregation', *Corrections & Mental Health: An Update of the National Institute of Corrections*, 21 June, 1–7.

Shaylor, C. (1998), 'It's like living in a black hole: Women of color and solitary confinement in the prison industrial complex,' *New England Journal on Criminal and Civil Confinement*, 24: 385–416.

Sheehy, D. (1888), *Prison Papers*, Dublin: Weldrick Brothers.

Shonin, E., Van Gordon, W., Slade, K. and Griffiths, M. D. (2013), 'Mindfulness and other Buddhist-derived interventions in correctional settings: A systematic review', *Aggression and Violent Behavior*, 18: 365–72.

Silverstein, T. (2011), 'Declaration', Exhibit 1, *Silverstein v. Federal Bureau of Prisons*, Civil Action No. 07–cv–02471–PAB–KMT, USDC Colorado, 2 April.

Simpson, W. (1840), 'Solitary confinement and the silent system', *The Lancet*, 34: 370.

Singer, R. G. (1971), 'Confining solitary confinement: Constitutional arguments for a "new penology"' *Iowa Law Review*, 56: 1251–96.

Sledge, W. H., Boydstun, J. A. and Rabe, A. J. (1980), 'Self-concept changes related to war captivity', *Archives of General Psychiatry*, 37: 430–43.

Smith, C. (2009), *The Prison and the American Imagination*, New Haven, Conn: Yale University Press.

Smith, G. W. (1833), *A Defence of the System of Solitary Confinement*, Philadelphia, Pa: Philadelphia Society for Alleviating the Miseries of Public Prisons. (Originally published in 1828 and 1829 as a series of articles in the *Philadelphia Gazette*)

Smith, P. S. (2004), 'Isolation and mental illness in Vridsløselille 1859–1873', *Scandinavian Journal of History*, 29: 1–25.

Smith, P. S. (2006), 'The effects of solitary confinement on prison inmates: A brief history and review of the literature', in M. Tonry (ed.), *Crime and Justice: A Review of Research*, Vol. 34, Chicago, Ill: University of Chicago Press, pp. 441–528.

Smith, P. S. (2008), '"Degenerate criminals": Mental health and psychiatric studies of Danish prisoners in solitary confinement, 1870—1920', *Criminal Justice and Behavior*, 35: 1048–64.

Smith, P. S. (2011), 'The effects of solitary confinement: Commentary on one year longitudinal study of the psychological effects of administrative segregation', *Corrections & Mental Health: An Update of the National Institute of Corrections*, 21 June, 1–11.

Sorokin, P. A. and Merton, R. K. (1937), 'Social time: A methodological and functional analysis', *The American Journal of Sociology*, 42: 615–29.

Speer, A. (2010), *Spandau: The Secret Diaries* (translated by Richard and Clara Winston), New York: Ishi Press International. (Originally published in 1975 by Verlag-Ullstein)

Spens, I. (1994), *Architecture of Incarceration*, London: Academy Editions.

Storr, A. (1988), *Solitude*, London: HarperCollins.

Strange, R. E. and Klein, W. J. (1973), 'Emotional and social adjustment of recent US winter-over parties in isolated Antarctic stations', in O. G. Edholm and E. K. E. Gunderson (eds), *Polar Human Biology*, London: William Heinemann Medical Books, pp. 410–16.

Suedfeld, P. (1974), 'Solitary confinement in the correctional setting: Goals, problems, and suggestions', *Corrective and Social Psychiatry*, 141: 10–20.

Suedfeld, P. (1978), 'Solitary confinement as a rehabilitative technique: Reply to Lucas', *Australian and New Zealand Journal of Criminology*, 11: 106–12.

Suedfeld, P., Ramirez, C., Deaton, J. and Baker-Brown, G. (1982), 'Reactions and attributes of prisoners in solitary confinement', *Criminal Justice and Behavior*, 9: 303–40.

Suedfeld, P. and Steel, G. (2000), 'The environmental psychology of capsule habitats', *Annual Review of Psychology*, 51: 227–53

Sundt, J. L., Castellano, T. C. and Briggs, C. S. (2008), 'The sociopolitical context of prison violence and its control: A case study of supermax and its effect in Illinois', *The Prison Journal*, 88: 94–122.

Svendsen, L. (2005), *A Philosophy of Boredom* (translated by John Irons), London: Reaktion Books. (Originally published in 1999 by Universitets Forlaget, Oslo)

Symes, C. (1999), 'Chronicles of labour: A discourse analysis of diaries', *Time & Society*, 8: 357–80.

Tapley, L. (2010), 'The worst of the worst: Supermax torture in America', *Boston Review*, November/December, 30–35.

Taylor, A. J. W. (1961), 'Social isolation and imprisonment', *Psychiatry*, 24: 373–6.

Taylor, A. J. W. (1989), 'Polar winters: Chronic deprivation or transient hibernation?', *Polar Record*, 25: 239–46.

Taylor, S. M. (2007), *Making Time: Why Time Seems to Pass at Different Speeds and How to Control It*, London: Icon Books.

Teagarden, E. (1969), 'A Victorian prison experiment', *Journal of Social History*, 2: 357–65.

Teeters, N. K. (1937), *They Were in Prison: A History of the Pennsylvania Prison Society, 1787–1937, Formerly the Philadelphia Society for Alleviating the Miseries of Public Prisons*, New York: The John C. Winston Co.

Teeters, N. K. (1943), 'Benjamin Rush, pioneer penal reformer', *The Prison Journal*, 23: 306–9.

Teeters, N. K. and Shearer, J. D. (1957), *The Prison at Philadelphia—Cherry Hill. The Separate System of Penal Discipline: 1829–1913*, New York: Columbia University Press.

Thoreau, H. D. (1965), *Walden or, Life in the Woods*, New York: Harper and Row. (Originally published in 1854 by Ticknor and Fields)

Throness, L. (2008), *A Protestant Purgatory: Theological Origins of the Penitentiary Act, 1779*, Aldershot: Ashgate.

Timerman, J. (1988), *Prisoner Without a Name, Cell Without a Number* (translated by Toby Talbot), New York: Vintage Books. (Originally published in 1981 by Alfred A. Knopf)

Toch, H. (1982), 'The disturbed disruptive inmate: Where does the bus stop?', *Journal of Psychiatry and Law*, 10: 327–49.

Toch, H. (1992), *Mosaic of Despair: Human Breakdowns in Prison*, Washington: APA. (Originally published in 1975 by Aldine)

Toch, H. (2001), 'The future of supermax confinement', *The Prison Journal*, 81: 376–88.

Tolle, E. (2005), *The Power of Now: A Guide to Spiritual Enlightenment*, London: Hodder Mobius. (Originally published in 1999 by New World Library)

Toohey, P. (2011), *Boredom: A Lively History*, New Haven, Conn: Yale University Press.

Tumim, S. (1993), *Doing Time or Using Time: Report of a Review by Her Majesty's Chief Inspector of Prisons for England and Wales of Regimes in Prison Service Establishments in England and Wales*, London: HMSO (Cm 2128).

Turner, R. (2000), 'Prison as monastery', in J. Evans (ed.), *Undoing Time: American Prisoners in their Own Words*, Boston: Northeastern University Press, pp. 216–19.

Turner, R. H. (1978), 'The role and the person', *American Journal of Sociology*, 84: 1–23.

Tyson, J. R. (1845), 'Letter to William Peter, Esq., 20 January 1845', *Pennsylvania Journal of Prison Discipline and Philanthropy*, 1: 85.

United Nations Committee against Torture (2006), *Conclusions and Recommendations of the Committee against Torture: United States of America*, 25 July, Geneva, Switzerland: Office of the United Nations High Commissioner for Human Rights.

United Nations General Assembly (2011), *Interim Report of the Special Rapporteur of the Human Rights Council on Torture and Other Cruel, Inhuman or Degrading Treatment or Punishment*, 66th session, 5 August.

United States Government Accountability Office (2013), *Improvements Needed in Bureau of Prisons' Monitoring and Evaluation of Segregated Housing*, GAO–13–429, Washington DC: Government Accountability Office.

Ursano, R. J., Boydstun, J. A. and Wheatley, R. D. (1981), 'Psychiatric Illness in U.S. Air Force Viet Nam prisoners of war: A five-year follow-up', *American Journal of Psychiatry*, 138: 310–14.

Useem, B. and Kimball, P. (1989), *States of Siege: US Prison Riots 1971–1986*, New York: Oxford University Press.

Vaux, R. (1872), *Brief Sketch of the Origin and History of the State Penitentiary for the Eastern District of Pennsylvania at Philadelphia*, Philadelphia, Pa: McLaughlin Brothers.

Vischer, A. L. (1919), *Barbed Wire Disease: A Psychological Study of the Prisoner of War*, London: John Bale, Sons and Danielsson, Ltd.

Wacquant, L. (2013), 'Foreword: Probing the meta-prison', in J. I. Ross (ed.), *The Globalization of Supermax Prisons*, New Brunswick, NJ: Rutgers University Press, pp. ix–xiv.

Wahidin, A. and Tate, S. (2005), 'Prison (e)scapes and body tropes: Older women in the prison time machine', *Body & Society*, 11: 59–79.

Waite, T. (1994), *Taken on Trust*, with a new postscript, London: Coronet Books, Hodder and Stoughton.

Ward, D. A. and Breed, A. F. (1985), *The United States Penitentiary, Marion, Illinois*, Consultants' Report Submitted to Committee on the Judiciary, U.S. House of Representatives, Ninety-Eighth Congress, Second Session, December 1984, Washington DC: US Government Printing Office.

Ward, D. A. and Kassebaum, G. G. (2009), *Alcatraz: The Gangster Years*, Berkeley, Calif: University of California Press.

Ward, D. A. and Werlich, T. G. (2003), 'Alcatraz and Marion: Evaluating super-maximum custody', *Punishment & Society*, 5: 53–75.

West, H. C., Sabol, W. J. and Greenman, S. J. (2010), *Prisoners in 2009*, Bureau of Justice Statistics Bulletin, December, Washington DC: US Department of Justice.

Wheeler, S. (1961), 'Socialization in correctional communities', *American Sociological Review*, 26: 697–712.

Wilde, O. (1891), 'The soul of man under socialism', *Fortnightly Review*, XLIX: 292–319.

Wilde, O. (1898), 'Don't read this if you want to be happy today', *Daily Chronicle*, 24 March.

Wines, F. H. (1895), *Punishment and Reformation: An Historical Sketch of the Rise of the Penitentiary System*, London: Swan Sonneschein and Co.

Wittmann, M. (2009), 'The inner experience of time', *Philosophical Transactions of the Royal Society–B*, 364: 1955–67.

Wood, S. R. (1845), 'Letter to the editor', *Pennsylvania Journal of Prison Discipline and Philanthropy*, 1: 203–6.

Wurmbrand, R. (1969), *Sermons in Solitary Confinement*, London: Hodder and Stoughton.

Zedner, L. (1995), 'Wayward sisters: The prison for women', in N. Morris and D. J. Rothman (eds), *The Oxford History of the Prison: The Practice of Punishment in Western Society*, New York: Oxford University Press, pp. 329–61.

Zehr, H. (1996), *Doing Life: Reflections of Men and Women Serving Life Sentences*, Intercourse, Pa: Good Books.

Zeldin, T. (1995), *An Intimate History of Humanity*, London: Minerva. (Originally published in 1994 by Sinclair-Stevenson)

Zeno (1968), *Life*, London: The Quality Book Club.

Zietz, H. (1961), 'Prisoners' views of time—by a lifer', *The Prison Journal*, 41: 50–2.

Zimbardo, P. and Boyd, J. (2008), *The Time Paradox: The New Psychology of Time*, New York: Free Press.

Zinger, I., Wichmann, C. and Andrews, D. A. (2001), 'The psychological effects of 60 days in administrative segregation', *Canadian Journal of Criminology*, 43: 47–83.

Zwerman, G. (1988), 'Special incapacitation: The emergence of a new correctional facility for women political prisoners', *Social Justice*, 15: 31–47.

Index